Culture and Belonging
in Divided Societies

Culture and Belonging in Divided Societies

Contestation and Symbolic Landscapes

Edited by Marc Howard Ross

PENN

University of Pennsylvania Press

Philadelphia

Published by
University of Pennsylvania Press
Philadelphia, Pennsylvania 19104-4112

Printed in the United States of America on acid-free paper
10 9 8 7 6 5   4 3 2 1

Library of Congress Cataloging-in-Publication Data

Culture and belonging in divided societies : contestation and symbolic
landscapes / edited by Marc Howard Ross.
    p. cm.
Includes bibliographical references and index.
ISBN 978–0-8122–4145–7 (alk. paper)
1. Cultural pluralism.   2. Multiculturalism.   3. Symbolism.   I. Ross, Marc Howard.
HM1271.C853   2009
305.8—dc22

                                                                2008047627

To Dan Bar-On,
who taught us so much about how and why
to listen to people's stories

Contents

Preface

Cultural expressions and enactments regularly produce nasty, and sometimes prolonged, disputes, whether the catalyst is music, graffiti, sculptures, flag displays, parades, pilgrimages, visits to sacred sites, secular and religious rituals, clothing and how it is (or is not) worn, museum exhibits, or films. What is striking about so many of these conflicts is their emotional intensity, despite the fact that in many cases what is at stake is often of little material value. This presents a problem to the dominant interest-based, rational-choice paradigm found in economics, political science, and sociology that gives a small role to such emotional expressions beyond labeling them irrational.

Yet because such conflicts are so widespread, surely these phenomena are worth understanding, especially when they are associated with some of the most intractable, long-term conflicts of our times involving racial, ethnic, and religious identities in a wide range of societies. For over a decade, I have been exploring these questions in my own work in three distinct ways. First, I have sought to better understand the deeper levels of these conflicts by asking what these emotional expressions tell us about the needs of the parties locked in disputes. Second, taking seriously the accounts that the parties to these conflicts offer reveals a great deal that is beneath the surface about the nature and intensity of the emotions that drive the conflict. Third, gaining a deeper understanding of the links between disputants' positions and their emotions helps us identify issues that any meaningful effort to mitigate or settle the conflict must address. My argument is not that emotions are all that matter in cultural conflicts, but because they often matter a good deal, diplomats, political makers, and other third parties who become involved in conflict mitigation efforts ignore them at their peril. Surely complex long-term conflicts such as those between Israelis and Palestinians, Catholics and Protestants in Northern Ireland, or black and white Americans are about not only emotionally powerful cultural issues and their underlying narratives, therefore attention to these matters as well as the parties' substantive interests must be integrated.

In the past decade, I have undertaken a number of studies of cultural contestation and as I approached the completion of a book describing and analyzing them, I organized a conference inviting scholars in American studies, anthropology, art history, history, religious studies, political science, and sociology whose work had been especially important to me in guiding the development of my ideas to discuss their own research and theories in this area. In some cases, these individuals worked on the same, or similar cases, to those that I had; in other cases, I was interested in expanding the analysis across time and space.

This book brings together the many insights from these scholars who share common interests in the dynamics of cultural contestation in ethnically and racially divided societies. Contributors were able to engage in productive conversations despite the very different disciplinary backgrounds and the very different contexts in which they had worked. Not that there was necessarily complete agreement on all questions; rather, the conversations and exchanges were productive in clarifying a number of issues that arose and the diversity of perspectives produced a rich set of answers to the key questions that the participants found very fruitful.

In the opening chapter of this book, I outline the key questions and concepts that organize this volume and offer a framework for situating the essays that follow. Each subsequent chapter examines issues of control over, and inclusion and exclusion from, a society's symbolic landscape as represented in visual images, physical objects, words, or sacred and solemn public celebrations. Attention to the symbolic landscape draws our attention to how and when contending groups recognize each other, how they refer to each other in group narratives, and how expressive culture is a tool in group conflicts to control the content of public representations and resource allocation. Representational battles that are played out through cultural expressions and enactments are hardly new; they are, however, understudied and undertheorized among students of conflict in general and ethnic conflict in particular. In addition, the focus here is not only on better understanding cultural contestation, but also using this understanding to identify opportunities for mitigating intense conflicts and for assisting peace efforts in those conflicts that are partially settled but hardly fully resolved.

There are a number of people and institutions to thank for their support of this project and their help in bringing this book to press. It was a pleasure to work with all of the contributors. Each person addressed the central concerns that I laid out at the start and engaged the ideas and cases others brought up in ways that one often aspires to, but does not find so often, in collective projects. Several groups at Bryn Mawr College provided the support needed to complete this especially the Center for Ethnicities, Communities and Social Policy (since renamed the Center for the Social Sciences), the Center for Visual Culture, and the Peace and Conflict Studies Program. Karen Sulpizio and Lorraine Kirschner provided administrative support for the logistics of the conference. The U.S. Weather Service provided accurate details on the snowstorm that arrived just in time to complicate our first day but provided a bonding experience for those in attendance. Peter Agree, University of Pennsylvania Press editor in chief, encouraged me to prepare the volume and offered a number of important suggestions that have greatly strengthened the final book. Carol Greenhouse, who reviewed the manuscript for the press, offered some particularly useful ideas about how to highlight the book's core argument. Finally, I wish to again thank Katherine Conner for her tremendous support in this, as in all my projects, and her careful, thoughtful suggestions about matters large and small that always improve the result.

Chapter 1
Cultural Contestation and the Symbolic Landscape
Politics by Other Means?

Marc Howard Ross

Cartoons of Mohammed in a Danish newspaper, the yearly visit of Japan's prime minister to a Shinto shrine honoring the country's war dead (including World War II war criminals), displays of the Confederate battle flag over the capitol of South Carolina, and French schoolgirls wearing Islamic headscarves have all set off political conflicts and sometimes violence in recent years. Why is conflict so intense over these cultural expressions? Why do people invest so much emotional energy in these battles? What is at stake in these conflicts and what does winning or losing represent? The answer explored here is that this cultural contestation is about inclusion and exclusion from a society's symbolic landscape and that such inclusion or exclusion tells us about the politics of acceptance, rejection, and access to a society's resources and opportunities.

This book brings together the insights on these questions from scholars in American studies, anthropology, art history, history, religion, political science, and sociology to explore their common interests in the dynamics of cultural contestation in ethnically and racially divided societies.

Each essay in this book focuses on questions surrounding control over, inclusion in, and exclusion from a society's symbolic landscape as represented in visual images, sacred sites, physical objects, words, music, images, media, or sacred and solemn public celebrations. Examining the symbolic landscape draws our attention to how and when contending groups recognize each other, how they refer to each other in their in-group narratives, and how expressive culture is a tool in group conflicts to control the content of public representations that shapes resource allocation. These battles are not necessarily for control of territory per se; rather, they focus on the representations found in a society's public space.

The core of the argument behind this project is that while ethnic conflict is about clashing interests and incompatible identities, it is the former that are most often analyzed and that too often the underlying issues of cultural and identity contestation are neglected. Yet a good deal of intense conflict cannot be explained simply by reference to competition over material interests. The essays in this volume seek to address this imbalance by taking identities seriously and not just as epiphenomena without making the claim that interests are unimportant. The goal here is to illuminate the contextual understandings that make conflict so emotionally intense using the concepts of cultural contestation, symbolic landscape, psychocultural narratives and dramas, and ritual and cultural performance. Each of these tools provides language to talk about cultural contestation and to help understand why and how at certain times cultural expressions and enactments exacerbate conflict and why at others they serve as tools for mitigation. In these processes, we see how more inclusive symbols and rituals can draw former opponents into a new relationship while more exclusive ones harden the lines of differentiation. In the analysis that follows, ethnic conflicts are not one-time matters; nor are they unchanging. Rather, the within- and between-group contextual meaning of events matters in great part when it alters the intersubjective understandings of local parties, at times operating as a significant force in larger societal transitions.

The remainder of this chapter introduces the key concepts for the study of cultural contestation intended to frame the subsequent chapters that address specific conflicts over cultural expressions and enactments such as festivals, flags and insignias, repatriation of remains and artifacts previously taken from native peoples, clothing, language, museums exhibitions, murals, monuments, memorials, sacred sites, literary and artistic presentations, and public buildings. First, it presents an overview of the concepts of culture and cultural contestation. Second, it discusses the idea of a symbolic landscape, focusing on which groups and people are present and which are absent in it and how different groups in society are portrayed when they are present. Third, it explains the concepts of psychocultural narratives and psychocultural dramas as tools for the analysis of cultural contestation and collective memory. Fourth, it connects narratives and dramas to rituals and cultural performances, suggesting important links between cultural contestation and the politics of inclusion or exclusion. Throughout I indicate links to these key questions to the volume's subsequent chapters.

Culture and Cultural Contestation

Culture has been an elusive concept with a wide range of shifting meanings and usages in the social sciences. As a result, it is sometimes proposed that the concept not be used at all. However, rather than seeking to resolve the differences among scholars across fields, it is more useful here to clarify how we use the concept of culture and how it informs the analysis we offer. To do this, it is helpful to identify the core of our definition of culture as a system of shared meanings and meaning-making through semiotic practices (Geertz 1973a, 1973b; Schweder and LeVine 1984; Wedeen 2002).

For many years, anthropology emphasized culture as a set of traits that distinguished one cultural group from another (Kroeber and Kluckhohn 1952). A major shift in how culture was understood occurred when, as D'Andrade (1984) observed, interest in cognition and cognitive framing came into prominence in the social sciences starting in the late 1960s. D'Andrade contended that the radical shift in the view of culture, from behavior that could be understood within a stimulus-response framework to a system of meaning, is found in a number of fields. It gave rise to an emphasis on culture as a system of meaning that helps people make sense of the world in which they live and interpret the actions of others (D'Andrade 1984: 88; Geertz 1973a, 1973b). It views culture as public, shared meanings whereas behaviors, institutions, objects, and social structures are understood not as culture itself but as culturally constituted phenomena (Ross forthcoming; Spiro 1984). This view of culture is particularly useful for the examination of politics and ethnic conflict, for it draws our attention to the competing identities and worldviews that clash and to the importance of understanding groups' fears, hopes, and interpretations of their own actions and those of others. It also opens the door to a less static view of culture than the trait-based formulations and invites investigation of the contextual definition and redefinition of cultural meanings.

Culture, from this perspective, is a worldview containing specific scripts that shape why and how individuals and groups behave as they do, and includes both cognitive and affective beliefs about social reality as well as assumptions about when, where, and how people in one's culture and those in other cultures are likely to act in particular ways (Berger 1995; Chabal and Daloz 2006). For purposes of political analysis, I emphasize that shared understandings occur among people who also have a common (and almost invariably named) identity that distinguishes them from outsiders. Culture, in short, marks what people experience as "a distinctive way of life" characterized in the subjective we-feelings of cultural group members (and outsiders), and expressed

though specific behaviors (customs and rituals)—both sacred and profane—which mark the daily, yearly, and life cycle rhythms of its members and reveal how people view past, present, and future events and
understand choices they face (Berger 1995). Cultural metaphors and
narratives have cognitive meanings that describe group experiences,
high affective salience that emphasizes unique intragroup bonds that set
one group's experience apart from that of others, and scripts that direct
action.

For Wedeen (2002) and others, Geertz overemphasizes the integration of culture and fails to consider ways that it is both contested and
never fully bounded. Wedeen contends therefore that culture should be
approached as semiotic practices of meaning-making that emphasize
what language and symbols do but also the effects of institutional
arrangements, structures of domination, and strategic interests (2002:
714). She makes the case that culture "designates a way of looking at
the world that requires an account of how symbols operate in practice,
why meanings generate action, and why actions produce meanings when
they do" (2002: 720), arguing that examining meaning-making practices helps us understand how particular meanings become authoritative.[1]

Often people have an image of culture as unified and monolithic,
which it rarely is. The fact that different individuals understand each
other and share a common identity does not imply that widely held
meanings are necessarily acceptable to all or that all share the same
intensity of identification (Cohen 1991). To the contrary, there are
invariably intense intracultural differences and conflicts over meaning
and identity, control over symbols and rituals, and the imposition of one
interpretation rather than another on a situation (Ross 2007; Scott
1985). In this same vein, Laitin contends that culture highlights points
of concern to be debated (1988: 589) and not just areas of agreement.
Sharing a cultural identity does not mean that people necessarily concur
on specifics, only that they possess a similar understanding of how the
world works.

Participating in a system of shared meanings is not the same as having
identical specific values or engaging in the same behaviors. As LeVine
argues, "Culture represents a consensus on a wide variety of meanings
among members of an interacting community approximating that of the
consensus on language among members of a speech-community" (1984:
68). However, this does not mean there is unity in thoughts, feelings,
behavior, and even conceptions of the social order. Within cultural communities one frequently finds intragroup conflict and competition, such
as between religious and secular Jews in Israel, Hindu nationalists and
socialists in India, and Republican and Nationalist Catholics in Northern

Ireland. Because culture and its narratives offer in-group agreement about meaning but not necessarily about substance, conflict and its management is (at least) a two-level game, with one level focusing on within-group differences and the second on what occurs between groups. Finally, it is crucial to recognize that common ground is often overestimated: what people who share a group identity *believe* is shared is often greater than what is *actually* shared.

Cultures and cultural differences do not themselves cause conflict (Eller 1999; Posner 2004), but are the lenses through which the causes of conflict are refracted (Avruch and Black 1993: 133–134). As a result, cultural meanings and the emotions associated with them are not invariant within a group and intergroup interaction and contestation in turn affect them. For example, in the Middle East and South Asia there are sacred sites that different religious communities have at times shared, while at other times as conflict between groups has intensified, exclusive claims for their use have increased. Cultural conflicts are not just out there ready to happen as Kaplan's (1993) "ancient hatreds" argument would have us believe. Rather, as conflicts evolve, the intensity of emotions surrounding cultural expressions and enactments sometimes increases and sometimes decreases.

Culture is a mechanism for connecting people across time and space and provides powerful tools for expressing inclusion and exclusion in a community. Although group conflicts invariably include differences over access to, or the allocation of, tangible resources such as land, government funds, or political positions, cultural contestation draws our attention to issues of identity, recognition, and inclusion and exclusion that quickly come into play when leaders and groups evoke cultural images that stir up deeply held and clashing feelings. In these conflicts, culture operates in what Eller (1999: 48) describes as a code for authentic and alternative groupness, and as the basis of context-specific political claims.

Cultural contestation is conflict that is ostensibly about cultural expressions or enactments that becomes intense when it engages core group identity issues (Ross 2007). Often it polarizes the participants, who tend to think in terms of mutually exclusive, zero-sum options. Cultural contestation can rarely be resolved through reference to higher order authorities or a shared set of standards because typically these do not exist or are not accepted by all sides. As a result, politics rooted in cultural and identity claims easily moves to mutual denial in which each party simply ignores or denies the claims of the other and is fearful at times that even acknowledging their existence weakens their own claims (Kelman 1987). These conflicts often revolve around existential issues involving group recognition, acknowledgment, and legitimation that become embodied in objects, places, cultural expressions, and enactments.

Cultural contestation can be significant analytically and practically in that the narratives that emerge often reveal the parties' deepest fears and threats and can lead to a richer understanding of a conflict's core issues. Such understandings can allow parties to offer guidance to those interested in conflict mitigation through the identification of central concerns that any settlement must address. In such situations, each side is wary of the other, making peacemaking and peacebuilding daunting. Yet because cultural identities are constructed, they can also be reconstructed as opponents develop more complex views of each other and come to realize that despite all that divides them, there are some important things they share and ways that their futures are interdependent. In this context, one-time opponents in search of peace discover new metaphors and images, build integrative narratives, and develop inclusive ritual expressions that communicate their shared past and linked future. The three chapters on post-apartheid South Africa and the two on Northern Ireland highlight this process in those regions.

Symbolic Landscapes

A society's symbolic landscape communicates social and political meanings through specific public images, physical objects, and other expressive representations. It includes public spaces and especially sacred (but not necessarily religious) sites and other emotionally important and visible venues, as well as representations associated with a group's identity found in the mass media, theater, school textbooks, music, literature, and public art. Symbolic landscapes reflect how people understand their world and others in it, but they can also be significant shapers of these worlds when they establish and legitimate particular normative standards and power relations within and between groups. As Cosgrove observes: "The landscape idea represents a way of seeing—a way in which some Europeans have represented themselves and to others the world about them and their social relationships with it, and through which they have commented on social relations. Landscape is a way of seeing that has its own history, but a history that can only be understood as part of a wider history of economy and society . . . whose origins and implications extend well beyond the use and perception of land; that has its own techniques of expression, but techniques which it shares with other areas of cultural practice" (Cosgrove 1998: 1).

Symbolic landscapes communicate inclusion and exclusion as well as hierarchy, and they portray dominant and subordinate groups in particular ways. The meanings a symbolic landscape conveys invite us to ask:

Who is present and who is absent in public representations? What are the qualities of those people and objects portrayed in it? Who controls the representations and to what extent are they contested? How is hierarchy portrayed and what qualities are associated with particular positions within a society? Each of the essays that follow addresses one or more of these questions about contestation and the symbolic landscape by analyzing many different forms it can take. For example, Greg Johnson discusses the powerful issue of repatriation politics in contemporary Hawai'i; Elaine Thomas and Britt Cartrite examine contestation of Islamic headscarves and regional languages in France; and Dominic Bryan, Clifford Stevenson, and Lee A. Smithey analyze controversy over flags, insignias, and murals in Northern Ireland.

Inclusion and exclusion are often powerfully expressed through the restriction or expansion of a society's symbolic landscape as the chapters that follow show. Exclusion of groups from the symbolic landscape is an explicit form of denial and assertion of power. In contrast, a more inclusive symbolic landscape is a powerful expression of societal inclusion that communicates a mutuality and shared stake in society. It renders the previously unseen visible, gives voice to those once voiceless, and can offer powerful messages to young people and help to reshape relations between groups as we see in the chapters on post-apartheid South Africa, Independence Mall in Philadelphia, and San Francisco's Chinese New Year festival. Inclusion offers acceptance and legitimation that can reflect and promote changes in intergroup relationships. Through inclusion, groups can more easily identify and help mourn past losses and express hopes and aspirations for a common future. As symbolic statements of acknowledgment, it is no wonder that particular sites and the representations they contain can become the source of intense controversy between groups but also within the previously socially invisible group. What stories do they choose to tell about themselves? How is this related to who can speak for the group? Who controls its narrative and the images associated with it? All of these issues can provoke thoughtful and heated discussion as in the case of the Holocaust Museum in Washington (Linenthal 2001a; Rassool and Prosalendis 2001) and the District 6 Museum in Cape Town described in Chapter 9 (Rassool and Prosalendis 2001).[2]

All groups have places that are sacred (Friedland and Hecht 1991), and these often are the most emotionally charged, treasured, and defended sites in the symbolic landscape, especially when they are threatened in ways that the group experiences as threats to itself.[3] These places can be religious or secular and mark key events in a group's past and are associated with emotionally significant victories or defeats, miracles, and the exploits of heroes (Levinson 1998). Sacred places containing relics linking a group's past to its present and future are particularly powerful emotionally (Benvenisti 2000), and often there are restrictions on admitting outsiders. Sharing these sites with others is frequently hard to even imagine, let alone achieve, as we see in Richard H. Davis's essay on Hindu nationalism and the conflict at Ayodhya. The emotional power of sacred sites is precisely what makes demands for exclusive physical control over them so common and so strident and why loss of control over a site easily heightens a group's vulnerability.

Psychocultural Narratives

Psychocultural narratives are explanations for events—large and small—in the form of short, commonsense accounts (stories) that often seem simple. However, the images they contain, and the judgments they make about the motivations and actions of one's own group and opponents, are emotionally powerful. Narratives are not always internally consistent. For example, group narratives often alternate between portraying one's own group as especially strong and as especially vulnerable—and the same holds for the portrayal of the opponent (Kaufman 2001). This can be seen among Jews in Israel and in the case of Hindus in India discussed in Davis's chapter.

Widely shared narratives meet a number of needs, and people are especially likely to call upon them when they are disoriented and struggling to make sense of events in situations combining high uncertainty and high stress. In such contexts, group narratives and the familiar shared images they draw upon link people together providing reassurance, relieving anxiety, and reinforcing within-group worldviews. However, we should also note that within-group narratives are never fully consistent, and that there is almost always variation in how members of an in-group understand and react to any narrative. As a result, narratives are best understood as existing at different levels of generality with specific parts that can be added, discarded, rearranged, emphasized, and deemphasized. All cultural traditions have access to multiple preexisting narratives and images that provide support for diverse actions in anxious times. Narratives, therefore, are not made from whole cloth but are grounded in selectively remembered, interpreted experiences and projections from them that resonate widely; yet there is no simple correspondence between narrative beliefs and action.

Psychocultural narratives matter because of the roles they play as reflectors, exacerbators or inhibitors, and causes of conflict. As reflectors, narratives tell us how those involved in a conflict understand it; and narratives can increase in-group conformity where such reflections of the "real world" provide significant cues to in-group members that make dissenting from a societal consensus potentially risky. For third parties, narratives can bring critical "hot spots" in a group's narrative to the surface and identify each party's central fears and concerns that must be addressed if a conflict is to move toward a constructive outcome (Volkan 1997). They also can reveal what each side needs to understand about the other since in many conflicts, one side has an incomplete, and often inaccurate, sense of what opponents need and what they think the conflict is about (Jervis 1976).

As exacerbators or inhibitors of conflict, narratives emphasize differences or commonalities among the parties that variously support continuing hostility and escalation or moderation and deescalation in response to an opponent. Sometimes a dominant narrative leaves no room for negotiation as was the case of Franco's national narrative that made regional languages incompatible with a Spanish identity and a unified Spain. However, following his death, the new government quickly endorsed a different way of thinking about being Spanish, that a person could have multiple identities, for example, as a Spanish citizen and a member of the Catalan or Basque nation. Whereas the first narrative about Spanish identity exacerbated conflict between the central government and Spain's historic nationalities, the post-Franco narrative diminished it.

Narratives play a causal role in conflict when they frame cognitions and emotions in ways that structure the actions individuals and groups consider as plausible, shaping what constitutes evidence and how it is to be used (Bates, de Figueiredo, and Weingast 1998; Kaufman 2001). As Smith notes in writing about myths of ethnic descent, "By telling us who we are and whence we came, ethnic myths of descent direct our interests like Weber's 'switchmen' and order our actions towards circumscribed but exalted goals" (Smith 1999: 88). When narratives portray no possible common ground between opponents, search for alternatives to fighting is unlikely. Thus there will be political pressures for leaders to pursue certain kinds of action, while other options will have already been eliminated from consideration. From this perspective, narratives do not force parties to take a particular action if for example they lack the capabilities or support, but narratives may be crucial in severely limiting the range of options taken seriously. Finally, at times it is useful to think about scripts within narratives that are particularly likely to be linked to action when they are linked to a specific situation (Peterson 2002, 2005).

Psychocultural narratives have a number of features that help in the analysis of cultural contestation as is seen in the chapters that follow. Narratives evoke past events as metaphors and lessons for the future; they emphasize collective memories; they are highly selective in terms of what is included and excluded; they identify group fears and threats to identity; they emphasize in-group conformity and externalization of responsibility; they evolve over time in response to changing events in any political context; they are not just verbal accounts, but they are also enacted in a variety of ways; and group narratives are ethnocentric and filled with moral superiority claims. These features are not mutually exclusive; many have overlapping elements, and considering connections among them helps spell out how narratives shape cultural contestation (Ross 2007).

Finally, in examining cultural contestation, it would be a mistake to not recognize that there is generally within-group diversity in any conflict. One reason is political difference concerning dangers to a group and who can best defend it. Another is that the linkage between events and narrative accounts of them is rarely direct. The generality of culture means that it can give rise to multiple narratives to cope with the same event or series of events. Linenthal (2001b) illustrates this idea especially well in his examination of how Oklahoma City residents, in particular, and Americans more generally, came to understand the 1995 bombing of the Murrah Federal Building that killed 168 people. He describes three different, but not necessarily incompatible, narratives to explain the attack and responses to it. The *progressive narrative* emphasized renewal and recovery as people struggled to rebuild the city and their lives. The *redemptive narrative* put the horrific events in a religious context, emphasizing the struggle between good and evil and ultimate redemption. The *toxic narrative* stressed the ongoing disruption and insecurity in many lives after the bombing and the losses that could not be restored. Linenthal's analysis shows how each of these narratives is deeply rooted in American culture. They exist side by side, he argues, and many survivors and family members of victims could readily identify how each of the three reflected their own experiences and emotions at different times.[4]

Narratives as Collective Memories

Ethnic groups commonly recount their narratives in a chronological fashion that blends key events, heroes, metaphors, and moral lessons (Kaufman 2001). These recountings can be usefully thought of as collective memories that connect people across time and space that are products of social interaction and individual memory processes (Devine-Wright 2003: 11). Collective memories, as Halbwachs (1980) and others have pointed out, are selective and what is emphasized is facilitated through socially produced mnemonic devices such as physical objects that serve as repositories of group memories. Social memory for Pierre

Nora is at odds with history and "takes root in the concrete, in spaces, gestures, images and objects" (1989: 9). However, it should be noted that what Nora (1989) terms *lieux de mémoire* (sites of memory) are best understood as not only physical sites of memory for they are more than simply physical locations that hold memories but can be thought of as images and expressions as well. For Connerton too collective social memory is clearly different from the more specific activity of historical reconstruction, which is more dependent upon evidence than is social memory (1989: 13–14). He argues, "We may say, more generally, that we all come to know each other by asking for accounts, by giving accounts, by believing or disbelieving stories about each other's pasts and identities. . . . We situate the agent's behavior with reference to its place in their life history; and we situate that behavior with references to its place in the history of the social settings to which they belong" (Connerton 1989: 21).

Groups, from this perspective, remember many of the same events, battles, and heroes that a historian might consider important. However, the explanations for them, and how the two modes of understanding interpret their significance, are generally highly divergent. In addition, although groups see collective memories as unchanging, objective accounts of a group's history, there are often major changes in emphasis and the specific events or people included in group narratives over several generations as well as variation in which memories are most salient across generations (Devine-Wright 2003: 13). Memories associated with historical events may often be far more recent and develop as political claim-making a good deal after an event takes place. For example, the French did not celebrate Bastille Day until a century after 1789; the 1690 Battle of the Boyne in Northern Ireland became significant only in the nineteenth century (Roe and Cairns 2003: 174); the 1838 Battle of Blood River in South Africa was unmarked for several decades after it took place (Thompson 1985: 164); and the close emotional connection between Jewish and Muslim identity and the ancient holy sites in the old city of Jerusalem have dramatically increased in the past century. All of these are examples that illustrate how the degree of emphasis on lessons and metaphors associated with particular events varies as collective memories evolve.

The objective manner in which collective memories are recounted should not blind us to their emotional significance as links between the individual and the group as well as between the past and present. Otherwise, how could we explain the strong reactions people have to totally nonutilitarian objects such as buildings, potsherds, and statues, not to mention pieces of cloth or household objects?

Connerton (1989) asks how collective memories are conveyed and sustained. Although he sees a role for unconscious dynamics, his main emphasis is on social processes that make connections to the past that are useful in the present: "We experience our present world in a context which is causally connected with past events and objects . . . [and] we may say that our experiences of the present largely depend upon our knowledge of the past, and that our images of the past commonly serve to legitimate a present social order" (Connerton 1989: 2–3).

For Connerton, the past matters because it shapes our present needs. My argument emphasizes the opposite relationship, namely that how we understand the past grows out of our present needs. However, like Connerton, I emphasize the role that social participation and especially ritual commemoration play in conveying and sustaining knowledge about the past, a topic considered in several chapters. For Connerton, commemorative ceremonies and bodily practices are important because they are performative and participation builds commitment to the group and to its core narrative. Like Halbwachs (1980), Connerton emphasizes that through group membership "individuals are able to acquire, to localize and to recall their memories" (1989: 36). Memories exist in relationships, and because the group is interested in the memories that "provide individuals with frameworks within which their memories are localized and memories are localized by a kind of [group] mapping" (Connerton 1989: 37).

Psychocultural Dramas

Psychocultural dramas are conflicts that arise over competing, and apparently irresolvable, claims that engage the central elements of each group's historical experience and contemporary identity (Ross 2007). Examples of them are found in each chapter here. The manifest focus of a psychocultural drama can be the allocation of material resources or can involve cultural differences over issues such as language, religion, social practices, or music and popular culture. At a deeper level, psychocultural dramas are polarizing events about nonnegotiable cultural claims, perceived threats, and/or rights that are connected to narratives and metaphors central to a group's core identity. As psychocultural dramas unfold, they produce reactions that are emotionally powerful, clearly differentiate the parties in conflict, and contain key elements of the larger conflict in which they are embedded. As psychocultural dramas unfold, their powerful emotional meanings link events across time and space, thereby increasing in-group solidarity and out-group hostility (LeVine and Campbell 1972; Volkan 1997).[5] Through the lens of psychocultural dramas, the multiple levels of these conflicts come into clearer view revealing both barriers to, and opportunities for, their constructive management.

The idea of the psychocultural drama is adapted from Victor Turner's (1957, 1974) concept of the social drama (Ross 2001). The term psychocultural, rather than social, emphasizes the deeply rooted identity dynamics in conflicts that link large-scale cultural processes through microlevel psychological mechanisms. The social dramas Turner analyzed are conflicts that are never fully resolved, but they are settled for a time when the conflict is redefined away from incompatible principles and toward the symbolic and ritual domain where disputants can emphasize shared concerns and superordinate goals. The social dramas Turner described took place in a society with shared core values. Yet despite shared values, conflict regularly arose over serious breaches in the social order where there is disagreement over the relative importance of the competing principles that groups or individuals invoke to support their divergent positions in the absence of a jural mechanism to choose among the competing principles (Turner 1957: 89–90).

Turner observed, "In a social drama it is not a crime [that constitutes the breach], though it may formally resemble one; it is in reality, a 'symbolic trigger of confrontation or encounter'" (Turner 1974: 38). As a social drama unfolds, tensions mount and the conflict escalates as each side works vigorously to strengthen its position and to draw in new allies. New issues are easily interjected into expanding conflicts, including memories of past disputes and latent feelings of hostility that resurface as social dramas unfold. Social dramas that are especially difficult to resolve involve structural contradictions between norms that cannot be easily settled in the absence of centralized authorities able to render an authoritative and acceptable decision. Some remain stuck and are periodically replayed, as in the case of Jerusalem's holy sites and black-white conflict in the United States. Lacking an obvious solution or a sanctioned effective decision maker, Turner emphasized the importance of ritual mechanisms of redress especially when jural mechanisms such as a judicial system, an administrative process, or a legislative process that the parties accept as legitimate either do not exist, or are inadequate because none of the competing principles is clearly more important than any of the others. In such conflicts, the scope and intensity of disputes quickly escalates and the initial conflict grows into a crisis.

Turner suggests that redressive action through ritual can follow mobilization of the wider society, including many who had little involvement in the original dispute. The performance of reparatory rituals refocuses people's emotional energy and situates the conflict in a context where disputants can emphasize shared norms and goals. The original conflict is not resolved in any profound sense because the competing norms are still present. Rather, the emotional significance of differences diminishes as part of mutual acknowledgment so that people can find a "solution" that lowers tension, as we see in Charlene Mires's analysis of the conflict over making visible the earlier presence of George Washington's slaves on what is now the home of the Liberty Bell on Independence Mall or the recent efforts to change Loyalist murals in Belfast that Lee A. Smithey discusses.

Turner posits that ritual is likely to be especially important as a mechanism of conflict mitigation in situations where structural conditions regularly give rise to hard-to-resolve conflict, a condition that is by no means limited to the specific communities he first studied. In many societies, for example, parties to such conflicts mark its termination with a ceremonial meal in which special foods are cooked and consumed together. In institutions such as courts or legislatures, decisions are taken and marked in a particular ritualistic fashion that separates the content of the outcome from the personalities of the parties. Turner's observation, that the intensity of social dramas can be diffused through the transformation of disputes over competing interests into ritual actions emphasizing what the parties share, has important general implications for mitigation of cultural conflicts when it becomes possible for opponents to participate in mutual or joint ritual expression, as we see in the three chapters on South Africa.

In observing emerging psychocultural dramas such as the conflict in Ayodhya that Richard H. Davis discusses, outsiders sometimes see leaders, such as the militant Hindu nationalists, articulating particularly venomous narratives and accuse them of manipulating vulnerable populations by sowing hatred. While this is surely the case at times, it is not the entire story. First, these charges imply that leaders know that they are recounting lies. This is not necessarily the case, and leaders often believe what they are saying for a number of reasons, most important for our purposes here is that the narrative they recount is one they have internalized for a long time. Second, because their account resonates so strongly with followers we should be asking why that is the case. The manipulation hypothesis suggests it is a matter of weakness and vulnerability, but there is good evidence that people often reject arguments that make little sense to them and are capable of resisting manipulation.[6] So what is going on here? One possible hypothesis is that the emotional plausibility of the leader's account is sufficiently compelling because it meets a need for clarity and nurturance in times of stress, uncertainty, and great fear. Focusing on the "buyers" and not just the "sellers" makes us recognize that the kernel of emotional truth in leader appeals must be sufficiently strong for followers to respond positively to leaders.

Ritual and Performance in Cultural Contestation

Psychocultural narratives and dramas are politically important because they evoke, build, and reinforce strong emotions that stake claims and mobilize actions in the name of the group. In such mobilization, cultural expressions and enactments are concrete actions that increase shared beliefs strengthening the emotional persuasiveness of political and social connectedness and requiring the defense of the group. Political claims are particularly compelling when they draw on culturally rooted shared images, metaphors, significant events, and personalities that connect in-group members across time and space. Through familiar and emotionally salient expressions, connections within a community are created, strengthened, and differentiated from out-groups. What is particularly important here is how convincing the imagined community becomes for people when they see themselves at risk as, for example, in Elaine Thomas's discussion of French fears for their culture in the face of Muslim immigration.

Expressions of community can be highly abstract or concrete. As with all symbols, their power lies not in their explicit content, but in how they are perceived in various social and political contexts. For example, flags and insignias are mere pieces of cloth of particular colors, but when they represent a nation at risk, they become a stimulus for the generation of intense pride and in-group solidarity and attacks upon them easily motivate counteraction including violence as Dominic Bryan and Clifford Stevenson point out in writing about insignias in Northern Ireland. Similarly, music, language, parades or festivals, theatrical performances, and clothing are some of the many ways that political identities are evoked, or group characteristics ascribed as M. Alison Kibler examines in her analysis of media portrayals of American minorities. What is important to realize is that it is frequently very ordinary objects or expressions that become politically powerful not because of their inherent qualities, but because of the meanings people attribute to them.

Ideas are emotionally powerful at times, however it is often only when people engage in actions or activities intimately linked to them that their full power is reached. These actions can be mundane or sacred, and often have a repetitive quality to them that enhances their emotional power. Ritual enactments, sometimes assisted by ancient objects, make emotionally significant connections between a group's past and present experiences as individuals participate in specific, often very ordinary, activities linking people across time and space. The demands on individual participants vary from very modest to extremely heavy. Some participants do nothing more than attend an event, or view it on television; others devote a great deal of time and personal resources to it including suspending their daily routines to participate as people on pilgrimages do.

Rituals are behaviors whose central elements and the contexts in which they take place are emotionally meaningful. Cultural performances as rituals communicate the core parts of a group's self-understood identity and history. Of particular interest here are those used to build or bolster political narratives and claims based on them.[7] As Connerton argues, repetitive cultural rituals are a crucial way of creating and solidifying collective memories that are transmitted over time (Connerton 1989; Jarman 1997). Participation in a wide range of activities such as festivals and commemorative ceremonies is important in Connerton's analysis in which he emphasizes that rites are not merely expressive; rites are not merely formal; and rites are not limited in their effect to ritual occasions (1989: 44). Rituals commemorate continuity and in so doing shape collective memory (Connerton 1989: 48). As noted above, invented rituals such as national holidays often begin long after the events they mark. In addition, "Ritual is not only an alternative way of expressing certain beliefs, but that certain things can be expressed only in ritual" (Connerton 1989: 54). Ritual has its own performative, formalized language encoded in postures, gestures, and movements (Connerton 1989: 58–59).

States are keenly aware of the value of ritual performances that enhance their legitimacy and the political loyalty of their citizens, and all states have ceremonial occasions, which are moments of high ritual that assert the state's power and legitimacy. State rituals mark occasions such as political transitions, national holidays, military victories, the deaths of leaders, and the achievements of past and present heroes. State rituals take many forms and vary along a number of dimensions such as their size, degree of organization, key participants, and the emotions they evoke. Some of these celebrations are planned in advance and follow a calendric cycle, while others are a response to unfolding events. These large-scale rituals involve elaborate pomp and ceremony, and often large numbers of people are present. However, not all ritual expressions of interest here are state organized or sanctioned. In addition, many cultural performances that are meaningful to one group are simply ignored by others. At other times, however, public cultural performances, such as Orange Order parades in Northern Ireland, are politicized and provoke counter demonstrations and alternative rituals (Bryan 2000; Jarman 1997). For example, Jewish Israelis celebrate the anniversary of Israel's independence each May, while Palestinian Israelis publicly commemorate "Al Nakba," the catastrophe, which places the same events in 1948 in an entirely different frame.

While there can be significant variation in the specifics of how celebrations are recounted and marked, a common feature is that they are occasions for retelling and enacting a group's narrative. Participation in cultural celebrations is a crucial mechanism for maintaining powerful psychocultural narratives and the memories associated with them, and there are always many ways to participate ranging from observing a performance that includes festive and solemn elements to taking part in one that requires months or even years of preparation and can involve high cost and risk to participants. Some are solemn and controversial, while others are mundane and not problematic. Enactments often reinforce the emotional salience of events in ways that are more powerful than verbal accounts alone (Jarman 1997; Verba 1961). As a result, the narrative's key metaphors and lessons become accessible for everyday political discourse and in periods of high stress, political leaders readily turn to its core images when they seek support for favored action strategies.

Plan of the Book

Each contributor reflects on how and when cultural expressions and enactments serve as a flash point in ethnic conflict. Because in many of these conflicts relatively little is at stake materially, the parties' deep emotional investment in the conflict requires explanation. Each author offers an analysis of cultural contestation and the symbolic landscape to make sense of how specific conflicts developed, escalated, and in some cases were managed constructively. These analyses communicate the complexity of culture and reveal some of the mechanisms that make culturally rooted conflicts so difficult to settle.

The essays reveal a broad agreement that culture frames conflict, even if cultural differences do not cause it directly, as the "ancient hatreds" or "clash of civilizations" arguments would have us believe (Huntington 1993; Kaplan 1993). Framing provides structure in ambiguous situations, evoking specific scripts so that groups in conflict can explain what took place to themselves and to outsiders. Frames draw on core beliefs about the world and human behavior, past experiences, and specific assumptions about opponents' motives to render an emotionally plausible account of a conflict that contains implicit or explicit assumptions of how to react to it. In some situations a single narrative emerges that is widely accepted as occurred in the United States following the September 11 attacks on New York and Washington that were viewed as a terrorist action and compared to the Japanese attack on Pearl Harbor in 1941.[8] Many times, however, multiple narratives are present and there is considerable in-group contestation around competing accounts that is played out. For example, in the Israeli-Palestinian conflict there have been hard-line narratives on both sides that deny the legitimacy of the national aspirations of the other, and more accommodating narratives that offer mutual recognition and tout the viability of a two-state solution as in everyone's self-interest.

At least four general hypotheses emerge that are consistent with the arguments and evidence found in the individual essays. First, while contestation around cultural expressions takes many forms, these disputes are most intense when the participants' core identities are threatened. Second, cultural expression itself does not cause intense conflict, but rather whether or not conflict occurs depends upon how particular cultural acts are interpreted. Cultural expressions reflect what people believe, yet cultural worldviews are also important when they frame political conflicts and make some forms of action and discourse more or less likely in the eyes of group members. Third, culture serves as a tool for the articulation of political demands and mobilization. At the same time, although some leaders use—and even manipulate—cultural expressions in their own interests, in many situations leaders make culturally based appeals that represent their long-held, sincere positions that are not merely developed for instrumental reasons. Finally, while it is easy to focus on culture as a divisive force as seen in terms such as culture wars or the clash of civilizations, cultural expressions and rituals can also play an important role in peacemaking as disputants find ways to express what it is that they have in common not just what divides them.

Cultural identities, from this perspective, provide both barriers to, and opportunities for, the mitigation of ethnic conflict. The hypothesis explored here is that movement toward constructive conflict management in long-term intergroup conflicts is tied to the development of inclusive narratives, symbols, and rituals in contexts where mutually exclusive claims previously predominated. In this way, conflict articulated around cultural issues can offer an opportunity to reduce the intense emotions associated with contested identities and can serve as powerful vehicles for bringing former opponents into new institutional arrangements and at the same time modifying a society's symbolic landscape, as has occurred in South Africa and to a lesser extent in Northern Ireland. Signed agreements between long-standing opponents are only one step in a peace process, and their implementation requires attention to its implementation in domains beyond formal governmental institutions, such as more inclusive expressions and enactments that communicate a new relationship among previously opposing groups.

This book explores cultural contestation in four groups of essays followed by an epilogue reflecting on the prior chapters. The first one examines sacred sites and identity in three different places offering broad analyses that examine the relevance and power of the past for political mobilization in the present. Sharing sacred spaces is especially difficult as we see in "The Rise and Fall of a Sacred Place: Ayodhya over Three Decades," in which Richard H. Davis examines intense contestation over control of a sacred site in the city of Ayodhya in Northern India. His chapter analyzes the mobilization strategies Hindu nationalists have employed to build support for the claim that a Muslim mosque was built over an older Hindu temple marking the birthplace of the God Rama. Greg Johnson's essay, "Social Lives of the Dead: Contestation and Continuities in the Hawaiian Repatriation Context," considers the intense debate over repatriation of native Hawaiian artifacts placing it in the context of powerful claims about cultural identity and belonging.

The next four chapters explore cases of identity conflict in liberal European democracies—two focusing on Northern Ireland and two on France. Dominic Bryan and Clifford Stevenson explore the efforts to design new, more inclusive flags and other identity markers in Northern Ireland in "Flagging Peace: Struggles over Symbolic Landscape in the New Northern Ireland." Then, in "Conflict Transformation, Cultural Innovation, and Loyalist Identity in Northern Ireland," Lee A. Smithey looks at grassroots efforts in Loyalist sections of Belfast to develop community-based murals that are less exclusive and conflictual than the paramilitary or triumphalist ones that were most common in the past. The next two essays turn to France. Elaine Thomas first analyzes the conflict over the issue of Islamic headscarves in schools in "Islamic Headscarves in Public Schools: Explaining France's Legal Restrictions" and Britt Cartrite explores competing French ideas about local identities in "Minority Language Policy in France: Jacobinism, Cultural Pluralism, and Ethnoregional Identities." Both emphasize the pressures France has felt to limit the expression of cultural diversity, especially in certain public spaces such as schools, while at the same time communicating the significant differences around issues of immigrant and regional minority rights that also exist. Here, the symbolic landscape is not the public space itself, but the expressions of identity through dress and language that people perform in it.

South Africa's symbolic landscape changed in major ways following the end of apartheid and the transition to majority rule. What happened to its symbolic landscape is the focus of three chapters. Sabine Marschall provides a critical look at new monuments in post-apartheid South Africa and asks how new monuments can serve both as contributors to reconciliation and division in her essay, "Symbols of Reconciliation or Instruments of Division? A Critical Look at New Monuments in South Africa." Crain Soudien investigates the expanding post-apartheid symbolic landscape in the Western Cape in "Emerging Multiculturalisms in

South African Museum Practice: Some Examples from the Western Cape." In "Strategies for Transforming and Enlarging South Africa's Post-Apartheid Symbolic Landscape" I emphasize how hard it is to alter culturally shared understandings of significant monuments following a regime change.

In the final section three historians examine the politics of changing the symbolic landscape in United States using cases drawn from African American, Asian, and white minorities at different points in time. Charlene Mires analyzes the recent controversy in Philadelphia surrounding the virtually untold and unknown story of the slaves George Washington maintained in the city while he was president and the conflict surrounding how to make this story accessible to the public in "Invisible House, Invisible Slavery: Struggles of Public History at Independence National Historical Park." Chiou-Ling Yeh considers the changing nature of Chinese New Year festivals as responses to the community's perceived political needs in "Politicizing Chinese New Year Festivals: Cold War Politics, Transnational Conflicts, and Chinese America." M. Alison Kibler looks at early twentieth-century Irish, Jewish, and African American protests and efforts to change how the group was portrayed in the mass media of the time—theater and movies in "Paddy, Shylock, and Sambo: Irish, Jewish, and African American Efforts to Ban Racial Ridicule on Stage and Screen." In his epilogue, Edward T. Linenthal examines several common themes across the chapters and links them to his own work over the past two decades that has focused on sacred and contested spaces in the American consciousness.

Focusing on the cultural dimensions of long-term ethnic conflicts is not intended to replace more traditional analysis that focus on interests, political structures, and ideologies. Rather, it is an effort to supplement them by highlighting an often neglected aspect of conflict that when ignored can easily increase a conflict's intractability. Finally, many of these essays illustrate ways that deepening our understanding of struggles over cultural expressions—from India and Hawaii, to Northern Ireland and France, to South Africa and the United States—may lead to more constructive dialogue between parties and further mutual efforts to resolve disputes.

Notes

1. Others such as Bourdieu (1977), Foucault (1979), and Swidler (1986) also emphasize culture as practice referring to both meaning-making and political relationships that privilege certain actions and groups over others.

2. There has been a particularly rich recent writing on the issue of landscape and memory in South Africa. For example, see Coombes (2003) and Rassool and Prosalendis (2001).

3. Group members easily feel a sacred site's power and its vulnerability. When I was in Sri Lanka in 1994, I visited the ancient city at Anuradhapura. It houses beautiful buildings and there are thousands of monks in flowing saffron robes and ordinary people in this important Buddhist pilgrimage center that contains a sacred Bohdi tree that is guarded day and night. It is said to have grown from a sapling from the tree under which the Buddha gained Enlightenment in 528 B.C. and was brought from India in the third century. The mood is calm and serene. A few years earlier a group of Tamil Tigers attacked Anuradhapura firing automatic weapons killing 180 people and wounding hundreds more. On my visit there I was told about the attack, but instead of focusing on the dead and wounded, my host said, "They tried to destroy our tree." For him, destruction of the tree would have been a far more deadly attack on Sinhalese Buddhists than the mortal one that took place.

4. Linenthal (2001b: 81–108) discusses a fourth narrative that focuses on the role of trauma in the aftermath of the bombing. This account, he argues, dominated the response of health professionals and some government agencies. It was significant in medicalizing and individualizing responses to the events, and providing health care professionals with a standard, acceptable formula for treating those touched by them.

5. Not all conflicts are psychocultural dramas. I exclude disputes that do not mobilize intense feelings and those which do not divide a community along group lines.

6. Early mass media research found that on topics on which people already had strong opinions, media campaigns often had little effect on their opinions even when the media messages were very clear.

7. Normally we think of people as performers, but Kirshenblatt-Gimblett (1998) argues that objects in museums, presentations or public exhibitions, festivals, fairs, and memorial and tourist sites perform as well. Performances, as she analyzes them, simultaneously reflect and produce plausible accounts of a group's past and present. This view of heritage can also include its commodification.

8. It should not be forgotten, however, that when the World Trade Center was bombed in 1993, the event was treated as a criminal action, not a terrorist attack.

Bibliography

Avruch, Kevin, and Peter W. Black. 1993. "Conflict Resolution in Intercultural Settings: Problems and Prospects." In *Conflict Resolution Theory and Practice: Integration and Application*, ed. Dennis Sandole and Hugo van der Merwe. Manchester: Manchester University Press, 131–145.

Bates, Robert H., Rui J. P. Jr. de Figueiredo, and Barry R. Weingast. 1998. "The Politics of Interpretation: Rationality, Culture and Transition." *Politics and Society* 26, no. 4: 603–642.

Benvenisti, Meron. 2000. *Sacred Landscape: The Buried History of the Holy Land Since 1948.* Berkeley: University of California Press.

Berger, Bennett M. 1995. *An Essay on Culture: Symbols, Structure and Social Structure.* Berkeley: University of California Press.

Bourdieu, Pierre. 1977. *The Logic of Practice.* Cambridge: Cambridge University Press.

Bryan, Dominic. 2000. *Orange Parades: The Politics of Ritual, Tradition and Control.* London: Pluto Press.

Chabal, Patrick and Jean-Pascal Daloz. 2006. *Culture Troubles: Politics and the Interpretation of Meaning.* London: Hurst.

Cohen, Raymond. 1991. *Negotiating Across Cultures: Communication Obstacles in International Diplomacy.* Washington, D.C.: United States Institute for Peace Press.

Connerton, Paul. 1989. *How Societies Remember.* Cambridge: Cambridge University Press.

Coombes, Annie E. 2003. *History After Apartheid: Visual Culture and Public Memory in a Democratic South Africa.* Durham: Duke University Press.

Cosgrove, Denis E. 1998. *Social Formation and Symbolic Landscape.* Madison: University of Wisconsin Press.

D'Andrade, Roy G. 1984. "Cultural Meaning Systems." In *Culture Theory: Essays on Mind, Self and Emotion,* ed. Richard A. Schweder and Robert A. LeVine. Cambridge: Cambridge University Press, 83–119.

Devine-Wright, Patrick. 2003. "A Theoretical Overview of Memory and Conflict." In *The Role of Memory in Ethnic Conflict,* ed. Ed Cairns and Michael D. Roe. Houndsmills, Basingstoke: Palgrave, 9–33.

Eller, Jack David. 1999. *From Culture to Ethnicity to Conflict: An Anthropological Perspective on International Ethnic Conflict.* Ann Arbor: University of Michigan Press.

Foucault, Michel. 1979. *Discipline and Punish: The Birth of the Prison.* New York: Vintage.

Friedland, Roger, and Richard Hecht. 1991. "The Politics of Sacred Place: Jerusalem's Temple Mount/al-haram al-sharif." In *Sacred Places and Profane Spaces,* ed. Jamie Scott and Paul Simpson-Housley. New York: Greenwood Press, 21–61.

Geertz, Clifford. 1973a. "Thick Description: Toward an Interprctive Theory of Culture." In *The Interpretation of Cultures,* ed. Clifford Geertz. New York: Basic Books, 3–30.

———. 1973b. "Religion as a Cultural System." In *The Interpretation of Cultures,* ed. Clifford Geertz. New York: Basic Books, 87–125.

Halbwachs, Maurice. 1980. *The Collective Memory.* New York: Harper and Row.

Huntington, Samuel. 1993. "The Clash of Civilizations." *Foreign Affairs,* 72, no. 3: 22–49.

Jarman, Neil. 1997. *Material Conflicts: Parades and Visual Displays in Northern Ireland.* Oxford: Berg.

Jervis, Robert. 1976. *Perception and Misperception in International Politics.* Princeton: Princeton University Press.

Kaplan, Robert D. 1993. *Balkan Ghosts: A Journey Through History.* New York: St. Martin's Press.

Kaufman, Stuart J. 2001. *Modern Hatreds: The Symbolic Politics of Ethnic War.* Ithaca: Cornell University Press.

Kelman, Herbert. 1987. "The Political Psychology of the Israeli-Palestinian Conflict: How Can We Overcome Barriers to a Negotiated Solution?" *Political Psychology* 8: 347–363.

Kirshenblatt-Gimblett, Barbara. 1998. *Destination Culture: Tourism, Museums, and Heritage.* Berkeley: University of California Press.

Kroeber, A. L., and Clyde Kluckhohn. 1952. *Culture: A Critical Review of Concepts and Definitions.* Papers of the Peabody Museum of American Archeology and Ethnology, 47, no. 1.

Laitin, David D. 1988. "Political Culture and Political Preference." *American Political Science Review* 82: 589–593.

LeVine, Robert A. 1984. "Properties of Culture: An Ethnographic View." In *Culture Theory: Essays on Mind, Self and Emotion*, ed. Richard A. Schweder and Robert A. LeVine. Cambridge: Cambridge University Press, 67–87.

LeVine, Robert A., and Donald T. Campbell. 1972. *Ethnocentrism: Theories of Conflict, Ethnic Attitudes and Group Behavior.* New York: John Wiley.

Levinson, Sanford. 1998. *Written in Stone: Public Monuments in Changing Societies.* Durham: Duke University Press.

Linenthal, Edward Tabor. 2001a. *Preserving Memory: The Struggle to Create America's Holocaust Museum.* New York: Columbia University Press.

———. 2001b. *The Unfinished Bombing: Oklahoma City in American Memory.* Oxford: Oxford University Press.

Nora, Pierre. 1989. "Between Memory and History: Les Lieux de Mémoire." *Représentations* 26: 7–24.

Peterson, Roger D. 2002. *Understanding Ethnic Violence: Fear, Hatred, and Resentment in Twentieth-Century Europe.* Cambridge: Cambridge University Press.

———. 2005. "Memory and Cultural Schema: Linking Memory to Political Action." In *Memory and World War II*, ed. Francesca Cappelletto. New York: Berg, 131–153.

Posner, Daniel N. 2004. "The Political Salience of Cultural Difference: Why Chewas and Tumbukas Are Allies in Zambia and Adversaries in Malawi." *American Political Science Review* 98, no. 4: 529–546.

Rassool, Ciraj, and Sandra Prosalendis, eds. 2001. *Recalling Community in Cape Town: Creating and Curating the District Six Museum.* Cape Town: District Six Museum Foundation.

Roe, Michael D., and Ed Cairns. 2003. "Memories in Conflict: Review and a Look to the Future." In *The Role of Memory in Ethnic Conflict*, ed. Ed Cairns and Michael D. Roe. Houndsmills, Basingstoke: Palgrave.

Ross, Marc Howard. 2001. "Psychocultural Interpretations and Dramas: Identity Dynamics in Ethnic Conflict." *Political Psychology* 22, no. 1: 157–178.

———. 2007. *Cultural Contestation in Ethnic Conflict.* Cambridge: Cambridge University Press.

———. Forthcoming. "Culture in Comparative Political Analysis." In *Comparative Politics: Rationality, Culture and Structure* (2nd ed.), ed. Mark Irving Lichbach and Alan S. Zuckerman. Cambridge: Cambridge University Press.

Schweder, Richard A., and Robert A. LeVine, eds. 1984. *Culture Theory: Essays on Mind, Self and Emotion.* Cambridge: Cambridge University Press.

Scott, James C. 1985. *Weapons of the Weak: Everyday Forms of Peasant Resistance.* New Haven: Yale University Press.

Smith, Anthony D. 1999. *Myths and Memories of the Nation.* Oxford: Oxford University Press.

Spiro, Melford. 1984. "Some Reflections on Cultural Determinism and Relativism with Special Reference to Emotion and Reason." In *Culture Theory: Essays on Mind, Self and Emotion*, ed. Richard A. Schweder and Robert A. LeVine. Cambridge: Cambridge University Press, 323–346.

Swidler, Ann. 1986. "Culture in Action: Symbols and Strategies." *American Sociological Review* 51, no. 2: 273–286.

Thompson, Leonard. 1985. *The Political Mythology of Apartheid.* New Haven: Yale University Press.

Turner, Victor. 1957. *Schism and Continuity in an African Society: A Study of Ndembu Village Life.* Manchester: University of Manchester Press.

———. 1974. *Dramas, Fields and Metaphors: Symbolic Action in Human Society.* Ithaca: Cornell University Press.

Verba, Sidney. 1961. *Small Groups and Political Behavior: A Study of Leadership.* Princeton: Princeton University Press.

Volkan, Vamik D. 1997. *Bloodlines: From Ethnic Pride to Ethnic Terrorism.* New York: Farrar, Straus, Giroux.

Wedeen, Lisa. 2002. "Conceptualizing Culture: Possibilities for Political Science." *American Political Science Review* 96, no. 4: 713–728.

Chapter 2
The Rise and Fall of a Sacred Place
Ayodhya over Three Decades

Richard H. Davis

On the morning of Wednesday, 6 July 2005, six young men wearing new clothes and new shoes arrived at the Faizabad bus station in eastern Uttar Pradesh.[1] They were pilgrims, they said, and wished to make a tour of the holy places in nearby Ayodhya, the birthplace of the Hindu god Rama. A driver named Rohan Ahmad offered to take them around in his Marshall jeep for a price of Rs 1,300. At Ayodhya, the six young men had the driver stop at a Hindu temple while they went in to seek the god's blessings. When they returned, one of the men put a revolver to the head of the driver, pushed him out, and took the car. They drove toward another Hindu place of worship, where a makeshift temple to Rama stood atop the debris of a ruined mosque. Unlike most other Hindu temples, this modest Rama shrine was surrounded by heavy security. The jeep apparently passed through the first checkpoint without incident. At the second security barrier, about 200 yards from the shrine, Central Reserve Police Force (CRPF) guards stopped the car. The men burst out of the jeep with guns firing. The security guards immediately took cover and returned the fire. One of the men detonated the car, along with himself, in an attempt to blow a hole through the security cordon. The attackers tried to fight their way toward the Rama temple, carrying a rocket-launcher, but by this time other security personnel had been alerted and the attackers were caught in a crossfire. The gun battle lasted ninety minutes, according to one account, and in the end all six men were killed. Several guards were also injured. Two unexploded rockets were found near the Rama temple, but the temple itself suffered no damage.

Subsequent investigations established that the attack was the work of Lashkar-e-Toiba, the "Army of the Pure," a terrorist organization based in Pakistan-occupied Kashmir. Known as the most brutal group active in the Jammu and Kashmir insurgency, the Lashkar-e-Toiba frequently employs small groups of *fidayeen* (suicide squads) to carry out attacks on secure sites in India. The iconoclastic attack on the Rama temple in Ayodhya was just such a *fidayeen* operation, and one that involved considerable planning and preparation. The task leader Yunus came from Pakistan through Kashmir to Delhi in August 2004. Others arrived separately over the next few months, and established themselves with pseudonyms and pseudo-lives. Two of the terrorists set up a vegetable stall in the weekly bazaar near their rooming house. Between January and June 2005, Yunus and the others made several reconnaissance visits to Ayodhya. In June 2005 guns and explosives were delivered to the *fidayeen*. They were brought in from Lashkar headquarters in Pakistan-occupied Kashmir concealed in a special compartment carved out of a Tata Sumo vehicle. As one police investigator noted, in operations of this sort the men come from one place and the weapons from another. In late June the men traveled separately by bus to Saharanpur, then regrouped and traveled on to Akbarpur. On 2 July they made a final reconnaissance of the Ayodhya complex. On 5 July they put on their new clothes and went by taxi to the Faizabad bus station to begin the operation. Just before the assault, one of the terrorists made a cell phone call, and had a message passed on to the Lashkar-e-Toiba leadership. This call was one of the threads that enabled investigators to unravel the connections between the attackers and their support network.

Responses to the unsuccessful plot were immediate and dramatic. The event was like a prism, and each constituent voice of the Indian political spectrum spoke out in its distinctive color. The Hindu nationalists took the most adamant stance. The irrepressible Chief Minister of Gujarat, Narendra Modi, hyperbolically proclaimed the attack "as important as 9/11." Sushma Swaraj, a spokesman for the Bharatiya Janata Party (BJP), maintained that the operation was not just an attack on a *bhautik sthan* (material place), but an assault on the *hindu aastha* (Hindu faith) itself. When reporters asked Prime Minister Manmohan Singh, who was attending a meeting of world leaders in the United Kingdom, about Swaraj's statement about Hindu faith, he carefully reframed the issue. "Any attack on places of worship is an insult to humanity," Singh observed. "As human beings we should all be concerned." The Congress Party leader of a secular ruling coalition, Singh wished to avoid any communal Hindu-Muslim interpretation of the event and instead portrayed it as a matter of a universal human right to religious practice. Meanwhile, several of the political leaders of the BJP, most notably L. K. Advani, found themselves in a quandary over how best to respond, caught between the "hardliners and the electoral calculations necessary to operate in a mainstream political system." (Advani's complex involvement with Ayodhya will reappear throughout this chapter.) Leaders of the primary Kashmiri separatist groups, for their part, condemned the attacks. They initially suggested that it might have been the work of Hindu extremists, and the next day clarified that assaults on religious places of worship were not acceptable in their understanding of Islam. For the Kashmiri separatists, the Ayodhya affair posed a dangerous threat to the peace talks between India and Pakistan, which they saw as the best hope for redressing their grievances. Others also recognized this threat. The English-language newspaper *Indian Express* stated in its editorial on the day of the attack, "By attempting an attack in Ayodhya, the site of so many grand passions, religious and political, the terrorists aimed at stirring up a communal conflagration perhaps leading to the disrupting of the peace process with Pakistan."

Any casual visitor to the target of this iconoclastic assault could be excused for wondering what all the fuss was about. At this place of "grand passions" stands a singularly unimpressive shrine with a few undistinguished images in it. From 1984, when a Hindu nationalist organization initiated a campaign to liberate the supposed site of the god Rama's human birth from a sixteenth-century Muslim masjid, until 1992 when the mosque was leveled, Ayodhya increasingly became the target of a nationwide mobilization that exacerbated tensions and conflicts between Indian religious communities. After the decisive destruction, debates over the site continued. The target was certainly not venerable in age, for it was only put up in 1992 after the leveling of the mosque. Yet the *Indian Express* was correct in its description. The shrine stands on a plot of land that had been, over the previous twenty-five years, the most discussed and most hotly contested site in India. Disagreements and disputes over what lay beneath the destroyed shrine and over what should now be constructed on the location acted as focal points for broader issues of political power, religious faith, and Indian national identity.

Yet despite the weight of recent events at Ayodhya, there were no evident repercussions after the Lashkar-e-Toiba raid, and it quickly disappeared from news coverage. In part, the event was pushed out of the headlines by a more deadly terrorist attack in London on 8 July. Something more was involved, however. Despite the widespread official alarm in the aftermath of the raid, it appeared as if Ayodhya might no longer be a site capable of stirring such grand passions among the Indian public as in the past.

Ayodhya as Sacred Space

The drama surrounding the so-called Ram Janmabhumi (Rama's Birthplace) in Ayodhya traces a rising action from 1984 up to the destruction of the Babri Masjid in December 1992, and falls off in ongoing disputes and controversies over the site after 1992. Undoubtedly it was a watershed event in the history of modern India. The grand passions that the *Indian Express* mentioned involved issues and tensions, political and cultural contestations that went to the heart of India as a national community, and those passions were embodied in an extensive public discourse within India. The Ayodhya affair has also instigated a tremendous amount of scholarly analysis of many of the issues involved: the history of the site, the historical development of Hindu nationalism, the history and sociology of communal violence involving Hindu and Muslim communities, the political and social ramifications of the event, and much more.[2] In accord with the themes of this volume, I wish to consider the events surrounding Ayodhya from the perspective of the symbolic landscape and the mobilization of sacred space.

Since the work of Mircea Eliade, the category of sacred space has been an important analytic topic in the history of religions. Eliade himself considered sacred space as one of the key principles by which human communities order their worlds. "The manifestation of the sacred ontologically founds the world," he writes (1959: 21). "In the homogeneous and infinite expanse, in which no point of reference is possible and hence no orientation can be established, the hierophany reveals an absolute fixed point, a center." He goes on to argue that religious humans consider sacred places to be outside human agency. Symbolically, they are revealed, not created. "This is as much as to say that men are not free to choose the sacred site, that they only seek for it and find it by the help of mysterious signs" (1959: 28). Following Eliade, historians of religion most often regard sacred space in terms of a continuing quality of select places. Indological studies of Ayodhya, similarly, have emphasized its antiquity as a pilgrimage spot.[3] And along the same lines, a great deal of the news coverage of the Ayodhya events in the American media emphasized the great age of the site and the (allegedly) ancient and ongoing controversies over it. But sacred places, I would emphasize, have their ebbs and flows, their times of creation and destruction, their moments of incendiary importance, and their periods of decline and lethargy. Contrary to the Eliadean symbolism of the eternality and inherence of sacred sites, I would stress the role of human agency in creating, sustaining, and at times abandoning or desacralizing sacred space. When we examine Ayodhya more closely as a place of cultural contestation within the Indian public sphere, it becomes apparent that it rose into prominence during the 1980s and 1990s through intentional mobilization by Hindu nationalist groups, and it appears equally to be retreating from cultural salience in the current decade.

My aim in this chapter is to sketch out the rise of the pilgrimage center Ayodhya into a place of grand passions. Participants in the struggle over Ayodhya characterized the contested site as a place on ongoing, continuous struggle over many centuries. Against this claim, I argue here that Ayodhya's nationwide significance resulted from a calculated and adept campaign to provoke a crisis, instigated by several interrelated groups of Hindu nationalists. I will trace some of the cultural and ideological background to their mobilization, centered on their theology of the land. The campaign led finally to the destruction of the mosque in December 1992. I conclude with brief comments on developments surrounding the site since 1992. In the aftermath of destruction, a combination of political calculations, unresolved archaeological debates, and legal stalemates have allowed Ayodhya to drop once again out of the public spotlight. I suggest this may represent a "good-enough" resolution to some irreconcilable conflicts at the heart of the Ayodhya controversy. Sacred space need not be sacred forever, and there are times when that is a good thing.

Destruction of the Babri Masjid

On another morning twelve and a half years before the Lashkar-e-Toiba raid on the Ayodhya site, 6 December 1992, another attack had occurred, with much more devastating results. A crowd estimated at over 300,000 people assembled that day for a rally in the old pilgrimage city. The leader of the BJP, L. K. Advani, and other Hindu nationalist leaders gave fiery orations. As the rally wore on, a group of activists or *kar sevaks* (voluntary workers) belonging to several other Hindu nationalist organizations broke away from the assembly ground and headed toward the place they identified as the Ram Janmabhumi, the birthplace of Rama. With little trouble they broke through police barricades and knocked down a chain-link fence that protected the sixteenth-century masjid that occupied the spot. With mattocks and axes the *kar sevaks* swarmed over the Babri Masjid and within a few hours they had leveled the old mosque to the ground.

The destruction of the Babri Masjid was not a random act of mob iconoclasm, but the outcome of an eight-year campaign led by two Hindu nationalist groups, the BJP and the Vishva Hindu Parishad or "World Hindu Congress" (VHP). Within this campaign, the electoral group BJP often articulated a more inclusive position, while the religious-cultural organization VHP took the more radical and uncompromising position, but the two agreed on its fundamental purposes. The campaign rested on three primary assertions. According to these groups, the Babri Masjid occupied the exact location where the Hindu god Rama, hero of the epic poem *Ramayana*, was physically born thousands of years earlier. For many centuries and up to the sixteenth century, they asserted, a great Hindu temple devoted to Rama had stood on the spot of Rama's birth, marking it as a holy place. And third, they averred, the Mughal conqueror Babur had destroyed the Rama temple in 1526 and appropriated the site by constructing an Islamic monument atop the ruins.

In April 1984 the VHP had initiated a campaign to reclaim the site for Hindus and construct on it a new Rama temple. They issued an ultimatum calling on state and national officials to hand over the Ram Janmabhumi. If the demand was not honored, they threatened a massive agitation led by the religious leaders of the Hindu faith.

All three tenets of the VHP campaign were debatable, and as the Ram Janmabhumi mobilization gained force in the late 1980s, vigorous debate did ensue. In November 1989 a group of secular historians from Jawaharlal Nehru University in Delhi issued a polemical pamphlet, "The Political Abuse of History," that called into question all the premises of the Ramjanmabhumi movement (Gopal et al. 1990). Proponents of the mobilization responded heatedly. Through the following several years, newspapers and magazines in India were filled with historiographical discussions of the life of Rama, medieval Hindu temple building, and Muslim iconoclasm in India. In these debates, however, the VHP held a religious trump card. Whatever the historical facts might be, they observed, their claims were ultimately matters of faith. The masses of the Hindu faithful, asserted the VHP, believed that Rama had been born at the site they identified as the Ram Janmabhumi. Secular historians might cast doubt on the factuality of this identification, but they could not refute tenets of religious belief. The leaders of the movement placed themselves in the role of agents of the will of the Hindu faithful.

According to the VHP and the BJP (which joined the campaign in 1988), Hindus had harbored a persistent grievance over Babur's supposed act of destruction. As the BJP put it, Hindus had been "waging unremitting struggle for centuries to repossess the birthplace of Sri Rama." According to the Hindu nationalist narrative, Ayodhya was just one front in a larger, centuries-long battle between two macrocommunities defined along religious lines: indigenous Hindus and invading Muslims. During medieval times Muslim warriors had conquered much of Hindu India, according to this story, and the new Muslim rulers had pursued a systematic policy of iconoclasm toward Hindu places of worship in an effort to convert the very landscape of India. But Hindus had zealously resisted. Within their version of events, the VHP identified themselves as only the latest "manifestation" of an ongoing effort: "The struggle for the liberation of Sri Ram Janmabhoomi and restoration of a magnificent Rama Temple at Ayodhya has been going on continuously, in one form or another, for several centuries. Many generations have participated in it and paid a heavy price in martyrdom. Only the perverse and blind will say that the Vishva Hindu Parishad is the originator of this struggle. VHP represents only the latest reincarnation or organised manifestation of this centuries old Hindu aspiration" (VHP 1991: i). But in fact, the VHP and the BJP had to work hard to create a movement to recapture the Ramjanmabhumi. When the VHP issued its call for liberation in 1984, the controversy over the site had never been more than a local concern, and even in Ayodhya itself the issue had been dormant for over thirty years. The VHP would seek to turn this forgotten local issue over a sacred place into a matter of pressing national concern.

The Mobilization of Sacred Space

To launch its mobilization the VHP employed a variety of media. They issued small stickers and greeting cards of Rama. Their artists designed a new poster depicting Rama as an adorable toddler behind bars—the infant god held prisoner in a Muslim institution at the site of his own birth. Another new poster showed Rama as a confident young warrior striding through the clouds, his bow and arrow at the ready for coming battle. The VHP commissioned an accomplished traditional architect to draw up plans for a new Ramjanmabhumi temple, designed to look like a twelfth-century North Indian temple. They put out a request to Hindus all over India and beyond to make special bricks inscribed with the name of Rama. Hindu communities throughout India and abroad were to hold special ceremonies to consecrate these bricks, and then send them to Ayodhya, where they would eventually be used to construct the new temple.

Other unanticipated developments assisted the VHP in its efforts to promote devotion to Rama and concern over his birthplace. In January 1987, just as the VHP campaign was picking up momentum, the national television network Doordarshan began to run a serial retelling of the story of Rama. It turned out to be an enormous hit, the most popular show ever to air on Indian television. Though he was not affiliated with the VHP, the director of the series Ramanand Sagar also sought to elevate Rama to the status of central deity for modern Hinduism, and he viewed the Ramayana story as a "symbol of national unity and integration" (Lutgendorf 1990; Rajagopal 2001). In the late 1980s Rama seemed to be everywhere you looked in India.

By 1990 the VHP and the BJP were ready to attempt a more ambitious and provocative leg in their campaign to liberate Rama's birthplace. The plan was to stage a nationwide Rath Yatra (or "chariot procession") across northern India, traversing some 6,000 miles, to drum up popular support for the Ayodhya movement. Advani as the leader of the BJP would preside over the procession in a Toyota flatbed truck fitted out with wooden cutouts to look like the kind of epic chariot Rama had ridden in the televised "Ramayana." The parade would halt every few hours along the way for rallies, speeches, and impromptu religious ceremonies. After a journey of thirty-five days the procession would reach Ayodhya. By then, organizers hoped, the procession would be joined by an irresistible congregation of followers and *kar sevaks*, and the work of converting the Babri Masjid into a Hindu temple would commence.

As Advani's Toyota-chariot rolled out of the Gujarati temple-town of Somnath on 25 September 1990, and proceeded eastward toward Ayodhya, civil disturbances followed in its wake. There was an unmistakable element of provocation in the procession, directed most immediately toward India's large Muslim population. The youth brigade, calling itself the Bajrang Dal ("Hanuman's army," after the famous monkey-warrior in the Ramayana), took to carrying tridents, bows, and other epic-period weapons. When the procession passed through Muslim neighborhoods, the ancient weapons were flourished and often put into action in street brawls. The chariot procession also posed a serious dilemma for ruling authorities. Prime Minister V. P. Singh, leader of the ruling coalition National Front, could not afford to allow the civil disturbances, nor could he take any chances on what might happen if the mobilization reached Ayodhya. Yet to stop the procession would involve acting against the BJP, a member of the governing coalition. The politically savvy Singh was also aware of the political consequences of appearing to act against the god Rama.

Finally on 23 October, seven days before the chariot was to reach Ayodhya, the Chief Minister of Bihar ordered police to stop the procession and arrest Advani and other leaders. Riots and mass arrests followed in many cities throughout India. Some 200,000 Indians were placed in detention, more than had been detained in India's other great moments of widespread civil protest and unrest, the 1942 Quit India movement and the National Emergency of 1975–1977. On 30 October, *kar sevaks* broke into the Babri Masjid and placed saffron banners, the symbolic color of Hindu nationalism, around the mosque's spires, but the masjid suffered only minor damage from this foray. On 7 November, the BJP withdrew support from Singh's coalition, and the National Front government fell.

The massive success of the 1990 Rath Yatra as a public mobilization, the unfinished business it left behind in Ayodhya, and the confusion over political authority it caused in Delhi, all paved the way toward the complete destruction of the Babri Masjid two years later, in December

1992. Once again Advani and the BJP leadership played an instigating role, but remained several hundred yards from the physical assault, which was carried out primarily by the young *kar sevaks* of the Bajrang Dal. Again Advani and other leaders were arrested and charged with incitement. Once again the events surrounding Ayodhya triggered mass violence. Within two months three thousand lives were lost in the communal disturbances.

As a watershed event in modern India, the Ayodhya campaign and its aftermath have been discussed by Indian observers and scholars from many different perspectives. Historians have carefully traced the history of Hindu nationalism from its origins in the colonial period. Archaeologists have debated the evidence for claims of an earlier Hindu temple at the Ayodhya site. Anthropologists have explored the social origins and repercussions of communal violence in contemporary India. Political scientists have discussed the various conditions that enabled Hindu nationalist political groups to move so rapidly from the periphery to the center of Indian public life. Cultural studies analysts have investigated the role of the media in promulgating Hindu nationalist ideology.

As a historian of Indian religions I have been particularly interested in the way Hindu nationalist groups appropriated and deployed existing Hindu images and practices, and invented new ones. The Ayodhya mobilization centrally concerned religious institutions, and the main instigator of the campaign was an organization devoted to the advancement of Hindu religious interests. Hindu nationalists sought to mobilize the religious sentiments of Hindus toward the broad political and social agenda associated with the term "Hindutva," literally Hindu-ness. In the process they transformed Hinduism itself. In this chapter I want to focus on one aspect of the Hindu nationalist religious ideology that infused the Ayodhya campaign, their theology of the land. In a modern nation-state that defined itself as multireligious and secular, proponents of Hindu nationalism sought through the Ayodhya campaign and others to remake the land of India and its sacred sites as essentially Hindu. The selection of the Ramjanmabhumi in Ayodhya as their exemplary target was a deft choice in this larger enterprise.

Theology of Hindu Land

The term "Hindutva" and the most succinct originating statement of Hindutva ideology come from the writings of Vinayak Damodar Savarkar, a nonreligious Maharashtrian brahmin. As a student Savarkar joined the extremist wing of the anticolonial movement, and in 1909 he was convicted in a conspiracy to assassinate a British colonial official and transported to prison in the Andaman Islands. During his confinement he began composing his best-known work, an essay entitled *Hindutva: Who Is a Hindu?* first published in 1922 (Savarkar 1989). As with many early twentieth-century Indian leaders and writers in the anticolonial movement, Savarkar was preoccupied with the theoretical and practical question of Indian unity. In the face of British colonial control, what could provide Indian subjects with the cohesive sense of shared identity and purpose that would give them the power to gain their independence?

On the title page of his essay, Savarkar answers his own question with a definition in Sanskrit verse. "A Hindu," he asserts, "means a person who regards this land of Bharatvarsha, from the Indus to the Seas, as his Father-Land as well as his Holy-Land that is the cradle land of his religion." In the essay he goes on to elaborate with a broad historical vision. From the earliest time of the Vedas right up to the present, he argued, the term *Hindu* had consistently referred to a single community of people who had occupied a territory they called *Hindustan*, the place of the Hindus. It is significant that Savarkar did not identify Hindutva precisely with Hinduism. Rather, he claimed, "Hinduism is only a derivative, a fraction, a part of Hindutva." In Savarkar's view, there were three fundamental constituents of Hindutva: a shared territory (*rashtra*), a common birth or shared ancestry (*jati*), and a common culture or civilization (*sanskriti*).

Unlike many of his contemporaries, Savarkar had no inclination to reform Hinduism, nor did he make any effort in *Hindutva* to identify central or essential Hindu beliefs or practices. Instead he defined Hinduism simply as "all the religious beliefs that the different communities of Hindu people hold." All these formed part of the common religious culture of the Hindu people. Indeed, within the broad definition of Hindutva, adherents of other religious groups that had originated in the Indian land, such as Jains, Buddhists, and Sikhs, might also partake of shared land, blood, and culture. However, the definition also pointedly excluded those who identified themselves with religious ideologies whose origins were foreign to the subcontinent, namely Muslims and Christians. Even though indigenous converts to Islam (who constituted, by some estimates, ninety percent of the Indian Muslim population) might share land and ancestry with Hindus, they had in Savarkar's view decisively broken with the common culture of Hindutva.

What is important in Savarkar's formulation for our purposes is his identification of the land of India "from the Indus to the Seas" as the very ground of Hindutva, and his exclusion of Muslims and adherents of other foreign ideologies from this common culture, even if they had occupied the same land for generations or centuries. While mainstream leaders of the independence movement articulated an inclusive "territorial nationalism" that would include all residents of India, Savarkar laid the ideological groundwork for a "cultural" or "religious nationalism" that would identify one cultural group, Hindus broadly defined, as the primary embodiment of nationhood. In subsequent writings, Savarkar developed a broad historical master narrative in which all Indian history consisted in a series of foreign invasions, starting with Alexander's raid in the fourth century B.C.E., and staunch Hindu struggles to combat these invaders and retain their independence (Savarkar 1971). Throughout the ages, in Savarkar's historical vision, Hindus have come together as a single community in times of threat to protect their Hindustan homeland.

Savarkar also served for several years in the late 1930s and early 1940s as the president of the Hindu Mahasabha, which was the primary Hindu nationalist political organization during this period. However, even under Savarkar's energetic leadership the Hindu Mahasabha played a marginal role in the politics of the independence movement. Soon after independence, Hindu nationalist politics was effectively barred for several decades, due to the involvement of an RSS member in the assassination of Mahatma Gandhi. Not until the 1990s, under very different conditions, would a Hindu nationalist electoral party emerge as a powerful voice in Indian politics.

Goddess of the Nation

While Savarkar viewed a common reverence for a shared territory as an essential component of Hindutva, other Indians during the colonial period began to envision this national landscape in divine terms, as a goddess. The new nation-goddess Bharat Mata (Mother India) made her first appearance in an 1882 work of historical fiction by Bankim Chandra Chatterji, *Anandamath*. In this novel set in the 1770s during the early years of British colonial rule, anti-British insurgents recruit the protagonist Mahendra, a rich villager who has lost his wealth and home, to join their cause. The leader of the group escorts the new recruit into an underground chamber, where he shows Mahendra three images of a goddess. First is a benign and bounteous form, the goddess as she used to be. Second, Mahendra sees a dark, naked, emaciated female, the goddess as she is now. Finally, the leader shows him a glorious ten-armed deity, each hand holding a different weapon, with her enemy sprawled at her feet—the goddess as she will appear in the future. The members of the cadre sing their praises to the goddess in a hymn, "Vande Mataram," (Victory to the Mother), where they celebrate both the glorious landscape and the bounteous fruits of the goddess, and also the tremendous power she holds latent within her.

Earlier Hindus had viewed individual elements of the landscape, including rivers like the Ganges, as goddesses. They had envisioned the earth itself as a goddess, Bhu Devi. But only in the colonial world of the late nineteenth century was a delimited portion of the earth's surface, the territory occupied by an incipient nation, transformed into a goddess. One historian speaks of Bharat Mata as a "Durkheimian goddess," a "sacred name for the collective self" of the Indian community as it came to imagine itself as a nation. While this is certainly one aspect of her being, she is also closely identified with the land itself, the divinization of a landscape that (as "Vande Mataram" puts it) "gives ease" to all those who depend upon her.

Chatterji's novel was enormously popular and influential in giving voice to the rising spirit of rebellion against British colonial control in the 1890s and 1900s, and "Vande Mataram" became the unofficial anthem of the movement for Indian independence. However, there was a problem with Bharat Mata. She was too Hindu. Although there was nothing particularly exclusive about the goddess evoked in "Vande Mataram," it inescapably drew on the iconography and devotional imagery of other Hindu deities. The urban elites who were organizing the Indian independence movement determined that they must avoid overt Hindu imagery in their mobilizations, to prevent non-Hindus from feeling excluded or marginalized. By the 1920s and 1930s, Bharat Mata largely dropped out of official view. Rabindranath Tagore composed an alternative anthem, and the official iconography of the Indian National Congress of that period revolved around austere aniconic images like the tricolor flag and the Gandhian spinning-wheel.

The nation-goddess returned briefly, and appropriately enough, around the time of independence. In the late 1940s and early 1950s, poster artists gave form to the unbound Mata arising, a new divine figure taking her place atop the globe. The goddess appears in a celebratory and generous mood in these depictions, with leaders of the independence movement like Gandhi and Jawaharlal Nehru either assisting her or receiving her blessings. In one poster by the artist Brojen, Gandhi actually cuts the shackles off Bharat Mata, as other well-known freedom fighters look on. The poster artists associate Bharat Mata repeatedly with the new map of India. After her appearance at the moment of national birth, however, Bharat Mata seems to recede from the public eye for several decades.

By the mid-1980s, the Hindu nationalists had resurrected her. However, she returned in a different form. If poster artists at the time of independence envisioned Bharat Mata as serene and bountiful toward her devotees, Hindu nationalist painters often depicted her as a militant goddess leading her minions into confrontation with their enemies

(Brosius 2007). No longer so accommodating, Bharat Mata now makes war on "foreign" elements of the Indian landscape, identified in one VHP pamphlet cover as snake-like Islam, Christianity, and American neocolonialism. If the Bharat Mata of the 1940s most resembled Laksmi, the Hindu goddess of prosperity, in the 1980s and 1990s she returned as an incarnation of Durga, goddess of war. On the fiftieth anniversary of Indian independence in 1997, the VHP staged a huge Bharat Mata Puja, a ceremonial worship of Mother India, at the Jawaharlal Nehru Stadium in the national capital. The goddess of the divinized land of India received her honor at the center of the public sphere.

Pilgrimage and the Mother Land

Pilgrimage to holy places is a long-standing and widespread practice in all Indian religions. Early on, Buddhists and Jains began to visit the important sites in the lives of their founders. The early Sanskrit epic *Mahabharata* takes the protagonists, the Pandavas, on a lengthy "tour of the sacred fords" that encompasses most regions of the subcontinent, and later Hindu orthodox literature reflects an enormous interest in the topic of pilgrimage. Indian Muslims undertake journeys to domestic holy sites, often those associated with Indian Sufi saints. So common was the practice of pilgrimage in India that a twelfth-century historian, Kalhana, estimated that in Kashmir no plot of land larger than a sesame seed lacked its own pilgrimage spot.

Within orthodox Hindu writings, pilgrimage is treated as *tirtha-yatra*, a journey to a holy place. Usage of the term *tirtha*, literally a "crossing place," is extended very early beyond river-fords to designate all sorts of places considered to be especially holy—not just rivers, but also lakes, mountains, forests, and even locations in cities. *Tirthas* may be sacred naturally, or they may be made holy by past acts of gods or by association with human saints. Hindu authors generally view pilgrimage as an individual act of renunciation and merit. Pilgrims begin their journey by announcing a resolution, which enumerates past sins and states an intention to expiate them through religious observance. One then adopts the ragged clothes of a mendicant and sets out on the journey. Once the pilgrim reaches the destination, there are ritual actions to be carried out, most commonly bathing. Acts performed at a *tirtha* are considered to be more efficacious than the same acts done elsewhere.

In 1983 the VHP undertook a pilgrimage, but it was a decidedly new kind of pilgrimage. If most pilgrimages are undertaken to gain personal or family merit (*punya*), as Hindu nationalist writer H. V. Seshadri observes (1988: 283), this one was a collective pilgrimage on behalf of social and national merit. In a nationwide public ceremony they called the

Ekatmata Yajna, or "sacrifice for unity," they set out on three *yatras* across the subcontinent. One proceeded from the holy city of Hardwar, where the waters of the Ganges River flow out from the Himalayas onto the plains, to Kanyakumari at the southern tip of India. Another went from Gangasagar, where the Ganges enters the Bay of Bengal in eastern India, to the temple site of Somnath on the western coast of Gujarat. The third traversed India north to south, from the Pasupatinath temple in Nepal to the Ramesvaram temple in Tamilnad. The routes were designed to visit as many existing pilgrimage spots along the way as possible. Each procession featured two decorated trucks. One held a large image of Bharat Mata, while the other held two enormous bronze water vessels. One of the receptacles held water taken from the holy Ganges River, while the other was filled with waters collected over the course of the procession.

Each day the processions moved along their routes and stopped at select locations. At each stop the VHP organized a two-hour program. The key part of each ceremony consisted in an exchange of waters. The locals donated water from local rivers and sources of holy water, which was deposited in one receptacle, and then received from the other receptacle water from the sacred Ganges, which they could use in their own local worship. By the time the processions reached their destinations, they had collected water "from all the sacred places, namely the four Dhams, the twelve Jyotirlingas, the fifty-two Shaktipeethas, Manasarovar, Nanak Sagar, Hemkund, and hundreds of sacred rivers, lakes, and wells" (Seshadri 1988: 279). A VHP leader, Swami Chinmayananda, explained the purpose of the pilgrimage was "to give an ideal acceptable to people of all religions, regions, and creeds and thus furnish a sense of national purpose and oneness to our national life" (Seshadri 1988: 279). Under the presiding gaze of Bharat Mata, the mixing of sacred waters served as a unifying metaphor for the Indian oneness the VHP sought to engender.

Purification of the Land

The success of the Ekatmata Yajna emboldened the VHP to undertake a larger and riskier project. In 1984 the group announced its plan to liberate three north Indian sites: Rama's birthplace in Ayodhya, Krishna's birthplace in Mathura, and a manifestation-place of Shiva in Varanasi. If the Ekatmata Yajna had adopted the ostensibly inclusive and unthreatening image of mixing holy waters, however, the new project linked the purity and unification of the Indian landscape with an inescapably confrontational anti-Muslim rhetoric. At each of the three sites stood an Islamic mosque. In each case the claim was made that the current mosque stood atop the ruins of a Hindu temple destroyed by Muslim conquerors. These mosques would need to be removed to allow the construction of new Hindu temples at each site. The VHP decided to focus their efforts first on the Babri Masjid in Ayodhya, and set in motion the events culminating in its destruction eight years later.

Rather than review those events, I would like to step back and view the Ayodhya campaign as part of a broader Hindutva discourse concerning Indian history, identity, exclusion, and the purity of the Indian landscape. Here again the writings of V. D. Savarkar offer the best starting point.

Savarkar's final work, *Six Glorious Epochs in Indian History*, was completed in 1963 when he was eighty years old. The six epochs of the title constituted a history of Hindu struggles to gain freedom from foreign domination, ending with the achievement of independence from British colonialism in 1947. Among the foreign threats, Savarkar devoted more than half his book to the fifth epoch, the medieval invasions of Muslim warriors. For Savarkar, Islamic invasions had more far-reaching ambitions than any earlier invaders or the British. While others sought only to dominate politically, Savarkar argues, "These new Islamic enemies not only aspired to crush the Hindu political power and establish in its place Muslim sovereignty over the whole of India, but they also had, seething in their brains another fierce religious ambition, not heretofore dreamt of by any of the old enemies of India. Intoxicated by this religious ambition, which was many more times diabolical than their political one, these millions of Muslim invaders from all over Asia fell over India century after century with all the ferocity at their command to destroy the Hindu religion which was the life-blood of the nation" (Savarkar 1971: 129–130). A central tactic in this war on Hinduism, according to Savarkar, was iconoclastic attacks on Hindu religious images and institutions: "Every Muslim aggressor went on demolishing Hindu temples at Mathura and Kashi (Benares). The most sacred idols in the various magnificent shrines from all over India right up to Rameswaram were not only purposely taken to the Muslim capitals like Delhi and plastered into the portal steps of their royal palaces, but, for the sole purpose of hurting the feelings of the Hindus and insulting them, they were also used as slabs and tiles for lavatories, water-closets, and urinals" (1971: 170). In the 1980s, new Hindu nationalist authors extended Savarkar's historical vision. The most effective and widely disseminated were the works of Sita Ram Goel, published by Voice of India. Goel asserted that "all masjids and mazars, particularly the Jami Masjids which date from the first Muslim occupation of a place, stand on the site of Hindu temples" (1990: 83). He goes on to provide lists of some two thousand Muslim monuments that allegedly occupy former Hindu temple sites or include Hindu materials in their fabric (1993: 255–374). His aim is comprehensive: every dilapidated temple ruin and every "Hindu element" in an Indo-Muslim structure should be perceived as evidence of what he calls an "Islamic theology of iconoclasm," carried out against Hindus. The overarching agenda of Goel's work, building on the historical narrative offered by Savarkar and other Hindu nationalist historians, is to persuade the Hindu population to view all Muslim structures as illegitimate, as polluting the sacred landscape of India. In the words of the BJP white paper on Ayodhya, Muslim buildings in India should serve as "ocular reminders" of a destructive past.

This representation of the medieval past is not just of historical interest, however, but meant to suggest a program for action in the present. If Muslims "stole" holy sites from Hindus in centuries past, Hindu nationalists can call upon present-day Hindus to take them back. The mobilization to recover Rama's birthplace in Ayodhya has certainly been the best-known and most consequential act of site-conversion, but by no means the only one. In *Wages of Violence* (2001: 107–108), Thomas Blom Hansen reports a local dispute from Thane City, near Bombay in Maharashtra.

On a hill north of Thane City stands a local Muslim *dargah* named for the medieval Sufi saint Haji Malang Baba. The dargah has been a pilgrimage site for centuries, and its annual fair attracts large crowds of Muslims and Hindus as well. Hansen observes that the dargah illustrates the "religious syncretism" common throughout India. While the tomb is undoubtedly a Muslim structure, worship at the site is managed by a Hindu brahmin family, many of the rites incorporate clearly Hindu elements, and the worshipers include adherents of both faiths.

Starting in 1988 the regional Hindu nationalist group Shiv Sena announced that the hill was in fact the location of an ancient Hindu shrine belonging to the Nath Panth, an order of yogis. Haji Malang, far from a saint, was a Muslim conqueror, they went on, who had destroyed the Nath shrine and constructed a fort and a tomb atop the hill. The local Shiv Sena leader, Anand Dighe, started a campaign to take back the hill. Every year at fair time crowds of Shiv Sena followers and sympathizers gather at the hill and Anand Dighe leads them in a procession to the dargah in dispute. Arrests generally follow, and then protests of the arrests. As Hansen summarizes, the Shiv Sena "has manufactured this recurrent conflict in order to project the party as the defender of a naive, good-hearted Hindu community, unaware until now of the Muslim 'theft' of this ancient place of worship" (2001: 108).

The Fall of Ayodhya

The fall of the Babri Masjid in 1992 was undoubtedly a significant event in modern Indian history. From one perspective it can be seen as the culmination of an audacious, adept, and successful public campaign carried out by Hindu nationalist organizations. The VHP, previously a rather peripheral religious interest group, became a major ideological force in the Indian public sphere. The BJP moved from the margins of Indian politics to the center. From just two seats in the Lok Sabha in 1984, it gained 118 seats in the 1991 election, and by 1998 it had become the dominant party in the ruling NDA coalition government. In their 1993 White Paper on the Ramjanmabhumi movement, the BJP envisioned this as a restoration of Hindu governance after a long "digression": "The nation in India always remained Hindu, whether the State was controlled by Turks, Afghans, Mughals, Portuguese, French, English, or Nehruvian Secularists. The Ayodhya movement became relevant and invincible when the postindependence digression in the national mind seriously undermined the ethos and traditions of the nation in India, and as a result, the state and the nation again got virtually divorced by the rupture of national identity and the mindless adoption of the Western as the modern" (BJP 1993: 15). For many of those whose lives were touched by the massive unrest, of course, the campaign was not something to be celebrated, but rather a terrible social tragedy. The consequences of the events reached far beyond Ayodhya and affected Indian public life in uncountable ways.

The failed terrorist incident of July 2005, however, may provide us with another dimension to the story of Ayodhya. The target was undoubtedly chosen by Lashkar-e-Toiba to constitute a symbolic attack on a highly charged Indian site, in hopes of kindling social animosities. In the terrorist scenario the Indian media and political elite played their roles in the immediate aftermath of the incident, with expression of alarm and anger. They feared, and with justification, that Ayodhya would once again be the central site, the *axis mundi* (to adopt Eliade's famous term) in an Indian landscape of communal violence. But the lack of any significant repercussions to the attack among the broader Indian public may help us to see that sacred sites, if created through political will, may also come to be ignored or forgotten.[4]

It is not possible here to retrace the peculiar denouement of Ayodhya in the aftermath of the 1992 destruction of the Babri Masji. When the smoke cleared, one key question was what would become of the site where the destroyed mosque had stood, the supposed birthplace of Rama. Several outcomes were proposed. The Hindu nationalists of course continued to insist on achieving the second part of their plan, to build a grand new Rama temple. They did succeed in establishing a small Rama shrine nearby (which the Lashkar-e-Toiba would attack thirteen years later), but the authorities prevented any large-scale construction at the site. Muslim organizations and others sympathetic to the aggrieved Muslim community urged a rebuilding of the Masjid, but this was not feasible in the face of fierce Hindu nationalist opposition. Others saw an opportunity for transforming the former masjid into a site for reconciliation. In early 1993 the news magazine *India Today*, for instance, ran a fascinating series of proposals from architects, urban designers, and lay readers for creating a new memorial at the location that would stress values of religious multiplicity, social tolerance, and secular politics above the site of past iconoclasm. But unresolved cultural disputes and political animosities were much too raw for such a monument to be physically realizable.

Instead, the site entered a kind of high-profile limbo. What was there before the Babri Masjid? What should be there after the Babri Masjid? These questions did not admit of unambiguous answers that all could agree upon, and so they entered finally into legal disputes. The Indian Supreme Court wisely dragged its feet on these issues, allowing grand passions to cool off. That very irresolution allowed Ayodhya to devolve from a flash point for cultural contestation in the 1980s and 1990s, into a present-day humdrum site of past disputes.[5] This may be the good-enough solution to Ayodhya's legacy as a sacred site.

Notes

1. The following account of the July 2005 attack on Ayodhya is based on the extensive newspaper coverage of two English-language newspapers, *Indian Express* and *The Hindu*, from 6 July to 24 July 2005.

2. A select list of scholarship, along with some valuable polemical writing, would include: Andersen and Damle (1987), Jaffrelot (1996), Hansen (1999), and Zavos (2000) on Hindu nationalism; the essays in Gopal et al. (1991) and Ludden (1996) for valuable perspectives on the Ayodhya affair; Bhattacharya (1991), Basu et al. (1993), and Brosius (2007) on Hindutva media and mobilizing strategies. Elst (1990) is an effective work of Hindu nationalist polemics, and Ahmad (2002) and Panikkar (2002) are strong counterpolemics. Madan (1997) offers a thoughtful reconsideration of the underlying issues. My previous contributions to this extensive literature include an iconographic study of the 1990 Hindu nationalist chariot procession (Davis 1996) and a brief cultural background of Hindu nationalism (Davis 2004).

3. See Bakker (1986) and Van der Veer (1992) for long-term accounts of sacred Ayodhya. For a more reflective treatment of Ayodhya as a sacred center, see Friedland and Hecht (1998).

4. For a long-range study of Somanatha, another Indian site with ups and downs as a sacred center, see Davis (1997: 88–112, 186–221) and Thapar (2004).

5. To pursue the archaeological and legal debates over Ayodhya since 1992, the interested reader may consult Mandal (1993), Noorani (2003), Shrimali (2003), and Hawkes (2004).

Bibliography

Ahmad, Aijaz. 2002. *On Communalism and Globalization: Offensives of the Far Right.* New Delhi: Three Essays.
Andersen, Walter K., and Shridhar D. Damle. 1987. *The Brotherhood in Saffron: The Rashtriya Swayamsevak Sangh and Hindu Revivalism.* Boulder, Colo.: Westview Press.
Bakker, Hans. 1986. *Ayodhya.* Gronigen: Egbert Forsten.
Basu, Tapan, Pradip Datta, Sumit Sarkar, Tanika Sarkar, and Sambuddha Sen. 1993. *Khaki Shorts and Saffron Flags: A Critique of the Hindu Right.* New Delhi: Orient Longman.
Bharatiya Janata Party. 1993. *White Paper on Ayodhya and the Rama Temple Movement.* New Delhi: Bharatiya Janata Party.
Bhattacharya, Neeladri. 1991. "Myth, History and the Politics of Ramjanmabhumi." In *Anatomy of a Confrontation,* ed. Sarvepalli Gopal. Delhi: Penguin Books, 122–140.
Brosius, Christiane. 2007. "'I Am a National Artist': Popular Art in the Sphere of Hindutva." In *Picturing the Nation: Iconographies of Modern India,* ed. Richard H. Davis. Hyderabad: Orient Longman, 171–205.
Davis, Richard H. 1996. "The Iconography of Rama's Chariot." In *Contesting the Nation: Religion, Community and the Politics of Democracy in India,* ed. David Ludden. Philadelphia: University of Pennsylvania Press, 27–54.
———. 1997. *Lives of Indian Images.* Princeton: Princeton University Press.
———. 2004. "The Cultural Background of Hindutva." In *India Briefing,* ed. Philip Oldenberg and Alyssa Ayres. New York: Asia Society, 107–139.
Eliade, Mircea. 1959 [1957]. *The Sacred and the Profane: The Nature of Religion,* trans. Williard R. Trask. San Diego: Harcourt Brace Jovanovich.
Elst, Koenraad. 1990. *Ram Janmabhoomi Vs. Babri Masjid: A Case Study in Hindu-Muslim Conflict.* New Delhi: Voice of India.
Friedland, Roger, and Richard Hecht. 1998. "The Bodies of Nations: A Comparative Study of Religious Violence in Jerusalem and Ayodhya." *History of Religions,* 38: 101–149.
Goel, Sita Ram. 1990. "Let the Mute Witnesses Speak." In *Hindu Temples: What Happened to Them (A Preliminary Survey),* ed. Arun Shourie, Harsh Narain, Jay Dubashi, Ram Swarup, and Sita Ram Goel. New Delhi: Voice of India, 62–181.
———. 1993. *Hindu Temples: What Happened to Them, Vol. II: The Islamic Evidence.* New Delhi: Voice of India.
Gopal, Sarvepalli, ed. 1991. *Anatomy of a Confrontation: The Babri-Masjid-Ramjanmabhumi Issue.* New Delhi: Penguin.
Gopal, Sarvepalli et al. 1990. "The Political Abuse of History: Babri Masjid-Rama Janmabhumi Dispute." *Social Scientist,* 18, no. 1–2: 76–81.
Hansen, Thomas Blom. 1999. *The Saffron Wave: Democracy and Hindu Nationalism in Modern India.* Princeton: Princeton University Press.
———. 2001. *Wages of Violence: Naming and Identity in Postcolonial Bombay.* Princeton: Princeton University Press.
Hawkes, Gillian. 2004. "The Archaeology and Politics of Ayodhya." In *Ayodhya 1992–2003: The Assertion of Cultural and Religious Hegemony,* ed. Richard Bonney. Delhi: Media House, 92–111.
Jaffrelot, Christophe. 1996. *The Hindu Nationalist Movement in India.* New York: Columbia University Press.

Ludden, David, ed. 1996. *Contesting the Nation: Religion, Community and the Politics of Democracy in India.* Philadelphia: University of Pennsylvania Press.

Lutgendorf, Philip. 1990. "Ramayan: The Video." *The Drama Review,* 34, no. 2: 127–176.

Madan, T. N. 1997. *Modern Myths, Locked Minds: Secularism and Fundamentalism in India.* Delhi: Oxford University Press.

Mandal, D. 1993. *Ayodhya: Archaeology After Demolition.* Hyderabad: Orient Longman.

Noorani, A. G., ed. 2003. *The Babri Masjid Question, 1528–2003: "A Matter of National Honour."* New Delhi: Tulika Books.

Panikkar, K. N. 2002. *An Agenda for Cultural Action, and Other Essays.* New Delhi: Three Essays.

Rajagopal, Arvind. 2001. *Politics After Television: Religious Nationalism and the Reshaping of the Indian Public.* Cambridge: Cambridge University Press.

Savarkar, Vinayak Damodar. 1971. *Six Glorious Epochs of Indian History,* trans. S. T. Godbole. New Delhi: Rajdhani Granthagar.

———. 1989. *Hindutva: Who Is a Hindu?* (6th ed.). New Delhi: Bharti Sahitya Sadan.

Seshadri, H. V. 1988. *RSS: A Vision in Action.* Bangalore: Jagarana Prakashana.

Shrimali, K. M. 2003. "Archaeology of Ayodhya: From Imbroglio to Resolution." In *The Babri Masjid Question, 1528–2003: "A Matter of National Honour,"* ed. A. G. Noorani. New Delhi: Tulika Books, 65–82.

Thapar, Romila. 2004. *Somanatha: The Many Voices of a History.* New Delhi: Penguin Books.

Van der Veer, Peter. 1992. "Ayodhya and Somnath: Eternal Shrines, Contested Histories." *Social Research,* 59, no. 1: 85–109.

Vishva Hindu Parishad. [1991]. *The Great Evidence of Shri Ram Janmabhoomi Mandir.* New Delhi: Vishva Hindu Parishad.

Zavos, John. 2000. *The Emergence of Hindu Nationalism in India.* New Delhi: Oxford University Press.

Chapter 3
Social Lives of the Dead
Contestation and Continuities in the
Hawaiian Repatriation Context

Greg Johnson

> The bones define what it means to be Native.—Kanalu Young,
> *Rethinking the Native Hawaiian Past*
>
> But with many of the old Hawaiian ways lost as oral traditions broke
> and went unrecorded, these ancestors wait as about twenty different
> native Hawaiian groups fight over how to rebury them. They argue
> over rituals and proper protocols, according to several members of
> the groups.—Sally Apgar, "Reclaiming History"

Law, Culture, and Religion

Western laws frequently reconfigure—if not entirely disfigure—native
cultures. To be equally sure, native cultures often have proven remarkably resilient to laws and forces they represent and advance. Though
these truisms have been amply attested and analyzed in venerable if now
tired ways, I would like to explore a context that exemplifies and illumi-
nates a somewhat different relationship between Western law and native
cultures—one where law has, in potent respects, stimulated "traditional" cultural activities, even when these activities take the form of
contestation and outright intracultural conflict. I will argue that these
conflicts are manifestations of living tradition, not merely products of
political fallout from engagement with "modernity." My argument is
made not in the service of defending law (in general terms or in specific
instances) but rather with the aim of contributing to cultural analyses
that wish to take seriously the properties and principles of tradition and
meaning without reifying the same.

The specific theoretical question I wish to illuminate is one central to this volume: How are cultures *constituted* through conflict? It is obvious enough that "cultures" struggle between and within themselves. Contributors to this book show how attending to such struggles reveals much about narrative processes and the relation of these to boundaries and divisions of various kinds. As Marc Ross writes in Chapter 1, the study of culture is most productive when framed as the investigation of competing identities. I hope to contribute to this mode of analysis by demonstrating how contestation is not only a consequence of culture, but is its very animating principle. To do so I will turn to repatriation contexts in Hawai'i, showing that laws designed to renew culture have done so precisely through generating unanticipated conflicts between Native Hawaiian groups. The analytic value of tracking these conflicts is found in how they push us to reject simplistic divisions between meaning-centric and power-centric views of culture.

Another of my theoretical motivations springs from a desire to address a long-entrenched crisis in approaches to religious conflict. Scholars, legal audiences, and the public have often reacted to religious struggles in two equally problematic ways. On the one hand, facile versions of cultural relativism coupled with a tendency to project onto other cultures and contexts a peculiarly Protestant ideal—which locates the "religious" as a domain of unassailable interior faith—have fostered a climate of noncritical engagement with the religious "other."[1] On the other hand, some observers have tended to view religious conflict as not "genuinely" religious and therefore fail to take seriously the ways symbols, myths, and rituals, for example, function and fluctuate in such settings of conflict. Both tendencies miss the opportunity to understand intrareligious conflicts as processes of identity formation and negotiation. I hope to contribute to a shift in analytical practice that is characterized by a willingness to view religious struggle as neither too holy to analyze nor too debased to take seriously.

Repatriation and Hawai'i

Repatriation politics in contemporary Hawai'i have been highly contentious and correspondingly visible in the media and public sphere over the past two decades, especially since the building boom of the 1980s and passage of the Native American Graves Protection and Repatriation Act (NAGPRA) in 1990.[2] Much of this activity shares a good deal with repatriation struggles engaged in by American Indians.[3] Like Native Americans, Native Hawaiians have experienced a cultural and political renaissance over the past thirty years and are increasingly vocal in announcing their terms of self-identification and put into practice such ideals by asserting control over their ancestors and their material heritage (see, for example, Ayau and Tengan 2002; Nihipali 2002). Also similar to Native Americans, many museums have collections of Native Hawaiian bones and objects that are potentially subject to repatriation on the basis of relatively new federal and state laws. Unlike American Indians, however, Native Hawaiians are not politically organized as tribes or nations.[4] Drafters of NAGPRA, however, were explicit in their desire to accommodate Native Hawaiian concerns, which had not a little to do with Senator Inouye's influence over the process and the outspoken testimony of Native Hawaiian representatives during the legislative history. To achieve this task—of rendering continental law in oceanic terms—Congress advanced a definition of "Native Hawaiian organization" (NHO) to construct Hawaiian groups as proxy tribes for legal purposes. The relevant portion of the statute reads:

(10) "Native Hawaiian" means any individual who is a descendant of the aboriginal people who, prior to 1778, occupied and exercised sovereignty in the area that now constitutes the State of Hawai'i.

(11) "Native Hawaiian organization" means any organization which (A) serves and represents the interest of Native Hawaiians, (B) has a primary and stated purpose the provision of services to Native Hawaiians, and (C) has expertise in Native Hawaiian Affairs, and shall include the Office of Hawaiian Affairs and Hui Malama I Na Kupuna O Hawai'i Nei. (Public Law 101–601, Section II: 6)

These definitions have—unwittingly, to be sure—provided Native Hawaiians a culturally recognizable template for constructing and advancing claims to authority: one that is polythetic in enabling claims that rely on sources as diverse as genealogy, geography, and religious pedigree, which is just the multilayered way Hawaiians have long reckoned authority. The consequence of this situation is that a law entailing considerably concrete effects is set into motion by remarkably subjective claims to identity, which in turn rely frequently upon nonfalsifiable and mutually exclusive religious assertions.

Predictably, these definitions have led to a variety of problems by way of their implementation. Who is able to fulfill the requirements of these definitions? A resounding answer has emerged: many, many groups—in three separate repatriation disputes there have been more than ten different NHO claimants, all of which represent their bases of authority in fairly exclusive terms. This has led to tremendous infighting, which will be described at greater length below. From observers—whether courts, the media, or academics—this situation has provoked a variety of comments, many less than charitable with regard to the integrity and sincerity of various claimants' positions. More generally, many observers have lamented that these multiple and conflicting claims are a barometer of the decayed state of Hawaiian culture. Implicit in this critique is the suggestion that repatriation conflicts of this sort are "merely political" and that the cultural and religious arguments advanced in this context operated more in the way of veneer than substance as Native Hawaiians tragically invoke culture to its own detriment. The quintessential conflict that has provoked such responses is the so-called Kawaihae (aka Forbes Cave) dispute. One of my principal aims is to read against the grain of popular representations of this conflict in order to argue for a more complex view of culture in and as contestation. Through sketching abiding Hawaiian ideas about the dead, describing a historical precursor to Kawaihae, and then turning to the conflict itself, I hope to leave readers with a sense that the dispute is Hawaiian to its very marrow.

The Meaningful Dead

A law intended to settle the fate of the dead has sent them on their (cultural) way.[5] Consider the following episodes that have transpired within the past fifteen years. Human remains erode out of the shoreline near the Maui surf town of Pa'ia and local groups coordinate efforts to move the remains inland for reburial. Only blocks apart in Honolulu, human remains are uncovered in the course of two real estate development projects. The respective projects—one a Whole Foods grocery store, the other a Wal-Mart—are stalled while the O'ahu Burial Council considers various neotraditional means for dealing with the dead in such contexts. Human remains to be repatriated and reburied from several museum collections are caught in limbo—stored in homes and garages—as various Native Hawaiian groups struggle over issues regarding authority and protocol for reburial. Numerous bones are returned to Kaua'i from the Smithsonian for reburial, but some islanders argue that the bones should not be returned to Kaua'i because they are those of Kamehameha's warriors and thus represent an invading force, not local people. Far more visible and contentious are the following two episodes, consideration of which is the principal task before us. In the first, two caskets which purportedly contain the bones of ancient kings were stolen from the Bishop Museum and, according to widespread rumors, reburied in the sacred Waipi'o Valley of Hawai'i Island. In the second, the Kawaihae dispute, eighty-three priceless objects are "loaned" by the Bishop Museum to a Native Hawaiian organization that subsequently reburies them in a cave and seals the entrance. After this point, thirteen more

NHOs emerge to seek repatriation of the same objects, with groups vehemently disagreeing as to whether the objects are funerary in nature or not. The dispute enters legal channels and a federal judge eventually orders the cave opened. The objects are removed and returned to the museum so that repatriation proceedings may begin anew. Clearly the dead matter in the Hawaiian present, if in decidedly peripatetic and contentious ways.

How do we make sense of this situation? Although I want to direct us to the importance of micropolitics in due course, macromeaning is perhaps a better starting point from which to answer this question. While resisting essentialist formulations that claim to locate the core of every cultural world, it must be said that in any cultural context certain conglomerations of ideas and values do generate considerable gravity. Such "core values," to use a quaint formulation, are often rather slow to change; or, rather, they change according to terms more of their own making than outside observers are usually able or willing to perceive. In the past and in the present, Hawaiian cultural values are seen most clearly in theories and practices surrounding the dead and their things.[6] Generally speaking, bones were and are used to honor or dishonor the memory of the person and lineages related to them. Furthermore, bones and related objects have been and are appealed to prospectively in order to anchor identity claims and legitimate assertions of *mana* and authority.

Just how the dead took on their specific meanings is, according to the revered Hawaiian historian David Malo, not clear: "a corpse was a very tabu thing in Hawaii nei. It was the ancients themselves who imposed this tabu; but the reason for it and the author of it have not been made known. The mere fact of the tabu was all that was known in Hawaii nei" (1951 [1898]: 96). While origins are hard to discern, practices are more readily apprehended. Generally speaking, mortuary rites in ancient Hawai'i involved several steps and possibilities, especially for the royal dead. First, the *tabu* or *kapu* referred to by Malo was enforced in response to the corpse's purportedly unclean or defiled (*haumia*) status (Malo 1951 [1898]: 97; Kamakau 1964: 35; see also Pukui, Haertig, and Lee 1972: 122). The *kapu* state of the corpse could last many days and much ritual attention was devoted to resolving the tension created by the presence of the dead among the living. The *kapu* surrounding common people usually lasted only several days, but *ali'i* (chiefs, royalty) were often subjected to protracted mortuary practices and correspondingly long *kapu* constraints. In many cases, the dead were stripped of flesh (regarded as the defiling component of the corpse) and the bones (*iwi*, regarded as the clean and immortal portion of the corpse) were washed before being buried, wrapped, bundled, or otherwise treated

(Malo 1951 [1898]: 105). The *iwi* of high ranking royalty were often placed in protected temple areas or in secret burial chambers in lava tube caves (Kirch 1985: 238–241). Even among commoners *iwi* were ritually treated in varying degrees (see, for example, Buck 1957: 567).[7]
Ancestral spirits, the *'aumākua*, were believed to maintain an attachment to their respective *iwi*, so care of the *iwi* was regarded as care for the *'aumākua*; defilement of the *iwi*, conversely, was regarded as defilement of the *'aumākua*, with potentially devastating consequences for the spirits and for the living (Kamakau 1964: 43). As sources of such *mana,* the *iwi* were also utilized for various ritual purposes, and sorcery in particular (Pukui, Haertig and Lee 1972: 29; Buck 1957: 569). For this reason even commoner *iwi* were secreted away in caves and burial pits during tumultuous times (Kamakau 1964: 38). The *iwi* also constituted tangible evidence of putative genealogical connections, an exceptionally important point in the context of a class-stratified society. Possession of or access to bones anchored one's claim upon a lineage connection— and all the entitlements and *mana* this might confer. For these reasons among others, the *iwi* were vigilantly protected and even relocated on occasion in order to protect them or to bring their power to a new place.
Active in the lives of the living, bones moved around—publicly and secretly, licitly and illicitly, and even in highly ritualized and society-wide contexts such as the parading of *kahili* (ritual staffs that served as a kind of royal standard and which were sometimes inlaid with human bone) and the annual Makahiki rite.[8] As a form of capital, the Hawaiian dead retained their currency through circulation.[9] Thus, contrary to some nonnative reactions predicated on a preference that the dead should be immune from the troubles of the living, the dead in Hawai'i were valued precisely through being harnessed to the interests of the living. While clearly so in the past, this is just as much the case now, and has been the case throughout the modern (postcontact) period. Indeed, modern circumstances—for example, the advent of Europeans, market economies, repatriation laws—have enabled the perpetuation of tradition through cultural disruption.
To give but one example of how this is so, consider the words of LaFrance Kapaka-Arboleda, a repatriation leader from Kaua'i. When I asked Ms. Kapaka-Arboleda about her passion for repatriation issues, she responded by telling me about her childhood.[10] She was the *hanai* (adopted) child of her grandparents, who were already quite old when she was born, having lived the majority of their lives in the nineteenth century. They impressed upon her the sacredness of the *iwi* and the importance of caring for them. Quickly, however, her story took a turn. Care for the dead, she conveyed, was significant precisely because of threats to them from a variety of sources, including exposure to the sun,

but most important from desecration by use of them in sorcery. One
protected bones from the living, which makes sense in a cultural context
defined by regular episodes of conquest and usurpation by proximate
others. "If bones fell to the other side," she said, "this was the ultimate
desecration" (compare Beckwith 1970: 274). Thus, Ms. Kapaka-
Arboleda framed her concern for the remains of the dead as a deep-
seated cultural heritage of preserving the *iwi* from threats external and
internal. For Ms. Kapaka-Arboleda, repatriation laws enabled care for
the dead, which in her view was not so much a matter of applying human
rights principles, rectifying colonial history, or any other abstract concern as it was a concrete means to carry out her cultural convictions as
mediated by her grandparents.

So with the dead plotted in a legal script, this is a story not about the
demise of tradition, but of its enactment in new contexts and under new
conditions, what Marshall Sahlins has playfully called the "develop-
man" of culture. In a classic essay, "The Economics of Develop-Man in
the Pacific," Sahlins grappled, as he has in many contexts, with the role
of "modernity" in shaping the cultural worlds of native peoples. In particular, Sahlins takes up the relationship of native thinking to nonnative
things, the effects of European goods on their conception of the good
life, as he quips. Showing his structuralist hand, he writes, "The first
commercial impulse of the local people is not to become just like us, but
more like themselves" (1992: 13). Even forces as material as the commodity trade, he insists, cannot be understood apart from their organization by cultural categories, impulses, and interests. While such a view
requires a dose of microcontextualization so that we attend to the ways
cultural categories are not homogeneously embraced and expressed,
even within acutely local settings, Sahlins's point is tremendously important for the project of coming to terms with how native peoples encoun
ter and inhabit "our" legal worlds. So, to be so bold, I offer my own spin
on Sahlins's formulation: The first *legal* impulse of the local people is
not to become just like us, but more like themselves. I quote him again
here to play out my substitutions in his words: "They related to European presence rather as producers than consumers. They would cre-
atively appropriate commerce [law] . . . to their own forms of life"
(1992: 16). This for Sahlins is no mere story about trade patterns and
patterning; it is a tale of the most traditional sorts: "'Tradition' is not
the dead hand of the past. On the contrary, 'tradition' is precisely the
way people always cope with circumstances not of their own doing and
beyond their control, whether acts of nature or of other peoples. Hence
tradition has changed in the past, and, by encompassing goods [laws]
and relations of the market [legal sphere] in its own terms, it would continue to do so" (1992: 21).

Sahlins provides us a good start not only in theory, but also in practice, for he has spent considerable energy analyzing Hawaiian relationships to nonnative realties from the time before Captain Cook's advent to the present, which is the same era that concerns us. One of his examples is particularly instructive, the case of *hula*. Contrary to those who describe *hula* as a fiction of the tour industry, Sahlins demonstrates that *hula* has retained a good deal of cultural meaning precisely through its ability to change in historically contingent but culturally orchestrated ways. He provides a similarly rich account of Hawaiian commodity consumption in another essay, charting a cultural continuity linking the display of *mana* to the display of goods across radically distinct historical periods, arguing that even the conspicuous consumption of chinaware by kings, for example, can only be understood when framed in cultural terms (1988: 28–36). "Not that the purpose of a historical ethnography is just to give salutary lessons in cultural continuity," he writes. "More important, the purpose is to synthesize form and function, structure and variation, as a meaningful cultural process, sequitur to a specific cultural order rather than an eternal practical logic" (1993: 11). Cautioned, then, against taking the mere arm of power to have the only hand in cultural processes, we move now to our cases.[11] Doing so, however, we will want to ask: How do we interpret power when it is exerted by an arm attached to the social body, rather than one that reaches in from the outside?

Kā'ai

> On the following night the venerable kahu, or guardian of the secret burial cave, was ordered to remove the stones that concealed the entrance. The coffins were then brought out by torch-light, and carried on board of the man-o-war, which brought them to Honolulu, where they were consigned to Governor Kekuanaoa.—W. D. Alexander (quoted in Rose 1992: 25)

To add substance to my claims about the social careers of the dead, I would like to trace the particular social life of the so-called *kā'ai*. These are the royal caskets that were stolen from the Bishop Museum, which I mentioned above. This momentous event took place in 1994, just as repatriation disputes were beginning to take on increased visibility in Hawai'i. Many observers—then and now—point to the removal of the *kā'ai* as the moment at which the Native Hawaiian repatriation movement took a turn toward "direct action." Some convey this sentiment in a positive sense: meaning, it was time for Kanaka Maoli (Native Hawaiians) to assert themselves in forceful terms. Speaking from a religious point of view, some Hawaiians have suggested that the removal was undertaken in response to visions (*hō'ailona*) sent from the *kā'ai*. From this perspective, the *kā'ai* were relocated in order to reconnect them with tradition and thus to rectify the political and religious trauma of Hawai'i Island chiefs being kept on O'ahu, a historic rival island. Others regard the removal as a theft and as a moment when some representatives of the Native Hawaiian community became belligerent, destructive, and counterproductive. Interestingly, a number of Native Hawaiians have expressed this view, adding to it their perception that the thieves also acted in a nontraditional manner by removing objects of cultural value from the public sphere. A piece of Hawaiian tradition "died" with the theft, they argued.[12]

While one can appreciate the gravity of such sentiments, it would seem to be the case that the apparent motivations of the thieves are quite "traditional" in the sense of seeking respect for and protection of the royal dead, which is historically a function of secret burial (Malo 1951 [1898]: 98). But so much is unknown here. Suppose the caskets were stolen in order to be placed on the black market for artifacts, for example. Fair enough—we can speak neither of the motivations of the thieves nor of the current status of the caskets with any confidence. That said, the mere fact of the caskets' removal and transit is enough to place their current fate squarely in a structure of remarkable duration. Removal from the Bishop Museum was but their most recent displacement. My aim is not to provide a full account of the social life of the *kā'ai*, which has been already been done by Roger Rose (1992), whose account I rely on here. Rather, my intention is to highlight aspects of this history as a means to begin suggesting by way of comparison how the contemporary Kawaihae dispute (our next example) might be regarded as something more than an index of the debased present.

To begin, then, with the things themselves. According to the renowned scholar of Hawaiian material culture, Peter Buck (Te Rangi Hiroa), the *kā'ai* are "Of peculiar construction, the two caskets are made after a similar pattern, having a head, neck, and somewhat cylindrical body without arms or legs. The neck is short and expands below into fairly square shoulders. This body is large enough to contain the bones of the trunk and limbs" (Buck 1957: 575). In their shape and features— particularly their mother of pearl eyes—the *kā'ai* are similar to various sacred *ki'i*, sculptures that represent and are regarded as conduits for *akua* (deities) and *'aumākua*.[13] Such *ki'i* are central, we should note, to the Kawaihae dispute.

In form and theory, the *kā'ai* physically represent the refashioning of the human dead into the living divine. In this refashioning, attributes of human sociality are not left behind but are in fact amplified. Namely, the former *ali'i* (noble) rank of the corpse and the *kapu* status of the *kā'ai* quite literally encase them, marking them off from the profane and common world. The very material of which the *kā'ai* caskets are woven, *'aha kapu* (sacred red coconut husk cordage), was the material historically used to mark off the sphere of the *ali'i* from that of the commoners, usually in the form of a rope cordoning off the royal compound (Rose 1992: 7; Valeri 1985: 296). Thus, quite apart from the actual bones and objects they may contain, the appearance of the *kā'ai* signals the presence of *mana*, both religious and political, which in the Hawaiian world are not neatly separable.[14] Correspondingly, to handle the *kā'ai* is itself a claim to being a legitimate conduit of *mana* and the wealth of authority this implies.

Rose devotes considerable effort to the project of assessing just whose bones are contained in these caskets. His study demonstrates that the very history of their mobility, which involves numerous episodes of interment and disinterment, renders any unambiguous conclusions untenable. This situation, of the things in dispute being objectively ambiguous, is found in parallel in the Kawaihae dispute. From an analytical perspective, these contexts may be usefully regarded not solely as contests over objects per se but as struggles over representations of them. Viewed in this manner, our attention turns to the ways in which these representations circulate as discourse. As Katherine Verdery argues, the very ambiguity of the dead is an enabler of their discursive potency: "Words can be put into their mouths—often quite ambiguous words—or their own actual words can be ambiguated by quoting them out of context. It is thus easier to rewrite history with dead people than with other kinds of symbols that are speechless" (1999: 29).

The potent story here is that the caskets contain the sacred remains of two ancient kings, Liloa and Lonoikamakahiki, the former thought to be from the fifteenth century, the latter from the sixteenth century (Buck 1957: 575).[15] Two observations merit emphasis. First, these monarchs likely have more symbolic value in the present than they had in their own day—Liloa and Lonoikamakahiki are regarded as predecessors in the line of King Kamehameha and therefore stand as emblematic of the power and promise the great king has betokened throughout Hawaiian history ever since his time. Second, discussion of them figures prominently in two of the sources most appealed to by Native Hawaiians in the present who wish to vitalize their cultural sense of self, Buck's *Arts and Crafts of Hawaii* and Malo's *Hawaiian Antiquities*. Thus, the *kā'ai* quite literally embody pre-European Hawaiian identity and are heavy with symbolic weight in the high gravity atmosphere of the present—a present in which discussions concerning restoration of the Hawaiian nation and its crown are heard with remarkable frequency, albeit this future is imagined in a diversity of ways.[16]

Whoever resides in the *kāʻai*, a sketch of their postmortem lives is as follows. It is worthwhile to quote Malo with reference to ritual procedures upon the death of a king:

[After being stripped of flesh and bundled] the bones were put in position and arranged to resemble the shape of a man, being seated in the house until the day of prayer, when their deification would take place and they would be addressed in prayer by the *kahuna* of the *mua*. The period of defilement was then at an end; consequently the king's successor was permitted to return, and the apotheosis of the dead king being accomplished, he was worshiped as a real god (*akua maoli*).

His successor then built for the reception of the bones a new *heiau*, which was called the *hale poki*, for the reason that in it was constructed a net-work to contain the bones, which, being placed in an upright position, as if they had been a man, were enshrined in the *heiau* as a god. (1951 [1989]: 105–106)

Buck adds, "The bones continued as the symbol of a deity, and the newly created deity demanded worship in the form of ritual services and offerings" (1957: 577). One can thus begin to understand the view of some contemporary Native Hawaiians when they assert that the *kāʻai* are divine and that they have been desecrated through their history of dislocation.

The site of the initial interment of the *kāʻai* is unknown. By the eighteenth century they were likely located in temples, with many accounts specifying Hale o Līloa in the Waipiʻo Valley and Hale o Keawe at Puʻuhonua o Honaunau on the Kona shore, both on Hawaiʻi Island. These and other temples were subjected to consequences of the abandonment of Hawaiian religion—with its foundation in the *kapu* system—in 1819. Namely, various elites who had abandoned the religion, Kaʻahumanu foremost among them, sought to desecrate temples to mark their affiliation with Christianity and to demonstrate to the unconverted that the *mana* of the dead was no more. Others who had not abandoned the *kapu* system sought to protect the temples and the dead residing in them. In this period of cultural ferment, numerous sets of human remains from the aforementioned temples, including the *kāʻai*, were removed and buried in a cave above Kealekekua Bay in the late 1820s. Their rest would not be long. In 1858 the cave was opened on the orders of Mataio Kekūanaōʻa, Governor of Oʻahu, who wished to have the royal dead collected on Oʻahu in the Royal Tomb at Pohukaina (Rose 1992: 11–24).

This was but a stop in their travels. From there the *kāʻai* were delivered to the Royal Mausoleum at Mauna ʻAla in Nuʻuanu Valley in 1865, once again at the behest of Governor Kekūanaōʻa. The Governor's intentions appear rather explicit in the inscription he had placed on the coffin containing the *kāʻai*. It read, "Liloa was the father of the celebrated King Umi, who is the progenitor of the present reigning family; and Lonoikamakahiki . . . the ancestor of H. R. H., M. Kekuanaoa" (Rose 1992: 26). Thus the royal dead were put to the service of advancing royal claims in the present. And this theme would continue. Some twenty years later the *kāʻai* received similar treatment at the hands of King Kalākaua's "Board for the Collection of Ancient Hawaiian History and the Genealogy of Hawaiian Chiefs." Rose reports that upon Kalākaua's death in 1891 his widow, Queen Kapiʻolani, had the casket—together with remains purported to be those of Kamehameha I—removed from the Royal Mausoleum and taken to her private residence. Kapiʻolani's actions, as well as those of her predecessors, may be interpreted as politically motivated, but such a view does not necessarily negate or exclude the possibility that they understood themselves to be acting in a long tradition of *mālama na iwi* (caring for the ancestors).

Some years later, in 1915, the status of the *kāʻai* became the subject of a legal dispute between Queen Liliʻuokalani and Prince Kūhiō in yet another struggle over genealogical legitimacy. The suit was eventually dropped, but interest in the *kāʻai* remained lively. The occasion of Liliʻuokalani's death in 1917 provoked the next movement of the *kāʻai*, this time to the Bishop Museum (Rose 1992: 29–30). Representatives of the museum urged that the *kāʻai* not be buried, as was being contemplated, on the grounds that the *kāʻai* are exceedingly rare and so well crafted. This argument has been embraced and rearticulated, as we will see, with reference to *kiʻi* and other objects in the Kawaihae dispute. Persuaded by such reasoning, Prince Kūhiō agreed to "loan" the objects to the museum, where they remained until 1994 (Rose 1992: 31). At that time, according to Hawaiian historian Davianna Pōmaikaʻi McGregor, the "Bishop Museum had planned to place the kaʻai in the Kalākaua crypt at Mauna Ala in Honolulu, while Native Hawaiians from Hawaiʻi Island had asked permission to instead inter the kaʻai in Waipiʻo Valley. Before any formal action was taken, the kaʻai were removed, and it is believed that they were taken back to their place of origin—Waipiʻo Valley" (2007: 287).

Suffice it to say, at each turn of their fate the *kāʻai* were subjected to intensely fraught micropolitical processes as a consequence of their widely shared if hotly contested cultural and religious meanings.[17]

Kawaihae (aka Forbes Cave)

Six years after two kaʻai burial caskets disappeared from the Bishop Museum in 1994, as many as eighty more Hawaiian artifacts may be gone from the museum as a result of a 1990 federal law requiring the return of objects from Native American graves.—Burl Burlingame (2000: 1)

If we can regard the careers of the *kā'ai* as an example of culture in action, so too we should be willing to consider recent and ongoing disputes over the Kawaihae objects in a cultural light. As a starting point in this consideration, it is instructive to emphasize a number of similar aspects between these contexts, some of which point to contiguity and continuity: Kawaihae as a sequitur to the *kā'ai*. Both entail struggles over the dead and things buried with them, that much is obvious and important. In the course of these contestations we note histories of transit, both back and forth between islands and institutions, but also in and out of the ground. Both have involved assertions that trafficking in the respective remains and relics and remains is dangerous, and both have involved untimely deaths that have been interpreted as evidence of such danger. Both have involved storage of human remains in private homes while legal matters were unfolding, and both have involved scrutiny by the public and high visibility in the media. Rumors of museum insiders assisting in the displacement of the objects have been circulated in both cases. In incidents separated by more than a hundred years, both contexts were subject to periods of media silence in response to pressure from the courts. Significantly, both situations have involved the Bishop Museum, which has in each instance provoked a state-wide conversation as to the status and role of the museum in preserving and perpetuating tradition.

In the case of Kawaihae, human remains—including funeral bundles—and objects were removed from a lava tube cave in 1905 by nonnative explorers, who then sold what they had taken to the Bishop Museum (Forbes 1905). Subsequent "explorations" of the same and adjacent caves resulted in further removal of bones and objects to the Bishop Museum and Volcanoes National Park through the 1930s. In the mid-1990s various NHOs, including a very prominent organization by the name of Hui Mālama I Nā Kupuna 'O Hawai'i Nei (Hui Mālama), began to request repatriation of the Kawaihae items under NAGPRA. Then, in the late 1990s, "the Forbes Cave human remains at Bishop Museum were supposedly given to Hui Malama and hidden . . . at a Hilo home of Hui Malama members" (Burlingame 2000: 2). Following this, in February 2000, a collection of eighty-three priceless objects was "loaned" to Hui Mālama by the museum. Shortly thereafter Hui Mālama members sealed the objects and human remains into the cave, constructing a barrier of rebar and concrete at the mouth of the lava tube. Several years of dispute followed as thirteen other Native Hawaiian organizations came forward to announce claims upon the objects. Many of these argued that the "repatriation" was fraudulent because not all of the NHOs had been consulted.

These contesting groups, however, were not merely disgruntled on grounds that they had not been consulted. Rather, as they began to announce their respective claims upon the objects it became clear that they imagined their relationships to them in vastly divergent ways. In the articulation of their differences with an eye to establishing standing under the statute, we see a poignant instance of law fueling tradition, if through catalyzing rivalry. Geographical proximity, religious lineage, and genealogical purity—particularly reckoned along lines of putative rank—became the means by which groups challenged one another's authority to speak of and for the objects and, by extension, of and for Hawaiian tradition writ large. A basic divide emerged that separated the groups into (a) those who regard the objects as *moepu* (funerary objects) and (b) those who regard the objects as nonfunerary. The former group has argued vehemently that the objects should remain buried; the latter group believes the objects were hidden in caves to prevent their desecration at the time of the fall of the *kapu* system. Further, some representatives of this group have asserted that the ancestors revealed the location of the objects to the nonnative explorers as the means by which to enable the objects' relocation to the museum where they would be preserved for future generations of Hawaiians to appreciate and learn from (see Johnson 2007).

As one can see, the provisions and definitions of NAGPRA opened a rather large can of cultural worms. In an attempt to address this context, a federal committee reviewed the situation several times, and their vicissitudes in addressing it are an indication of the complexity of the dispute (NAGPRA Review Committee 2003, 2004, 2005). By 2005 the matter became a legal dispute when two of the claimants filed suit against Hui Mālama and the Bishop Museum (Kobayashi 2005). One of the claimants was Abigail Kawananakoa, a descendant of Prince Kūhiō, who had loaned the *kā'ai* to the Bishop Museum. She has asserted that the theft of the *kā'ai* provoked her to action in defense of her ancestors and all they stand for and that Kawaihae is the front line of that battle (Apgar 2004). Her hallmark assertion has been that she stands and speaks for the *ali'i* of the past as an *ali'i* in the present. In contrast to her purportedly royal status, she has declared that others, and especially members of Hui Mālama, are *maka'āinana*—commoners—who have no right to handle or speak for the dead and their things (see, for example, Apgar 2005).

Whether or not Kawananakoa is a legitimate heir to the *kā'ai* or a legitimate claimant with regard to Kawaihae, her linkage between these contexts is significant. If we understand these disputes as ways in which the ancestors and their putative authority are appropriated in the present, then both contexts must be appreciated for their magnitude. Both pertain to the same area of Hawai'i Island, the historically powerful region extending from the Waipiʻo Valley to the north to the Kealakekua Bay area to the south. This area is the homeland of Kamehameha and his ancestors. Here Hawaiian religion and politics reached their most elaborate expressions in the decades surrounding European contact. Magnificent *heiaus* offer physical evidence of the power of this place—indeed Kawaihae Caves are located in a gulch above Puʻu Kohalā, the temple at which Kamehameha is said to have fulfilled sacrifices necessary to accomplish his goal of uniting the islands. By the same token, this area was hardest hit by the encroachments of European influence. After Kamehameha's death the foundations of Hawaiian religion were shaken with widespread abandonment of the *kapu* system and shortly thereupon Christianity became increasingly influential, and one classic marker of this was destruction of temples at converts' hands, as noted above. Thus, it is not too simplistic to say that "traditional" Hawaiian religion received its most complex expressions and was most powerfully challenged within decades along the Kohala and Kona coasts. Hawaiians have been engaged in playing out the ramifications of this era ever since. Reconnecting to the meaning of this time and place is widely regarded as a function of possessing and controlling tangible links to them, the prime examples of which are royal bones and royal objects. Thus, struggles over the *kāʻai* and the Kawaihae objects are not merely about the stakes of representing the past but are about reconstituting the power of the past in the present and asserting *kuleana* (responsibility) to care for the past.

Just as contemporary Christians are hardly unanimous in their accounts of how the historical Jesus ought to be regarded and worshiped today, so too do Hawaiians challenge one another as to what Hawaiian religion and culture mean in the present—and who has the authority to determine this. But is there a "pure" origin point in either case? Is it a function of the "terror of history" that Christians in the present diverge in their views of Jesus and Hawaiians fight over the terms of tradition? Such questions strike us as misguided in a variety of ways, and it is easy enough to reject entropy theories of culture in principle, but—as courts and other audiences have shown—this is harder to do in practice. Legal audiences in particular seem to seek out "purity" when assessing cultural claims, which is an understandable function of cognitive and ideological frames shaped by strict evidentiary requirements parsed on empirical grounds. But cultural disputes are not so easily reckoned, of course. It is a simple but often forgotten step in the comparative study of cultural conflict to remind ourselves that even the most apparently stable traditions have always been defined through identity making and marking processes that are products of internal and external challenges. No challenge, no response; no threat, no distinctions; no struggle, no marked content. In view of such dynamics, tradition is not most usefully regarded as "the" source of identity but as a resource for and product of staging identities. While courts may shrug or shiver at such an account of culture in practice, Sahlins's charge to take cultural meanings seriously as organizing principles in action is made all the more urgent by the recognition of the stakes of tradition as discourse.

"Traditional Hawaiianness"—the authority to define tradition in the present—is the discursive turf of the Kawaihae struggle. For each group, indeed for each person, the stakes are somewhat different, certainly multiple, and variable in their articulation and coherence. Here is the core paradox: that the parties should disagree so powerfully that they engage Western courts to express and pursue their different aims while simultaneously agreeing about general terms of the conflict—the dead are powerful, that control of them matters, and that for these reasons proper treatment of the dead is the *kuleana* (responsibility) of the living. Consider language found in the following declaration of a number of the groups supporting burial of the objects:

> We believe in maintaining the sanctity of the Kawaihae burial caves. The ceremonial burial of iwi kupuna (ancestral Native Hawaiian remains) and moepu (funerary objects) involves great secrecy in order to protect the burial site and ensure the peace and sanctity of ancestors who have passed away, as well as the spiritual, physical, and psychological well-being of their descendants. The desecration of burials . . . results in great cultural and religious harm to both the ancestors and to the descendants, as well as spiritual exile in the afterlife for people implicated in the re-desecration. . . . We support efforts to repatriate ancestral remains and funerary objects to their rightful resting place through the NAGPRA process. (He Ho'olaha 2006)

Opposing groups have expressed their position in equally strong religious terms, complete with parallel references to the spiritual wrath to be incurred by those who violate the will of the ancestors.

Indeed, various representatives of NHOs whom I have interviewed worded their religious commitments to the dead so fiercely that they have threatened violence if their views do not prevail. Frankly, I do not take most of these threats to violence literally—one was announced by an older man who relies on oxygen and a wheelchair to get through his days. Rather, they are another indication of the sincerity and cultural gravity of their positions—fighting for the dead is a cultural conviction. And even here, when cultural contests threaten to explode into contests of force, traditional signifiers define the rhetorical battle—all four speakers who announced threats made special reference to the cultural means to carry out their actions: two referred to their shark tooth clubs, two referred to *lua* (Hawaiian martial arts). Even force, or at least its threat, is culturally configured. Here again modern repatriation laws provide the context for the articulation of cultural sentiments, however agonistic they may strike us.

Late in the summer of 2006, a judge ordered the cave opened and the objects removed. Reports from the two major Hawaiian newspapers are instructive here, particularly in the way their reporting echoes sentiments expressed in the *kā'ai* context. The *Honolulu Star-Bulletin* reported the following: "Ancient Hawaiian artifacts buried in a cave for more than five years have been returned to the Bishop Museum, said Laakea Suganuma, president of the Royal Academy of Traditional Arts. . . . Suganuma said the museum, which completed the task last week with United States District Judge David Ezra's consent, took more than a week to find and recover the artifacts, a task made difficult because some were buried under rocks or behind cement walls" (Kubota 2006: 1). A *Honolulu Advertiser* reporter wrote:

Published reports that cultural objects were collected by state authorities from a Big Island cave and turned over to the Bishop Museum are being met with mixed—and emotional—reactions by the Hawaiian community. . . . One faction is rooting for their return to the museum. . . . But another faction argues that the explorers who first removed them from the caves and turned them over to the museum were thieves. "Moving them to the Bishop Museum creates a real problem culturally, spiritually and politically for the Hawaiian community," said Jon Osorio, chairman of the Center for Hawaiian Studies at the University of Hawai'i-Manoa. "Those people who believe they were moepu (funerary objects) are going to be outraged and will be devoted to getting them returned." (Pang 2006: 1)

Now that the objects have been returned to the museum, the process of deciding which claimants will have control of them begins anew. Meanwhile, Volcanoes National Park is just initiating repatriation processes regarding the Kawaihae objects in its collection, so the future of the past remains considerably open-ended.

The Cultivation of Politics as Culture

Just when and why the dead and their things took on such cultural prominence for Hawaiians is a matter of speculation, though desires to marshal postmortem evidence to claims of social standing surely matter here. What is entirely more certain is that the dead have long anchored for Hawaiians their particular "science of the concrete." Indeed, the physical instability of the dead is precisely an index and enabler of their cultural and ideological potential. With the living seeking to harness the discursive potential of the dead, ancestors are made to work very hard in the context of novel political struggles. Remaining consistent across fairly significant shifts in Hawaiian society are the ways in which the dead metonymically anchor and signify the core nexus of Hawaiian identity: assertions of genealogical *mana* that map the speaker's authority with reference to lineage and place. This mapping is also, of course, a moral cartography—those who properly care for the dead in the present affirm and display their moral bearings as a putative function of fidelity to tradition. That such claims and actions may be regarded as political is clear, but this recognition does not cancel out culture. Two truisms, then, must be appreciated in their conjunction and in practice: (1) that "power" is everywhere and (2) that power, short of brute force, cannot persuade absent of shared referents.

Despite my attention to "traditional" detail in attempting to make sense of particular moments of the Polynesian postmortem, I remain convinced that micropolitical processes are at the root of "culture." Surely geography, modes of subsistence, language, blood, and other "facts" matter, culturally speaking. A long line of thinkers have taught us to see that such facts do not stand as meaningful outside of social constructions of them. It is precisely the social nature of cultural symbolism that interests me here, for I understand social construction to be a function of making through marking, of distinctiveness through deliberate distinction—of interested as well as happenstance affiliations and estrangements. But from the roots of power culture flowers in ways that become far more elaborate than the mere needs of power dictate. The florescence of culture—an always intricate system of symbols, meanings, and values—can be circulated, elaborated, and otherwise engaged in a variety of ways not determined by ideological needs alone. When ideological ends are sought, however, culture stands at attention to be marshaled to the cause. This analysis is, of course, redolent of a rather flat-footed Marxian paradigm of base and superstructure. A crucial difference from this old paradigm is itself not particularly new—namely, I wish to nuance but not negate the priority of Marx's schema, being more suggestive, I hope, of the basic power of symbols. Thus, I invoke Jean and John Comaroff's neomodern mantra—to find power in meaning and meaning in power (1992), but with a conjectural trajectory: power is at once primary and tertiary, meaning secondary. Without the cultural repertoire of secondary meaning, there could be no culturally recognizable tertiary articulations of it. Power, in other words, requires meaning to be persuasive rather than merely forceful (see Lincoln 1989). That the dead should matter in reckoning authority seems to be a broadly human fact; just how they should matter for Hawaiians is a cultural one. For Hawaiians to fight over the dead they must agree upon the meaning of them, if in ways divergent enough to allow for battles both rhetorical and physical. In this formulation power takes on meaningful elaborations and is then ripe for rearticulation as hegemony or, by way of subversion, counterhegemony, and the forms of the latter two include intracultural conflict.

We might want to erase or challenge the order and causal links I have set out, in which case we might suggest that social worlds are driven by three principal engines (ideology, culture, and hegemony), the first marked by raw power, the second shared discourse, the third by persuasive and interested discourse. Further, some might argue that the second term in my formula—culture—is always already hegemonic, if by degrees. I find this formulation sound; my investment in setting culture apart for analysis is to underscore the relevance of meaning, symbol, and value, but this is not to suggest that these ever float free of interested uses of them. One might imagine, as others have, that "culture" is a "conversation," which I find instructive. Insofar as this analogy is apt, we want to note that the notion of "conversation" runs quite a gamut— from idle chatter to argument, for example. Culture as conversation can be viewed in similar terms—we must have "shared symbols" even to engage in idle chatter, and it is precisely our "shared symbols" that enable us to argue and to express ourselves so decisively in the process. An analytic that wishes to view cultural conversations without reference to power, is, in my view, the study of something akin to idle chatter, and consequently should be itself relegated to that status. An analytic that wishes to view cultural conversations as forums of persuasion and, on occasion, argumentation, gets much closer to studying social processes in meaningful terms. In the context we have considered, it is one thing to describe Hawaiian views of the dead in abstract terms and quite another to see the social lives of the dead in practice.

Just what might motivate the expression of meaningful power in these ways is never predictable, as our tale of the lively dead illustrates. What can be said with confidence is this: to read either crosscultural or intracultural politics in merely ideological terms—for example, to see only the coercive force of external laws disfiguring native traditions—is to remain blind to the cultural (con)text. For this reason it is critical that we do not abandon attempts to understand intracultural politics in "cultural" terms, however much we might be interested in power and politics, for these are not ultimately separable from the cultural lives of those who lead them. "Culture" provides the bases of group identity and solidarity, but it is also the principal resource for mobilizing authority in the course of reckoning internal disputes. So, when groups wage internal struggles in cultural terms, this does not necessarily signal the demise of "culture," but rather signals the activation of it.

Notes

I would like to thank Marc Ross, Halealoha Ayau, and John Charlot for their helpful and challenging responses to drafts of this chapter.

1. On this line of analysis, see, for example Lincoln (1996) and Masuzawa (2005).

2. The Hawaiian repatriation context is addressed at greater length in my book, *Sacred Claims: Repatriation and Living Tradition* (2007).

3. On NAGPRA generally and its relationship to American Indian contexts, see Fine-Dare (2002), Brown (2003), McKeown and Hutt (2003), and Johnson (2005).

4. This may change in the relatively near future if a version of the Native Hawaiian Government Reorganization Act passes. This bill been stalled for several years as legislators struggle over the political stakes of enabling the formation of a Native Hawaiian government modeled on the limited sovereignty of federally recognized tribes.

5. For a trenchant analysis of the political and cultural valences of dead bodies and their sociobiographies, see Verdery (1999). Verdery's analysis is focused on postsocialist contexts but has considerable relevance to repatriation issues generally. For an engaging example of the social life of the dead, see Starn (2004).

6. On Polynesian theories of death and dying generally, see Charlot (2003).

7. Kamakau, however, gives the impression that many times commoners' corpses were disposed of without specific treatment of the *iwi* (1964: 39).

8. On *kahili*, see Buck (1957: 579–580). For an example pertaining to the circulation of Captain Cook's bones in Makahiki ceremonies, see Sahlins (1981: 24).

9. My emphasis on the social careers of the dead owes a good deal of inspiration to the seminal volume, *The Social Life of Things: Commodities in Cultural Perspective*, edited by Arjun Appadurai (1986), and in particular to Patrick Geary's essay therein, "Sacred Commodities: The Circulation of Medieval Relics."

10. The following material relies upon an interview I conducted with Ms. Kapaka-Arboleda on 30 July 2004 in Līhuʻe, Kauaʻi. She died in 2006.

11. For a critical response to Sahlins that wishes to place more emphasis on external pressures and, at the same time, render problematic questions of cultural authorship and agency, see Asad (1993: 3–10). For a view sympathetic to Sahlins's formulations, with particular relevance to Hawaiian history and historiography, see Dening (1995).

12. Still others have suggested that removing the *kāʻai* was the right thing but object to the means by which this was accomplished as not being *pono* (correct). Acting in a *pono* manner is a highly held Hawaiian value, so much so that the "spirit" of an act is often regarded as being more important than the act itself. This point has been raised in the Kawaihae context as well. On the concept of *pono* in traditional contexts, see Charlot (1985: 2).

13. On Hawaiian sculpture, see Cox and Davenport (1988) and Dodd (1967).

14. On the relationship of politics and religion in Hawaiian society, see Charlot (1985).

15. Alternative accounts name Liloa's famous son ʻUmi as occupying one of the *kāʻai*. See, for example, Rose (1992: 13).

16. On imagined nations see, among others, Anderson (1991) and, more recently, Taylor (2004).

17. See the recent feature film *Night Marchers 2: Return of the Ka'ai* (2006) to get a sense of how the *kā'ai* have entered the pop culture imagination in Hawai'i. According to the film's promotional blurb, it depicts what happens when "stolen relics unleash an ancient curse upon the Hawaiian islands."

Bibliography

Anderson, Benedict. 1991. *Imagined Communities: Reflections on the Origins and Spread of Nationalism.* London: Verso.

Apgar, Sally. 2004. "Reclaiming History: Hawaiian Groups Decry the Bishop Museum's New 'Native' Status." *Honolulu Star-Bulletin* (2 August). Retrieved 6 August 2004, from http://starbulletin.com/2004/08/02/news/story5html.

———. 2005. "Showdown Over Artifacts Unearths Spiritual Divide." *Honolulu Star-Bulletin* (19 September). Retrieved 3 March 2006, from http://starbulletin.com/2005/09/19/news/index1.html.

———. 2006. "Judge Orders Disputed Cave Artifacts Retrieved." *Honolulu Star-Bulletin* (29 April). Retrieved 2 May 2006, from http://starbulletin.com/2006/04/29/news/story06.html.

Appadurai, Arjun, ed. 1986. *The Social Life of Things: Commodities in Cultural Perspective.* New York: Cambridge University Press.

Asad, Talal. 1993. *Genealogies of Religion: Discipline and Reasons of Power in Christianity and Islam.* Baltimore: Johns Hopkins University Press.

Ayau, Edward, and Ty Tengan. 2002. "Ka Huaka'i O Na 'Oiwi: The Journey Home." In *The Dead and Their Possessions: Repatriation in Principle, Policy and Practice,* ed. C. Fforde, J. Hubert, and P. Turnbull. London: Routledge, 171–189.

Beckwith, Martha. 1970. *Hawaiian Mythology.* Honolulu: University of Hawaii Press.

Brown, Michael. 2003. *Who Owns Native Culture?* Cambridge: Harvard University Press.

Buck, Peter. 1957. *Arts and Crafts of Hawaii.* Bernice P. Bishop Museum Special Publication, 45. Honolulu: Bishop Museum Press.

Burlingame, Burl. 2000. "Fate of Some Bishop Museum Artifacts Debated." *Honolulu Star-Bulletin* (25 March). Retrieved 19 July 2006, from http://starbulletin.com/2000/03/25/news/story1.html.

Charlot, John. 1985. *The Hawaiian Poetry of Religion and Politics.* Honolulu: Institute for Polynesian Studies.

———. 2003. "Polynesian Religions." In *Macmillan Encyclopedia of Death and Dying,* ed. Robert Kastenbaum. New York: Macmillan Reference, 679–680.

Comaroff, Jean, and John Comaroff. 1992. *Ethnography and the Historical Imagination.* Boulder, Colo.: Westview Press.

Cox, J. Halley, with William Davenport. 1988. *Hawaiian Sculpture* (Rev. ed.). Honolulu: University of Hawai'i Press.

Dening, Greg. 1995. *The Death of William Gooch: A History's Anthropology.* Honolulu: University of Hawai'i Press.

Dodd, Edward. 1967. *Polynesian Art.* New York: Dodd, Mead & Company.

Fine-Dare, Kathleen. 2002. *Grave Injustice: The American Indian Repatriation Movement.* Lincoln: University of Nebraska Press.

Forbes, David. 1905. "Letter to William T. Brigham." In *Protect Kawaihae Iwi Kupuna and Moepu Information Packet.* Hui Malama I Na Kupuna O'Hawai'i Nei (Fall 2005).

He Hoʻolaha. 2006. "Declaration Calling for the Protection of the Iwi Kupuna (Ancestral Remains) and Moepu (Funerary Objects)." Retrieved 25 August 2006, from http://66.102.7.104.

Johnson, Greg. 2005. "Narrative Remains: Articulating Indian Identities in the Repatriation Context." *Comparative Studies in Society and History*, 47, no. 3: 480–506.

———. 2007. *Sacred Claims: Repatriation and Living Tradition*. Charlottesville: University Press of Virginia.

Kamakau, Samuel. 1964. *Ka Poʻe Kahiko: The People of Old*, trans. Mary Kawena Pukui. Arranged and edited by Dorothy Barrère. Honolulu: Bishop Museum Press.

Kirch, Patrick. 1985. *Feathered Gods and Fishhooks: An Introduction to Hawaiian Archaeology and Prehistory*. Honolulu: University of Hawaiʻi Press.

Kobayashi, Ken. 2005. "Kawananako Seeks Transfer of Artifacts." *Honolulu Advertiser* (20 August). Retrieved 20 August 2005, from http://www.honolulu advertiser.com/2005/08/20/NEWS23.

Kubota, Gary. 2006. "Reburied Cave Items Finally Back at Museum." *Honolulu Star-Bulletin* (8 September). Retrieved 8 September 2006, from http://starbul letin.com/2006/09/08/news/story02.html.

Lincoln, Bruce. 1989. *Discourse and the Construction of Society: Comparative Studies of Myth, Ritual and Classification*. New York: Oxford University Press.

———. 1996. "Theses on Method." *Method and Theory in the Study of Religion*, 8: 225–227.

Malo, David. 1951 [1898]. *Hawaiian Antiquities*, trans. Nathaniel B. Emerson. Honolulu: Bernice P. Bishop Museum Special Publication No. 2.

Masuzawa, Tomoko. 2005. *The Invention of World Religions: Or, How European Universalism Was Preserved in the Language of Pluralism*. Chicago: University of Chicago Press.

McGregor, Davianna Pōmaikaʻi. 2007. *Nā Kuaʻāina: Living Hawaiian Culture*. Honolulu: University of Hawaiʻi Press.

McKeown, Timothy C., and Sherry Hutt. 2003. "In the Smaller Scope of Conscience: The Native American Graves Protection and Repatriation Act Twelve Years After." *UCLA Journal of Environmental Law and Policy*, 21, no. 2: 153–213.

Native American Graves Protection and Repatriation Act (NAGPRA). Public Law 101–601 (25 U.S.C. 3001), 1990.

NAGPRA Review Committee. 2003. *Official Summary of the Twenty-Fifth Meeting of the Native American Graves Protection and Repatriation Act Review Committee*. St. Paul, Minn. 9–10 May. Retrieved from www.cr.nps.gov/nagpra/REVIEW/meetings/MINUTES.HTM.

———. 2004. *Official Summary of the Twenty-Seventh Meeting of the Native American Graves Protection and Repatriation Act Review Committee*. Washington, D.C. 17–18 September. Retrieved from www.cr.nps.gov/nagpra/REVIEW/meetings/MINUTES.HTM.

———. 2005. *Official Summary of the Twenty-Ninth Meeting of the Native American Graves Protection and Repatriation Act Review Committee*. Honolulu. 13–15 March. Retrieved from www.cr.nps.gov/nagpra/REVIEW/meetings/MINUTES.HTM.

Nihipali, Kunani. 2002. "Stone by Stone, Bone by Bone: Rebuilding the Hawaiian Nation in the Illusion of Reality." *Arizona State Law Journal*, 34, no. 1: 28–46.

Pang, Gordon. 2006. "Hawaiians React to Artifact Reports." *Honolulu Advertiser*

(9 September). Retrieved 11 September 2006, from http://the.honoluluadvertiser.com/article/2006/Sep/09/In/FP609100328.html.

Pukui, Mary Kawena, E. W. Haertig, and Catherine E. Lee. 1972. *Nānā I Ke Kumu: Look to the Source.* Honolulu: Hui Hanai.

Rose, Roger. 1992. *Reconciling the Past: Two Basketry Kāʻai and the Legendary Līloa and Lonoikamakahiki.* Honolulu: Bishop Museum Press.

Sahlins, Marshall. 1981. *Historical Metaphors and Mythical Realities: Structure and History in the Early History of the Sandwich Islands Kingdom.* Ann Arbor: University of Michigan Press.

———. 1988. "Cosmologies of Capitalism: The Trans-Pacific Sector of 'The World System.'" *Proceedings of the British Academy,* 74: 1–51.

———. 1992. "The Economics of Develop-Man in the Pacific." *Res,* 21: 12–25.

———. 1993. "Goodbye to *Tristes Tropes*: Ethnography in the Context of Modern World History." *Journal of Modern History,* 65: 1–25.

Starn, Orin. 2004. *Ishi's Brain: In Search of America's Last "Wild" Indian.* New York: Norton.

Taylor, Charles. 2004. *Modern Social Imaginaries.* Durham: Duke University Press.

Valeri, Valerio. 1985. *Kingship and Sacrifice: Ritual and Society in Ancient Hawaii,* trans. Paula Wissig. Chicago: University of Chicago Press.

Verdery, Katherine. 1999. *The Political Lives of Dead Bodies: Reburial and Post-Socialist Change.* New York: Columbia University Press.

Young, Kanalu. 1998. *Rethinking the Native Hawaiian Past.* New York: Garland.

Chapter 4
Flagging Peace
Struggles over Symbolic Landscape in the New Northern Ireland

Dominic Bryan and Clifford Stevenson

Half way along the Cave Hill Road in north Belfast is what is locally known as an interface. The junction near the Cave Hill pub demarcates the "loyalist," Protestant, Westlands Road area from the predominantly Catholic, Irish republican area known as Little America.[1] Three lampposts at the junction each display two flags, the Union Jack and the Ulster flag (a red cross of St. George with a six-pointed star and red hand in the center) to demarcate the boundary. The flags were put up in late June at the start of the marching season, a period of Protestant parading that culminates with the Twelfth of July, the annual commemoration of the victory of Protestant King William over Catholic King James at the Battle of the Boyne in 1690. The flags are left in place long after this period of commemoration is over. Indeed, in many areas they are never removed and serve to demarcate territory into the winter months when the wind and rain reduce them to tatters.

The meaning of these flags can be understood on a number of different levels. Like many societies throughout the world, in Northern Ireland there are commemorative events where local and national identities are displayed. Loyalists describe such displays as part of their tradition, their culture. The flags that they display on these occasions also mark territory and offer a different message to people who live in or near the area. These flags are not simply a reflection of local communal identities, but are also markers of physical ethnopolitical boundaries and, more particularly, of areas controlled by paramilitary groups. It is too simple to interpret these displays only as reflections of Protestant community identity given that the flags are put up by groups connected to paramilitary organizations, which despite the 1994 paramilitary cease-fires and subsequent political agreements, have continued to offer the threat of violence. Yet opposition to displays of these flags from both outside and inside the Protestant community (and there is evidence of plenty of opposition inside) remains muted, and despite a government policy to promote "A Shared Future" (Office of the First and Deputy First Minister 2005), its implementation often reflects a reluctance to challenge the power of these local paramilitary groups directly.

This chapter surveys the symbolic landscape of Northern Ireland before and after the peace process, particularly with reference to flags to analyze ways that it is and is not shifting. We argue that the symbolic landscape in Northern Ireland is complex and the use of symbols and emblems cannot be simply read as a reflection of people's identities. It is also part of localized power structures linked to potential and remembered violence and ongoing struggles and contests both internal to their own communities and to the boundaries between communities. To do this we explore how flags and other contentious symbols are used, looking at policy initiatives to reduce conflict over symbols and offering the possibility of more inclusive representations and difficulties in moving "toward constructive conflict management in long-term intergroup conflicts" (Ross, Chapter 1, this volume). In this analysis, we describe how symbols both include and exclude, and how the meaning of particular symbols shifts across contexts in which they are used and viewed (Bryan and Gillespie 2005; Bryan and Stevenson 2006; Bryan 2007). It describes exclusive symbolic displays in the region over time and concludes with some thoughts on how the context of the symbolic landscape has changed since the 1998 Belfast Agreement and the more recent 2007 creation of a powersharing government headed by the once archenemies Rev. Ian Paisley (Democratic Unionist Party) and Martin McGuinness (Sinn Féin).

Flags and Emblems in Northern Ireland

Both the general public and politicians have long paid a great deal of attention to the use of symbols in the politics of Northern Ireland, and they are frequently engaged and enraged by contestation over symbolic displays. Public events with their attendant rituals are often the site of public disorder, while displays of flags and poppies, pictures of the Queen and sports shirts have all ended up in the courts at one time or another. Researchers studying Northern Ireland have also paid great attention to the role of symbols in the region's long-term conflict (Bryan 2000, 2007; Bryan and Gillespie 2005; Bryan and McIntosh 2007; Brown and MacGinty 2003; Bryson and McCartney 1994; Buckley 1985; Feldman 1991; Harrison 1995; Jarman 1993, 1997; Loftus 1990, 1994; McCormick and Jarman 2005; McIntosh 1999; Nic Craith 2002; Rolston 1991, 1992, 1995, 2003; Ross 2007; Santino 2001). Flags and emblems, as well as memorials and parades, are the language through which identity politics is expressed and contested.

Northern Ireland came into being as an autonomous region in 1921 when the British granted self-rule to the Irish in the south with their large Catholic majority after a bitter war between the British Army and Irish republicans. The Irish Free State declared itself the Republic of Ireland in 1948, and they did not relinquish their formal claims to the six counties in the north until 1998. The northeast corner of Ireland with its Protestant majority and a Catholic minority remained part of the United Kingdom and became Northern Ireland when the island was partitioned. Its Protestants continued to express their loyalty to the British throne while Catholics suffered from discrimination and exclusion. The Ulster Unionist Party (UUP), whose first Prime Minister boasted that "we are a Protestant Parliament and a Protestant State" (McIntosh 1999: 42), ruled Northern Ireland until 1972, constantly warning of the threat offered by the disloyal Catholic population and by the claims made by the Republic of Ireland on the six counties.

In this political context, the rituals and symbols that the rival ethnopolitical communities displayed were a frequent source of conflict. Many public events and most state occasions were marked by symbolic expressions and their accompanying contestation. The Union flag and the Ulster flag were routinely flown on many government buildings, not only on designated flag days as in the rest of the United Kingdom, but also on additional days including 12 July, the most significant day in the Protestant symbolic calendar (Bryson and McCartney 1994: 76–78). Indeed, some unionist-controlled local councils still fly the flag every day of the year not only on official buildings but also on public facilities such as swimming pools. The Union flag was also flown from police stations, fire stations, and other services, as well as from many Protestant churches. This relationship between the popular and official flying of these flags has an important bearing on flags as both a reflection and cause of conflict in Northern Ireland.

In contrast, we are not aware of any official occasions when the green, white, and orange of the Irish Tricolor, the national flag of the Republic of Ireland, were ever displayed in Northern Ireland. In fact, until the 1970s, when it was used on popular occasions, the police never greatly tolerated display of the Tricolor. The Civil Authorities (Special Powers) Act of 1922 was used to restrict parades and other displays of a broadly Irish nationalist character (Jarman and Bryan 1998: 41–53). In 1958 Northern Ireland's Minister of Home Affairs, Edmond Warnock, announced the banning of a St. Patrick's Day parade saying: "so long as this Government lasts and so long as I am Home Affairs Minister, I shall not permit the republican flag to be carried in Derry City" (Farrell 1980: 199).

In 1954 the Northern Ireland Parliament passed the Flags and Emblems (Display) Act that gave the police the power to order a person who publicly displayed an "emblem" to remove it, or for the officer to remove it, if the officer felt it would lead to a breach of the peace. If the person failed to obey the constable's order, they would be cited for an offense. At one level, this proposition was not in itself totally unreasonable, but what made the Act controversial and partisan was the section that declared that the definition of "emblem" includes any flag except the Union flag (Bew et al. 2002: 97; Patterson 1999). Rev. Ian Paisley successfully exploited this legislation on many occasions in the 1960s. For example, in September 1964 he threatened to remove a Tricolor from the window of the Republican Party offices on the Falls Road (a Catholic/nationalist area of Belfast). It is perhaps ironic that given the threat to public order the police removed the "offending" flag, which in itself led to a serious riot. Civil rights demonstrations after 1967 were frequently met by counterdemonstrators waving Union flags which the police rarely, if ever, removed giving a clear message to all sections of the population.

From the founding of Northern Ireland, the unionists controlled its public space. Protestant fraternal organizations, notably the Orange Order, the Black Institution, and the Apprentice Boys of Derry organized hundred and even thousands of parades that dominated the roads of Northern Ireland through the summer months (Bryan 2000). In contrast, public expressions of Irish nationalism were only allowed in predominantly Catholic areas and even then displays of the Irish Tricolor often led to police intervention (Jarman and Bryan 1998).

The development of a civil rights movement in 1967 demanding an end to discrimination against Catholics threatened the status quo. The Protestant dominated Royal Ulster Constabulary (RUC) generally viewed the civil rights marchers as a threat to public order and responded with increasing levels of violence. Intimidation and fears in both ethnopolitical communities produced increased residential segregation and greater territorial demarcation with Catholics moving out of Protestant areas and Protestants moving from Catholic areas. The public order situation was so bad that following riots after an Apprentice Boys parade in Derry in August 1969, the British government introduced soldiers who were to remain for over thirty years to undertake policing functions. Catholic resistance moved from supporting the nonviolent civil rights movement toward backing the growing Irish Republican Army (IRA) that declared itself the defender of the community (English

2003: 81–119). Politically, there was a parallel shift so that rather than demand rights within Northern Ireland, Catholics withdrew into "ghettos" which the IRA labeled as "No Go" areas for the British Army and police and focused on the reunification of the island. Within these areas the Irish Tricolor was hoisted as a sign of resistance and, in later years, it often had the letters I, R, and A written across it.

Within working-class Protestant areas, increasing disillusionment with the inability of the unionist administration and the security forces to deal with the apparent threat of the IRA led to increased support for their own paramilitary groups, the Ulster Volunteer Force (UVF) and after 1972, the Ulster Defense Association (UDA). While they "patrolled" their own areas their strategic response to IRA attacks was frequently sectarian murder of any Catholic they could find. These groups also developed their own symbolic repertoire of flags and emblems that were displayed in Orange Order and other parades by flute bands supporting these organizations.

Patterns of violence between the paramilitaries, the police, and British army troops stationed in the region continued for twenty-five years before the 1994 ceasefire. During that time, 3,500 people were killed and many thousands more injured.[2] From 1969 until 1994, the period commonly referred to as "The Troubles," urban areas of Belfast and Derry and rural border areas such as South Armagh were important sites of violence. Funerals, emotive events at any time, became part of the political and symbolic landscape as coffins draped in national flags or carrying paramilitary regalia and pictures of guns being fired over coffins of dead comrades were a regular part of the daily news despite the best efforts of the RUC to stop such expressions. Events like Bloody Sunday (1972), Bloody Friday (1972), the Hunger Strikes (1981), the Enniskillen bomb (1987), the Teebane massacre (1992), the Shankill bomb (1993), the Omagh bomb (1998), and so many more, became part of local folklore. In a less violent expression of their differences republicans and loyalists revealed their anger and rage, recognized their heroes and enemies, and expressed their intractable positions in the hundreds of wall murals that sprung up throughout the region (Rolston 1991, 1992, 1995; Jarman 1997). The number of parades increased with republicans commemorating internment, Bloody Sunday, and the Hunger Strikes and the Orange Order introducing "mini-Twelfth parades" in the first few weeks each July. In addition, many loyalist bands developed their own parades,[3] and at various points peace groups developed public campaigns as did organizations supporting republican and loyalist prisoners. Many of these expressions ended in public disorder that the police controlled using baton round guns.

After the IRA, UDA, and UVF announced ceasefires in 1994 and a tentative peace process began, symbolic contestation become even more intense and a principal means for the two sides to express their differences. From 1993 republicans were allowed to hold demonstrations in the center of Belfast, and since 1998 St. Patrick's Day events attended by thousands of people (including many of whom vigorously waved Tricolors) have been organized in the city. By way of contrast, there were still many hundreds more Orange Order and other parades reflecting Protestant and unionist identities than there were Irish nationalist ones. A central source of conflict developed around the protests of residents in a number of predominantly Catholic areas against the Orange Order parades that marched through their neighborhoods. In the past, the RUC had always permitted these parades, but the changed political context then led to changes in policing strategy. The RUC first blocked a number of parades in between 1995 and 1997, most particularly a July Orange parade at Drumcree Church outside Portadown, County Armagh although twice at the last moment they relented and allowed it to proceed. Blocking parades from walking their "traditional routes" and other decisions over the next few years led to such widespread public disorder the British Government was forced to introduce completely new public order legislation for Northern Ireland (Bryan 2001). A new Parades Commission, rather than the police, would decide whether a parade would be permitted, what route it might take, how many bands would be permitted, and what time of the day they could march. In addition, they effectively required negotiations between the marchers' and residents' groups as a precondition for granting permits to march along routes through disputed areas. In some areas, such as Portadown, there were years with violence and standoffs with the security forces, but over time this new strategy has proved successful in lowering tensions.

Government and local council buildings remained ongoing sites of symbolic contestation as well. Once direct rule was introduced in 1972, the United Kingdom government buildings often flew flags on official days, which was, in effect, a reduction from the practice under the pre-1972 unionist regime. However, the Union flag still flew over police stations and law courts. Significantly, popular flying of flags during the 12 July period increased greatly as part of the increased making of territorial space. Flags had long been flown on people's houses during the marching season, but increasingly flags were mounted on lampposts and left up all year round. Most local councils under unionist control not only flew the Union flag, but often the Ulster flag, every day of the year, as well as on all buildings and amenities within their control. In contrast a number of nationalist councils stopped flying the Union flag altogether and either flew a council flag or no flag at all. Bryson and McCartney (1994: 78–79) describe the nationalist controlled Derry City council's unsuccessful attempts to resolve the contestation over the flag by flying the Crimson flag associated with the Protestant defense of the city in 1688–1689. However, this did not satisfy unionists who saw the removal of the Union flag as the central issue.

Contemporary Symbolic Landscape

Following the 1994 ceasefires, the political parties gradually moved to the table and in 1998 in talks presided over by United States Senator George Mitchell reached an agreement that offered the possibility of political powersharing. Reaching it was long and arduous and there were a number of issues that still remained unsettled including paramilitary weapons and police reform. The symbolic landscape was so contested that the 1998 Belfast Agreement said nothing specific about the issues of parades or flags other than: "All participants acknowledge the sensitivity of the use of symbols and emblems for public purposes and the need in particular in creating new institutions to ensure that such symbols and emblems are used in a manner which promotes mutual respect rather than division. Arrangements will be made to monitor this issue and consider what action might be required" (20).

The agreement established ten government departments whose control was to be divided among the major political parties. After the 1998 Assembly election, the Ulster Unionist Party and the Social and Democratic Labour Party (SDLP) controlled three departments each, while Ian Paisley's Democratic Unionist Party and Sinn Féin controlled two each. As soon as local rule began the next year, there were immediate disputes around the flying of the Union flag over government buildings. Sinn Féin's Ministers of Health and Education asked for the Union flag not to be put on buildings they controlled. In response, an Education Department building in Bangor, County Down, a predominantly Protestant area, had all the lampposts surrounding it bedecked in Union flags the following day. In 2000, with no agreement on the flying of flags on government buildings, the British Secretary of State Peter Mandelson decided to introduce legislation at Westminster. The Flags (Northern Ireland) Order 2000 designates the government buildings and the particular days on which the Union flag should be flown. The list of seventeen designated days, which included many of the birthdays of the Royal family, did not name the Twelfth of July but did include St. Patrick's Day (Bryan and Gillespie 2005; Bryan 2007).

The legislation did not apply to the twenty-six local councils in Northern Ireland, however, and the issue of what flag to fly, when to fly it, and where, remains contentious in almost every council. The policy adopted depends on which political parties control each council. Those controlled by a combination of the UUP and DUP usually had the flag flown on all official buildings and other services. In some councils where there was no majority the compromise seemed to be to follow the designated days as for government buildings. Although Sinn Féin has a policy of flying both the Union and Tricolor flags on buildings, in practice they follow the same policy as that held by the SDLP in councils they control: they usually opted for flying no flag at all. When Alex Maskey became the first Sinn Féin councilor to become Mayor of Belfast (in 2002), he did hang both flags in his office within the City Hall, but the Union flag remained on the building.

The use of flags and emblems on the streets and in the housing estates of Northern Ireland has an altogether more complex dynamic. As discussed above, some displays of flags have always accompanied the Twelfth of July celebrations and the marching season although the number of flags flown, where they are flown, the length of time they are up, as well as the variety of flags flown in loyalist areas have all increased *[new para?]* dramatically since the mid-1990s. *[Policy]* While there are displays of republican flags and other symbols, particularly around an increasing number of memorial sites, they still do not come close to the number in loyalist Protestant areas. In July 2006, just prior to the Twelfth of July, we counted the symbols and emblems on every main road and urban area in Northern Ireland. We found 4,136 emblems, 3,638 of which were flags on main roads alone, and it is clear that there are many more in residential areas. Two months later, just after the twenty-fifth anniversary commemorations of the hunger strikes, 737 republican symbols were enumerated, of which 556 were flags and forty-four murals, and there were still 1,754 loyalist emblems displayed. In 1997 there was no reduction in the numbers of flags in the July period but a significantly greater number had been taken down by September.

The patterns to these displays are very familiar. By far the largest percentage of flags appears in working-class loyalist areas. However, none *[Relation?]* were found in more middle-class areas unless they are put up around an Orange hall in the center of a town or village. While the proliferation of *[Cultural Clash]* flags that are displayed is partially connected to Protestant dissatisfaction with the peace process and the involvement of Sinn Féin in government, of greater significance has been the intra-loyalist contest between the paramilitary groups and their factions. The sometimes violent feud between the UVF and the UDA on the Shankill Road in West Belfast reached a murderous peak in August 2000 and led to widespread use of paramilitary flags demarcating areas different loyalists controlled. In addition, a split in the UVF in 1996 (with a faction in County Armagh styling itself the Loyalist Volunteer Force (LVF) led to more flag and mural displays. Further, friction within the UDA itself has led to continued symbolic assertiveness in a number of areas. Thus, in many areas since the late 1990s Union and Ulster flags have been accompanied by a range of loyalist paramilitary flags, and territorial demarcation among Protestant working-class groups has accompanied the longer tradition of distinguishing unionist and Catholic nationalist areas. In other words, the meanings of some of the loyalist displays are aimed at other loyalists as much as nationalists.

It is clear that to describe the "Protestant community" as flying flags to express their identity during the marching season is far too simplistic. In nearly all middle-class residential areas, there are no flags flown. This has probably as much to do with the influence of property ownership and house prices as the political sentiments of the Protestants who live there. However, even in working-class areas the meaning of the symbolic landscape is complex. In the survey we conducted in July and September 2006, most flags around Orange halls and most Orange Order flags were taken down soon after the Twelfth of July celebrations and our research shows that it is not, in the main, members of the Orange Order who put flags up. Rather, it is the committees that run the 11 July bonfire celebrations, those involved with the numerous loyalist flute bands and groups closely connected with the loyalist paramilitaries who put up most of the flags.

Indeed, the general public understands this quite well. In the 2007 "Northern Ireland Life and Times Survey" (http://www.ark.ac.uk/nilt/) respondents were asked who they thought usually put up Union flags on lampposts. They were offered choices, of which they could pick more than one, including the town council (10.5 percent), political parties (19.1 percent), cultural groups (13.2 percent), paramilitaries (55.6 percent), other groups (11.4 percent), and isolated individuals (24.7 percent). From the results it is clear that people believe, in the main, that paramilitary groups hang the Union flag on lampposts. Interestingly, when asked the same question about the Irish Tricolor, the results were virtually the same. So, the massive displays of flags left on lampposts are not simply read by people (Protestant or Catholic) as a display of loyalty by supporters of the Orange Order around the Twelfth of July, but rather are understood as markers of paramilitary control. Even more striking, when asked if they "support flag flying on lampposts in your own neighborhood," an overwhelming 80 percent of people said "no" although the opposition was ten percent higher among Catholics than Protestants (Table 4.1). Interestingly, class differences were also modest and seventy-four percent of the working-class respondents do not support flag flying in their area.

These results provide us with a complex picture with regard to the popular use of flags in contemporary Northern Ireland. Rather than

Table 4.1. In General, Would You, or Do You Support Flag Flying on Lampposts in Your Own Neighborhood?

	Catholic*	Protestant*	No Religion	Total
Yes	9.1%	18.4%	5.8%	13.1%
No	85.3%	75.0%	88.9%	80.9%
Other	.8%	2.1%	.6%	1.4%
Don't know	4.8%	4.5%	4.7%	4.6%
Total	100.0%	100.0%	100.0%	100.0%

simply an expression of a loyalist identity within the Protestant community, both Protestants and Catholics recognize the flags as assertions by people and groups with paramilitary connections aimed at marking their territories. Yet, these local understandings while reasonably accurate are not complete since other groups such as local marching bands with no paramilitary connections are also involved with putting up flags at times.

Policies for Inclusiveness and Shared Space

Thus far we have concentrated on the divisive role symbols play in Northern Ireland. However, it is worth looking at how the peace process, the 1998 agreement, and resulting new political structures and legislation have created alternative symbolic representations. For some of the new institutions symbolic representations could be uncontroversial. For example, the new symbol for the Northern Ireland Assembly is the image of a flax plant, important in the historic local linen industry, and government departments adopted a hexagonal design based upon the shape of the rocks of the Giants Causeway in County Antrim (Bryan and McIntosh 2007: 129).

However, police reform included both renaming of the Royal Ulster Constabulary (RUC) and the search for a new badge. Catholics resented the RUC, which was over ninety percent Protestant and associated with long-term discrimination. The RUC badge consisted of a crown above an Irish harp. While unionists received a promise from Prime Minister Tony Blair that the RUC would not be disbanded, the independent report set up under the 1998 Agreement, *A New Beginning: Policing in Northern Ireland* (Patten et al. 1999), suggested major changes including a renaming and a new badge (98–100). For unionists this was too much yet for nationalists the proposed reforms did not go far enough.

Behind the conflicting unionist and nationalist views were different beliefs about the role of the RUC in the Troubles. During the debates an enormous amount of time was spent discussing symbolic issues, particularly the question of the badge. Finally, the decision over the new badge was left to the new Police Board that included representatives of all the main political parties except Sinn Féin, which had refused to participate in it. The new renamed Police Service of Northern Ireland (PSNI) adopted a badge displaying a laurel leaf, a torch, a crown, a shamrock, a harp, and scales surrounding the cross of St. Patrick all set on a six-pointed star. The greatest point of controversy surrounded the use of the crown, the shamrock, and the harp with the crown. Though the Patten Report (1999: 98–100) had recommended that the new badge contain no symbol connected with the British or Irish states in order to make it neutral, Secretary of State Peter Mandelson ruled that the new badge could include symbols to make it inclusive as opposed to neutral. As a result, the design of the new badge grew out of horse-trading between the UUP and SDLP. Following its adoption there has been very little controversy which itself could be seen as an indicator of its success. Perhaps this is, ironically, because there are so many symbols on the badge that the individual components are difficult to discern, having the end effect of producing the neutral emblem originally envisaged by Patten (Bryan and McIntosh 2007: 129–130). It is also worth noting, in regard to policing, that the Union flag no longer flies from police stations.

In addition to these specific examples, a new legislative and policy framework has started to shape the symbolic landscape. The 1998 Fair Employment and Treatment Order has put pressure upon both the private and public sector to change practices making discrimination on the grounds of religious belief and political opinion unlawful both in the work place and in the provision of goods, facilities, and services. The Fair Employment Code of Practice states that employers are required to identify any practices that do not provide equality of opportunity and that they should "promote a good and harmonious working environment and atmosphere in which no worker feels under threat or intimidated because of his or her religious belief or political opinion" (Equality Commission for Northern Ireland 1998: 19). The Code of Practice further encourages employers to undertake action by considering: "Ending displays at the workplace of flags, emblems, posters, graffiti, or the circulation of materials, or the deliberate articulation of slogans or songs which are likely to give offence to, or cause apprehension among, any one section of the population" (Equality Commission for Northern Ireland 1998: 50). While this legislation has meant that employers cannot fly Union flags from their buildings, unionist-controlled local councils do not see it as applying to them, and continue to display the flag arguing that as a layer of government they should fly the "national flag."

The Equality Commission, set up under the Agreement, has attempted to put pressure on some of the ~~councils~~ citing the 1998 Northern Ireland Act which makes it a statutory duty for a public body to carry out its function with due regard to the need to promote "equal opportunity between persons of different religious belief, political opinion, racial group, age, marital status or sexual orientation" and with regard to "the desirability of promoting good relations between persons of different religious belief, political opinion or racial groups" (Section 75). This has made local councils go through a process of consultation over their policies, including those on flying flags, but as far as we are aware, it has yet to force any significant change in policy for any council as regards the flying of the Union flag (Bryan and Gillespie 2005: 35–43).

More broadly the Government has introduced the policy of *A Shared Future* whose overall aim is: "to establish, over time, a shared society defined by a culture of tolerance: a normal, civic society, in which all individuals are considered as equals, where differences are resolved through dialogue in the public sphere, and where all individuals are treated impartially. A society where there is equity, respect for diversity and recognition of our interdependence" (OFDFM 2005: 7). This policy includes "tackling the visible manifestations of sectarianism and racism" by "freeing the public realm (including public property) from displays of sectarian aggression" and "reclaiming shared space" by "developing and protecting town and city centres as safe and welcoming for all people of all walks of life" (OFDFM 2005: 18).

The PSNI is now designated as the lead agency for dealing with the popular flying of flags. To do this, they developed a protocol that aims to "remove the display of paramilitary flags or flags of a sectarian nature," but also to "develop a strategic and graduated response to the flags issue which involves consultation, shared understanding, negotiation and, if necessary, proportionate and legal use of enforcement methods." They will undertake "the removal of all flags and emblems from arterial routes and town centres" and "the control of displays of flags and emblems in particular areas: for example, mixed and interface areas and near buildings such as schools, hospitals, places of worship and community halls." However, "they will undertake this process with the support of communities and their representatives" (Bryan and Stevenson 2006: 65–75). In practice the police are working to persuade groups not to put up paramilitary flags and to take down all the flags they put up after a period of time. Note that while they talk about support of "the community" this often effectively means garnering cooperation from the local paramilitary leaders. Judging from our survey, while there seems to have been little success in removing flags from arterial routes and town centers, greater efforts do seem to be made to remove flags at the end of the marching season. The aim of the policy is to return the flying of flags to a practice symbolizing commemoration and celebration and away from long-term marking of territory (Bryan and Stevenson 2006).

Another development relevant to the changing symbolic landscape is attempts to neutralize or reduce territorial symbol marking through the transformation of previously exclusive events into more inclusive, shared ones. The most obvious example of this has been the St. Patrick's Day Carnival in Belfast. When the event was first organized in the center of Belfast in 1998 people generally viewed it as republicans claiming their space in a city center from which they had been excluded in the past. The organizers tried to persuade the Belfast City Council that the event deserved council backing and public funding. Over the years there have been annual debates over whether the event had become sufficiently inclusive, in other words whether Protestants felt involved enough to merit public funding. Central to this argument is that St. Patrick was a saint for all of Ireland and that St. Patrick's Day is recognized and to a certain extent celebrated in Protestant churches and within the Protestant community. In 2006 the City Council began running the event itself and there is now an attempt to evaluate whether St. Patrick's Day offers the possibility of being a more inclusive event that could improve community relations (St. Patrick's Day Project 2006). At the St. Patrick's Day carnival in 2007 stewards asked people carrying Tricolor flags and entering the Custom House Square area of the city where the major events take place, to put the flags away. In return they were offered green flags with a shamrock on it. While the requests were not always complied with, our monitoring showed that most people put their Tricolor flag away, and our survey of the event suggested that around eighteen percent of the attendees were Protestant, up from twelve percent the previous year.

Conclusion

There has been recognition among policy makers from government, local authorities, and institutions such as the police that the transformation of society in Northern Ireland requires addressing the way contentious symbols are displayed. Symbolic displays are not simply a by-product of social and political events, but central to how people experience them. Yet because the two communities' political interests differ, symbols and rituals involving flag displays remain sites of contestation. In addition, in the present period, construction of exclusive, local memorials expressing understandings of the past are increasing in both cities and rural areas, and could become very contentious in the near future. At the same time, there are very real attempts to create inclusive symbols and rituals and to share public spaces in ways that they have never before.

Perhaps recent developments offer us some important clues. Following nine years of conflict over a range of issues unresolved in 1998, especially police reform and decommissioning IRA weapons, the DUP and Sinn Féin negotiators reached an agreement that allowed them to form a new government in 2007. As a result, in May, a new devolved government of Northern Ireland led by First Minister and leader of the Democratic Unionist Party (DUP), Rev. Ian Paisley, and Deputy First Minister, Sinn Féin's Martin McGuinness, took office. Over the past forty years, no single person has symbolized Unionist opposition to Irish republicans more than Paisley, who in the 1960s drew upon his fundamentalist religious positions to oppose the developing Civil Rights movement and attempts by the dominant Ulster Unionist Party (UUP) to negotiate powersharing with Irish nationalists. Paisley created the DUP in 1972 as an alternative to the UUP and was involved in numerous campaigns, marches, and rallies warning successive British governments that any softening of their political stances toward Irish republicanism would be met with bitter opposition within the Protestant community. After the Irish Republican Army (IRA) announced its 1994 ceasefire and the British, Irish, and American governments began brokering a peace agreement between political parties in Northern Ireland, Paisley and the DUP walked out of the talks, refusing to sit with Sinn Féin. After the multi-party agreement was signed in 1998, Paisley mobilized opposition within the Protestant community, calling for a rejection of the referendum on it. His strident opposition to a government that included Sinn Féin clearly struck a chord within the community and the DUP's vote significantly increased in successive elections, making them the largest unionist political party and ensuring that no administration could exist without the DUP's support.

Martin McGuinness is widely understood to have been a senior IRA member in Derry in the 1970s. While he has been central to the development of Sinn Féin in the 1980s, many believe he also served on the IRA's Army Council during some of that period. Clearly unionists see him, along with Gerry Adams, as symbolizing modern Irish republicanism against which they have fought for decades. When he became Minister of Education in the first administration after the 1998 Agreement, many Protestants found it very difficult to come to terms with what they saw as a terrorist in government.

This is why recent pictures of Paisley and McGuinness together were (and to many still are) momentous. There was much discussion before their first public meeting as to whether the two men would shake hands. Paisley made it clear that he would not be seen shaking hands with McGuinness, yet it appears to observers that the two men got on. They have been pictured apparently sharing jokes and at ease in each other's company, so much so the press nicknames them "the chuckle brothers." While there has so far been no symbolic handshake, the changes in the relationship between the two and their sharing the region's leadership positions and willingness to appear together in public are enormously important. This is in stark contrast to David Trimble (UUP) and Seamus Mallon (SDLP) who were First and Deputy First Minister in the first administration after the 1998 Agreement who failed to convey symbolically the possibility that they could work well together to solve problems of the region following three decades of violence (Bryan and McIntosh 2007: 133–136).

To date, there has not been, and will not be, an easy transformation of the symbolic landscape in Northern Ireland. Yet, it is wrong to underestimate the potential for continuing change as Protestants and Catholics in the region establish a new relationship with each other. There are indications that the mutually exclusive symbols that previously dominated Northern Ireland's symbolic landscape are on the decline or being modified and there are increasing efforts to create inclusive symbols and events emphasizing mutual recognition and things that Protestants and Catholics in the region share. This process is influenced by policy and legislation, but it is ultimately rooted in the new, changed political context.

Notes

This research was originally funded by the United Kingdom's Economic and Social Research Council and then further funded by the Office of the First and Deputy First Minister in Northern Ireland. Thanks are due to Gillian McIntosh and Marc Howard Ross for their suggestions on reading drafts of this chapter.

1. Protestants in Northern Ireland are variously described as Unionist, those favoring the continuing union between Northern Ireland and Great Britain, and loyalists, who are those who are more culturally oriented and emphasize their loyalty to the British crown. However, the term loyalist is most commonly used locally to describe those people who support paramilitary groups like the Ulster Volunteer Force (UVF) and Ulster Defence Association (UDA). Catholics, in contrast, are variously described as republicans and nationalists; while both favor reuniting the island of Ireland, the former have been more willing to endorse the use of violence while the latter have endorsed politics as their preferred method.

2. The population of Northern Ireland is about 1.5 million meaning that the death rate was roughly equivalent to the United States battle deaths in the Vietnam War.

3. One counting in the mid-1990s estimated that there were about 3,500

parades in the region each year and about 80 percent of them were politically reflected the Unionist community (Jarman 1997).

Bibliography

Bew, P., P. Gibbon, and H. Patterson. 2002. *Northern Ireland 1921–2001: Political Forces and Social Classes*. London: Verso.

Brown, Kris, and Roger MacGinty. 2003. "Public Attitudes Towards Partisan and Neutral Symbols in Post-Agreement Northern Ireland." *Identities: Global Structures in Culture and Power*, 10: 83–108.

Bryan, D. 2000. *Orange Parades: The Politics of Ritual Tradition and Control*. London: Pluto Press.

———. 2001. "Parade Disputes and the Peace Process." *Peace Review*, 13, no. 1: 43–50.

———. 2007. "New Colours for the Orange State: Finding Symbolic Space in a Newly Devolved Northern Ireland." In *Devolution and Identity*, ed. J. Wilson and K. Stapleton. Aldershot, Hampshire: Ashgate.

Bryan, D., and G. Gillespie. 2005. *Transforming Conflict: Flags and Emblems*. Belfast: IIS.

Bryan, D., and G. McIntosh. 2007. "Symbols and Identity in the 'new' Northern Ireland." In *Devolution and Constitutional Change in Northern Ireland*, ed. P. Carmichael, C. Knox, and R. Osborn. Manchester: Manchester University Press.

Bryan, D., and C. Stevenson. 2006. *Flags Monitoring Project 2006: Preliminary Findings*. Retrieved from http://www.asharedfutureni.gov.uk.

Bryson, L., and C. McCartney. 1994. *Clashing Symbols: A Report on the Use of Flags, Anthems and Other National Symbols in Northern Ireland*. Belfast: Institute of Irish Studies.

Buckley, A. 1985. "The Chosen Few: Biblical Texts in the Regalia of an Ulster Secret Society." *Folklife*, 24: 5–24.

English, R. 2003. *Armed Struggle: The History of the IRA*. London: Macmillan.

Equality Commission for Northern Ireland. 1998. Fair Employment in Northern Ireland—Code of Practice. http://www.equalityni.org.

Farrell, M. 1980. *Northern Ireland: The Orange State*. London: Pluto Press

Feldman, A. 1991. *Formations of Violence: The Narrative of the Body and Political Terror in Northern Ireland*. Chicago: University of Chicago Press.

Harrison, Simon 1995. "Four Types of Symbolic Conflict." *Journal of the Royal Anthropological Institute* (n.s.), 1: 255–272.

Jarman, N. 1993. "Intersecting Belfast." In *Landscape: Politics and Perspectives*, ed. B. Bender. Oxford: Berg.

———. 1997. *Material Conflicts: Parades and Visual Displays in Northern Ireland*. Oxford: Berg.

Jarman, N., and D. Bryan. 1998. *From Riots to Rights: Nationalist Parades in the North of Ireland*. Coleraine: Centre for the Study of Conflict.

Loftus, B. 1990. *Mirrors: William III and Mother Ireland*. Dundrum: Picture Press.

———. 1994. *Mirrors: Orange and Green*. Dundrum: Picture Press.

McCormick, J., and N. Jarman. 2005. "Death of a Mural." *Journal of Material Culture*, 10, no. 1: 49–71.

McIntosh, G. 1999. *The Force of Culture: Unionist Identities in Twentieth Century Ireland*. Cork: Cork University Press.

Nic Craith, Máiréad. 2002. *Plural Identities-Singular Narratives: The Case of Northern Ireland*. Oxford: Berghahn Books.

Northern Ireland Life and Times Survey. Retrieved from http://www.ark.ac.uk/nilt/.

Office of the First and Deputy First Minister. 2005. *A Shared Future.* Retrieved from www.asharedfuture.gov.uk.

Patten, C. et al. 1999. *A New Beginning: Policing in Northern Ireland—The Report of the Independent Commission on Policing for Northern Ireland.* Retrieved from http://www.nio.gov.uk/a_new_beginning_in_policing_in_northern_ireland.pdf.

Patterson, H. 1999. "Party Versus Order: Ulster Unionism and the Flags and Emblems Act." *Contemporary British History,* 13, no. 4: 105–129.

Rolston, B. 1991. *Politics and Painting: Murals and Conflict in Northern Ireland.* London: Associated Universities Press.

———. 1992. *Drawing Support 1: Murals in the North of Ireland.* Belfast: Beyond the Pale Publications.

———. 1995. *Drawing Support 2: Murals of War and Peace.* Belfast: Beyond the Pale Publications.

———. 2003. *Drawing Support 3: Murals of War and Peace in the North of Ireland.* Belfast: Beyond the Pale Publications.

Ross, Marc Howard. 2007. *Cultural Contestation in Ethnic Conflict.* Cambridge: Cambridge University Press.

Santino, J. 2001. *Signs of War and Peace: Social Conflict and the Use of Public Symbols in Northern Ireland.* Hampshire: Palgrave.

St. Patrick's Day Project. 2006. Retrieved from http://www.qub.ac.uk/schools/IrishStudies/NewsandEvents/News/#d.en.64122.

Chapter 5
Conflict Transformation, Cultural Innovation, and Loyalist Identity in Northern Ireland

Lee A. Smithey

Walking through the streets of loyalist[1] working-class East Belfast or the Shankill Road, one encounters political and cultural expressions ranging from hastily daubed slogans and acronyms of paramilitary organizations to flags, banners, and elaborate wall murals. The murals celebrate historic victories and crises in loyalist mythology, commemorate fallen comrades and neighbors, and valorize paramilitary organizations and local bands. They have become hallmarks of Northern Ireland's Troubles, and in recent years have become the subject of a growing tourism industry. Scholars have noted the functions murals serve in expressing communal identity and ideology, marking territory, and delivering statements beyond the locale in which the murals reside (Jarman 2005; Rolston 1991). I will focus on the role murals and other cultural expressions play in expressing and shaping communal identity and communicating beyond the community, and I argue that they constitute mediums through which communities and their leaders can experiment with a community's symbolic landscape and shift the focus of their collective identity from defensiveness and exclusivity to one that is more inclusive and empowering.

Walking through East Belfast, one now comes across murals featuring local historical and cultural topics such as the building of the passenger liner *Titanic* and C. S. Lewis's *The Lion, the Witch, and the Wardrobe*. The redesign of paramilitary murals and modification of other traditional forms of cultural expression reflect shifts in historical perspective, offer alternative cultural expressions and a means of pursuing collective grievances, and generally shift the tone of loyalism, even if only relative to the traditional ubiquity of martial themes that have reinforced siege mentalities and alienated Catholic nationalist communities.[2] Murals and other forms of publicly expressing loyalist identity provide windows onto a critical process in conflict transformation: changing perceptions of the conflict and softening out-group boundaries by redefining collective identities in ways that are empowering and yet less polarizing.

This essay is part of a larger research project examining a growing shift among loyalists as they attempt to enhance their political cachet by modifying public expressions of collective identity, such as parades and bonfires that have traditionally been seen by Northern Ireland's Catholics and many outsiders as intimidating and triumphalist. Collective action and collective identity are mutually recursive, and a change in one signals or requires a change in the other. To the extent that loyalists begin to publicly emphasize features of their identity, often through cultural expressions and enactments, that are not defensive or retributive expressions toward Catholic nationalists and republicans, they signal a new orientation across the political and sectarian divide. While they aim to maintain in-group solidarity and ontological security through these practices, they also lower the salience of sectarian and ethnopolitical boundaries that have helped fuel conflict in Ireland.

Local community leaders and activists play an important role in experimenting with the boundaries of communal identities, using their own intimate and internalized sense of their communities to carefully choreograph innovative public expressions of loyalism. This process contributes to conflict transformation in Northern Ireland as loyalists attempt to empower themselves, diminish the intensity of their siege mentality, and orient themselves in a more cooperative way to new political and economic circumstances in the region. Here, I present a model for grassroots conflict transformation, emphasize the importance of identity in ethnopolitical conflict in Northern Ireland, and detail the role murals play as a medium for the expression of and innovation in loyalist collective identity. I use as an illustration the ability of *local* leaders to maintain and yet reorient loyalist worldviews and narratives in ways that could improve the environment for community relations work and continued political progress toward a shared democratic future.

Ethnopolitical Identity and Conflict

Polarized ethnic identities have become a widely recognized factor exacerbating allegedly intractable conflicts as groups develop contradictory, negative, and mutually reinforcing out-group stereotypes. In extreme conflict situations, groups can become so polarized that the conflict itself constitutes a fundamental element in groups' inverse identities. Adversaries' identities can become defined in such a way that they are mutually exclusive of one another, indivisible, and nonnegotiable. They become inseparable from conflict that tends to be seen in zero-sum terms reflecting exclusive definitions of "us" and "them." Using this calculus, any gain by one side amounts to an unacceptable loss by the other side, and to each group, it seems as if their very existence is under threat. Such groups respond defensively, and further modify their own worldviews to distinguish their opponents in even more stark terms (Brewer and Higgins 1998; Coy and Woehrle 2000; Kriesberg, Northrup, and Thorson 1989; Northrup 1997; Tajfel 1981; Waddell and Cairns 1986). Such conflicts are often called "intractable" because the vicious cycle involving identity and retributive collective action becomes almost seamless. As Northrup (1992) points out, a cultural "collusion" can develop between adversaries in ethnic conflict. When groups define themselves and each other in terms of the conflict, they collude in perpetuating the psychological bases for destructive conflict. Giving up the conflict is akin to giving up an important part of their own identity.

Identity plays such a crucial role in these conflicts because shared schema for perceiving the world around them direct ethnic groups to interpret their actions and those of their opponents in ways that protect in-group ontological security. Ross (2001) calls these schema "psychocultural interpretations" or "the shared, deeply rooted worldviews that help groups make sense of daily life and provide psychologically meaningful accounts of a group's relationship with other groups, their actions and motives" (159). We refer to worldviews that become widely shared as "collective identities" that are constructed and reconstructed from origin myths, historical narratives, commentary on contemporary states of affairs, and teleological visions (especially when religion serves as a resource for identity construction) (Brewer and Higgins 1998; Higgins and Brewer 2002).

Polarized communal identities are constructed and reconstructed on a daily basis over long periods of time, sometimes spectacularly (through intimidation and direct attacks), symbolically (public rituals, flags, and emblems), and sometimes in quite mundane ways (what newspaper one buys, where one shops, or where one attends school). Each becomes invested with emotional value, and one of the greatest challenges in addressing intractable conflict in divided societies lies in slowing and reversing a vicious and yet often subtle cycle of out-group prejudice, dehumanization, coercion, and fear. To the extent that opponents in a conflict situation ignore, condone, or openly advocate intimidation or violence, they will heighten out-group boundaries and cast responsibility for violence on one another. Intergroup boundaries can become so rigid and others vilified and dehumanized to such an extent that group members become more likely to sanction and employ the use of lethal force, fueling a cycle of fear, retribution, and division.

In intractable conflicts, according to social identity theorists, natural tendencies to create in-group/out-group distinctions become heightened as each group feels under threat and rallies around increasingly defensive collective identities seeking to maintain ontological security. However, the process is not aberrant; the construction of in-group and out-group identities is part and parcel of social life. Cognitive psychologists, through social identity theory, assert that all people have a limited capacity for processing stimuli from the world around them. They simplify the world though social schemata, stereotypes, or ideologies, thus meeting a need for ontological coherence and maintaining a positive sense of self-worth, self-efficacy, and self-authenticity. The combination of these drives produces solidarity and in-group cohesion, while strongly differentiating one's own group from out-groups facilitates the process (Cairns 1994; Gecas 2000; Melucci 1995; Tajfel 1982).

In societies that have become deeply divided and in which groups have come to fear one another, the options of leaving one's own group are limited, either because the social solidarity costs are so high or there simply are not other groups readily available to which one can switch. As Cairns (1994) has put it, "What I hope Social Identity Theory will do is influence people to see the conflict as a form of behavior which is determined by essentially normal psychological processes, but normal psychological processes which are operating in exceptional circumstances" (14). Those circumstances include a long history of colonialism, resistance, discrimination, open conflict, and in many cases poverty. Political struggles of this sort that involve core group identities (consider Israel and Palestine, Rwanda, and the former Yugoslavia) have proven particularly contentious and susceptible to intractability (Kriesberg 1998b; Northrup 1989).

In Northern Ireland, a range of political, religious, and ethnic traditions tend to align broadly into Protestant unionist/loyalist and Catholic nationalist/republican blocs that maintain incompatible views on the history and sovereignty of six of the nine counties of Ulster that make up Northern Ireland. Religious sectarianism, language, music, and communal values, to name a few, are employed to distinguish one community from another or signal out-group differences, either through public display, such as ritual, or in discourse and narrative within and between groups.

Over centuries of conflict in Ireland and over the course of the "Troubles," from approximately 1968 to 1998, Northern Ireland has become a deeply divided society in which Protestants and Catholics have been pushed and pulled into segregated public spheres. British colonialism,

Protestant unionist rule through the middle of the twentieth century, paramilitary intimidation, and radical political movements have each contributed to the trend. Protestants and Catholics motivated by fear, anger, habit, and tradition have routinely segregated themselves in education, housing, sports, and arts, to name a few domains. While a great deal of attention is paid to the working-class communities in which paramilitarism and the state's counterterrorism efforts have been focused, ethnopolitical division is subtly perpetuated or allowed to continue throughout society (Liechty and Clegg 2001).

Conflict Transformation

Conflict in Northern Ireland has taken remarkable turns toward peace in recent years. Tentative and secretive back-channel contacts and negotiations in the early 1990s led to the 1994 ceasefires, followed by difficult negotiations that produced the Belfast Agreement (often called the Good Friday Agreement) and powersharing governance in the form of the Northern Ireland Assembly. The assembly collapsed in the wake of an espionage scandal in 2002 but was restored in the spring of 2007, again after much political turmoil and negotiation, under the leadership of erstwhile adversaries Ian Paisley and Martin McGuinness of the Democratic Unionist Party and Sinn Féin, respectively. Throughout the political peace process, careful negotiations, impression management, risk-taking, and artful diplomacy on the part of politicians and influential leaders in civil society have made an imperfect but viable plan for democratic politics possible.

A comprehensive attempt to make sustainable politics work in Northern Ireland will have to consider the immense influence of polarized ethnic identities. Political peace processes are essential to the transformation of ethnopolitical conflict into constructive politics, but they are inevitably tied to grassroots community relations. Over time, as conflicts become inseparable from the cultures and identities of the communities in which they are waged, political negotiations become increasingly difficult. Political leaders' abilities to make compromises and embrace new initiatives are enabled and limited by their support bases and the extent to which their respective communities have become alienated from one another and feel that their traditions and identity are under threat. If agreed structural arrangements that facilitate political cooperation allow the cultural and psychological underpinnings of division to persist, they bring the sustainability of peace into question. Rev. Gary Mason of the East Belfast Mission, who has undertaken a great deal of community development work in the area characterized the challenge: "I think my worry always about this peace process is if you do end up building a benign apartheid, there's nothing to say that in ten or fifteen years the thing cannot begin all over again, but you know there are big questions. How do you heal memories? How do you get people to engage genuinely? There are lots of models out there. But what is genuine engagement? What does that mean? And, how do you stop people when the doors are closed, the curtains are closed, telling stories, passing pain, hatred, and sectarianism down to another generation?"[3] The persistence of mutually polarized social worlds and identities remains an important concern with which practitioners and scholars continue to wrestle as peace processes are largely dependent on changes in grassroots identities and aspirations that have often been forged and hardened over decades of violent conflict.

A great deal of effort has been directed at undermining prejudice and stereotyping, especially among youth in Northern Ireland, in attempts to "transform" conflict. Conflict transformation involves *both* a shift away from coercive means of conducting conflict to persuasion or reward *and* subjective redefinitions of out-groups (Kriesberg 1998a).[4] Unlike conflict resolution initiatives, which tend to focus more narrowly on encouraging adversaries' representatives to negotiate over discrete aspirations and grievances, often with the assistance of a third-party neutral mediator, conflict transformation efforts recognize the importance of building and improving *relationships* at multiple levels, from grassroots to the "highest" levels of politics. A conflict is in a state of transformation when fundamentally polarized in-group and out-group perceptions have begun to change, albeit slowly and incrementally, and when each side's narratives and the society's symbolic landscape become less polarizing (Ross 2007). These shifts can be understood as both indicators of social structural and political change and as prerequisites for future change. Emotions, identities, ideologies, prejudices, and the rituals and expressions that express and sustain them in both Protestant and Catholic communities must begin to accommodate one another such that an increasing level of trust can be established that enables conflict resolution work to establish an infrastructure of nonviolent politics and cooperation in civil society (Lederach 1997). Ethnopolitical identities in this model are sturdy to be sure, but they are also malleable, opening possibilities for the mitigation of deeply polarized collective identities.

Transformation Within Communities and Traditions

Cultivating pliable collective identities remains a central challenge for peacebuilding in Northern Ireland. I argue here that much of the critical work of developing less polarized collective identities takes place *within* even the most traumatized communities, and I offer examples from loyalist neighborhoods in Northern Ireland where mural redesign projects and other innovations in traditional cultural expressions may contribute to reshaping contours of loyalist identity. In urban communities, where the violence of the Troubles has been concentrated, organized violence and cultural expressions exert an influence within communities and foster stark out-group divisions, often between Protestant and Catholic neighborhoods that adjoin one another. This chapter focuses primarily on loyalist East Belfast, but I hasten to reemphasize that while contention between urban loyalist and republican areas can be particularly severe, sectarian and political division in Northern Ireland is perpetuated across the region in rural and middle-class communities, often through the daily structuration of parallel Protestant and Catholic lifeworlds.[5]

A great deal of time, effort, and resources have been expended in Northern Ireland over the past twenty-five years in important programmatic attempts to improve community relations (Bloomfield 1997; Fitzduff 2002). Some refer disparagingly to the "community relations industry" of professional researchers, trainers, administrators, and youth and community workers who have worked to bridge the sectarian gap, most often among youth. Mediation programs, cross-community clubs, art initiatives, international travel programs, and sports tournaments, to name a few, have aimed to diminish alienation and fear generated by three decades and more of ethnopolitical conflict. Research by Gidron, Katz, and Hasenfeld (2002b) shows that peace and conflict resolution organizations (PCROs) in Northern Ireland have made significant, if sometimes subtle, contributions that can prove difficult to quantify (Gidron, Katz, and Hasenfeld 2002a; Schubotz and Robinson 2006). Still, the challenge of overcoming the polarization of Protestant and Catholic communities remains, as evidenced by high levels of residential segregation and the continued prominence of ethnopolitical identities (Poole and Doherty 1996; Shuttleworth and Lloyd 2006).

Much of the community relations work carried out by PCROs has been based on contact theory which holds that bringing groups (usually youth) who are alienated from one another into contact can help break down stereotypes and prejudices, opening the way for dialogue and mutual understanding. Research has focused on determining the most conducive circumstances in which contact produces the desired results (Amir 1969; Cairns 1994; Connolly 2000; Hewstone and Brown 1986; Pettigrew 1998). During the 1990s, however, many community relations practitioners found that bringing Protestant and Catholic groups together for brief periods of time was less effective than they had hoped, especially if each group lacked a critical level of self-awareness regarding their own identity, history, and fears. Thus, "single-identity" work, as it has been called, became prominent among practitioners (Church, Visser, and Johnson 2004; Hughes 2003). The work is premised on the idea that groups of people who are not confident in their own identity are more likely to feel anxiety in their encounters with members of other communities, to respond aggressively, and are less likely to overcome stereotypes and broaden their identification outside of their traditional community (Niens, Cairns, and Hewstone 2003).

I propose we can take the single-identity lesson further by seeking to identify and better understand attempts developed *within* communities to define, critique, and modify their own senses of identity. According to Schubotz and Robinson's (2006) analysis of the 2005 "Young Life and Times Survey" in Northern Ireland, 45 percent of respondents identified their family as the most important influence on their views about the other religious community. Nineteen percent identified friends as most influential, predictably suggesting that out-group attitudes are sustained within communities. Contact theory research finds that projects designed and executed with the initiative or approval of local community leaders allow greater freedom for participants to experiment with new orientations toward out-groups (Amir 1969; Pettigrew 1998). When local community leaders and authority figures undertake to alter or selectively emphasize familiar expressions of communal identity, they do so with a credibility and legitimacy that is often not part of programmatic community relations initiatives.

Leadership and Collective Identities

Less polarizing worldviews are best developed as closely as possible to sources of communal legitimacy through internal transformation that emphasizes the articulation of constructive alternative visions from *within* each communal tradition. Liechty and Clegg (2001) have stressed the importance of internal or local transformation in their excellent work on religious sectarianism and reconciliation: "What is far more constructive is for a community to learn to hear its own ancestral voices anew, with or without the aid of outside voices . . . When destructive ancestral voices are countered from within the tradition, they are weakened and silenced as effectively as they ever can be" (178).

Research shows that leaders have the ability to shape collective identity and its cultural expressions (Brewer 2003). This is true only within limits, however, because authority is a communal product. Pierre Bourdieu's (1991) work on politics proves useful here because he recognizes that authority is not something that political leaders possess; authority is a resource within their constituencies which they access. Leaders command cultural capital that allows them to speak in such a way that their language is recognized as legitimate; they are able to tap into wells of meaning that make up collective identity. With that ability, they represent the group to itself in innovative ways, but leaders who go too far in jettisoning the cultural trappings of their community often find themselves with diminished influence in the community. As Lederach (1997) argues, leaders "are under tremendous pressure to maintain a position of strength vis à vis their adversaries and their own constituencies. . . . This, coupled with a high degree of publicity, often constrains the freedom of maneuver of leaders operating at this level" (40). And yet, they must seek some measure of freedom to maneuver in order to be effective negotiators. Politicians in Northern Ireland are no strangers to the dilemma. Since the early 1980s, Sinn Féin's political leadership has worked tirelessly to hone the party's ability to utilize the deep well of republican myth, both claiming the cachet of the armed struggle and cultivating politics as an equally powerful strategy in the hearts and minds of the republican movement (Shirlow and McGovern 1998).

Gormley-Heenan and Robinson (2003) refer to this careful dance as "elastic band leadership." Leaders in negotiations must deliver their constituencies, so they must pay careful attention and present themselves as the receptacles of core beliefs and commitments. However, in order to be effective negotiators, they must also stretch their constituents to embrace new ideas and jettison some former commitments (such as "not one inch" or "not one bullet," in the Northern Ireland case). The process of introducing new ideas and opening the community to new possibilities can be a slow one. Collective identities must have ontological continuity; they must have authenticity and be recognized as bearing the imprimatur of the community. Moving too quickly can endanger ontological security and create a backlash and a retreat to insularity.

The potential also exists for local figures in communities to innovate and contribute to the constructive reframing of their communal identities, and consequently, the way in which conflict is conducted. Referring to peace processes in South Africa and Northern Ireland, Brewer (2003) states, "In some cases local spaces are opening up in which, for example, grassroots peacemaking and reconciliation are possible, and in which new identities can be experimented with and perceived as possible or in which existing identities come to be seen as more flexible and inclusive than previously imagined" (163). In these cases, collective identities and their cultural expressions can be subtly altered in ways that are ontologically consonant, but that open the group's orientation to hear their adversaries in a new constructive way or at least minimize the alienating effect of a particular cultural expression. Liechty and Clegg (2001) refer to this process as "mitigation" and define it as ". . . the capacity to lessen or eliminate possible negative outcomes of a belief, commitment, or action. What cannot be negotiated can sometimes be mitigated" (229). In short, practices that threaten and intimidate out-groups can be modified so that they are less likely to cause offense and feed destructive relations.

Action, Identity, and Feet-First Persuasion

Similarly, McCauley (2002) calls for "feet-first persuasion" noting a "power of small steps to motivate larger steps in the same direction." One might consider it a slippery-slope model. The central mechanism lies in the setting of precedents within communities. There is something to be said for instances of innovation, moments in which groups redefine themselves and even conduct conflict with opposing parties in less destructive ways. Even experimentation can set precedents for further development, at least in part because action and identity are recursively related. The actions that groups or communities carry out both reflect and contribute to the formation of their collective identities. Rituals and expressions that feature less exclusive narratives and images can open the way to a shared symbolic landscape and enhance the potential for cooperation and coexistence.

Because intractable conflict is driven largely by polarized communal identities and the mode of conflict methods employed, it is important that transformation include changes in both of these factors. In many cases, experimentation with a new collective action or a new twist on an old tradition can trigger a reassessment of collective identity. McCauley (2002) captures this in his discussion of dissonance theory: "When we act in a way that is inconsistent with our attitudes and values, we are likely to change our beliefs to rationalize the new behaviors. The motivation for the change is to avoid looking stupid or sleazy to ourselves or others" (253). There are times during which a movement toward persuasive conflict methods, toward a more constructive stance, can provoke a constructive redefinition of collective identity. Somewhere in this cycle of action and identity, change takes place, both in the kinds of actions in which communities engage when they encounter one another and the construction of meaning and identity.

Influential meaning makers (intellectuals, artists, writers, poets, political and civic leaders) articulate group identity through various media that represent communities to themselves. In the process of disseminating rhetoric within the community and promoting persuasive or rewarding actions over others, they may incrementally influence communal preferences concerning the conduct of conflict. Though this chapter does not attempt to formally assess levels of local support for these initiatives or degrees of implementation, they are among the factors that will determine the extent to which initiatives can help undermine polarization between Catholic and Protestant communities in Northern Ireland. Further research assessing the success or failure of these and similar projects will reveal the ability (or inability) of alienated and traumatized communities to contribute to postconflict peacebuilding in Northern Ireland.[6]

Murals and Loyalist Cultural Innovation

Of particular relevance here is a new trend of cultural innovation developing within loyalist communities. Initiatives are emerging that aim to reform cultural practices such as paramilitary murals, Orange Order parades,[7] and bonfires, to make them less offensive to nationalist and republican communities, the British and Irish governments, and the international community. On 12 July each year, the Orange Order celebrates the victory in 1690 of King William III's victory over the Jacobite forces of James II at the Battle of the Boyne. The Twelfth celebrations are preceded on the Eleventh night by the burning of large bonfires in Protestant communities across Northern Ireland. Tricolor flags of the Republic of Ireland and other nationalist or republican symbols are often burned with the bonfires.

The Orange Order in recent years has moved to make Twelfth parades more family-friendly by sponsoring historical reenactments, fun fairs, and Ulster-Scots musical performances. Indeed, in 2006, the British government pledged £104,000 to support the creation of an "Orangefest" to make the Twelfth celebrations more welcoming to tourists (BBC 2006b). Belfast City Council has pledged £90,000 in a scheme to downsize enormous Eleventh-night bonfires to symbolic beacons (BBC 2006a). Plans have been proposed in some neighborhoods to ensure that flags and banners do not linger on lampposts after the summer parading season has passed (see Bryan and Gillespie 2005). Leaders in loyalist communities presumably hope through these initiatives to maintain solidarity within their communities, diminish the sense of isolation and exclusion they have experienced, and develop political advantage by undermining the charges of triumphalism often leveled against them. This focus is particularly timely, as the British and Irish governments turn their attention to loyalist communities in an attempt to win support for devolution and decommissioning of loyalist paramilitary organizations.

Murals in Northern Ireland have become one of the more famous expressions of collective ethnopolitical identity. Historically, they have been found primarily in loyalist neighborhoods. The practice can be traced to the turn of the twentieth century and became increasingly common as partition was established in 1920. The Northern Ireland state that followed ensured unionist ascendancy, and murals became a widely accepted way for Protestant communities to declare their support for unionist politics, and Protestant expressions of British loyalty were approved if not officially sanctioned by the unionist-controlled Stormont government. Early murals featured reproductions of King William of Orange crossing the Boyne River atop his steed during the Battle of the Boyne in 1690. Not surprisingly, murals have been connected to annual Twelfth commemorations of the same battle in which the forces of the Protestant "King Billy" defeated the deposed Catholic King James II and his Jacobite army. During the Twelfth holidays, murals were often unveiled and retouched to complement a range of other traditional activities such as the erection of arches, bunting, and flags, the painting of curbstones, and of course, parades by the loyal institutions, such as the Orange Order (Bryan 2000; Jarman 1997; Rolston 1991).

As Rolston (1991, 1992) reports, the comfortable relationship between Protestants and the British government became strained with the advent of the Troubles in the late 1960s, and as the local Stormont government was superseded by direct rule from Westminster. Loyalist murals declined amid unionist and loyalist confusion over their new status as British citizens who were increasingly dissatisfied with British policy in Northern Ireland. The murals that did appear largely abandoned the traditional themes of Britishness and Protestant ascendancy and turned to iconic references to Ulster,[8] such as the flag of Northern Ireland, which features the Red Hand and St. George's cross. Through the late 1980s and 1990s, loyalist murals proliferated and became militant, featuring loyalist paramilitary organizations such as the Ulster Volunteer Force (UVF), the Ulster Defense Association/Ulster Freedom Fighters (UDA/UFF), and the Red Hand Commando. Younger politicized painters commonly produced images of balaclava-clad paramilitary members wielding automatic weapons surrounded by flags, slogans, and emblems. Intimidating murals such as these in both loyalist and republican neighborhoods are common and have served to mark territory and project threat to outsiders while discouraging dissent within communities. In loyalist communities, paramilitary murals have also been used to distinguish territory controlled by rival paramilitary organizations.

Like other forms of collective cultural expression, murals represent communities to themselves and help define collective identity in a number of ways: through shaping collective memory, commemorating lost comrades and community members, declaring that the community is under pressure or attack, or memorializing a long history of sacrifice.

Figure 5.1. UVF mural in West Belfast, a typical paramilitary representation.

Rolston (1992) describes the expressive character of murals: "Through their murals both loyalists and republicans parade their ideologies publicly. The murals act, therefore, as a sort of barometer of political ideology. Not only do they articulate what republicanism or loyalism stands for in general, but, manifestly or otherwise, they reveal the current status of each of these political beliefs" (27). Murals exhibit political ideology, and in the case of Northern Ireland's loyalists, the decline and resurgence of mural painting as well as its content have reflected the broad outlines of the unionist and loyalist psyche. This, incidentally, is not to say that all residents of loyalist neighborhoods appreciate or condone paramilitary activity or the murals that valorize them and mark territory. In fact, murals are often placed without the consent of local residents under an unspoken threat of intimidation that ensures paramilitary organizations can claim territory as they see fit through the placement of murals. Nonetheless, Neil Jarman argues that murals have not just reflected but have promoted solidarity in both loyalist and republican neighborhoods. From the beginning, "Murals helped to transform 'areas where Protestants lived' into 'Protestant areas,'" and "All murals create a new type of space, they redefine mundane public space as a politicized place and can thereby help to reclaim it for the community" (Jarman 2005:176, 179).

However, as Jarman argues, collective expressions such as murals can also be appropriated in innovative ways for new agendas and thus, I would argue, have the potential to shape collective identity. In a similar fashion, they could perform the mitigating work of redefining collective identities in less polarizing ways. To examine this idea, I consider the role that murals have played recently within local initiatives to redevelop some of Belfast's struggling working-class neighborhoods. In these instances, local organizations, many with hardline loyalist credentials, have undertaken to modify cultural expressions, in particular murals, in order to improve their neighborhoods. These initiatives take up some of the aspirations of the earlier community arts program but also aim to enrich loyalist identity.

Local leaders, for example ex-combatants and Orangemen, grasp the depth of trauma their communities have experienced, even if they have contributed directly or indirectly to that trauma. They are themselves deeply immersed in loyalist communal identities, but for a variety of reasons, they perceive a need to reframe loyalism in new ways that are less intimidating and offensive. *Newsnight*, a BBC news television program, cleverly borrowed one of their video segment titles, "The Writing on the Wall?" from a mural redesign initiative in East Belfast titled, "The Writing's Not on the Wall" (2003b). The titles refer to a growing recognition among Protestants that a return to majoritarian governance is impossible. Powersharing is inevitable, especially in a Europe where borders are dissolving. Some loyalists understand that working-class Protestants need to adapt to new political circumstances and develop the necessary political skills to effectively engage nationalists and advocate for their communities.

Murals have provided one avenue for experimenting with the reframing of loyalist identity, and loyalist paramilitary organizations in some areas have agreed to relinquish militant murals to be replaced by "cultural murals" that present historical themes or other features of communal life that loyalists can claim as their own. In other cases, murals have begun to take on a political tone that is not militaristic, but that still expresses loyalist grievances and concerns in more articulate ways than the iconic murals of the 1980s and the militaristic murals of the 1990s could (though these are still quite common). In either case, one finds a growing recognition, identified by Jarman, that murals, by virtue of their media appeal can deliver messages beyond the confines of the neighbor-

Figure 5.2. Titanic mural in downtown Belfast, a source of Protestant pride.

hoods in which the murals are painted (Jarman 2005). Indeed, several of these projects have gained significant media attention.

Recently founded loyalist cultural organizations have redesigned paramilitary murals to display nonsectarian and nonexclusive local historical themes, such as the building of the Titanic. The most extensive of the mural schemes in East Belfast was developed by a coalition of local clergy, community development organizations, representatives from local paramilitaries, and statutory bodies such as the Northern Ireland Housing Executive, and Police Service of Northern Ireland (PSNI), a collaboration that is notable on its own in terms of the cooperation between a range of state and nonstate organizations. In all, at least nine murals were placed or redesigned featuring local historical themes that included: the building of the *Titanic* in the East Belfast shipyards, the famous footballer George Best, Protestant reformers, a local primary school, Belfast native C. S. Lewis's novel *The Lion, the Witch, and the Wardrobe,* and Northern Ireland's football team.

The mural project constitutes one manifestation of an effort to recast the loyalist narrative and of a broader shift among some loyalist paramilitary commanders (especially older ones) who want to avoid a return to open conflict in Northern Ireland. They want to maintain their place within communities as defenders, perhaps not against republican attack, but against poverty and unemployment. As one commander said, "We've been part of the problem, we need to be part of the solution." Mural redesigns have allowed loyalist leaders to test the waters of becoming involved in community development, and may also have begun to shift the balance of the content of loyalist identity. Instead of loyalism being associated primarily with the violence of the Troubles, it begins to take on new dimensions. "Cultural murals" highlight community history and achievements and thus sustain community identity while simultaneously tweaking the community's symbolic landscape by replacing overtly sectarian themes with others that define "us" without direct reference to "them." Even murals that make political arguments about grievances in the Protestant community, such as the conditions placed on parades or the disbanding of the Royal Ulster Constabulary (which Protestants have seen as a crucial bulwark against republican violence) signal an engagement in political discourse that is more nuanced and constructive than murals that emphasize the paramilitary defense of loyalist neighborhoods, tit-for-tat retribution between loyalist and republican paramilitaries, and factional infighting among loyalist paramilitaries.

One is then led to ask several questions: Who is most credible in loyalist communities and therefore capable of developing and advocating the transformation of cultural expressions? How do they manage cultural capital to best effect? Which of their initiatives prove successful and why? At what point and under what circumstances do new cultural initiatives fail? Do they fail because they are perceived as alien and become labeled as disloyal or treacherous? Is there evidence that, when successful, they open the door for improved community relations and political cooperation? If so, can these initiatives be encouraged and sponsored by other parties to the conflict or external actors? Answers to all of these questions cannot be offered here, warranting further culturally and psychologically based research into the transformation of similarly intractable conflict situations.

Conclusion

The mitigation of intimidating or polarizing cultural expressions is a modest but important contribution to improved community relations. Jim Wilson, a local loyalist community activist interviewed by the BBC in

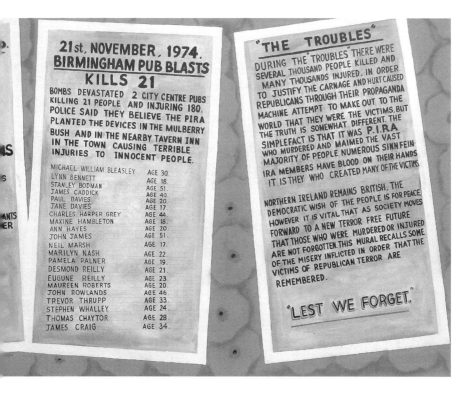

Figure 5.3. "Lest We Forget" mural in Belfast.

2003, acknowledged, "There's only so far you can go in asking people to remove murals, you cannot wipe away history and you cannot wipe away what has happened in this country in the last thirty-five years just by taking murals down" (BBC 2003b). Nevertheless, the process is critical to breaking down the deep psychological barriers that have perpetuated intractable conflict in Northern Ireland. We need not be naïve either and trumpet mural redesign and new parading policies as the ultimate indicators of change in loyalist paramilitaries or other loyalist organizations. Paramilitary murals are still commissioned, and paramilitary leaders are careful not to appear as if they are selling out their organizations, and they will be wary of removing their murals without reciprocation among rival paramilitary organizations (BBC 2005).

Political self-interest also drives participation in these and similar schemes. Under a growing recognition that loyalism has a poor public image, replacing sectarian murals can provide positive media spin and new political advantages. A subtle and incremental softening of in-group and out-group boundaries is desirable, but in the long run, cosmetic changes without cross-community engagement runs the risk of glossing over the pain and trauma of decades of sectarian violence. Only shared justice and reconciliation work will ensure a sustainable peace. For now, mural redesign schemes, for example, do not often constitute cross-community work, though a recent mural redesign of a particularly offensive mural in the staunchly loyalist neighborhood of Tullycarnet commemorates the bravery of a Catholic from the Falls Road who was the only person from Northern Ireland to receive the Victoria Cross for bravery during World War II. According to Frankie Gallagher, a resident of Tullycarnet and a member of the Ulster Political Research Group, which is associated with the UDA,

We brought Catholics, from Dublin and Donegal and all over, into Tullycarnet Estate, who had never been before. And they marched up the middle of the road with an Orange flute band, with a military band, and everybody just walked up the middle of the road around to the community centre where we all had a knees-up after it, and it was fantastic. So there's an educational side, there's a capacity-building side, there's a confidence-building side, and there's a dealing-with-the-past side, and there's this thing: Do you learn anything from it not to make the same mistake in the future?[9]

The development of this sort of new inclusive narrative reveals a potential for community workers and former combatants in Northern Ireland to develop symbols and narratives that challenge old psychological and emotional barriers.

The British government obviously hopes to replicate the Tullycarnet experience. In July 2006, the Northern Ireland Office Minister David Hanson announced a £3.3 million funding package called "Re-Imaging Communities Programs" (BBC 2005). Whether the intervention of a state bureaucracy will undermine the authenticity of local efforts remains to be seen. Across the political divide, nationalists are predictably skeptical. SDLP politician Alban Maginness responded with incredulity to the NIO funding scheme, "It is clear that any paramilitary murals designed to intimidate or mark out territory should be removed. . . . Indeed their very existence is illegal. That is why today's announcement really beggars belief" (BBC 2005).

Modifying or mitigating offensive cultural expressions and hardened in-group and out-group boundaries is a delicate undertaking. It is most effective when leaders with credibility and legitimacy draw on familiar resources such as the language and ethos of the community. Radical departures are likely to be seen as betrayal within the group and departures from the long-established scripts of intergroup relationships are likely to be met with skepticism across ethnopolitical divides. Nonetheless, the softening of out-group boundaries is critical for long-term conflict transformation in Northern Ireland, and further research is needed to identify the conditions under which initiatives such as the mural redesign projects develop and how they can be encouraged, remembering that the credibility of local voices is a critical component in the constructive transformation of hardened ethnopolitical attitudes. Those voices will often belong to individuals who are reviled in out-groups, and in some quarters within groups. The process is bound to prove slow and contentious but necessary.

Notes

1. "Loyalism" refers to an ideological or cultural commitment, held by many Protestants who insist on Northern Ireland's remaining part of the United Kingdom while also defending Protestant culture, faith, and identity. Loyalists are often from working-class backgrounds, some of whom are involved in or would support paramilitary organizations. "Unionism" refers to a political orientation that emphasizes loyalty to the British crown and a commitment to Northern Ireland's position within the United Kingdom. Parties such as the Ulster Unionist Party (UUP) and the Democratic Unionist Party (DUP) represent unionist aspirations through constitutional politics. There is often considerable overlap between loyalism and unionism, as loyalists are unionists politically and often vote for the DUP instead of the much smaller loyalist Progressive Unionist Party. "Nationalism" refers to political positions held primarily by Catholics that advocate a united Ireland and emphasize civil equality for all, especially for Catholics, who have historically not enjoyed full political and economic access. "Republicans" constitute a subset of nationalists who insist on equality and a united Ireland and have been willing to employ both violent and political means.

2. It is worth noting that historical murals can also express sectarianism and militancy depending on their content. Images of weapons and violence, even in the context of Cromwell's seventeenth-century campaign to pacify Ireland can alienate and intimidate Irish Catholics.

3. Interview, July 2005.

4. Kriesberg (1998a) offers an immensely useful scheme for classifying conflict methods on a tridimensional continuum with poles representing coercion, persuasion, and reward. Methods characterized primarily by coercion, as opposed to persuasions and reward, are more likely to polarize opponents and diminish the potential for constructive dialogical relationships.

5. Census data from 2001 show that 66 percent of the population live in areas that are either more than 99 percent Protestant or 99 percent Catholic (up from 63 percent at the 1991 census) (Brown 2002). Recent research by Shuttleworth and Lloyd (2006) using 2001 census data indicates that levels of segregation have probably remained the same throughout the 1990s, findings that moderate but do not extinguish concerns about levels of division between Catholics and Protestants. For example, only 5 percent of students attend integrated schools in Northern Ireland (Northern Ireland Council for Integrated Education 2004), though in 2001, the Northern Ireland Life and Times Survey reports that 73 percent of respondents felt the government should encourage more mixed schooling (Queen's University Belfast and University of Ulster 2001).

6. I use the term "postconflict" here to refer to the study of peace and reconciliation efforts after peace accords have been reached. The terminology, however, is actually a misnomer. In many if not most of these situations, the conflict is more correctly understood to have entered a new phase of diminished violence.

7. The Orange Order is one of several all-male fraternal organizations that dedicate themselves to the preservation of the Protestant faith and British sovereignty in Ireland. The Orange Order is the best-known, though others (some closely affiliated with the Orange Order) include the Apprentice Boys of Derry, the Independent Orange Order, the Royal Black Preceptory, and the Royal Arch Purple.

8. The northernmost region of Ireland and the political borders of Northern Ireland are often called Ulster.

9. Interview, January 2008. See also BBC (2003a).

Bibliography

Amir, Yehuda. 1969. "Contact Hypothesis in Ethnic Relations." *Psychological Bulletin* 71: 319–342.

BBC. 2003a. "Catholic Face in Loyalist Estate." Retrieved from http://news.bbc.co.uk/2/hi/uk_news/northern_ireland/4259524.stm.

———. 2003b. "Picture Politics." *Newsnight.* Retrieved from http://news.bbc.co.uk/2/hi/programmes/newsnight/3147185.stm.

———. 2005. "Old Masters Change Murals." Retrieved from http://news.bbc.co.uk/go/pr/fr/-/2/hi/uk_news/northern_ireland/4562793.stm.

———. 2006a. "Beacons 'Could Replace Bonfires.'" Retrieved from http://news.bbc.co.uk/1/hi/northern_ireland/5170364.stm.

———. 2006b. "Order to Receive Government Cash." Retrieved from http://news.bbc.co.uk/1/hi/northern_ireland/5131470.stm.

Bloomfield, David. 1997. *Peacemaking Strategies in Northern Ireland: Building Complementarity in Conflict Management Theory.* Basingstoke: Macmillan.

Bourdieu, Pierre. 1991. *Language and Symbolic Power,* ed. J. B. Thompson. Cambridge, Mass.: Harvard University Press.

Brewer, John D. 2003. *C. Wright Mills and the Ending of Violence.* New York: Palgrave Macmillan.

Brewer, John D., and Gareth I. Higgins. 1998. *Anti-Catholicism in Northern Ireland, 1600–1998: The Mote and the Beam.* London: Macmillan.

Brown, Paul. 2002. "Peace but No Love as Northern Ireland Divide Grows Ever Wider." *Guardian,* 4 January, p. 3.

Bryan, Dominic. 2000. *Orange Parades: The Politics of Ritual, Tradition, and Control.* London: Pluto Press.

Bryan, Dominic, and Gordon Gillespie. 2005. *Transforming Conflict: Flags and Emblems.* Belfast: Institute for Irish Studies, Queen's University.

Cairns, Ed. 1994. *A Welling Up of Deep Unconscious Forces: Psychology and the Northern Ireland Conflict.* Coleraine: Centre for the Study of Conflict.

Church, Cheyanne, Anna Visser, and Laurie Shepherd Johnson. 2004. "A Path to Peace or Persistence? The 'Single Identity' Approach to Conflict Resolution in Northern Ireland." *Conflict Resolution Quarterly* 21: 273–293.

Connolly, Paul. 2000. "What Now for the Contact Hypothesis? Towards a New Research Agenda." *Race, Ethnicity, and Education,* 3: 169–193.

Coy, Patrick G., and Lynne M. Woehrle. 2000. *Social Conflicts and Collective Identities*. Lanham, Md.: Rowman and Littlefield.

Fitzduff, Mari. 2002. *Beyond Violence: Conflict Resolution Process in Northern Ireland*. New York: United Nations University Press.

Gecas, Viktor. 2000. "Value Identities, Self-Motives, and Social Movements." In *Self, Identity, and Social Movements*, vol. 13, ed. S. Stryker, T. J. Owens, and R. W. White. New York: Aldine de Gruyter, 93–109.

Gidron, Benjamin, Stanley Nider Katz, and Yeheskel Hasenfeld. 2002a. "The Efficacy of the Peace and Conflict-Resolution Organizations: A Comparative Perspective." In *Mobilizing for Peace: Conflict Resolution in Northern Ireland, Israel/Palestine, and South Africa*, ed. B. Gidron, S. N. Katz, and Y. Hasenfeld. New York: Oxford University Press, 202–223.

———. 2002b. *Mobilizing for Peace: Conflict Resolution in Northern Ireland, Israel/Palestine, and South Africa*. New York: Oxford University Press.

Gormley-Heenan, Cathy, and Gillian Robinson. 2003. "Political Leadership: Protagonists and Pragmatists in Northern Ireland." In *Researching the Troubles: Social Science Perspectives on the Northern Ireland Conflict*, ed. O. Hargie and D. Dickson. Edinburgh: Mainstream, 259–272.

Hewstone, M. and R. Brown. 1986. *Contact and Conflict in Intergroup Encounters*. London: Blackwell.

Higgins, Gareth I. and John D. Brewer. 2002. "The Roots of Sectarianism in Northern Ireland." In *Researching the Troubles: Social Science Perspectives on the Northern Ireland Conflict*, ed. O. Hargie and D. Dickson. Edinburgh: Mainstream, 107–121.

Hughes, Joanne. 2003. "Resolving Community Relations Problems in Northern Ireland: An Intra-Community Approach." *Research in Social Movements, Conflicts and Change* 24: 257–282.

Jarman, Neil. 1997. *Material Conflicts: Parades and Visual Displays in Northern Ireland*. New York: Berg.

———. 2005. "Painting Landscapes: The Place of Murals in the Symbolic Construction of Urban Space." In *National Symbols, Fractured Identities: Contesting the National Narrative*, ed. M. E. Geisler. Middlebury, Vt.: Middlebury College Press, 172–192.

Kriesberg, Louis. 1998a. *Constructive Conflicts: From Escalation to Resolution*. Lanham, Md.: Rowman and Littlefield.

———. 1998b. "Intractable Conflicts." In *The Handbook of Interethnic Coexistence*, ed. E. Weiner. New York: Continuum, 332–342.

Kriesberg, Louis, Terrell A. Northrup, and Stuart J. Thorson. 1989. *Intractable Conflicts and Their Transformation*. Syracuse, N.Y.: Syracuse University Press.

Lederach, John Paul. 1997. *Building Peace: Sustainable Reconciliation in Divided Societies*. Washington, D.C.: United States Institute of Peace Press.

Liechty, Joseph, and Cecelia Clegg. 2001. *Moving Beyond Sectarianism: Religion, Conflict, and Reconciliation in Northern Ireland*. Blackrock, Colo.: Columba Press.

McCauley, Clark. 2002. "Head-first Versus Feet-first in Peace Education." In *Peace Education: The Concept, Principles, and Practices Around the World*, ed. G. Salomon and B. Nevo. Mahwah, N.J.: Lawrence Erlbaum Associates, 63–71.

Melucci, Alberto. 1995. "The Process of Collective Identity." In *Social Movements and Culture*, vol. 4, *Social Movements, Protest, and Contention*, ed. H. Johnston and B. Klandermans. Minneapolis: University of Minnesota Press, 41–63.

Niens, Ulrike, Ed Cairns, and Miles Hewstone. 2003. "Contact and Conflict in Northern Ireland." In *Researching the Troubles: Social Science Perspectives on the*

Northern Ireland Conflict, ed. O. Hargie and D. Dickson. Edinburgh: Mainstream, 123–139.

Northern Ireland Council for Integrated Education, 2004. "Just Who Will Drive the Movement for Integrated Schools in Northern Ireland?" *Parliamentary Monitor* (April).

Northrup, Terrell A. 1989. "The Dynamic of Identity in Personal and Social Conflict." In *Intractable Conflicts and Their Transformation*, ed. L. Kriesberg, T. A. Northrup, and S. J. Thorson. Syracuse, N.Y.: Syracuse University Press, 55–82.

———. 1992. "The Collusion of Enemies: Identity and Conflict in Northern Ireland." Program on the Analysis and Resolution of Conflict, Maxwell School of Citizenship and Public Affairs, Syracuse University.

———. 1997. "Identity Theory." In *Protest, Power, and Change: An Encyclopedia of Nonviolent Action from ACT-UP to Women's Suffrage*, ed. R. S. Powers, W. B. Vogele, C. Kruegler, and R. M. McCarthy. New York: Garland, 239–241.

Pettigrew, Thomas F. 1998. "Intergroup Contact Theory." *Annual Review of Psychology* 49: 65–85.

Poole, Michael A., and Paul Doherty. 1996. *Ethnic Residential Segregation in Northern Ireland*. Coleraine: University of Ulster.

Rolston, Bill. 1991. *Politics and Painting: Murals and Conflict in Northern Ireland*. Rutherford, N.J.: Associated University Presses.

———. 1992. *Drawing Support: Murals in the North of Ireland*. Belfast: Beyond the Pale Publications.

Ross, Marc Howard. 2001. "Psychocultural Interpretations and Dramas: Identity Dynamics in Ethnic Conflict." *Political Psychology* 22: 157–178.

———. 2007. *Cultural Contestation in Ethnic Conflict*. Cambridge: Cambridge University Press.

Schubotz, Dirk, and Gillian Robinson. 2006, "Cross-Community Integration and Mixing: Does It Make a Difference?" *Research Update*, Retrieved from http://www.ark.ac.uk/publications/updates/update43.pdf.

Shirlow, Peter, and Mark McGovern. 1998. "Language, Discourse and Dialogue: Sinn Fein and the Irish Peace Process." *Political Geography* 17:171–186.

Shuttleworth, Ian, and Chris Lloyd. 2006. "Are Northern Ireland's Two Communities Dividing? Evidence from the Census of Population 1971–2001." *Shared Space* 2: 5–13.

Tajfel, Henri. 1981. *Human Groups and Social Categories: Studies in Social Psychology*. Cambridge: Cambridge University Press.

———. 1982. *Social Identity and Intergroup Relations*. New York: Cambridge University Press.

Waddell, Neil, and Ed Cairns. 1986. "Situational Perspectives on Social Identity in Northern Ireland." *British Journal of Social Psychology* 25: 25–31.

Chapter 6
Islamic Headscarves in Public Schools
Explaining France's Legal Restrictions

Elaine R. Thomas

In February 2004, the French National Assembly approved a law prohibiting "the wearing of signs or dress by which students conspicuously express a religious affiliation" in the nation's public schools. While formally applicable to signs of all religions—headscarves, yarmulkes, and overly large crosses are all banned—the law was clearly passed mainly in response to concerns about Muslim students wearing headscarves. The proposed law was drawn, selectively, from the recommendations of a special investigatory commission appointed by President Jacques Chirac in July 2003 to investigate "the application of the principle of secularism in the Republic" and led by immigration expert Bernard Stasi. The widely publicized conclusions of this Commission sought to harness the broad public legitimacy of *laïcité* (secularism or nondenominationalism) to the project of developing a new shared consensus about how best to integrate France's sizable, and increasingly visible, Muslim religious minority.[1] However, when the new law was proposed, it provoked a national public debate of rare intensity over France's symbolic landscape and the terms of inclusion in it, a case of cultural contestation that has visibly divided France's leading prosecularist organizations, political parties, and other major political groupings (17 January 2004, *Le Monde*; 24 January 2004, *Le Temps*).

Both the intensity of controversy surrounding the headscarf issue and the new law itself astonished many observers outside of France, not only in the United States and Arab countries, but even within the rest of Europe (Vidal 2004: 6–7; 11 December 2003, *Le Monde*; 18 December 2003, *Le Temps*; 2 January 2004, *Le Point*). What accounts for the unusually intense emotions surrounding this question in France and the determination of the French government, supported by a clear majority of

French public opinion[2] and many French intellectuals from across the political spectrum, to pass such controversial and restrictive new legislation on this issue?

In reality, this question can be seen as having two rather different faces. The first face of the question has to do with the apparent disparity between cause and effect, with the fact that (mere) headscarves have provoked such a seemingly disproportionate reaction in France. Students can readily be found wearing headscarves to school in the United States, Canada, Britain, and other many countries where they generally pass almost without notice, their relative novelty and a non-Muslim majority population notwithstanding. To explain France's adoption of its striking new law, one must therefore first explain why the headscarves issue has proven so sensitive in France, regularly occasioned such public furor since its first emergence in 1989, and now commanded the attention of a prestigious national commission of experts, the president, and the National Assembly. In responding to this first face of the question, an appreciation of French understandings of citizenship and secularism, the particularities of French history and tradition associated with those concepts, and the nature of prevailing French psychocultural narratives surrounding them is essential.

There is also a second face of the question, however, which has to do with why, in 2004, this law was adopted. The new law marks a break in French policy, and cannot be accounted for by reference to long-term continuities of French political tradition alone. In order to understand the departure marked by this law, as opposed to France's ongoing interest in the headscarf issue, one needs to look more closely at the practical difficulties associated with earlier policy responses and at the changing social, political, and legal context within which the Stasi Commission was appointed and arrived at its recommendations. Dissatisfaction with earlier policy responses, especially by school officials charged with implementing them at the local level, played a key role in convincing the Stasi Commission to recommend reform. The new law also became more attractive and politically acceptable to many as issues of sexist community pressures pushing girls to wear headscarves were increasingly highlighted in respectable public discourse and incorporated into prevailing psychocultural narratives. Though these issues and arguments were not entirely new, mobilization by new feminist groups organizing within disadvantaged neighborhoods and related political actions increasingly drew them to public attention in the months prior to Chirac's appointment of the commission. Meanwhile, contrary to commonly held expectations that the rise of human rights norms and institutions internationally should have a liberalizing influence, developments in

international human rights law—particularly at the European level—
helped to legitimate rather than prevent restrictive policy reform in this
area in France. Increasing public focus on restrictive community pressures on Muslim girls in France and developments in European law
helped set the stage not only for surprisingly wide-ranging political and
intellectual support of the new law within and beyond the Stasi Commission itself, but also for a key change of position by France's Conseil
d'Etat, the highly influential judicial body that had, until then, consistently stood against outright prohibition of headscarves in schools.[3]

The first part of this chapter looks at why the headscarves issue has
been such an emotionally intense case of cultural contestation in
France. It considers the historical factors contributing to this intensity
and how distinctive French conceptions of citizenship and *laïcité* (secularism or nondenominationalism) have reinforced both the headscarf
issue's perceived significance and the political appeal of particular one-
sided, and sometimes conflicting, psychocultural narratives about why
headscarves are worn. The second part of the chapter then turns to the
practical considerations and recent social, political, and legal developments that together contributed to shaping the most recent round of
cultural contestation over headscarves and help to account for France's
2004 change in headscarves policy.

The Intensity of the Headscarf Issue in France

France has reacted more strongly than other countries of immigration
to the presence of "Islamic" headscarves (*foulards*) in its public schools.
According to official French sources, a total of 1,256 *foulards* were
reported in France's public schools at the start of the 2003–2004 school
year. Only twenty of these cases were judged "difficult" by school officials themselves, and only four students were expelled (10 December
2003, *Le Monde*). Considering that France's Muslim population is currently estimated at five million and is predominantly young, French public reaction to the problem of students in headscarves appears strikingly
disproportionate.

France's intense, and to many outside observers seemingly overblown,
reaction to this issue has been significantly shaped by France's republican tradition of thinking about citizenship, the relationship of citizenship to membership in social and religious groups, and most
importantly secularism or *laïcité*. The terms of public "common sense"
on these issues in France form a peculiar political cultural backdrop
against which the headscarves issue has repeatedly emerged as a leading
national issue.

Citizenship and Group Membership

Among French proponents of the law, citizenship is commonly exalted as a realization of individuality. For supporters, this individuality of the citizen is further equated with emancipation of the individual as a rational agent from groups secking control of their members though force or superstition.[4] As a passage of the Commission's report tellingly declared: "The secular state, guarantor of freedom of conscience, protects not only freedom of religion and of speech but also the individual; it allows all freely to choose, or not, a spiritual or religious option, to change it, or to renounce it. It makes sure that no group, no community can impose on anyone a membership or denominational identity, especially because of his or her origins" (Commission de Réflexion sur l'Application du Principe de Laïcité dans la République 2003: 14).[5]

This understanding of citizenship and identity is closely linked to particular psychocultural narratives that have contributed to fueling the headscarves issue in France. For instance, many proponents of the new law point to growing numbers of students in "Islamic" attire as evidence of sexual oppression and rising religious and traditional pressures on Muslim girls in France. Some influential French feminist critics have recently likened these pressures to those forcing women to wear the veil in Iran or other parts of the world (for example, Djavann 2003).

Among the new law's critics, by contrast, one finds others challenging those narratives and seeking to articulate an understanding of citizenship more compatible with individuality as expressed in and through membership in particular social and religious groups. Demonstrations against the new law organized by the small, extremist Party of the Muslims of France (*Parti des musulmans de France*, PMF) and joined by one of France's largest Muslim organizations, the Union of Islamic Organizations of France (Union des organisations islamistes de France, UOIF), appealed to this alternative view of individuality in relation to group membership. Marches in Paris and provincial cities, which assembled between 5,000 and 10,000 participants, featured slogans such as "Neither brother, nor husband, we have chosen the headscarf" and "the veil is my choice" (18 January 2004, *Le Télégramme*; 18 January 2004, Agence France Press; 19 January 2004, *Le Temps*). Certainly, it could be argued that these demonstrations were unrepresentative of the views of France's Muslim population. According to surveys in 2003, eighty-one percent of Muslim women in France never wore headscarves outdoors.[6] Of 300 women from Muslim families, 49 percent actually favored a law against visible religious and political symbols in the schools, while only 43 percent opposed it (Ifop 2003). Nonetheless, the message sent by these protests attests tellingly to the savvy of even relatively "fundamentalist"

Muslim groups in France in understanding, and frontally challenging, the underlying theoretical premises about citizenship, individuality, and (religious) group membership shaping the positions and associated narratives of their republican adversaries.

Interestingly, however, the message of these new social actors actually shared significant common ground with that of their opponents. Both camps present the individual as external to, and thus capable of choosing, even its closest social, cultural, and religious ties. Neither side has championed the position exemplified by communitarian political theorist Michael Sandel, skeptical for his part of the very possibility of individuals as agents of choice fully external to their own "constitutive attachments" (1982: 175–183). Still, this shared ground has by no means resolved the debate given widely differing narratives about why, whether, and at what age girls may be "freely choosing" to don their headscarves.

Laïcité and Its Explanatory Limits

The French concept of *laïcité* and the peculiar historical tradition associated with it are also undeniably key to understanding the intensity of this debate in France. The bearing of secularism, as understood by many French supporters of *laïcité,* on rights to freedom of public religious expression is particularly important in this regard. The liberal tradition of separation of church and state, more familiar to American observers, historically developed largely to protect religion from the state, to ensure the state's neutrality and protect individuals in their faith from undue state pressure or interference. State neutrality and freedom of religion are thus key to what secularism is understood to be about in the liberal tradition.

By contrast, the French republican conception of *laïcité* developed primarily in reaction to the traditional political power of the Catholic Church. Thus, whereas Americans historically sought to protect religion from the state, France's combat for *laïcité* sought to free the state from undue religious influence. The historical circumstances that contributed to forming the notion of *laïcité* as it developed in France gave the notion of secularism a much more anticlerical and less "antistate" emphasis there. That republican emphasis continues to significantly mark the instinctive reactions of the French public today to issues concerning the place of religion in the public sphere and, above all, within public institutions charged with forming citizens. In its report, the Stasi Commission clearly distinguished the meaning and entailments of *laïcité* from other (more liberal) notions of separation of church and state, explaining: "According to the French conception, *laïcité* is not a mere 'boundary keeper' that should be limited to ensuring that the separation between the state and religions, between the political and spiritual or religious spheres, is respected. The state permits the consolidation of shared values that establish the social bond (*le lien social*) in our country" (15).

As presented by the commission, this understanding of *laïcité* is in turn closely tied to the republican model of citizenship's relation to group membership. The commission thus presented defense of *laïcité* as grounds for setting limits to citizens' expression of "difference," and even to cultural and religious identification itself. The commission argued: "The exacerbation of cultural identity should not become a fanatical defence of difference, bringing with it oppression and exclusion. In a secular society, each person must be able to take some distance with regard to tradition. That does not involve any renunciation of oneself but rather an individual act of liberty that allows one to define oneself in relation to one's cultural and spiritual references without being subjected to them" (16).

In another particularly striking passage, just after remarking that "secularism can allow the full intellectual blossoming of Islamic thought free from the constraints of power," the report continued: "Beyond the status of religions, the requirement of *laïcité* also calls on everyone to work on him or herself. Through secularism, the citizen gains protection of his freedom of conscience; in return, he must respect the public space that everyone can share. Demanding state neutrality does not seem very compatible with the display of an aggressive proselytism, particularly within the schools. Being willing to adapt the public expression of one's religious particularities and to set limits to the affirmation of one's identity allows everyone to meet in the public space" (16).

In contrast with this tradition, in Britain, Denmark, and other European countries with established state churches, separation of church and state was never so clearly instituted. Such historical differences have no doubt also contributed to the sometimes puzzled reactions of other Europeans to recent French discussions (Vidal 2004: 6–7). As comparatively oriented scholars have rightly emphasized, these diverse historical traditions continue to play an important role in shaping political choices related to the recognition of religious differences in the public sphere, choices again coming to the fore as Europe's Muslim population grows and becomes more settled (Soper and Fetzer 2003).

The particularities of France's tradition of *laïcité* alone cannot explain the decision to legally restrict the wearing of religious signs, however. Were that the case, such legislation should already have been passed in response to France's first national controversy over students in headscarves, the *affaire du foulard* of 1989. In reality, however, that initial controversy led to a very different, more decentralized, case-by-case approach to addressing the issue.

Also tellingly, the present law was not supported by several leading French organizations widely known for their long-standing firm support of *laïcité*.[7] Like French feminists, the teachers' unions, and France's major political parties, the *laïque* camp itself was quite divided internally by the issue (Tevanian 2004: 8; 17 January 2004, *Le Monde*; 24 January 2004, *Le Temps*). Jean Bauberot, a leading French expert on *laïcité*, was in fact the one member of the Stasi Commission who abstained from endorsing its recommendations (11 December 2003, *Le Monde*). However important the French republican model of citizenship and secularism was for turning students' headscarves into a major national issue, these ideas alone do not explain the recent change in French policy.

Why France's Approach to Headscarves Changed

The 2004 law marked a clear departure from France's previous approaches to the headscarves issue. Such a decided change cannot be explained solely in terms of the French republican tradition of *laïcité*, a constant since the first *affaire du foulard* began in 1989. Why then did the Stasi Commission opt to recommend a departure from standing policy and practice on this issue?

Answering this question requires one to look beyond French understandings of citizenship and *laïcité* and other constant features of the French republican model. More short-term contextual factors are essential to explaining France's new resolve to legislate against headscarves and other religious signs. Most significantly, practical problems associated with existing policy, the role of new feminist groups in changing public perceptions of Muslim women's interests, and perceived openings in European human rights law must be taken into account.

The Alternative, Case-By-Case Approach

From 1989 to 2004, French policy regarding headscarves was based on the 1989 opinion of the Council of State. In contrast to the new prohibition on religious signs, the approach associated with the Council of State decision was one of qualified laissez-faire. The decision underscored students' rights to freedom of religion and religious expression, including the wearing of religious signs. These rights could be abrogated only where overridden by other considerations. The decision allowed for school officials to prevent a student from wearing her headscarf only if and where required by the schools' obligation to prohibit "acts of pressure, provocation, proselytism, or propaganda," to ensure safety and security, to prevent "any perturbation of the course of teaching activities, [or] of the educational role of teachers and any troubling of order within establishments," and to ensure that students fully followed their required courses of study (Commission 2003: 29–30; 10 December 2003, *Le Monde*). This policy clearly left generous room for discretion by local school officials and sometimes permitted expulsion of students who refused to uncover their heads. Notably, however, this approach did *not* deny students' rights to wear headscarves on grounds of any a priori conflict with the principle of *laïcité*.

Dissatisfaction with Existing Policy

In 2004, the 1989 Council of State decision still had its supporters. Intellectuals often praised the decision for duly recognizing the inherent multiplicity of symbols' potential meanings and effects. Some also praised it for delegating authority to the local level, and for promoting constructive negotiation and discussion between local educational authorities, parents, and students (10 and 11 December 2003, *Le Monde*; 19 and 23 December 2003, *Le Figaro*; 14 January 2004, *Le Monde*).

Despite its long list of considerations that could, in principle, trump students' rights to religious expression, the 1989 decision did not grant headscarf opponents very much. In practice, few headscarves could be shown to cause any of the specific problems mentioned. The Council of State decision kept school officials' reaction to headscarves within bounds, forcing teachers and administrators to show that particular headscarves really did pose irresolvable problems before expelling students wearing them.

Many teachers and school administrators were clearly dissatisfied with this approach, which posed a variety of difficulties for them. Although decision-making was delegated to the local level, schools were not allowed to pass stricter local rules of their own that simply prohibited headscarves from being worn. French courts repeatedly ruled that such blanket prohibitions, which many schools tried to pass in the interest of clarity and simplicity, were contrary to the Council of State's decision (Commission 2003: 30; 10 December 2003, *Le Monde*). Any punishment of a student for wearing a headscarf thus had to be justified on a case-by-case basis. Some principals resented the way this requirement forced them to play the "bad cop" vis-à-vis particular students and their families. Nor did they relish having to make the highly contestable case-by-case judgment calls that the 1989 Council of State ruling required (Public Senat 2003). Indeed, a number of local administrators' decisions made within that framework were legally challenged, with decisions sometimes overturned in court (10 December 2003, *Le Monde*). Not surprisingly, this proved an approach with which the very school officials to whom the ruling sought to devolve greater authority were largely dissatisfied. Though the appointment of mediators from 1995–2004 made some cases more manageable, legal conflicts continued and many administrators remained dissatisfied. While the leading public education unions were divided on whether to support the law, those representing school principals and school inspectors voted in favor (17 January 2004, *Le Monde*). A CSA survey of French teachers subsequently found some three-quarters of them also in support (5 February 2004, *Le Monde*).

The Stasi Commission was, by its own account, particularly moved by testimony solicited from teachers and administrators (Commission 2003: 40–44). Three-quarters of the Commission's members themselves were or had been teachers, school administrators, or professors. Backing a stricter and clearer approach, the Commission stressed the need to support public teachers and principals who they saw as abandoned by the state in difficult local situations that were often difficult for them to manage on their own (40–44). Prime Minister Jean-Pierre Raffarin expressed hope that the law would help "to protect state servants who feel vulnerable" (16 December 2003, *Le Monde*.) As Commission member Patrick Weil explained after the Commission's report was issued, "We felt that it [the school system] had been overtaken, that it was no longer in control of the situation. That incited us to act" (13 December 2003, *Libération*).

Pro-Christian Prejudice Thinly Veiled?

It seems unlikely, however, that a majority of the French public rallied behind the new law mainly in the interest of helping school principals avoid legal challenges, so one might very well ask whether French public support for the law was not simply guided by religiously traditionalist desires to secure predominance for Christianity over other religions within France's contested symbolic landscape. While it would doubtless be rather naïve to think that concerns about the declining symbolic predominance of Christianity marked by Islam's increasing inclusion in France's symbolic landscape played no role in generating support for the new law, such concerns received little play in public discussion of the new policy. Indeed, not even religious officials or far-Right politicians adopted positions congruent with such an interpretation.

Many derided the new law as an attack on Muslims thinly disguised as an evenhanded prohibition of religious signs in general (for example, 16 December 2003, *Le Monde*; 18 December, *Le Temps*). Large crosses, as critics quickly pointed out, are not particularly in vogue, and wearing a cross is not a religious obligation. One might therefore be tempted to argue that the French were really just seeking a way to permit only typical symbols of Christian identity (such as small crosses), selectively protecting France's Christian minority without admitting it.

Clever though this may seem, this reading did not square very well with the actual pattern of support and opposition that developed. Christianity in France has long been more beleaguered by secularism than it is today by the rise of Islam, and those most explicitly concerned with Christianity's place in France tended to oppose the new law rather than to support it. Catholic, Protestant, and Orthodox church officials all criticized the proposed law for being antireligious and warned Chirac against passing it (9 December 2003, *Le Temps*). Nor was the law supported by the far-Right National Front (FN), which preferred to see Christianity's privileged position in France upheld much more overtly. When the new law was proposed, FN leader Jean-Marie Le Pen denounced it as an effort to delude the public into focusing on the veil while ignoring the "real" problem: "massive immigration" (5 December 2003, *Libération*). Similarly, an editorial in the FN weekly *National Hebdo* argued: "The solution to this problem rests in assimilating those who accept being assimilated and returning to their countries of origin those who do not. Legislating about the veil at school is legislating on the accessory. It is taking a measure that risks resolving nothing, but just exacerbating the conflicts and turning itself back against the French loyal to the religion of their father" (26 December 2003, *Le Figaro*).

The fact that the FN itself was so outspokenly opposed to the law also makes interpretations of the law as a move to co-opt the FN's supporters more problematic than one might first assume.

The Headscarf as a Symbol of Women's Submission

To explain the surprisingly wide-ranging coalition that supported the 2004 law, one must look beyond Le Pen and the far-Right to the part played by other actors, particularly new feminist groups. To make sense of their role, one needs to understand how French observers have come to "read" the headscarf. Unlike political t-shirts, headscarves do not come inscribed with words specifying the messages they are intended to convey. Such messages are thus imputed to them by those who see or imagine the garment, and patterns of interpretation are culturally variable. This situation generates considerable potential for crosscultural misunderstandings. French and non-French observers, for example, often tend to "read" the scarf as a sign conveying very different messages.

Non-French observers often imagine a student attending class with her hair covered as someone willingly engaged in a freely chosen expression of her religious identity or cultural tradition, or as guided by personal modesty. Thus, they often imagine the headscarf as a t-shirt reading, "I believe in Allah," or "I'm proud to be a Muslim!" Why, they wonder, would the French prohibit such declarations of piety and cultural pride?

By contrast, when the French picture such a student, they more often tend to imagine her as an unwilling victim of sexist familial or community pressures. For many French observers, a headscarf looks more like a t-shirt that says, "I'm just a girl, and I know my place," or "Don't hit me! I accept my submission." Deciphering the message that way, they are more indignant at the idea of girls being forced to wear such signs. These different interpretations are, of course, closely tied to the different psychocultural narratives about when and why women veil that have surrounded this cultural controversy.

Who is right? The available evidence fortunately allows us to go beyond such generalizations as the fact that signs have multiple meanings, or that all signs may be subject to discrepancies between the message emitted and the one received. On the basis of interviews conducted with French young women wearing headscarves, we can fairly reach some conclusions about why they are worn and what they mean. In reality, it is fairly clear that there are *both* students in France wearing headscarves as a matter of personal religious conviction *and* those who do not want to wear headscarves but are forced to do so by familial or community pressure (Gaspard and Khosrokhavar 1995).[8] Others wear them for personal security, in response to peer pressure, or for other complex combinations of reasons.

It is the fact of female students being forced to wear signs read as saying, "I'm just a girl and I know my place" that particularly galls many people in France. In contrast to its position in 1989, the French Council of State in early 2004 expressed its support for a law prohibiting such signs. Explaining this change, members of the Council of State characterized sexually inegalitarian community pressures on girls as a factor marking a significant change from the situation in 1989 (28 January 2004, *Le Figaro*).

It is difficult to say whether such pressures at the local level really have increased. The phenomenon of *parents* pressuring their daughters to wear headscarves was also widely noted back in 1989. However, there was little or no discussion then of the role of *community* pressure and intimidation by other students, or local gang leaders, in pushing girls to dress this way. Since 1989, the terms of the French national discussion of the issue have clearly changed in this regard, and changes in prevailing psychocultural narratives about why students wear headscarves have in turn factored in changing the position of members of France's Council of State, the highly influential court which had long played a vital role in upholding a more case-by-case approach.

In particular, the prevalence of narratives about unwanted community pressures on girls to wear "signs" allegedly expressing acceptance of a subordinate and submissive social role has grown significantly since 1989. As the commission's report noted (29), the Council of State's 1989 decision made no reference to issues of sexual equality. The omission was not then surprising; back in 1989, arguments centered on concerns about sexual equality were less common and first appeared only in news-papers of the far-Left and were then picked up mainly by feminists within the Socialist Party.[9] The new centrality of those issues in the head-scarves debate of 2003–2004 in part reflected the influence of recent actions and publicity by groups representing women from the under-privileged suburban areas (*banlieues*) where North African immigrants are concentrated.

The activities of the organization Ni putes, ni soumises (Neither Whores Nor Submissives) (NPNS) and the network of local associations associated with it were illustrative in this respect. In late 2002, Sohane Benziane, an adolescent from the public housing projects of Vitry-sur-Seine was burned alive in a cellar, a victim of local male aggression. Reports of this horrifying incident helped draw public attention to vio-lence against women in France's poor neighborhoods. Very shortly thereafter, a movement calling itself "Ni putes, ni soumises" was launched together with NPNS cofounder Samira Bellil's (2002) widely read autobiography, *Dans l'enfer des tournantes* (In the Hell of the Gang Rapes), a hard-hitting account years of abuse at the hands of oppressive male youth from the rough-and-tumble district where she grew up.[10]

Despite its relatively small membership,[11] NPNS soon won consider-able attention from the media and French officials. NPNS leaders were even invited in March 2003 to meet directly with Prime Minister Jean-Pierre Raffarin, who then embraced NPNS demands congruent with the united right UMP's own emphasis on security (10 March 2003, *Le Monde*). Leaders from NPNS were later invited to present their testi-mony to the Stasi Commission.[12]

The message NPNS conveyed was highly critical of traditional Islam, machismo, and sexist family and community pressures to which many young women of France's immigrant suburbs are subject (see, for exam-ple, Macité Femmes n.d.). Calling for a "generational struggle," the movement has decried such pressures as impeding the emancipation of France's "women from below." The recent rise of this movement has drawn public attention to divisions within "immigrant" groups in

France, particularly tensions between more conservative elements and feminists sharply critical of tradition.

Given this context, the French public has become acutely aware that veiling, even if it is limited to the wearing of a headscarf, is far from being consensually accepted within France's Muslim population. Cases of girls forced to adopt more "modest" Islamic dress by community pressure, threats, or intimidation have been widely publicized. Just before the Stasi Commission's report was released, the popular magazine *Elle* published an open letter by sixty well-known women, Muslim and non-Muslim, calling on Chirac to ban the "veil"[13] (12 December 2003, *New York Times*), surely contributing to rising public awareness of sharp divisions among Muslims themselves in France. This pattern of organizational activity, popular mobilization, and media coverage has thus played a key role in shaping French public perceptions of "the veil" (*le voile*) and increasingly influenced psychocultural narratives about the constraints leading some girls to wear it. While France's response to this perceived situation may be misguided, it is not at all surprising in this context that demands for public intervention to "save" girls from veiling have arisen.

For its part, the Commission heard not only from representatives of NPNS but also from several other French feminists militantly opposed to the veil, including Chahdortt Djavann, the Iranian-born novelist and author of *Bas les voiles!* (Down with the Veils!). By contrast, though they were the main group targeted by the Commission's recommendations, only two students actually wearing Islamic headscarves were invited to testify. Nor did other feminists opposed to the new prohibition receive the same attention. As one commission member later noted, an atmosphere developed within which it became almost impossible to defend the right to wear headscarves without being cast as sexist and reactionary (Bauberot 2004).[14]

France's Domestic War on Terrorism?

One could be tempted to regard France's new law as a delayed response to 11 September and related fears about connections between Islamic fundamentalism and international terrorism. As Silverstein notes in an article on the headscarf law, after September 2001 in particular, "Many journalists and politicians began to worry that the French suburban housing projects (*cités*) had become nodes in a global jihad network stretching from Algeria to Chechnya to Afghanistan" (2004, para. 8). In a similar vein, Kramer (2004) argues that it was after September 2001 that "an increasing number of Muslim schoolgirls started attempting to enter classrooms draped in clothing that had less to do with the places their families came from than with a kind of global ur-Islam" (66).[15]

In support of this interpretation, one might also point to France's expulsion of several foreign-born fundamentalist imams shortly after the new law was recommended. Do these deportations not suggest that the law emerged largely from new state concerns about terrorist threats associated with fundamentalism's rise in French suburbs? A dramatic front-page article in the *Wall Street Journal* (9 August 2004), in part titled, "Trying to Pre-Empt Terrorism," clearly invited that interpretation.[16] It presented the deportations of eight imams during the first months of 2004 as a "new" practice driven by a far-reaching French "campaign against extremism."[17] The headscarves law, in turn, was characterized as part of the same hardheaded crackdown.

Such explanations of the background to the headscarf law undoubtedly resonate with American readers. They conform neatly to prevailing perceptions of 9/11 as a watershed moment in world history and reinforce familiar claims that Al Qaeda's attacks inaugurated a scared new world joined in a global war on terror, terrorism, and "radical" Islam. Even the French were, after all, on board, at least at home.

Fears of terrorism associated with radical, transnational Islamic movements are certainly familiar in the French context, but they have not followed exactly the same chronology as in the United States. September 2001 was arguably less of a new turning point in this regard in France, where recent fears of this kind date back to the 1995 bombings in Paris by French-born supporters of the Algerian Front islamique de salut (Silverstein 2004: para. 9).

Moves toward a new law banning religious signs in schools arose from a somewhat different, if not unrelated, set of concerns. Fears about radical, intentionally provocative and disruptive, expressions of Islam and, above all, fundamentalism (*intégrisme*) were frequently mentioned during public discussions of the law. By contrast, however, concerns regarding transnational Islamic networks sowing the seeds of terrorism did not figure in the Stasi Commission's report, and they played almost no part in the public debates that followed. Arguments for the new law clearly did not center on preventing such developments. In fact, in striking contrast to the terms of recent American discussion of the dangers of Islamic fundamentalism, there was no mention of "terror," "terrorism," or "terrorists" at all in either the Stasi Commission's seventy-eight-page report or Chirac's key speech on it (19 December 2003, *Le Monde*).

If preventing terrorism had been a driving motivation behind the quest for a new law, then one would expect to have heard that reason clearly invoked, if not by leading public figures, then at least by some important supporters of the policy. After all, pointing to dangers of terrorism is generally thought to be quite effective for boosting public support of potentially repressive and controversial new measures. Yet, such appeals were notably absent. Contrary to what some American reports have suggested, the idea that the new headscarves law arose from a concerted new French effort to crack down on potential terrorists is unwarranted. More than anything, such reports have reflected the dominance of the frame by which the American media interpret current tensions surrounding Islam in France through a terrorism-centered post-9/11 lens.

Of course, the French media have also tended to employ certain stock ways of framing the conflict. These frames are somewhat different from those found in other countries, however. The French media, for example, are quick to invoke "republican" values and closely linked the issue of Islamic fundamentalism to women's subordination and well-known French historical conflicts over church-state relations.

The European Court of Human Rights

One might well ask why the rising influence of international and European human rights law did not prevent France from passing its unusual new restrictions on the right to freedom of religious expression. In reality, the authority of the European Court of Human Rights (ECHR) did influence the Stasi Commission's reasoning and conclusions, but not as one might have expected. Perhaps anticipating concerns of the Council of State, which evaluates potential legislation partly in terms of its compatibility with international commitments, the Stasi Commission was clearly concerned that any new French legislation should be able to pass eventual scrutiny by ECHR. The commission's official report therefore discussed relevant precedents and how a national law prohibiting religious signs in public schools could potentially satisfy the European court's standards. The commission noted that the European Convention on Human Rights and Fundamental Freedoms protects religious liberty, but that this right is not absolute. Moreover, the commission stressed, the approach of ECHR to interpreting this requirement has involved "a recognition of the traditions of each country, without seeking to impose a uniform model of the relationship between church and state" (21).

One of the recent precedents identified by the commission as relevant in this respect was the court's 13 February 2003 decision on the case *Refah Partisi* [Prosperity Party] *and Others v. Turkey*. This case challenged the Turkish government's banning of the Islamic Prosperity Party, primarily on grounds that the ban was in conflict with freedom of expression and freedom of association. ECHR decided in favor of the Turkish government in this case, ruling that the party's political project posed dangers to the rights and liberties guaranteed by the Turkish constitution, including that of *laïcité*. In other words, where *laïcité* is constitutionally guaranteed—as it also is in France—ECHR was, this precedent suggested, willing to allow state measures to defend *laïcité*, even if they restricted other rights included in the convention (Commission 2003: 21).

Is it a coincidence that the commission's own recommendation of a new law banning the wearing of conspicuous religious signs in the public schools was set forth in the context of a report on the French tradition of *laïcité* and the conditions for its continued application in France today? Awareness of the ECHR and the need to satisfy its standards helps explain why defense of the new law prohibiting headscarves and other religious signs centered to such an extent on reference to the principle of *laïcité*, despite the fact that France's tradition of *laïcité* actually does *not* by itself account for the recent change in policy. Paradoxically, despite its institutional role in upholding universal human rights, the European court's influence did not lead to a more liberal policy. On the contrary, raising objections about the wearing of headscarves to a level of principle sufficient to satisfy ECHR standards took regulations restricting headscarves off the relatively pragmatic terrain that the Council of State had insisted upon in its 1989 decision. In practice, France's concern about the ECHR's standards favored official emphasis on *laïcité* and the republican tradition, thus reinforcing tendencies to concentrate precisely on the most symbolically and emotionally charged dimensions of the headscarves issue.

Conclusion

Since its first eruption in 1989, the issue of whether female students should be allowed to come to public schools wearing "Islamic" headscarves has proven a case of intense cultural contestation in France. The issue has raised fundamental questions about the terms of inclusion of visible signs of Muslim cultural identity and of Islam as a growing minority religious tradition in France's public symbolic landscape, thereby also raising questions about how and whether everyday practices within schools and other public institutions should transcend particular religious identifications. Because of its connections to France's highly conflictual history of church-state relations and to French republican understandings of citizenship and *laïcité*, the issue has long been more emotionally charged in France than in many other national contexts. Until 2004, however, public concern and attention to the issue never translated into an all-out ban on students' wearing of headscarves and other religious signs. Instead, policy followed a case-by-case approach upheld since 1989 by France's Council of State.

To understand France's recent change of policy on headscarves as opposed to the issue's emotional intensity, however, one needs to look beyond the long-standing symbolic significance of the issue in France. Local school officials' dissatisfaction with earlier policy approaches; increasing attention to feminist arguments favorable to state prohibition of headscarves, particularly arguments about the need to protect students from community pressures; and developments in European human rights law all played an important role in bestowing greater legitimacy on the new, more restrictive policy. These developments together helped to garner surprisingly wide-ranging political support for the new policy in France, not only from intellectuals and political leaders but also from the Council of State itself. The Stasi Commission report's discussion of other recent cases decided by the European Court of Human Rights appeared to be aimed at preempting arguments that the new bill was contrary to international law, arguments one would have expected the Council of State to consider. However, it is interesting to note that a key factor explaining the Council's change of position, cited by members themselves, was instead changing French social realities, particularly new, sexually inegalitarian community pressures on female students. The Council of State's new position thus appears to have been decisively influenced by changing public interpretations of headscarves and the rise of corresponding new narratives about why they were worn. Understanding the most recent French round of cultural conflict over the headscarves issue and the new policy that followed thus requires attention both to historically rooted French understandings of citizenship and *laïcité* and to more short-term factors, particularly dissatisfaction with the open-endedness of previous policies; recent developments in European human rights law; and increasing attention to gender-related concerns highlighted by feminists speaking on behalf of Muslim and other women from France's disadvantaged suburbs.

The 2004 French law aimed to promote integration and bolster social consensus regarding the terms on which France's ethnic and religious minorities of postwar immigrant origin are to be integrated. It is, however, a risky policy. Many moderate Muslims who are not particularly committed to wearing headscarves themselves may see France's latest "scarf hunt" as evidence of a certain public, officially sanctioned, "islamophobia." Indeed, some of France's more radical new Islamic organizations, such as the PMF and the UOIF, have clearly sought to encourage that interpretation. The danger is that the law may alienate relatively secular and moderate French Muslims, even turning them toward radical organizations seeking to rally them as outcast victims, thereby worsening existing social and cultural tensions in France.

The Stasi Commission itself as well as many intellectuals and the mainstream French media clearly aimed to discourage that kind of critical interpretation of the new law, instead stressing its congruence with republican principles and its feminist and liberatory rationales. The ability of the French mainstream media and French intellectuals to define the terms of national debate around Islam and the everyday behavior of France's Muslim citizens currently faces rising new challenges, however. As self-conscious organization of France's Muslim minority develops, new groups claiming to represent it have gained more voice in recent years. At the same time, commentators from elsewhere in Europe and around the world have been much quicker to comment on France's handling of its "diversity" issues than they were during the first headscarves debate in 1989–1990, widening the array of "respectable" perspectives now demanding consideration. So far, neither of these changes has led to any liberalization of French policy, which has instead taken a somewhat more restrictive turn. Even the widely noted influence of the European Court of Human Rights has not for now prevented France from pursuing its increasingly restrictive national policy course in this area. Ultimately, however, these underlying domestic and international changes are bound to make France's handling of its diversity issues ever more challenging.

Notes

An earlier version of this chapter, "Keeping Identity at a Distance: Explaining France's New Legal Restrictions on the Islamic Headscarf," was published in *Ethnic and Racial Studies* 29 (March 2006): 237–259. I would like to thank the Chaire de Recherche du Canada en Mondialisation, Citoyenneté et Démocratie, directed by Jules Duchastel at the Université du Québec à Montréal, for supporting the research and writing of this chapter. I am also grateful to Marc Ross and three anonymous reviewers for helpful comments on earlier drafts.

1. France's Muslim population, Europe's largest, is estimated at approximately five million. Wholly reliable figures are lacking, however, since France prohibits collecting of census data on religion. A 1994 survey by *Le Monde* found that 27 percent of Muslims in France were "believing and practicing" (Caldwell 2000).

2. Surveys of CSA, Ifop, and BVA before the law was passed in the Assembly found anywhere from 57 percent to 72 percent in favor (8 December 2003, *Libération*).

3. France's highly respected and influential supreme administrative court, the Council of State (Conseil d'Etat) issues opinions on all proposed legislative measures before they are submitted to the parliament. Members of the government can also seek advice from the Council of State on particular legal and administrative issues, as the Minister of National Education first did in regard to

the headscarves question in 1989. For more extensive discussion of this body and its functions, see http://www.conseil-etat.fr, and Langrod (1955: 676).

4. In the words of Commission member Ghislaine Hudson, "Le fait de demander que l'école soit un milieu protégé des influences religieuses et politique, parce que c'est un lieu de formation d'esprit, ne vise pas a exclure mais à s'intégrer et donc à s'émanciper" ["Demanding that the schools be a milieu protected from religious and political influences because they are a site of personal and intellectual development does not aim to exclude but to integrate and thus to emancipate"] (11 December 2003, *Le Monde*). All translations from French sources are my own unless otherwise noted.

5. Here my analysis closely follows that of Pierre Birnbaum (see 13 December 2003, *Libération*).

6. Results reported in *Elle*, 15 December 2003. Also see the very diverse reactions to the proposed law on the part of Muslim women questioned in " 'Si c'est ça, je ne me sens plus française' " (18 December 2003, *Libération*).

7. Important prosecular groups opposing the law included the Ligue de l'enseignement, Ligue des droits de l'homme, Mouvement contre le racisme et pour l'amitié entre les peuples (MRAP), and Fédération des conseils de parents d'élève (FCPE).

8. It is unfortunately impossible on the basis of this work to put any percentages to these different possibilities; for that, a more representative study with a larger sample would be required.

9. Most notably, *Lutte Ouvrière* (20 October 1989) linked the headscarves issue to Muslim girls' submission to their fathers and brothers, complaining of families constraining girls to wear the veil. Even within the LCR, the hard line against headscarves on feminist grounds was in 1989–1990 a minority position; the majority position instead stressed anticolonialism and opposed a firm crackdown. The feminist hard line was also taken within the PS by feminists including Yvette Roudy and Geneviève Domanach-Chich. There again, however, it remained a relatively subordinate line of argument (see *La Croix*, 26 October 1989, and *Le Quotidien de Paris*, 24 October 1989).

10. Bellil's book was released just five days after the murder of Sohane Benziane. On Bellil's role in NPNS, see Mouedden (2004).

11. In summer 2006, NPNS claimed just 6,000 members (MSNBC, 7 June 2006, http://www.msnbc.msn.com /id/12812170/).

12. Though previously active on the political left, NPNS's president, Fadela (Fatiha) Amara, was in 2007 appointed Secretary of State for Urban Policies in the UMP government of François Fillon. Born to a large Algerian Kabyle family, Amara was raised in the French town of Clermont-Ferrard.

13. The two terms most often used in France, *le foulard* (the headscarf) and *le voile* (the veil), are sometimes used to refer to the same garments, but they are not synonymous and have different political connotations. The former (*foulard*) refers specifically to a headscarf, a garment covering the head, ears, hair, and usually the neck. The latter (*le voile*) is a more inclusive term. Many in France now do refer to *foulards* as *voiles*, but the term *voile* can also refer to various types of large gowns or cloaks worn over other clothes. A full-length burka or chador, for instance, would be a veil, but certainly not a headscarf. The term *voile* therefore lends itself more readily to conceptual inflation and has more often been used by those seeking to dramatize issues of "Islamic" women's dress in France, whereas the term *foulard* has often been preferred by those seeking to de-dramatize the issue.

14. I refer here to Bauberot's presentation at the May 2004 meeting of the French-Canadian Association for the Advancement of the Sciences (Acfas) rather than the text of the paper.

15. Compare Kepel's (1994) much subtler, and earlier, account of the connection between veiled students and international Islamic currents.

16. The telling full title of the article was "Fighting Words—French Move Fast to Expel Foreigners Espousing Violence—Nation Targets Several Imams from a Muslim Populace Poorly Integrated in Society—Trying to Pre-Empt Terrorism."

17. *Le Monde* (21 August 2004) reported the number of deportations during this period as only seven, that is, half the number of allegedly dangerous "Islamists" deported by Interior Minister Charles Pasqua a decade before. Deportation of imams was thus not a "new" practice that took hold only post-9/11 as the *Wall Street Journal* suggested.

Bibliography

Bauberot, Jean. 2004. "Les mutations actuelles de la laïcité en France au miroir de la Commission Stasi." Paper presented at the Seventy-second Congress of Acfas, Montréal, Québec, 10–14 May.

Bellil, Samira. 2002. *Dans l'enfer des tournantes*. Paris: Éditions Denoël.

Caldwell, Christopher. 2000. "The Crescent and the Tricolor." *Atlantic Online* (November): 286. Retrieved from http://www.theatlantic.com/doc/200011/france-muslims.

Commission de Réflexion sur l'Application du Principe de Laïcité dans la République. 2003. *Rapport au Président de la République*. Paris: La Documentation Française.

Djavann, Chahdortt. 2003. *Bas les voiles!* Paris: Gallimard.

Gaspard, Françoise, and Farhad Khosrokhavar. 1995. *Le foulard et le république*. Paris: Découverte.

Ifop. 2003. "Les femmes musulmanes en France." Retrieved 7 June 2004, from http://www.ifop.com/europe/ sondages/opinionf/musulmane.asp.

Kepel, Gilles. 1994. *À l'Ouest d'Allah*. Paris: Seuil.

Kramer, Jane. 2004. "Taking the Veil: How France's Public Schools Became the Battleground in a Culture War." *New Yorker* (22 November): 59–71.

Langrod, Georges. 1955. "The French Council of State: Its Role in the Formulation and Implementation of Administrative Law." *American Political Science Review* 49, no. 3: 673–692.

Macité Femmes. n.d. "Le Manifeste des femmes des quartiers." Retrieved 24 February 2004, from http:// www.macite.net/home/article.php3?id_article = 29.

Mouedden, Mohsin. 2004. "Le mouvement 'Ni P . . . , Ni Soumises' sert-il la cause des femmes?" Retrieved 23 February 2004, from http://www.saphirnet .info/imprimer.php?id = 938.

Public Senat. 2003. "Louise Arvaud, Principal du collège Beaumarchais Paris 11è." Retrieved 4 June 2004, from http://www.publicsenat.fr/dossiers/ open_video_special_laicite.asp?video; eq20030909_01&player = windows&debit = bas.

Sandel, Michael. 1982. *Liberalism and the Limits of Justice*. Cambridge: Cambridge University Press.

Silverstein, Paul. 2004. "Headscarves and the French Tricolor." *Middle East*

Report Online 13, no. 4. Retrieved from http://www.merip.org/mero/mero
013004.html.

Soper, J. Christopher and Joel Fetzer. 2003. "Explaining the Accommodation of
Muslim Religious Practices in France, Britain, and Germany." *French Politics* 1,
no. 1: 39–59.

Tevanian, Pierre. 2004. "Une loi antilaïque, antiféministe et antisociale." *Le
Monde Diplomatique* 599: 8.

Vidal, Dominique. 2004. "Exception française." *Le Monde Diplomatique* 599: 6–7.

Chapter 7
Minority Language Policy in France
Jacobinism, Cultural Pluralism, and
Ethnoregional Identities

Britt Cartrite

France has long been seen as an archetype of the nation-state. French identity and French language policies are generally understood as, at least since 1539, tightly intertwined and set France on a path of homogenization. Since the French Revolution, the centralizing and standardizing needs of state required French rejection of subnational identities and, in particular, regional languages. As a result, recent changes in legal policies and, perhaps most interesting, official rhetoric which seem to suggest an acceptance of regional languages are conceptualized as a profound identity shift within France, a contest to redefine the nation that has profound implications for the future of France. While immigrant minorities, particularly Muslims, have drawn the most attention and emotional reactions in recent decades, regional and national minorities within France have also sought greater recognition and political rights which have the potential to significantly alter the French state should these movements build in intensity.

Political mobilization on the basis of ethnic cleavages entails two nontrivial necessary, if insufficient, conditions. First, potential ethnic activists must perceive themselves as members of a subgroup within the society (Gellner 1983). Second, there must be an evaluation by potential activists that such social cleavages represent the legitimate basis for political mobilization.[1] The state plays a significant role in determining the likelihood of each of these conditions being met. Post-Revolutionary France, representing in many respects an extreme example within Europe in terms of its history of homogenizing policies, has for decades sought to undermine subnational identities in rhetoric ("France one and indivisible") and practice (such as the banning of local languages in school), providing at least a partial explanation for the relative paucity of ethnopolitical mobilization by regional minorities when compared to similar groups in neighboring countries such as Spain, Belgium, the United Kingdom, and others.

The story of France as a homogeneous, centralized society, which dominates scholarly, official, and popular understandings of France and the French, is a powerful one, yet is ultimately unsatisfying. A reexamination of both the historical record and official rhetoric suggests a persistent counternarrative of France as a culturally plural space. If indeed such an alternative narrative exists within France, shifts in the official rhetoric and official policies should be understood not as a profound reshaping of French identity but as the apparent rise of this alternative narrative to challenge the hegemonic Jacobin discourse. In addition, the great resistance to a recognition of the possibility of multiple identities or hyphenated identities in France makes countries like France very different from Spain or Canada where there is widespread acceptance of the idea that a person can strongly hold both a national, regional identity and be a loyal citizen of the state at the same time.

Yet the implications of a shift in how the French view the legitimacy of regional identities may not merely be manifest in the potential for increased tolerance of subnational identities. Such a shift may serve to facilitate both the recognition of subnational ethnic cleavages within France and the legitimization of political activism based on those cleavages. A shift in the framing of the legitimacy of ethnic identities may thus result in reducing French exceptionalism in this regard, subjecting the French state to the devolutionary and even secessionist pressures evidenced in its neighbors.

"Les langues régionales sont une richesse de notre patrimoine culturel" (Péry 1998: 2).[2] With this bold opening statement in a letter dated 29 October 1997 then Prime Minister Lionel Jospin charged Deputy Nicole Péry with undertaking an inventory of the state of regional languages within France as well as proposing policies for extending their teaching. The proximate cause of this charge was the Council of Europe's passage of the European Charter for Regional or Minority Languages and the subsequent debate of whether or not France should, or even could, sign and ratify the charter.[3] For those unfamiliar with French attitudes and policies toward regional languages, this statement may hardly seem bold. Yet the Prime Minister anticipated some of the potential arguments against the mission later in the same letter: "The time is past when the State could consider the teaching of these languages as likely to threaten national unity. If, as it is today prescribed in our Constitution, 'the language of the Republic is French,' it remains to give appropriate support to the teaching of regional languages" (2).[4] Indeed, August 2000 would see the resignation of Interior Minister and prominent socialist politician Jean-Pierre Chevènement over the issue of limited self-government in Corsica which, he argued, would lead to the break-up of the French Republic itself.

This tension between visions of France as a culturally and linguistically plural society and France as "one and indivisible" results from two distinct framings of French identity itself. The clearly hegemonic discourse, strongly associated with Jacobin thought has antecedents extending back at least to the sixteenth century and views regional languages and identities as, at best, residues of an earlier, predemocratic period that should rightfully fade into nonexistence: the French "melting-pot" allows for individuals of a very wide array to become French, with an implicit proviso that they learn French and consider themselves to be French.[5] However, in terms of the number of "national minority"[6] groups, France has long been the most heterogeneous country in Western Europe. Jospin's statement suggests a counter to this dominant frame, offering a vision of France as containing a plurality of languages and cultures and, indeed, suggesting that French exceptionalism can be partially understood as a function of this heterogeneity.

This chapter argues that the conceptualization of a pluralist French identity is, in fact, evident in the historical and discursive record, although the linkage of homogeneity to Jacobin republicanism and the success of democratic institutions following 1871 greatly subordinated it. During this period, there was a great effort to alter France's symbolic landscape and to operationally transform a multilingual country into one where only French was used in public and private settings. In comparing the interpretations of the two traditions of key events in French language policy and evaluating the explanatory power of the homogeneity narrative, I highlight both the sources and evidence of this alternative, subordinate tradition and argue that what is new in this dynamic is not a new conceptualization of French identity, but rather that heterogeneity and republicanism are increasingly linked in public discourse in ways that presents a real opportunity for decoupling the more traditional Jacobin homogeneous formulation without representing either a profound sea change in French self-conceptualizations or a necessarily fundamental threat to the Republic itself; indeed, by reframing the debate in these terms, one can imagine that integrationists could occupy the discursive space of the True France (*la France profonde*) that to date has been a monopoly of the assimilationists. My argument makes clear that cultural contestation around what it means to be French and who gets to determine the answer to this question involves both the mobiliza-

tion of discourse and resources in ways that have significant consequences for the nature of the French state.

Pre-Revolutionary Policy

The question of which came first, assimilation as a central component
of French identity or assimilation as a necessary component of the
expansion of the French state, is perhaps a chicken-and-egg dilemma
lost in the mists of time. What almost all studies, both scholarly and official, agree upon is that the Ordonnance de Villers-Cotterêts of 1539 represents the first attempt to establish by royal edict French as the national
language: "And because such things [doubts and uncertainties] frequently occurred with the interpretation of Latin words contained in the
said decrees, we wish that henceforth all judgments, together with all
other proceedings, whether of our sovereign courts and other subordinate and inferior courts, or accounts, inquiries, contracts, warrants, wills
and any other acts and processes of justice or such as result from them,
be pronounced, recorded and issued to the parties in the French
mother tongue, and in no other way (art. 111)." By replacing Latin,
French became the official language across a territory that already consisted of numerous regional languages (*patois*).

As the French state continued its territorial expansion during the
seventeenth and eighteenth centuries, edicts were issued that extended
this policy to the newly acquired areas: Béarn (1620), Flanders (1684),
Alsace (1685), Roussillon (1700), Lorraine (1748). The establishment
of the Académie Française in 1635 was intended to regulate French pro-
nunciation and grammar and elites across France and elsewhere
adopted this standardized language (Grillo 1989: 29). Attempts to stan-
dardize French were undertaken with an eye toward facilitating the further spread of the language, such that by the end of the eighteenth
century, the impact of great writers was felt and French had become the
preferred language for aristocrats across Europe (Wardhaugh 1987:
100–101).

The Revolution

The Revolution radically altered French national minority policy.
Despite an apparent initial rejection of homogenization by the National
Assembly in 1790, when legislation requiring the translation of all laws
and decrees into local vernaculars, according to the mainstream narrative Jacobin revolutionaries quickly resumed the homogenizing policies
of the *Ancien Regime*. In response to surveys undertaken by Grégoire and
Barère regarding the use of French outside the capital and the apparent

linkage between antirevolutionary resistance and the use of local vernaculars, official policy quickly advocated stamping out local languages in
an attempt to secure the gains of the Revolution.

Yet in the first years of the Revolution there was no clear policy regarding the promulgation of standard French throughout the Republic. On
the one hand, standardization and centralization were the hallmarks of
Jacobinism as local institutional variations gave way to a uniform, rational system (Jacob and Gordon 1985: 112). Indeed, the very notion of
citizenship for the Jacobins was civic rather than ethnic. Regional languages were seen as an artifact of political institutions rather than as the
determining factor of those institutions (Safran 1999a: 85). On the
other hand, Rousseau's notion of the social contract asserted that what
mattered in building a nation was a commitment to a common legal,
political, and economic entity and the shared values those institutions
entailed; for him, language was not a defining characteristic of a "people" (Geary 2002: 63; Hobsbawm 1992: 19–20). Indeed, policies undertaken in 1792 seemed to be leading toward a kind of linguistic
federalism, with bilingualism and accommodations for local languages
to be provided (Grillo 1989: 36). Thus arguments could be made either
for a homogenizing policy or for permitting local languages.

However, increasingly the revolutionaries began to assert that French
needed to be established as the single language of the Republic, arguing
that linguistic diversity inhibited social equality and was inefficient and
cumbersome for administration, and it was felt that a single language
would facilitate the free exchange of revolutionary ideas.[7] Furthermore,
French could bind all citizens more tightly together in the face of the
counterrevolutionary attacks the Republic began to suffer. In 1794 Abbé
Grégoire published a government-ordered study in which he stated: "It
is no exaggeration to say that at least six million Frenchmen, particularly
in the countryside, do not speak the national language; that an equal
number are more or less incapable of sustaining a coherent conversation; that as a result, the number of true speakers does not exceed three
million, and that the number of those who write it correctly is probably
even smaller" (Grillo 1989: 24).[8]

Grégoire also found at least thirty dialects or distinct languages in use
at the time of the Revolution. Such linguistic heterogeneity was of great
concern to the threatened revolutionaries and their image of a homogeneous French Republic. Interestingly, Grégoire himself did not argue
for a monolingual France; rather, he argued for bilingualism, asserting
that regional languages "exist . . . and their disappearance would be very
regrettable; the important thing is that all Frenchmen understand and
speak the national language, without forgetting their individual dialects" (Jacob and Gordon 1985: 114).

Not everyone agreed, however, and, based at least in part on counter-revolutionary resistance in outlying areas, some argued that ethnolinguistic groups represented "a dangerous reactionary particularism or, at best, as symptoms of an irrelevant primordialism" (Safran 1999a: 117). For example, some months prior to Grégoire's report, Bertrand Barère de Viezac, in a report to the Committee of Public Safety, stated: "federalism and superstition speak low-Breton; emigration and hate for the Revolution speak German; the counter-revolution speaks Italian, and fanaticism speaks Basque" (Jacob and Gordon 1985: 114). This harder line eventually won the day and a series of laws were published later in 1794 to officially ban all languages other than French in public service and education (Safran 1999b: 42). However, the internal and external troubles of the Republic, when combined with the limited capacity of the government to penetrate the countryside, meant that the masses continued to speak their *patois* during and after this period.

Napoleon to 1870

The period between the First and Third Republics was to see France struggle through a series of external wars and internal revolutions leading to the end of the First Empire (1814), the Bourbon Restoration (1815), the July Monarchy (1830), the Second Republic (1848), and the Second Empire (1852). Perhaps not surprisingly, initiatives regarding the extension of French throughout the country were relegated to the back burner for much of this period. Officially, however, the policies of 1794 were pursued. In the 1820s it was decreed that "all acts of civil status (of persons) be written in French, which is the only official language. Hence the patois of the different regions in France are forbidden" (Safran 1999b: 42). And in 1845 a French official instructed a group of teachers to "remember that you have been posted here [Brittany] exclusively to kill the Breton language" (Jacob and Gordon 1985: 115). However, such official proclamations yielded little fruit and Safran suggests that French was expanding throughout elite circles in France, quite possibly of its own accord rather than due to the efficacy of official policy, while the masses continued to speak the local language (1999b: 42–43). What is clear is that the inauguration of the Third Republic, after defeat by Prussia, found that French was not the primary language for fully half of its citizens (Weber 1976: 70).

The Third Republic

Following wartime defeat by the Prussians and the internal turmoil of the Paris Commune, the newly established Third Republic found itself faced with a number of serious problems. The political impasse between the three distinct camps of monarchists (Bourbonist, Orleanist, and Bonapartist) that had allowed the Third Republic to be formed represented a shaky foundation for a state which reasonably saw itself as a great power suffering from internal weaknesses. This "provisional" government, which would last until the Nazi occupation of 1940, would undertake policies that, both through intent and effect, would drastically undermine local languages and identities in favor of French.

Eugen Weber finds that the gulf between the city and countryside in 1871 was vast indeed: "Léon Gambetta put all this in a nutshell in 1871: the peasants were 'intellectually several centuries behind the enlightened part of the country'; there was 'an enormous distance between them and us . . . between those who speak our language and those many of our compatriots [who], cruel as it is to say so, can no more than stammer in it'; materiel property had to 'become the means of their moral progress,' that is, of their civilization. The peasant had to be integrated into the national society, economy, and culture: the culture of the city and of the City par excellence, Paris" (1976: 5).

Of all the various initiatives undertaken during the Third Republic to bring the parts of France together, the one generally given the most credit for advancing a national identity was the initiation of *compulsory* free public education in French under Jules Ferry in 1877. While free schools had been established in 1832, insufficient resources and their voluntary nature limited their nationbuilding impact (Ager 1999: 26; Weber 1976: 303). In addition to teaching all students only in French, the *symbole* came into use: Any student heard speaking in *patois* would be made to wear a token around their neck; the actual object varied, but included cardboard tickets, a bar or stick, a peg, a paper ribbon or metal object, or a brick. The bearer of the object could pass it along by catching and denouncing "another student using the local language. At the end of the day, the student with the *symbole* would then be punished."[9] This method, which continued in some parts of the country well into the twentieth century, was particularly resented, yet also appears to have been effective in reducing the usage of local languages among children.

As with public education elsewhere, French schools also inculcated a shared history and civic values across the country, further helping to break down local identities. And the increasing numbers of girls in school further undermined another source of persistent localism, as young people of both sexes learned and were required to use the national language. As a result, the extension of compulsory education served to expand French and the national identity in dramatic fashion so that most *patois*-speaking communes in 1863 were largely French-speaking by 1914.

Other reforms of the period would also undermine national minority identities. The construction of roads and railways increased communication between various regions. Military service brought men from across the country together with standard French as their *lingua franca*. Industrialization led to increasing urbanization and an increasing sense of shared identity. Under the aegis of the French state, the effect of these various policies, rather than exacerbating the differences among various groups, was instead to bring individuals together as French citizens with a common language and culture, in short, the creation of the French nation.

Interestingly, two unexpected dissents emerged during this drive to proactively create the French nation. First, in a celebrated 1882 speech entitled *Qu'est-ce qu'une nation?* (What is a nation?), the historian Ernest Renan, hailing from Brittany, articulated a profoundly civic notion of French identity, representing in some respects a return to Revolutionary Jacobinism. Renan discounted the role of "race, language, [shared] interests, religious affinity, geography and military exigencies" as the generators and distinguishing features of a nation. Instead, any national group required only two things: first, a common, albeit inevitably factually inaccurate, historical heritage and, second, the will to retain that shared heritage (1996: 57–58). Recalling Rousseau's social contract in many ways he argued that anyone wishing to join in the retention and expression of the common heritage was a member of the nation. This position of assimilation as a voluntary option, while clearly associated with Rousseau and therefore reasonably associated with Jacobin thought, stands in stark contrast to Third Republic efforts undertaken to homogenize France linguistically and culturally.[10]

A second important effect of the period was an increasing anti-Semitism, exploding in the Dreyfus Affair, which occupied the French imagination for over a decade in the years surrounding the turn of the century (Bredin 1983: 515–516). During the years of the Second Republic and Second Empire, Jews were assimilating at a remarkable pace; in many ways they represented the ideal Jacobin citizen, with loyalties to France based purely on a love of the Republic rather than on any sentimental attachment to a local region (Safran 1995: 4). However, in 1894 Alfred Dreyfus, the only Jew on the general staff, was convicted of spying for the Germans based on the handwriting (which only vaguely resembled Dreyfus's) on a scrap of paper found in a wastepaper basket by a cleaning woman, evidence that anti-Semitic officers forged.

Although the government soon uncovered the actual spy, Major Esterhazy, it argued that staining the honor of the military and the state was not worth the price of one Jew. This line polarized French society between conservatives, the government, the Church, and the military on one side and progressives on the other. Various trials would last more than a decade and cause the collapse of a government before Dreyfus was finally declared innocent of all charges.

The link between nationbuilding in the Third Republic and anti-Semitism is twofold. First, Jewish assimilation was in part a function of revolutionary secularization. To the extent that the Catholic Church was reintegrated into French identity in the Third Republic, even long-assimilated Jews became questionable Frenchmen. Second, while the Ferry laws were actively seeking to undermine provincial identities, at the same time the peasant as the romantic archetype of the Frenchman with close ties to the hallowed soil reinvigorated ties between urbanites and the countryside. Jews, however, rarely had such close associations with the peasantry; as a result, their association with *la France profonde* was tenuous, even when Jews could trace their inhabiting of French towns back many generations. During the Dreyfus Affair it was claimed that Jews were more susceptible to being spies than others because their lack of a home territory in France rendered their allegiance to the nation questionable. Thus Jews, living in French cities for centuries and fully accepting Republican ideals and assimilating into the national identity and in many respects resembling the archetypal civic citizen, were suspect because of a lack of ties to the countryside which the Romantics and the Third Republic had reified as essential to being French.

What this explosion of anti-Semitism illustrates is that membership in the French nation under the Third Republic had a stronger ethnic component than the dominant narrative recognizes. To be French required an association with the land and an acceptance of the French language and culture, in contrast to the arguably Jacobin rhetoric of Renan and others. What must be emphasized was the overall efficacy of this approach to nationbuilding: these policies to some degree reflected an abandonment of Revolutionary ideals and created a new group of "outsiders" from citizens long-assimilated and committed to Republican ideals while simultaneously reducing the degree of linguistic heterogeneity within France.

The Interwar Years

Although World War I and the interwar years were to occupy much of the attention of French policymakers in the years following the Dreyfus Affair, the policy of undermining local identities continued. The French rejected a Breton delegation to the Paris Conference, stating that

"France has no minorities" and in 1924 leaders of an Alsatian autonomy movement were put on trial and convicted. World War I had created a heightened loyalty to France, and the educational system continued to strengthen that through its highly nationalistic history curriculum.

Abroad, France played an active role in the League of Nations Minority Treaties system, seeking to ensure the viability of new states ostensibly created along ethnic lines according to the Wilsonian principle of self-determination, as well as participating in League Mandates in the Middle East. France retained its extensive overseas empire as well. Thus while domestically the Third Republic was increasingly successful in building a French identity and a monolingual society by undermining national minority identities and retaining its empire abroad, in Eastern Europe it pursued policies supporting national minorities in their quest for independence. This seeming hypocrisy did not go unnoticed by domestic national minorities; however, these voices were quite muted and the pressing economic and social concerns of the interwar years crowded out minority concerns from the national agenda.

The Nazi Occupation and Vichy Regime

During their occupation of Belgium the Nazis renewed the German policy of World War I of encouraging Flemish separatism and support for the occupation through a relatively extensive devolution of institutional capacities for Flemish-speaking areas. In France, however, the Nazis were much less decisive. On the one hand, there were some early negotiations with, especially, the Flemish and Bretons for special provisions in exchange for cooperation; the Bretons eventually were to form an SS unit during the war to fight for the Nazis. However, the newly established Vichy regime also needed to be placated and, despite their location in Southern France occupying almost all of the regions where Occitan was spoken, Vichy leader Marshal Petain retained aspirations of influence and control in all of France, hoping to keep the country intact. As a result, few concessions were made to national minorities, although the Vichy did approve the teaching of Breton language and history in primary schools in that region.

While there was some limited collaboration with the Nazis by Bretons, Flemings, Alsatians, and Italian-speakers in southeastern France, this did not result in any special provisions for national minorities during the Occupation, although some limited promises were made to the Bretons early on and Alsace and Lorraine were reannexed by the Reich.[11] Furthermore, support for the Nazis was limited at best, and some of the most significant support for the Resistance was also found in these areas. Nazi policy was a balance between encouraging collaboration and retaining the cooperation of the Vichy regime and its aspirations for the appearance of controlling France, with the tendency being to support the latter over the former.

The Fourth Republic

Following liberation in 1944, the Fourth Republic was faced with a number of difficulties in addition to the national minority issue. During the roundup and prosecution of Nazi collaborators, which occurred across the country, the French were particularly harsh toward the Bretons despite any clear evidence that Breton collaboration differed from that in the rest of France: 2,000 arrested, 1,000 sent to camps, sixty sentenced to death, fifteen executed, 1,000 others killed in reprisals (Reece 1977: 166–172), indicating a return to the sentiment, if not the actual policy, of Barère in 1794. By and large, however, the task of rebuilding France economically and attempts to maintain the Empire occupied the attention of political leaders during this period.

Interestingly, a major symbolic piece of legislation was passed regarding national minorities during this period. The Loi Deixonne of 1951 provided for the elective teaching of Breton, Basque, Catalan, and Occitan after school at all levels.[12] However, the wording of the law originally permitted no more than one hour per week of such instruction, subsequently expanded to three hours in 1975, and effectively prohibited teaching at the primary school level. Furthermore, almost no funding or training was provided to teachers. As a result, the law was little more than symbolic and generated more frustration than hope for national minorities (Safran 1999b: 44; Oakes 2001: 118; Ager 1999: 31; Jacob and Gordon 1985: 120–122).

Regional organizations also were created during the 1950s although not expressly to articulate the interests of national minorities; rather, they were part of a limited effort to decentralize the centralized state. In 1954 regional interest groups were recognized and institutionalized as the *Comités d'expansion économique,* and in 1955 twenty-two *circonscriptions d'action régionale* were created. These moves toward decentralization represented the beginning of a shift away from more extreme Jacobin views and had spillover potential to increase support for regional identities. By and large, however, the governmental instability of the Fourth Republic, coupled with the more pressing concerns of rebuilding France and Western Europe and dealing with wars in their crumbling empire, left little energy for significant demand-making or initiatives regarding national minorities or decentralization more generally.

The Fifth Republic

After the turmoil of the Algerian War and the collapse of the Fourth Republic, the fortunes of French national minorities gradually improved. While institutional provisions for these groups would continue to lag behind accommodations realized by other groups in neighboring states, a clear shift in the national perception regarding the legitimacy of these groups was occurring. Interestingly, and perhaps relatedly, there was an increasing sense of the French language being under attack especially from English. Thus legislation providing increasing provisions for national minorities occurred at the same time that efforts were undertaken to protect the French language from outside influences.

Supporting Regional Languages

In many respects the early national minority policies of the Fifth Republic were extensions of those of the Fourth: symbolic pronouncements with little implementation. In 1963 the *Délégation à l'Aménagement du Territoire et à l'Action régionale* (DATAR) was established as an adjunct to the Prime Minister's office. The following year the *Commission de Développement économique regional* (CODER) was instituted but, indicative of the prevailing symbolic nature of national minority policy, the CODER had a strictly administrative, not budgetary, role. In addition, there were increasing numbers of broadcasts in some regional languages, although many were either of dubious quality or limited to one regional dialect, thus circumscribing their potential audience (Safran 1999b: 54).

During the heady days of May 1968, during which the continued survival of the Republic was in doubt in some circles, the radical left linked with regional movements[13] to advocate decentralization of the French state and declared the peripheral regions of France to be "internal colonies." A referendum on decentralization was slated for the following year. However, the initiative became, in effect, a vote on support for De Gaulle himself and was defeated by groups who, under other circumstances, would likely have voted in support for the measure (Beer 1980: 37).

Despite this apparent setback for regionalism, regional groups continued to evolve, although government policies were primarily symbolic. There was however, some transformation of the *loi Deixonne* into an effective instrument for promoting regional identity. Corsican was included as a covered language in 1974, while the next year the one hour of elective language study for high school students was expanded to three. Despite these modifications, the Ministry of Education in 1976 argued that the law was essentially a "dead letter" (Jacob and Gordon 1985: 121). The relative lack of substantive progress regarding regional identity led Michel Denieul, the Cabinet Director of the Minister of Education, to remark in 1976: "Not to recognize the existence of such a cultural patrimony would be to deny a reality tangible everywhere and to impoverish a national treasure which is, on the whole of our territory, the sum of special relationships between the soil and the men who succeeded one another upon it. Founded on the awareness and the importance of these differences, this teaching [of regional languages] must naturally be conceived of in the absolute respect for our national unity which could not be questioned again by an artificial opposition between local cultures and the national reality incarnated by the State" (Jacob and Gordon 1985: 121).

When the Haby Committee proposed increasing the teaching of regional languages in 1976, the government opposed it and, in fact, Occitan was removed from some examinations and support for Breton bilingual classes was tepid (Ager 1999: 32). Thus while official policy continued very lukewarm and largely symbolic policies, there was an emerging sense both within and outside government that a change in spirit as well as policy was necessary if the government was to support regional languages and identities.

The election of Socialist François Mitterand as President in 1981 institutionalized exactly that shift in attitude. Elected on a platform that supported and encouraged cultural pluralism and limited decentralization, which clearly supported national minority identity, the early years of Socialist rule represented tangible gains for national minorities. Mitterand had argued as early as 1974 that

The Socialist party has always decided to choose the development of the personality. And when one considers Brittany, Corsica, the Basque country, and the Languedoc region, too, it is true that the attempt to suffocate all the means of expression of original languages—for the structures of languages are also the deeper structures of the brain, touching the very essence of being—it is true that economic colonialism . . . and a certain reflex of centralistic domination of a colonialist nature—all that should be corrected. . . . At one time the kings of France, the Jacobins, Bonaparte . . . were right . . . in their efforts to [fight against] centrifugal tendencies . . . Very well, it was necessary to make France. But . . . the necessary unity has become uniformity, in which individual being is stamped out . . . . [Now we must respect] the right to be different. (Safran 1989: 123)

The rapid passage and 1982 signing of the Loi Defferre, implementing administrative decentralization and establishing direct election to regional councils (institutionally between the French state and local communes), while not targeted specifically to national minorities, represented a significant shift away from traditional Jacobin centralism. In addition, Corsican autonomy laws in 1982 and 1983 gave the Corsicans a directly elected popular assembly with control over regional matters such as agriculture, fishing, communications, land-use planning, transport, technological research, vocational training, education, and culture. This approach was seen as a possible model for accommodating other national minorities. The 1982 Giordan Report recognized the existence in France of authentic "regional and minority cultures" and argued that their languages and cultures be preserved and promoted by government subsidies and overseen by a National Commission for Minority Cultures (Jacob and Gordon 1985: 126). It argued that political citizenship is dependent on social and cultural citizenship; for the latter two to be meaningful, the state needed to abandon its myopic view of Parisian language and culture in favor of accepting the linguistic and cultural diversity within the Hexagon (Safran 1989: 125). And the Savary Circular of that same year stipulated (Ager 1999: 33):

The state should be responsible for the teaching of regional languages.
Regional languages should be taught from Kindergarten to University with the status of a separate discipline.
Teaching should be based on the expressed wishes of both teacher and pupil.

However, this initial momentum regarding national minorities did not sustain itself. In 1985 the Conseil National des Langues et Cultures Régionales (National Council for Regional Languages and Cultures) was established; there were prominent members of government at the initial meetings and regional movements sought to have it address a wide array of concerns. However, funding for the council was uncertain from the very beginning, and the victory of the Gaullist-Giscardist alliance in 1986 with the ascension of Jacques Chirac to prime minister virtually ensured that funding would continue to be a problem (Safran 1989: 138–141). In the end, the council only met three times and yielded no concrete results. No other initiatives of note were undertaken between 1983 and 1988 after only two years of intense activity; economic malaise once again came to dominate the political agenda.

Despite the apparent waning of interest on the Left for national minority issues and the success of the Right in 1986, the progress on decentralization and recognition of regional identity was not completely undone. Rather, the government returned to a tepid and symbolic approach to the issue. In 1988 teaching of regional languages was redefined and teaching in the Lycées somewhat expanded. Additional languages were added to the list in subsequent years. In 1994 teachers of regional languages in private bilingual schools began to be paid by the state, an improvement of their status.

More recently a debate regarding national minority rights has emerged in the wake of the approval of the Council of Europe's 1992 European Charter for Regional and Minority Languages. The government initiated a study by Nicole Péry, a member of the National Assembly from the Basque region, which was subsequently completed by Breton mayor Bernard Poignant (1998). It argued that regional languages represent a valuable part of French culture and tradition and efforts to support them should be expanded. It also advocated ratification of the European Charter as part of a broader policy of encouraging national minority identities, arguing that encouraging cultural pluralism within France could actually serve to secure French in the European Union and globally. However, the report concluded that the most important first step is the signing and ratification of the Charter. While it has subsequently been signed (7 May 1999), it has not been put to the Assembly for ratification.[14]

Protecting French Internally and Externally

Interestingly, the postwar period, which has seen a slow increase in provisions recognizing linguistic pluralism within France, has also been witness to increasing concern for the French language both domestically and abroad. Once considered one of the preeminent international languages, in 1945 French was made a working language of the United Nations by only one vote (Jacob and Gordon 1985: 118). Recent decades have seen efforts to protect French in three particular ways: (1) promotion of the international status of French (*francophonie*); (2) reinforcing the use of proper grammar; and (3) inhibiting the inclusion of foreign, and especially Anglo-American, words (Safran 1999b: 46).

French weakness during the Second World War and the subsequent collapse of the French empire served to undermine the stature of French abroad. In reaction to this, in 1966 the Haut Comité de la Langue Français was established for the promotion of French abroad and its protection at home. In addition, the government spent large sums subsidizing French in the former colonies, especially in Africa, encouraging *francophone* literature abroad, and signing agreements with *francophone* countries. One ambitious project was a five-year plan focusing on cooperation between France and Quebec on matters of language, education, and culture, although this was interpreted by some as an attempt by De Gaulle to attack Anglo-Saxon hegemony.

In 1964 René Etiemble published the first in a series of books pointing to the increasing inclusion of Anglo-American terms and pronuncia-
tions in French and labeling the phenomenon *franglais* (Ager 1999:
98–100). While others had pointed to the incursion of foreign words
before, Etiemble's work appeared shortly after the independence of a
number of French colonies, when the status of French internationally
was in question. As a result, his findings struck a particularly sensitive
chord: the need to protect and preserve the French language and culture.

In 1972 the Haut Comité set up "terminology commissions" in each
Ministry attempting to ensure relevant technical terminology was of
French origin. A series of ministerial decrees between 1973 and 1983
addressed the replacement of English words with French in vocabulary.
And in 1975 the Bas-Lauriol law was passed, requiring the use of French
in commerce, advertising, and other business transactions, imposing
fines for violations. However, these efforts were undermined by inadequate funding, a lack of agreement on an "authorized" French, and the
absence of provisions to reinforce French in scientific and educational
gatherings (Safran 1999: 49).

In 1994 the minister of culture and *francophonie*, Jacques Toubon, prepared new legislation to reiterate and extend the Bas-Lauriol law, and
both the necessity for his proposals and the motivations behind it were
hotly debated. While the law increased the fines for violating its provisions from those of the earlier law, it was also restricted to ensure free
speech. Furthermore, the continued lack of agreement on standard
French undermined the application of the law, both practically and in
the eyes of the Constitutional Council. It is questionable whether such
laws can ever be as broadly effective as their supporters hope (Ager
1999: 114–115).

What is clear is that there is a growing sense that French language and
culture are under attack, externally with regards to its international
status and internally through the incorporation of Anglo-American
phrases. Interestingly, this turn toward protecting French may partially
explain increased support for local languages in two ways. First, the
effort to protect the language from outside threats serves to open a functional space for local languages domestically. Second, by promoting cultural pluralism at home, the government can then argue for the
relevance of French abroad as an international example of cultural pluralism.

Conclusion

This chapter has focused on the impact of language policy on national
minorities in France, excluding an evaluation of the implications for

immigrant groups. This emphasis is intentional for a number of reasons. First, the 1992 Charter for Regional or Minority Languages, the consideration of which prompted the Péry and Poignant reports, itself expressly excludes from its purview the consideration of policies toward both dialects and immigrant languages; thus while shifts in French conceptualizations of the legitimacy of non-French identities may indeed impact immigrant groups (and inform policies directed at them), such effects would be ancillary to the more direct issue of national minority languages.

The focus of the Charter, perhaps unintentionally, raises the deeper issue of the differences between national minorities and immigrants vis-à-vis the state and, therefore, the focus of this chapter. Will Kymlicka (1995), among others, notes that although both types of groups are defined in terms of their distinctiveness from the dominant identity, the two types make very different claims (and therefore present very different threats) to the state. Immigrant groups tend to make claims seeking increased access to state and society as they seek to integrate (if not assimilate) into the host polity. National minorities, however, represent in real terms potential nation-states themselves. They are most readily defined in terms of a distinct language, even when that language has effectively died (Horowitz 1985). They, almost by definition, tend to associate themselves historically with a particular territory. And they frequently adopt the language of unjust coercive absorption by the state and a need to "right historic wrongs" or even, in the case of the Quebeçois, to "reconquer the conquest." Thus national minorities, rather than immigrant groups, tend to be the basis for autonomist movements and secessionists, with the Irish, Scots, Basques, Bretons, Catalans, Flemish, and Corsicans as only some of the examples evidenced in Western Europe. And, as a result, ethnopolitical mobilization by such groups threatens the integrity of existing states in ways that political activism by immigrant groups does not.

Within France there is evidence for two competing conceptualizations of French society. The arguably hegemonic discourse since the Revolution has been that of homogeneity, associated during this period particularly with the Jacobins and republicanism. Clearly, however, there exists an alternative framing of France as a heterogeneous society with historical roots at least as deep as the homogeneity model, although admittedly this latter framing has been largely subordinate for most of the nineteenth and twentieth centuries. This chapter suggests that a surprising resurfacing, in official discourse, of this latter framing is underway in France. The significance of such a shift lies in the potential change to the conditions necessary for ethnopolitical mobilization: the recognized existence of cultural cleavages in society and the acceptance of the claim that such cleavages represent the legitimate basis for political mobilization.

In terms of the first condition, the Jacobins appear to have understood that the elimination of cultural cleavages necessarily removes them as a potential political issue. And indeed French policy, particularly in the Third Republic, was remarkably successful in reducing the salience of linguistic cleavages in France, as the society was within the span of a couple of generations transformed into an overwhelmingly homogeneous society. Possibly equally important to note, however, is that despite decades of relatively successful policies, by the 1970s both Mitterand and Denieul, among others, articulated the persistence of national minority identities as self-evident, having been maintained in the periphery by small groups of activists against French policy. Why ethnic identity has such a strong appeal for some is beyond the scope of this chapter, but it appears to be the case that the homogenization of French society reached its peak sometime in the first half of the twentieth century (as measured by the number of speakers of minority languages or support for national minority political parties) and has begun a slow decline.

However, the mere existence of cultural pluralism does not render inevitable ethnopolitical mobilization; rather, some articulation of the legitimate association of political institutions with social cleavages is required. Clearly not all cleavages represent widely accepted bases for political contestation. Yet the political principle of nationalism, which associates nations with political institutions, likely increases the probability that cultural cleavages will be understood, at least by nondominant groups, as legitimate sources for the articulation of political grievances.

In this light, the Jacobin formulation appears to have been something of a gamble: the legitimacy of the French state rests significantly on its representation of the French people, defined at least partially in linguistic terms (Cartrite 2003). To the extent that the French state includes non-French people, the legitimacy of its rule over them may be called into doubt (as the articulation of "internal colonialism" expressly does). But the impact of the potential success of framing France as a culturally plural society is less clear.

One consequence could reasonably be that this alternative formula decouples the legitimacy of the French state from the French nation, allowing the legitimacy of that state to derive from alternative sources such as democracy. At a minimum this shift would undermine the potential for catastrophe articulated by Chevènement and others. As a result, French national identity might move in the direction of Spanish, Italian, Canadian, or even British identity, in which national minorities may feel themselves, reasonably and legitimately, to be members both of their ethnic community and of the national identity at the same time, even if the national identity itself is closely associated with a dominant ethnic group.

Alternatively, this reframing of the legitimacy of national minority identity may represent a normative opening in French society for the advancing of claims for the protection of cultural distinctiveness that may serve to enhance these as yet generally disregarded social cleavages. As Kymlicka notes, "Sustaining a societal culture in the modern world is not a matter of holding ethnic festivals, or having a few classes taught in one's mother tongue as a child. It is a matter of creating and sustaining a set of public institutions that will enable a minority group to participate in the modern world in its own language" (Kymlicka 1998: 34). While the ability of national minorities in France to persist in precisely such conditions suggests that what may ultimately be required for the survival of a national identity is merely the devotion of a small number of activists, Kymlicka highlights what often becomes among the most basic political demands for such groups: policies and institutions designed to protect, and even extend, the minority identity. The acknowledgment of the legitimacy of national minority identity in France, represented in recent official rhetoric, may make legitimate state opposition to policies protecting those identities less tenable, increasing the likelihood that the first necessary condition for ethnopolitical mobilization will continue to be satisfied.

Interestingly, efforts at decentralization may have a related, if unintended, effect on ethnopolitical mobilization in France. Proposals to reform the unitary French state, some of which have been implemented, echo the broad language of federalism and the principle of subsidiarity at work in the European Union: democratic and functional efficacy are best realized when competencies rest at the lowest functional level for them to be effective. While some functions are best addressed at the level of the state, others may require aggregation up to the level of the European Union or disaggregation down to some relevant substate level. With the partial exception of proposals for Corsican institutions, the decentralization debate in France has been conducted largely in these terms.

However, national minorities often seek to have subnational institutional boundaries approximate the cultural boundaries and to use those bodies both to implement additional policies aimed at revitalizing the identity and to differentiate the region from the larger polity (Miodownik and Cartrite 2006). Thus Breton nationalists successfully led efforts within the Breton regional assembly to unanimously request in 2004 a referendum that the department of Loire Atlantique (part of the Pays de la Loire region), with the historic Breton capital of Nantes, be appended to the current Breton region (consisting of the four departments of Finistère, Ille-et-Vilaine, Morbihan, and Côtes d'Armor). The Alsatian parties Alsace d'Abord and Pour L'Alsace, representing the right and left extremes of the political spectrum respectively, currently call for the merging of the two Alsatian departments into a single entity. And both Basque and Catalan parties in France seek to have departments corresponding to their ethnic boundaries created out of existing departments. In addition, the argument that some policies are best addressed at a subnational level raises the possibility for asymmetric federalism, in which some regions are granted particular competencies not extended elsewhere, as is currently the case in the United Kingdom, Belgium, Canada, and Spain. National minorities frequently claim that their ethnic distinctiveness itself necessitates competencies beyond those granted to other regions, a principle enshrined in the Spanish Constitution of 1977.

Thus the shift in how the French understand the relationship between French and national minority identity, while an arguably necessary revision to the long-dominant Jacobin homogeneous formulation, may open the way to potentially significant institutional and social change whose endpoint is unclear. Indeed, it may be the case that as the French narrative evolves, it necessarily generates pressures for devolution and even autonomy, but such processes may themselves undermine more extreme calls for secession by some nationalists by shifting the bases for the legitimacy of the French state away from the protection of the French nation (narrowly conceived) and toward arguments of democratic legitimacy. This may also shift the debate surrounding immigrant minority rights in a similar direction, although that linkage appears more tenuous. What is clear is that while the two framings of French identity both enjoy long historical pedigrees, the shift from Jacobin homogeneity to cultural pluralism is likely to have an array of significant impacts on French society and the Republic itself.

The issue of the recognition of national minority languages and rights continues to be highly contested in French politics, although in some respects it has been overshadowed, in particular, by ongoing debates surrounding the integration of Muslim immigrants into French society. This chapter has argued that since the French Revolution there have been two alternating poles in the state's treatment of national minorities. Rather than thinking of the recent overtures to minority rights as a novel reframing of French identity, this relatively recent shift is better understood as the resurgence of the narrative of France as a culturally plural society. What does appear novel is the seeming association of decentralization and minority rights with democratic values, a linkage long monopolized by Jacobin visions of French identity and society.

While the significance of a renewed contestation of French identity should not be understated, nor should an assessment of Jacobinism as being on the wane, it appears that the two framings of French identity, and the policies they imply, are increasingly contested.

Notes

1. For a comparable argument regarding the emergence of Catholic political activism in Western Europe, see Kalyvas (1996: 8).

2. "The regional languages are a richness of our cultural heritage." All translations are by the author.

3. By the date of the letter, eighteen countries had signed the Charter (opening for signatures was on 11 May 1992) and four had ratified the charter, with a fifth ratification (which would put the Charter into force) expected later that fall.

4. The translations here are my own.

5. As a country with the highest European rates immigration since 1800, France has applied this same standard to immigrants demanding that they, and their children, become monolingual French speakers and adopt French cultural practices and norms in their daily lives (Horowitz 1992).

6. "National minorities" is a term developed under the League of Nations that continues to be used in the European context. Although it is not clearly defined, the term refers to groups understood to be culturally (in practice linguistically) distinct from the dominant identity that also claim some historical association with territory in the state; in the American context such groups would be classified as "indigenous minorities."

7. It must be noted, however, that this was not an attempt to reformulate the "nation" along ethnic lines. Indeed, the overtly functional arguments of the Jacobins stand in stark contrast to contemporary thinkers such as Herder and the Göttingen historians, along with early philologists and following in the tradition of Herodotus, who argued that language was the quintessential demarcation of a nation across time and space. For an extended discussion of Herodotus and the tradition of ethnic citizenship, see Geary (2002: 22–46).

8. Interestingly, the sum of Grégoire's figures varies widely from the twenty-five million that a 1793 census had determined to be the population of France, the results of which he certainly would have been aware.

9. Interestingly, this technique was adopted from the Jesuits, who had used it to enforce Latin against French (Weber 1976: 313).

10. The issue of voluntary association versus compulsory membership in the nation lies at the core of Rousseau's conceptualization of the social contract and is obscured by Renan. Both strands, while in tension, are reasonably associated within Jacobinism.

11. During the occupation some Alsatian activists apparently hoped for a special status within the Reich, but the region was institutionally assimilated, quashing such aspirations and significantly weakening Alsatian support for the German occupation.

12. Corsican was added as a language in 1974. The law now permits teaching in Gallo, Alsatian and Lorraine, Tahitian, and four Melanesian languages in addition to the five languages earlier stipulated (Oakes 2001: 116). The law also

stipulates a variety of Occitan dialects for instruction, rather than singling out any one of them as representative of the region.

13. Traditionally national minority movements were linked with conservative elements dating back to the Revolution.

14. The French government, under Prime Minister Jean-Pierre Raffarin in an announcement on 6 September 2002 in Alsace, has proposed amending seven articles of the French Constitution to refer to decentralization ("Decentralization" 2002), allowing subnational jurisdictions to "experiment" with transfers of competence for a period of five years ("Raffarin Defends" 2002). While not targeted directly at national minorities, this proposal represents both a continued shift away from Jacobin unitarism and a potential opening of new opportunity structures for the organized ethnic communities to exploit.

Bibliography

Ager, Dennis. 1999. *Identity, Insecurity, and Image: France and Language.* Philadelphia: Multilingual Matters Ltd.

Beer, William R. 1980. *The Unexpected Rebellion: Ethnic Activism in Contemporary France.* New York: New York University Press.

Bell, David A. 1995. "Lingua Populi, Lingua Dei: Language, Religion, and the Origins of French Revolutionary Nationalism." *American Historical Review* 100, no. 5: 1403–1437.

Bredin, Jean-Denis. 1983. *The Affair: The Case of Alfred Dreyfus,* trans. Jeffrey Mehlman. New York: George Braziller.

Cartrite, Britt. 2003. "Reclaiming Their Shadow: Ethnopolitical Mobilization in Consolidated Democracies." Ph.D. diss., University of Colorado at Boulder.

"Decentralization: The Local Referendum in the Constitution." 2002. *Agence France Presse* (4 October).

Geary, Patrick J. 2002. *The Myth of Nations: The Medieval Origins of Europe.* Princeton: Princeton University Press.

Gellner, Ernest. 1983. *Nations and Nationalism.* Ithaca: Cornell University Press.

Grillo, R. D. 1989. *Dominant Languages: Language and Hierarchy in Britain and France.* New York: Cambridge University Press.

Hobsbawm, Eric. 1992. *Nations and Nationalism Since 1780.* 2nd ed. New York: Cambridge University Press.

Horowitz, Donald L. 1985. *Ethnic Groups in Conflict.* Los Angeles: University of California Press.

———. 1992. "Immigration and Group Relations in France and America." In *Immigrants in Two Democracies: French and American Experience,* ed. Donald L. Horowitz. New York: Columbia University Press, 3–35.

Jacob, James E., and David C. Gordon. 1985. "National Minority Policy in France." In *National Minority Policy and National Unity,* ed. William R. Beer and James E. Jacob. Totowa, N.J.: Rowman & Allanheld, 106–133.

Kalyvas, Stathis N. 1996. *The Rise of Christian Democracy in Europe.* Ithaca: Cornell University Press.

Kymlicka, Will. 1995. *Multicultural Citizenship: A Liberal Theory of Minority Rights.* New York: Oxford University Press.

———. 1998. *Finding Our Way: Rethinking Ethnocultural Relations in Canada.* Toronto: Oxford University Press.

Miodownik, D., and B. A. Cartrite. 2006. "Demarcating Political Space: Territoriality and the Ethnoregional Party Family." *Nationalism and Ethnic Politics* 12: 53–82.

Oakes, Leigh. 2001. *Language and National Identity: Comparing France and Sweden.* Philadelphia: John Benjamins.

Péry, Nicole. 1998. *Rapport d'Etape: Langues et Cultures Régionales.* Retrieved 19 November 2006, from http://www.ladocumentationfrancaise.fr/brp/notices/984000481.shtml.

Poignant, Bernard. 1998. *Langues et Cultures Régionales: Rapport de Monsieur Bernard Poignant, Maire de Quimper, à Monsieur Lionel Jospin, Premier Ministre.* Retrieved 19 November 2006, from http://www.ladocumentationfran caise.fr/brp/notices/984001448.shtml.

"Raffarin Defends to the Senate His Text on Decentralization." 2002. *Reuters* (29 October).

Reece, Jack E. 1977. *The Bretons Against France: Ethnic Minority Nationalism in Twentieth-Century Brittany.* Chapel Hill: University of North Carolina Press.

Renan, Ernest. 1996 [1882]. "What Is a Nation?" In *Nationalism in Europe, 1815 to the Present: A Reader,* ed. Stuart Woolf. New York: Routledge, 48–60.

Safran, William. 1989. "The French State and Ethnic Minority Cultures: Policy Dimensions and Problems." In *Ethnoterritorial Politics, Policy, and the Western World,* ed. Joseph R. Rudolph, Jr., and Robert J. Thompson. Boulder: Lynne Rienner Publishers, 115–157.

———. 1995. "The Dreyfus Affair, Political Consciousness, and the Jews: A Centennial Retrospective." *Contemporary French Civilization* 19, no. 1 (Winter–Spring): 1–32.

———. 1999a. "Nationalism." In *Handbook of Language and Ethnic Identity,* ed. Joshua A. Fishman. New York: Oxford University Press, 77–93.

———. 1999b. "Politics and Language in Contemporary France: Facing Supranational and Infranational Challenges." *International Journal of the Sociology of Language* 137: 39–66.

Wardhaugh, Ronald. 1987. *Languages in Competition: Dominance, Diversity, and Decline.* New York: Basil Blackwell.

Weber, Eugen. 1976. *Peasants into Frenchmen: The Modernization of Rural France, 1870–1914.* Stanford: Stanford University Press.

Chapter 8
Symbols of Reconciliation or Instruments of Division?
A Critical Look at New Monuments in South Africa
Sabine Marschall

In any new sociopolitical order, memory is called upon to (re)shape identity and the symbolic landscape in the light of new priorities. Institutionalized and officially endorsed in public commemorative monuments, memory is invariably political and tied to the value systems of an imagined community. In the current post-apartheid South African context, commemorative monuments can make previously silenced voices heard; they can be empowering by affirming the identity and restoring the dignity of marginalized groups; they can be important instruments of healing and reconciliation; and they can facilitate an inclusive process of nation-building (Marschall 2003, 2004). But monuments can also be highly problematic and contested structures, as this chapter shows. In principle, contestation is not negative. The fact that new commemorative projects almost always stir debate and are levied with objections or outright criticism by disapproving groups or individuals, can be interpreted as a positive sign of an active civil society and a participatory democratic order (Gillis 1994). One might even argue that there is not enough contestation and public debate about monuments and the ways in which they authorize specific versions of the past in the emergent democratic society of present-day South Africa.[1]

While controversial debate over the meaning of the past may be constructive, involving fruitful processes of negotiation and emergence of new identity discourses, it may also be counterproductive or even destructive. It is precisely because monuments affirm group identity that they can be contentious and divisive, serving as symbols of unity for one group pitched against another. Monuments can potentially threaten the project of nation-building by enforcing partisan identities; they can be contested by members of the very "community" they are meant to represent; they can lead to the disempowerment of some people in the process of empowering others; they can encourage the obliteration of memories that are not aligned with official discourses of public memory; and they can perpetuate and reinforce questionable racial, ethnic, and gender stereotypes (Ashplant et al. 2004; Connerton 1989; Hall 1999–2000; Levinson 1998).

Moving from national to provincial and then local community level, this chapter discusses some of these negative side effects by focusing on three case studies of new monument initiatives in the province of Kwa-Zulu-Natal (KZN). Throughout South Africa, the current enthusiasm for building new monuments and erecting bronze statues is prompted in large part by the need for "redress," that is, the desire to "correct" the biased symbolic landscape inherited from the colonial and apartheid eras. This is amplified by the national government's strategic decision to refrain from wholesale destruction of apartheid-era heritage and complement rather then replace monuments that whites, and especially Afrikaners, believed expressed their historical narrative and their political and economic domination.

In a larger context, the post-apartheid commemorative project is fueled by four major forces, namely the government, acting on behalf of "the people" and intent on implementing specific sociopolitical agendas; the heritage conservation and management sector, now concerned about the preservation of previously neglected heritage; the growing tourism industry with its commercial interests and promises of economic development and employment creation; and the general public or civil society, ostensibly represented through the government, but in reality fragmented and often at odds with national identity discourses. In principle, these four forces are closely interlinked and often form a complex mutually beneficial alliance with shared goals and interests. For instance, the state may want to promote specific heroes and key events in the emergence of the post-apartheid order; the heritage sector identifies sites, often fragile, associated with such leaders and events and protects them from neglect or erasure through development; the emergent cultural and heritage tourism sector, constantly in need of new attractions, exploits such sites and their inspiring narratives for local destination branding and tourism development efforts; and local communities are proud to see their heroes celebrated or glad to have their suffering officially acknowledged while potentially simultaneously benefiting in material terms (Marschall 2005).

However, in practice new monument projects can become contested precisely because stakeholders affiliated with each of these sectors may be pitched against one another. The Robben Island World Heritage Site (a former maximum security prison, where many political prisoners, including Nelson Mandela, were held), for instance, represents a great success for those affiliated with tourism interests, exceeding their highest expectations, but for the conservation sector (represented primarily by the Robben Island Museum), the insatiable tourist interest and the tourism sector's development agenda constitute a serious threat to the authenticity of the site. For the African National Congress (ANC)-led national government, Robben Island is an important symbol, whose meaning has been shaped in accordance with the experience of former political prisoners affiliated with the ANC. But opposition political forces and other groupings in society criticize the visitor representation of the island and the official interpretation of its symbolic significance for its neglect and outright omission of alternative memories and narratives (Coombes 2003; Deacon 1998, 2004; Kruger 2000).

In many other post-apartheid heritage initiatives throughout the country competitive claims are staked to the public memory of key events of the past, especially associated with the struggle for liberation. Several scholars have pointed out with respect to different sites, how the ANC as the ruling party is often well positioned to fashion a narrative in which the local community story coincides with the party's own interpretation of the event and how the ANC-led government appropriates private and community memories for the sake of a national identity agenda that largely overlaps with party-political principles (Baines 2007; Coombes 2003; Hansen 2003).

This context of ANC dominance in the general project of reshaping South Africa's symbolic landscape is important to understand and partly explains the vigorous drive of specific communities and political opposition forces to represent their own narratives, as will become evident in this chapter. KZN is racially and ethnically one of the most diverse provinces in the country and in addition there are significant ethnically based ideological agendas and group-specific claims for recognition that often overlay, and sometimes contradict, the national agenda of reconciliation and nation-building. If KZN is hence a region with a narrative and a set of heroes somewhat at odds with those in other parts of the country, upon closer examination it becomes evident that similar local versus national tensions exist in most parts of South Africa. It is partly as a concession to regionally based opposition forces and their specific agendas of identity formation that the post-apartheid government resolved to decentralize the country's heritage management, relegating control to the provinces and even local level (Graham et al. 2000; Hall 2005, 2006; Hart and Winter 2001).

After the 1994 elections, the Western Cape and KZN were the only provinces where the ANC did not obtain a majority and it is here that heritage is arguably most contested and politicized. In the Western Cape, where the New National Party retained control of the government until 2000, virtually no new commemorative initiatives were seriously pursued until power in the region shifted. KZN, ruled until recently by the Inkatha Freedom Party (IFP), on the contrary, experienced a flurry of activity in the field of public memorialization. The roots of the IFP can be found in a Zulu cultural organization called Inkatha, founded by the Zulu King Solomon in the 1920s, based upon which Gatsha Mangos-uthu Buthelezi, formerly a member of the ANC Youth League, estab-lished the Inkatha National Cultural Liberation Movement in 1975. In 1990, this organization was formally turned into a political party, the IFP, with Buthelezi as president (IFP 2007). The IFP has always been domi-nated by Zulu speakers and its political agenda has historically tended to emphasize Zulu nationalist values. During the apartheid era and even beyond, the political landscape in some parts of South Africa, most nota-bly in KZN, was marked by intense competition and political violence between ANC and IFP supporters.[2] After a decade of IPF control, in 2004 the ANC won the provincial elections for the first time, a fact that is likely to have a tangible effect on the region's symbolic landscape in the future.

Memory and Identity

Memory theorists distinguish between different categories of memory, including mimetic memory, communicative memory, or cultural mem-ory, the latter being the subject of Jan Assmann's (2002) influential book of the same title. Cultural memory refers to a sense of meaning within a culture and it incorporates all other types of memory. It refers to the cultural sphere which connects tradition, historical conscious-ness, and self-definition (2002: 24). In contrast to communicative mem-ory, a concept developed by Maurice Halbwachs, which is shared informally, cultural memory requires careful induction. It is always dependent on media and politics and can be concretized only artificially through institutions, such as museums, archives, and monuments.

Assmann explains that the function of cultural memory in relation to social communication parallels that of individual memory in relation to consciousness. For Assmann, the primary organizational forms of cul-tural memory are rituals and festivals whose repetitive character serves the dissemination and transfer of specific knowledge and the reproduc-tion of cultural identity. As repetition is a basic principle of every con-nective structure, ritual ensures the coherence of the group in place and time (2002: 24; A. Assmann 2003: 15). Apart from repetition, representation and visualization constitute important aspects of ritual. Monuments provide the *locus* of private and official acts of ritual. By offering a ready-made stage, they invite, even call for, the more or less elaborate *mise-en-scène* of public commemorative action. They also often textually and/or visually represent the past and encourage the visitor to visualize past events. Monuments represent, control, and authorize preselected memories; they aim to create a specific historical consciousness and identity. Monuments can become contested and divisive because they are often so narrow in focus—representing selected memories, or what Nora (1989) calls "history" as opposed to "memory"—and so authoritative, foregrounding and officially endorsing one version of the past over other plausible alternatives. In this way, any particular symbolic landscape emphasizes and privileges certain narratives (and associated heroes) over others.

Nora's insistence that we need *lieux de mémoire*, sites of memory, because there are no longer real environments of memory (*milieux de mémoire*) has been criticized or rather qualified, especially with respect to its application to the non-European context (for example, Ben-Amos and Weissberg 1999; Lambek and Antze 1996). However, many of Nora's observations are very relevant in present-day South Africa, where migration, fragmentation of traditional family units and destruction of community cohesion as a result of political and socioeconomic pressures, as well as more recent social changes induced by the HIV/AIDS pandemic, have impacted negatively on the oral tradition. It is frequently lamented how little South Africa's youngsters know about important persons and events even in the recent past and monuments are called upon to fill the gap.

I want to clarify that the term "monument" in the context of this chapter refers exclusively to intentionally constructed, commemorative monuments, not to landmark buildings or features of nature declared a national monument. Much has been written about potential ways of distinguishing between monument and memorial (for example, Danto 1987; Rowlands 1999; Dubow 2004), but clear distinctions are agreed upon neither in South Africa nor internationally. Hence, in this chapter, the terms monument and memorial are used in accordance with the official designations of the respective sites and otherwise largely interchangeably, as is common practice in ordinary South African language usage and in the media. It is noteworthy though that some individuals (scholars, heritage officials, artists, architects, and so forth) hold strong and often divergent views about the distinction between the two terms, a fact which invariably influences their reading of the current post-apartheid commemorative effort.[3]

National Legacy Projects in KZN

It is no coincidence that the South African government, especially at the national level, tends to endorse resistance narratives as the basis of a new cultural memory and foundation myth for a nonracial, democratic society. Being well aware of the potential divisiveness of heritage, the focus on anticolonial and anti-apartheid resistance was chosen precisely because individuals of all racial and ethnic groups have a share in this historical experience. In 1996 the Department of Arts, Culture, Science and Technology (DACST) developed the National Legacy Project consisting of nine state-funded heritage ventures (mostly monuments and museums) located throughout the country which commemorate acts of resistance and historical events and persons perceived as building blocks in the emergence of the post-apartheid order. It was meant to "counter" the country's skewed landscape of memory by representing previously marginalized groups and narratives now deemed of national significance, thereby becoming focal points of a newly defined national identity in the making.

Two components of the Legacy Project were established in KZN. The first one is the Ncome monument and museum near Dundee, built in 1998 opposite the Afrikaner nationalist monument of Blood River to commemorate the fallen Zulu warriors of the famous battle of Blood River (1838). The Ncome project, perhaps more than any other monument initiative in South Africa, was meant to be about reconciliation—in the narrow sense between the two warring parties of the past, Zulus and Voortrekkers, and in a broader sense about black and white in the present. The date of the battle, 16 December, is now celebrated as a public holiday called Day of Reconciliation; at the unveiling of the new monument, reconciliatory tones prevailed in official speeches and some important symbolic gestures of reconciliation were made (Ross 1998; Khumalo 1998; Bishop 1998).[4]

However, the unveiling ceremony was marred by interference from Afrikaner right-wingers, who displayed their strong resistance to the idea of reconciliation (Milazi 1998). There are still occasional racial incidents involving black visitors at Blood River, especially on 16 December (for example, "Racist Remarks Spark Strong Response" 2004). Most dramatically, the planned pedestrian bridge, originally intended as a symbol of reconciliation linking both monuments, has never been built and there is strong opposition to its construction among members of the Afrikaner community. As Jabu Maphalala, one of the members of the Ncome monument committee aptly put it, "the bridge must start in the mind" (personal conversation 2005).

Both Dlamini (2001) and Girshick (2004) have closely analyzed the

Figure 8.1. Ncome. The heritage site constructed a short distance from the Afrikaner memorial at Blood River.

Ncome monument and museum in the context of the Legacy Project and the coalition politics of the time, notably the tension between the ANC and its national agenda of reconciliation and nationbuilding versus the IFP and its partisan Zulu nationalist aims. But the Ncome project has an important prehistory, which may explain why it became such a bold statement of Zulu resistance. In 1994, the state-funded Voortrekker Museum in Pietermaritzburg, then in charge of the administration and development of the Blood River battlefield, embarked on ambitious plans for upgrading the site by adding a museum with various visitor amenities. An application with plans for the proposed development was considered by the KZN Regional Office of the National Monuments Council (NMC) toward the end of 1994, but rejected both for aesthetic reasons and because it was felt that such an initiative would warrant consultation with the KwaZulu Monuments Council (KMC) and the constituencies it represented (letter, Hall to Director of Museum, 15 December 1994). The KMC administered heritage conservation in the former "homeland" of KwaZulu, to which the eastern bank of the river and the historical battlefield belonged, although an amalgamation of the two conservation management bodies was anticipated.

In March 1995, the architect was informed of the approval of the proposed development on condition that a broad process of consultation with various cultural formations and communities be instituted and that "some sort of Zulu focus" be added, most likely a statue, but ultimately to be decided upon through the consultation process (letter, Hall to Meiring, 16 March 1995). NMC Regional Manager, Andrew Hall, wrote to his counterpart at the KMC, Barry Marshall, that the boundaries of the officially protected battlefield should be extended across the river and emphasized the desirability of a future reinterpretation of the entire site, which would in effect give previously marginalized communities a chance to have a say in the creation of the museum exhibition (letter, Hall to Marshall, 21 September 1995). By September 1995 it emerged that the Blood River management was planning to erect a large *indlu* (round thatched hut) for craft sales or exhibition purposes on either side of the existing 1938 ox-wagon monument (made by Coert Steynberg), but was not prepared to spend enough money to produce a significant icon in representation of the Zulu perspective. The museum building was by now almost completed and two bronze plaques, one in Afrikaans and one in isiZulu, were affixed on either side of the entrance (unveiled in November 1995), speaking of reconciliation between Zulu and Afrikaner. Yet the museum exhibition and most notably the video shown in the auditorium presented the battle exclusively from an Afrikaner nationalist perspective (the video was changed after 2002), and by the end of 1998, the NMC had still not declared the eastern side of the battlefield a national monument.

This procrastination, indeed unwillingness, in effecting significant changes to the Blood River site must have played a role in the national government's later decision to include Ncome into the National Legacy Project.[5] For conservative Afrikaner nationalists, Blood River is hallowed ground, a sacred place, closely linked to their sense of identity and the foundation myth of the Afrikaner "nation." Friedland and Hecht (2005) show how sacred places can become powerful symbolic focal points in the building of nation and it appears that virtually all new nations "need" such places. If none presents itself naturally, a site can also be made into or constructed as a sacred place. For the post-apartheid nation, this process is currently underway with respect to Salvokop Hill outside Pretoria, the site of the new Freedom Park, South Africa's heroes' acre and foremost national monument in the making. The battlefield of Blood River traditionally fulfilled this function for Afrikaner nationalists and they clearly would consider any significant change on this site as a direct attack on their heritage and identity.

Hence the construction of a separate Zulu monument on the other side of the river was a victory for conservative Afrikaner nationalists, as they "got away" with making virtually no changes to "their" site. As Dlamini (2001) has shown, it was also a victory for Zulu nationalists, as it allowed them to make a significant statement fostering partisan Zulu ethnic agendas, furthermore at the expense of the national government.[6] From the perspective of the ANC, the Ncome project can also be viewed as a victory, because—being part of the Legacy Project—it allowed the national government to retain ultimate control over this contentious site and preempted the IFP-led provincial government from devising its own commemorative venture, as occurred at other sites in the province. Furthermore, many visitors are indeed likely to interpret the new monument as a symbol of reconciliation. But many visitors are also likely to recognize the symbolic intervention at this battle site as an apartheid-style solution, because the two monuments, supposedly repre- senting two "communities," now face each other like hostile camps divided by a river without a bridge. The Ncome monument is a classic example of the post-apartheid add-on (or extend-rather-than-revise) approach to redressing the imbalance of the apartheid-era symbolic landscape—a strategy that has been criticized as falling short of real transformation (Rassool, Witz, and Minkley 2000; Rassool 2001). It invariably perpetuates and solidifies—rather than challenges—notions of "community" and sometimes stereotyped identity patterns established in the past and bolstered by apartheid ideology.

Girshick (2004) argues that Ncome is more about celebrating resistance than symbolizing reconciliation and raises the question whether reconciliation and redress are indeed always compatible goals. What needs to be considered here is that reconciliation may mean different things to different people. This point has been forcefully made by Cox (2003: 160) in the context of the Confederate memorial at Arlington Cemetery across the Potomac River from Washington, D.C. According to her, not everyone agrees that this monument is a symbol of reconciliation, but it does so from the perspective of white Southerners, who have long railed against the "biased" interpretations of the war by Northern historians. One might say that at Ncome a bold statement of resistance, a radical Zulu nationalist perspective, might be necessary in order to achieve a balanced representation of the past, and an effective counterpoint to the conventional Afrikaner version of the battle.

However, reconciliation is also always a work in progress and to what extent monuments or other symbolic gestures contribute to its success is difficult to measure. The initial exhibition inside the Ncome museum was soon changed, not least perhaps as a result of turbulent internal politics within the DACST.[7] Much of the originally displayed ethnographic material has been removed and the focus is now on the representation of the battle and the historical circumstances that surrounded the conflict. This notwithstanding, the exhibition still clearly represents the battle from a Zulu (some might argue Zulu nationalist) perspective with some displays making direct reference to those in the Blood River museum, alerting the visitor to contradictions, discursively interrogating some of the key contentions and discrediting some of the "evidence" on which the Afrikaner narrative is based.[8] On the other side of the river, the biased video shown in the Blood River museum has been replaced and the exhibition has evolved over time, now acknowledging the existence of other perspectives on the battle and its historical context. In their predominantly one-sided, nationalist orientation, both museums nevertheless remain mirror images of each other.

Irrespective of their intended meaning, not all visitors will interpret the museum displays, the architectural and sculptural shapes, the iconographic and symbolic references in exactly the same way. The architectural shape of the Ncome monument, for instance, was meant to symbolize the hornlike Zulu battle formation, but it could also be read more abstractly as an embracing shape reaching out in an inclusive gesture of reconciliation. Much depends furthermore on the narrative and attitude of the guide; differences between the accounts that those at the museum provide and those that visitors bring themselves; and the predispositions that different visitors hold before they arrive at a site can significantly affect the lessons people take away from their visitor experience.

Heritage as Political Battleground in KZN

While the Ncome initiative was begun very swiftly, the second national Legacy Project located in KZN experienced a number of delays and was the subject of much political and bureaucratic wrangling (Dlamini 2001). This project in honor of Albert Luthuli (1899–1967), former ANC president and Nobel Peace Prize laureate (1960), includes the restoration of his house in Groutville north of Durban, an adjacent museum and a life-size public bronze statue in kwaDukuza (formerly Stanger). The town of kwaDukuza is named after King Shaka Zulu's royal kraal, which was located in the vicinity of the modern town at the beginning of the nineteenth century. The town's most prominent heritage object has long been the Shaka memorial (erected in the 1930s), which some believe to mark the famous king's burial place.

In the statue, Luthuli is presented in a three-piece western suit with hat in hand. It now forms a distinct counterpoint to the Shaka memorial and opens up alternative models of identification for people of Zulu descent. Luthuli was an elected tribal chief, but also a learned urban man, a Christian, and a modern politician whose beliefs in detribalization, formal education, and western paradigms contrast with narrow discourses of traditionalist ethnic identity (as symbolically represented by the Shaka icon). While Ncome was one of the first Legacy Projects to be implemented, Luthuli was one of the last. One might speculate that the Ncome monument, with its focus on the precolonial Zulu "nation" and its proud militaristic tradition, was highly welcome in a province governed by the IFP, while the Luthuli project—indisputably associated with the ANC—received less pressing attention in the prevailing political climate. It was perhaps no coincidence that the Luthuli statue was eventually unveiled and the museum opened in the same year (2004) when the ANC won the elections in KZN.

Stereotypes

The last ten years have seen a strong trend—both politically and economically motivated—to equate KZN with Zululand or the "Zulu Kingdom," as the province is glamorously marketed by Tourism KZN nationally and internationally. As the home of the historical Zulu kingdom and the site of many historic battles between the Zulu people and various parties of white opponents (Voortrekkers and British forces) many monuments, memorials, and statues in KZN invariably refer to Zulu heritage. Following the national initiative at Ncome, the provincial heritage agency, Amafa akwaZulu-Natali (Amafa), promoted the erection of Zulu memorials on other battlefields in KZN, notably Isandlwana, where the British suffered an unexpected defeat in 1879, and the nearby site of Rorke's Drift.[9]

Amafa's flagship project is the new Spirit of eMakhosini monument near Ulundi, unveiled on 3 May 2003 by Prince Gideon Zulu and King Goodwill Zwelithini—members of the royal Zulu house—alongside Chief Buthelezi, long-term leader of the IFP, and himself affiliated with the royal clan. Called kwaNkomba (*nkomba* means "to show"), the impressive sculptured monument overlooks the scenic Makhosini valley, the "cradle" of the Zulu nation, where many of the early kings were buried. Surrounded by giant aluminum casts of different animal horns, the centerpiece of the monument is a realistically rendered traditional Zulu beer pot or *ukhamba,* cast in bronze. According to van Vuuren (personal e-mail communication 2006), the icon of the pot was chosen because it is an object found in all households—from kings to commoners, from Africa to Europe—but in this specific context, a more ethnic and gender exclusive reading arguably presents itself, as the object is strongly associated with both ancestor worship and traditional practices of male bonding.

A series of small bronze relief plaques encircling the base projects the viewer into an imaginary past with scenes from traditional Zulu life. They are replete with well-known stereotypical icons: the Zulu warrior, the bare-breasted maiden, the submissive married woman preparing food or serving her husband.[10] At the base of the pot is a head ring or *inkatha* (after which the IFP takes its name), the ring traditionally employed to carry heavy loads on the head. According to the official

Figure 8.2. The Spirit of eMakhosini monument near Ulundi.

onsite guide, it symbolizes "the coming together of all races"—an interpretation which inscribes the monument with a reconciliatory, inclusive meaning somewhat in contradiction to its exclusive ethnic and gender iconography and symbolism.

Hewison (1987) provocatively suggests that heritage can not only lead to the manufacture of a suitable past but also become a veritable industry. The Spirit of eMakhosini monument is part of the eMakhosini Ophathe Heritage Park, which is meant to become one of the country's major heritage tourism attractions. Its meaning cannot be fully understood without considering its positioning within the framework of two closely allied contexts: the flourishing heritage field with its emphasis on reordering the past guided by a particular politics of memory, and the budding tourism sector, thriving on stereotypes and characterized by complex interactions between consumption, leisure, economic empowerment, and memory. Perhaps not surprisingly, the officially endorsed representation of the past in public commemorative monuments and heritage sites shows striking parallels with the rearrangement and reauthorization of the past as exhibited in South African history museums. Soudien (Chapter 9 of this volume) distinguishes a number of different approaches currently dominating the field of museum exhibitions, one of which he calls the Nostalgia Style. Driven by discourses of nostalgia, this usually narrow, ethnic-based exhibition style provides an unsullied, innocent representation of the past. Strongly supported by

Figure 8.3. Bronze relief from the eMakhosini monument.

the tourism industry, it promotes tropes of timeless beauty and offers "authentic" representations of what life was like in the past, suggesting that remnants can still be found in modern descendants. The same pattern can be observed in cultural villages, as observed by Witz, Rassool, and Minkley (2001).

The Spirit of eMahkosini monument clearly falls into this category. Exploiting the aura and mystique associated with royal graves, the monument conjures up a sense of grandeur about these early Zulu kings and their noble subjects, and while this serves as a springboard for the appreciative perception of the Zulu "nation" today, it potentially triggers further interest in Zulu heritage sites and cultural tourism "products." The commemoration of a glorious past, about which historical details are blurred but sketchily surviving in the oral tradition and local myths, easily captures the imagination of foreign tourists. It can also be a source of pride and inspiration for locals, for whom such validation of their cultural heritage and traditional value systems is implicitly championed as a backbone for moral regeneration. Jan Assmann (1999: 29) calls this familiar pattern, found in many societies in the world, *Mythomotorik*—a type of remembrance focused on an unrecoverable past, which becomes glorified as a heroic or golden age to serve as a counterimage to the negativity of the present. Such remembrance provides the energy, and functions as a motor for the creation of a new and better order. The vigorous embrace of highly stereotyped images of King Shaka and the Zulu people, images often based on colonial invention and reinforced by apartheid ideologues, also reflects an escape from the uncertainties and instability associated with post-apartheid identity discourses.[11]

The Indian Monument

The notion of KZN as the "Zulu kingdom" is not only problematic because the historical Zulu kingdom covered but a portion of the modern province, but also because it negates the history, presence, and contribution of KZN's non-Zulu inhabitants. The province's diverse, multicultural mix of people includes the world's largest Indian community outside of India, most of which is concentrated in the Durban area. Having moved my discussion from national to provincial commemorative initiatives, I now want to focus at the local level with a monument proposal initiated by members of the Indian community in Durban that is intended to acknowledge the contribution made by South Africans of Indian descent, who arrived in the colony of Natal as indentured laborers beginning in the 1860s. The project dates back to the centenary celebrations of 1960, when the 1860 Indian Settlers Foundation (now called 1860 Heritage Foundation) was established with the aim to build a multifunctional monument, containing a museum, a theatre, and various activity rooms. Over the years the Foundation approached four subsequent city mayors to obtain a site, but to no avail (Gokool quoted in Govender 2004 and personal communication 2005). Only when the present (ANC-dominated) council came to office did the idea fall on fertile ground in principle, although nothing ever happened in practice toward its implementation.

When the initiative was reported in the press in 2000, it triggered some debate, notably within the Indian community itself (see, for example, Yoganathan 2000; Mhlanga 2000; "This is welcome recognition of Indians' contribution" 2000; Naidu 2000a; Naidu 2000b). Most outspoken among the critics was then University of Durban-Westville academic, Sanusha Naidu (2000a, 2000b), who accused the ANC of merely wanting to capture the "Indian vote." Naidu (2000a) argued that an "Indian monument" would perpetuate apartheid-era concepts of distinct racial communities and encourage people to think of themselves as being

Indian first and then South African, in ways that were at odds with the
ANC's commitment toward building a nonracial society. Like other critics, Naidu took issue with the post-apartheid concept of the Rainbow
Nation with its diverse array of cultures arguing that it tended to replicate the fixed, static, and clearly bounded racial and ethnic categories
established during the colonial era and entrenched by apartheid. The
notion of homogeneous communities and ethnic groups has long been
a focal point of academic critique, but it appears that the majority of
ordinary South Africans, including the political leadership, are still
strongly inclined to think in such categories. As Annie Coombes (2003:
4) recently pointed out, "the single most frequently used justification
for much government expenditure in the public heritage sector is a
much vaunted recourse to an ideal of 'community.'"

It is no coincidence that the fiercest critique of the Indian Monument
emerged from academic circles, whereas many newspaper articles suggest that the initiative enjoyed much popular support within the community. Generally speaking, South Africans of Indian descent tend to be
conservative people, whose sense of identity has been shaped during the
colonial and apartheid eras. They often foster a strong sense of community and awareness of difference, motivated by feeling defensive and
beleaguered in the face of persisting racism, from both whites and
blacks. The community is fragmented along ethnic, religious, class, and
language lines, but a monument of this nature could become a unifying
symbol and community focal point. It would be a public statement
acknowledging Indian contributions and it might constitute a lasting justification of the Indian presence in a climate increasingly marked by the
growth of African nationalism.

As the prominent Indian writer and community activist, Ashwin Desai
(personal conversation 2005), puts it, two basic strategies of survival
present themselves to a minority group such as the Indians in South
Africa: either "you keep your head down" and become invisible, or you
assert yourself and make yourself indispensable to the new order. The
Indian monument proposal is an initiative in pursuit of the latter strategy. It fits the pattern of what Harrison (1995: 261) calls "innovation
contests"—the invention or competitive elaboration of traditions and
symbols that represent a specific group and make it visible in the larger
societal spectrum. In the current South African climate characterized by
an escalation in the quantity and complexity of monuments and other
symbols every group is easily drawn into the competitive race for asserting its identity through heritage. In short, one almost needs a monument to remain visible in the expanding symbolic landscape.

If there is broad consensus on the need for generating a symbolic representation of group identity, the question still beckons what form this

representation should take. Gokool (personal communication 2005) envisages the Indian monument as a functional community building, but others might prefer a commemorative structure or statue prominently displaying some powerful symbol of unity. In innovation contests new symbols often resemble those of other groups, despite serving to differentiate one group from others. The reason is that the aim of inventing these symbolic representations is not only an assertion of group identity, but also a statement of equality with other groups, especially those acknowledged as dominant (Harrison 1995: 262). As Harrison puts it, "The newly-created symbol must therefore resemble the corresponding symbols of rival groups and belong to the same genre, as well as differ from them" (262). This is poignantly evident in S'bu Ndebele's (now Premier of KZN) public endorsement of the Indian monument initiative in 2000, when he prominently urged that a "lasting monument" should be erected in honor of the Indian community in Durban: "Just as we have a monument for the 1820 British settlers in Grahamstown, the Indian community, too should be *similarly* honoured" (Yoganathan 2000; my emphasis).

Need for Community Participation

The tendency of monuments to reflect and reinforce existing societal structures and notions of community and to perpetuate commonly held images and stereotypes is well-known and by no means unique to South Africa. But perhaps it is exacerbated here by the lack of critical public debate—both around monuments and around issues of group identity. With respect to the Indian monument proposal, Desai suggests that ordinary people should be involved to decide "whether there should be a memorial and, if so, what form it should take and who should drive the process" (Govender 2004). He advocates opening the debate about Indian history and identity—a monument in his view closes that debate (personal conversation 2005).

Despite much talk to the contrary, there is still an overwhelming tendency in South Africa today to implement heritage projects in a top-down fashion, resulting in a lacking sense of ownership by local people. This problem has been discussed, among others, by Wells (2004) in the context of the Egazini monument in Grahamstown and by Hansen (2003) in the context of the Emlotheni Memorial in Port Elizabeth. It is an area of concern that the National Heritage Council is intent on addressing through the development of strategic policy. Ironically, when a fundamental revision of the structures and policies around heritage were being discussed during the immediate postelection period, broad consensus emerged about the need for community participation (Pistorius 1996: 14) and the new National Heritage Resources Act stipulates that "public interest and involvement in the identification, assessment, recording and management of heritage resources" (NHRA 1999: Point 13e) must be encouraged and promoted. Yet, research has shown that the idea of true community involvement and democratization of the heritage sector has thus far received little attention. As Julia Wells observes, monuments and other heritage projects are often driven by local and national government, while relevant stakeholders are relegated to the position of informants (Wells 2004: 1). "Consultation" is primarily about telling people what has been decided. While it must be acknowledged that community participation is difficult to achieve without turning it into a process model, the result of the current top-down approach is often that inclusive goals are not achieved, and many locals feel alienated and excluded. Lack of identification with the monument explains why many new monuments in South Africa are not being respected, properly maintained, and even sometimes vandalized by members of the same "community" they are meant to represent.

Contestation over Benefits

In any society, monuments and other elements in the symbolic landscape can become focal points of contestation over the political, social, or religious values they symbolize. In the specific South African context, however, another dimension plays an important role, namely the fact that monuments are being promoted as vehicles to the attainment of economic benefits. As a result, monuments can become divisive and contentious not only over their symbolic meaning, but over the issue of who benefits most from their existence. In a context of abject poverty, high unemployment, and underdevelopment, initiators of monuments—whether they emanate from the private or public sector—invariably need to promise economic benefits, mostly through tourism, to "sell" their proposal. Some political officials are deeply concerned about the need for transforming the landscape of memory and consider symbolic measures such as the establishment of heritage sites or renaming of streets as just as important as building houses and providing services. However, anecdotal evidence suggests that many ordinary people do not share this sentiment. People often criticize the expense of building new monuments, or even that of removing existing ones, pointing out that the money would be better spent on helping the poor meet their basic needs of survival.

In this context, the success of a monument, or the level of general acceptance of a new heritage initiative, hinges crucially on whether or not people's high expectations of economic development and financial gain are being met. If tourist numbers remain low or surrounding communities do not see tangible and immediate benefits from the visitor flow, the result may be disillusionment, a lack of care and lack of identification with the monument—no matter what it may symbolize. Even worse, if one individual or group is seen to benefit to the exclusion of others, the monument can stoke resentment, jealousy, and internal divisions, sometimes even making it the target of sabotage and vandalism. This situation is most likely to prevail when people believe in promises of tangible benefits rather than in intangible symbolic values that allow the monument to be appreciated and respected as an intrinsic benefit. This might involve a learning process that will take time, but even more it might depend on a genuine broad-based improvement of the majority's economic situation.

Conclusion

This chapter neither intends to deny that monuments, memorials, and public art interventions can make a valuable contribution to reconciliation in societies marred by conflict, nor does it necessarily consent with the multitude of local critics who condemn South Africa's current commemorative drive as a waste of public funds in a context marked by pressing needs of basic survival. Although one might rightfully argue about the processes and practices associated with their conception and the visual and textual language in which they communicate, I acknowledge monuments as important symbolic markers that can substantially reshape the symbolic landscape by making previously neglected voices heard and promote new historical discourses and identity projects.

But monuments are also always problematic, as they communicate notions of inclusiveness and exclusiveness; represent one-sided, often ideologically charged accounts of the past and parade specific value systems (furthermore often derived from one particular group) as societal norms. Despite being erected in the spirit of nation-building as symbols of unity and reconciliation, in multicultural, historically divided societies such as South Africa, monuments still end up pitching one racial or ethnic group against another, because monuments are inevitably exclusive to some extent in order to be meaningful as symbols of group identification based on selected cultural values. The three case studies discussed in this chapter each illustrate what I see as key problems associated with post-apartheid monument effort.

The Ncome monument and museum, being a national project, was meant to facilitate redress and reconciliation, an objective that it no doubt successfully achieves for some visitors, especially perhaps foreign tourists. But for others, the very presence of the structure, juxtaposed to the existing Afrikaner nationalist monument, provides a material expression of the Other's claim for group recognition. Not only does the new monument literally appear to be pitched against the old enemy, thus perpetuating divisions of the past, but it furthermore promotes a partisan identity in some ways at odds with the country's nation-building agenda.

Yet there is another level of division, another dynamic of cultural contestation, namely in-group conflict and disagreement over meaning. Dlamini's (2001) analysis of the original museum exhibition at Ncome revealed that the latter projected a specific notion of "Zuluness" that excluded the representation and contribution of other black communities in the area (this has meanwhile been partially corrected). Even more so, the Spirit of eMakhosini monument and a number of other "Zulu monuments" in the rural areas of KZN perpetuate ethnic, racial, and gender stereotypes and project a glorified, nostalgic vision of a precolonial Zulu past, which celebrate the Zulu royal house and its proud militaristic tradition, as well as bolstering local tourism marketing campaigns that "sell" the province of KZN as the "Zulu kingdom." While such identity discourses are presumably attractive to the traditional Zulu leadership, IFP supporters, some Zulu communities, and probably foreign tourists, on the whole such monuments forge a symbolic landscape from which not only other racial groups are excluded, but which remains questionable as a larger model for contemporary African group identity in present-day South Africa.

In-group contestation no doubt also explains why the Indian monument proposal has not yet come to fruition, despite a principally supportive city council. The extremely fragmented nature of the Indian population group renders the notion of an Indian monument as a symbol of unity and community identification questionable and naïve. But even if it were to succeed on this level, the project is problematic, because it perpetuates and fortifies a concept of racially defined "community" inherited from the colonial and apartheid era. It highlights one of the key challenges faced by the post-apartheid government and South African society at large: on the one hand, the national objective to create unity and forge nonracial imagined communities based on shared values; on the other hand, an encouragement for celebrating cultural diversity through the fostering of separate racially and ethnically defined "community" heritage, which often replicates apartheid-era strategies pursued in the name of separate development.

In the specific South African context marked by poverty and scarce resources, such dynamics of cultural representation and contestation are furthermore overlaid by conflict over economic benefits. The government's strong emphasis on community empowerment and sustainable heritage conservation through tourism-derived economic development can foster resentment and rejection among those who lose out on promised resources and opportunities associated with monument projects. The state-supported focus on conserving previously neglected heritage invariably results in public resources being withdrawn from the sites and identity symbols of previously privileged groups. The withdrawal of state subsidies, coupled with media-supported public discourses about the dubitable worth and significance of such monuments, signals a threat to white minority identity and drives such groups into the defensive, even if they no longer identify with the specific values these monuments were once intended to represent.

Below the surface celebrated in the speeches of public officials, the tourism marketing literature, and the tour guide narratives presented to foreign visitors at post-apartheid monument sites, ordinary people often find that they do not actually share the interpretation of "their" history, experience, and identity as portrayed in the new monument. This is likely to change only when the government no longer builds monuments on behalf of "the people," but ordinary South Africans themselves become more active participants and significant shapers of their own symbolic landscapes. This development presumes the strengthening of civil society, accompanied by vigorous and constructive public debate, in a political climate in which the new democratic order is consolidated and critique is no longer perceived as a threat.

Notes

1. This chapter is part of a larger research project on Commemoration and Heritage in post-apartheid South Africa, funded by the National Research Foundation of South Africa.

2. Violence and civil strife peaked during the fragile negotiation period of the early 1990s, as the state instigated conflict within the black community, especially between members of the ANC and the IFP. In the area of Thokoza on the East Rand approximately, 800 people died and about 600 families were displaced, their homes ruined, between 1990 and 1994 as a result of community violence fueled by the IFP-ANC conflict (Kgalema 1999; Davenport and Saunders 2000: 562). The IFP threatened to boycott the 1994 first democratic elections until only two weeks before the election date. In KZN "faction-fighting" between IFP and ANC supporters lasted long into the post-apartheid period, especially in the Richmond area.

3. Dubow (2004), for instance, while acknowledging the virtual interchangeability of the two terms, considers "memorials" to be structures and institutions whose essence is reflective and contemplative, while "monument" refers to historical markers, as well as structures that are predominantly celebratory and potentially self-aggrandizing: "Monuments outwardly proclaim something. Memorials invite introspection and interpretation" (2004: 375). On the basis of similar distinctions, many local scholars criticize the present development of the

commemorative sector in South Africa, arguing that the government is clearly building monuments, while the country really needs memorials (for example, Dubow 2004; Maré 2002a, 2002b; Nettleton 2003). Others, especially architects, tend to criticize that the country's commemorative structures are erroneously referred to as monuments, while they should really be called memorials, until such time that they are proclaimed a monument by the national conservation authorities (for example, Frescura personal communication 2002; Greef personal communication 2004).

4. For a more detailed description of the changes in this holiday and controversy over its meaning, see Ross (2007: Chapters 8–9) and Chapter 10 in this volume.

5. Girshick (2004) established that Ncome was not part of the preliminary list of sites selected for the Legacy Project, but only included as an afterthought. This occurred in early 1998 as a result of Lionel Mtshali's intervention, who had taken over the portfolio of the DACST from Ben Ngubane in September 1996. Like Ngubane, Mtashli was a member of the IFP in the ANC-led Government of National Unity, but he was also a prominent Zulu nationalist, who had picked up the idea of the Ncome project from Chief Mangosuthu Buthelezi. It is difficult to determine the origins of the idea, but Hall reports that Barry Marshall, director of the KMC, had long cherished the idea of a Zulu counterpart to the Blood River monument (Hall e-mail communication 2007).

6. Dlamini found that the representation of the battle in the newly opened Ncome museum drew substantially on the radical Zulu nationalist interpretation of the event, which rejected the Afrikaner perspective. He concludes that the national Ncome project has been hijacked by Zulu nationalist forces, exploiting a national "heritage" resource for the revival of ethnic nationalism (2001: 132).

7. When Ben Ngubane returned to the Ministry (in 1999), he clashed badly with Musa Xulu, the staunch IFP loyalist who had been the driving force behind the implementation of the Ncome project. Xulu was suspended (in mid-2000) and subsequently dismissed on charges of misconduct (Hall e-mail communication 2007; South Africa Government Information 2000).

8. For instance, a copy of the alleged treaty between Piet Retief and King Dingaan is displayed with the accompanying text questioning how the latter, who was illiterate, could have signed his name "King Dingaan." This particular display is important in terms of its content, because it discredits a piece of paper that has long played a crucial role in legitimizing Afrikaner claims to the land. Furthermore, and perhaps more importantly, it makes a fundamental point about historiography and its methodology in direct response to the Blood River museum. In the latter museum, both the video and the wall panels emphasize that the Afrikaner version of the battle is entirely based on "written sources," presumed to be reliable and accurate (according to an older, Western school of thought), while the Zulu version is based on oral history, implied to be largely fictitious.

9. The new Zulu memorial at Isandlwana, initiated by Amafa but financed almost entirely with funds raised from the traditional Zulu leadership, was unveiled on 21 January 1999. The day marks the one-hundred-twentieth anniversary of the famous Anglo-Zulu battle, in which the British army, led by Lord Chelmsford and equipped with Martini Henry rifles, was defeated by 24,000 Zulu warriors in the service of King Cetshwayo equipped with the *iklwa* stabbing spear (Laband 1995). Despite this glorious victory, the Zulus themselves suffered defeat at the nearby mission station of Rorke's Drift, where another conflagra-

tion ensued a few days later, ultimately sealing the expansion of British colonization. A bronze memorial representing the fallen Zulu warriors was commissioned by Amafa and installed on the site in January 2005.

10. Discussions of these and similar images among Zulu mother-tongue students at the University of KwaZulu-Natal regularly reveal high levels of identification and pride, even among emancipated, westernized, urban black females,
who commonly understand such representations as respectable symbols of "culture."

11. For a more detailed discussion of post-apartheid monument initiatives in
KZN, see Marschall 2008.

Bibliography

Ashplant, Timothy G., Graham Dawson, and Michael Roper, eds. 2004. *The Poli-
tics of Memory: Commemorating War.* London: Transaction Publishers.
Assmann, Aleida. 2003. *Erinnerungsräume. Formen und Wandlungen des kulturellen
Gedächtnisses.* Broschierte Sonderausgabe. Munich: C. H. Beck.
Assmann, Jan. 1999. "Kollektives und kulturelles Gedächtnis. Zur Phänomenolo-
gie und Funktion von Gegen-Erinnerung." In *Orte der Erinnerung. Denkmal,
Gedenkstätte, Museum,* ed. Ulrich Borsdorf and Heinrich Theodor Grütter.
Frankfurt: Campus, 13–32.
———. 2002. *Das kulturelle Gedächtnis. Schrift, Erinnerung und politische Identität in
frühen Hochkulturen.* 4th ed. Munich: C. H. Beck.
Baines, Gary. 2007. "The Master Narrative of South Africa's Liberation Struggle:
Remembering and Forgetting June 16, 1976." *International Journal of African
Historical Studies* 40, no. 2: 283–302.
Ben-Amos, Dan, and Liliane Weissberg, eds. 1999. *Cultural Memory and the Con-
struction of Identity.* Detroit: Wayne State University Press.
Bishop, Craig. 1998. "Reconciliation at the River." *Natal Witness* (17 December).
Connerton, Paul. 1989. *How Societies Remember.* Cambridge: Cambridge Univer-
sity Press.
Coombes, Annie E. 2003. *History After Apartheid: Visual Culture and Public Memory
in a Democratic South Africa.* Durham: Duke University Press.
Cox, Karen L. 2003. "The Confederate Monument at Arlington: A Token of Rec-
onciliation." In *Monuments to the Lost Cause: Women, Art, and the Landscapes of
Southern Memory,* ed. Cynthia Mills and Pamela H. Simpson. Knoxville: University of Tennessee Press, 148–162.
Danto, Arthur. 1987. *The State of the Art.* New York: Prentice Hall.
Davenport, Rodney, and Christopher Saunders. 2000. *South Africa: A Modern History.* 5th ed. London: Macmillan.
Deacon, Harriet. 1998. "Remembering Tragedy, Constructing Modernity: Robben Island as National Monument." In *Negotiating the Past: The Making of Memory in South Africa,* ed. Sarah Nuttall and Carli Coetzee. Cape Town: Oxford
University Press South Africa, ch. 11.
———. 2004. "Intangible Heritage in Conservation Management Planning: The
Case of Robben Island." *International Journal of Heritage Studies* 10, no. 3 (July):
309–319.
Dlamini, Nsizwa. 2001. "The Battle of Ncome Project: State Memorialism, Dis-
comforting Spaces." *Southern African Humanities* 13: 125–138.
Dubow, Neville. 2004. "On Monuments, Memorials and Memory: Some Precedents Towards a South African Option." In *To Repair the Irreparable: Reparation*

and Reconstruction in South Africa, ed. Erik Doxtader and Charles Villa-Vicencio. Claremont: David Philip, 359–378.

Friedland, Roger, and Richard D. Hecht. 2005. "Place Memory, and Identity: Some Theoretical Reflections on the Power of Place." Paper presented at *Contesting Culture, Narratives, Dramas and Representing Identity,* conference at Bryn Mawr College, Pa. February.

Gillis, John R. 1994. "Introduction: Memory and Identity: The History of a Relationship." In *Commemorations: The Politics of National Identity,* ed. John R. Gillis. Princeton: Princeton University Press, 3–24.

Girshick, Paula. 2004. "Ncome Museum/Monument: From Reconciliation to Resistance." *Museum Anthropology* 27, no. 1: 25–36.

Govender, Suthentira. 2004. "Foundation's 40-Year Wait for 1860 Memorial." *Sunday Times* (1 August).

Graham, Bill, G. J. Ashworth, and J. E. Tunbridge. 2000. *A Geography of Heritage: Power, Culture and Economy.* London: Arnold.

Hall, Andrew. 2005. "Initiating a Review of National Heritage Legislation in the South African Experience." In *Legal Frameworks for the Protection of Immovable Cultural Heritage in Africa,* ed. Webber Ndoro and Gilbert Pwiti. ICCROM Conservation Studies, 5: 36–41.

———. 2006. "Rethinking Heritage Conservation in South Africa in the Post-Apartheid Era: Innovation in Policies and Legislation Since 1994." In *La Dimensión Social del Patrimonio,* vol. 1. Buenos Aires: Centro Internacional para la Conservatión del Patrimonio Argentina, pp.31–35.

Hall, Stuart. 1999–2000. "Whose Heritage? Un-settling 'The Heritage,' Re-imagining the Post-nation." *Third Text* 49 (Winter): 3–13.

Hansen, Birthe Rytter. 2003. "Public Spaces for National Commemoration: The Case of Emlotheni Memorial, Port Elizabeth." *Anthropology and Humanism* 28, no. 1 (June): 43–60.

Harrison, Simon. 1995. "Four Types of Symbolic Conflict." *Journal of the Royal Anthropological Institute* (n.s.), 1: 255–272.

Hart, David, and Sarah Winter. 2001. "The Politics of Remembrance in the New South Africa." In *Archaeologies of the Contemporary Past,* ed. Victor Buchli and Gavin Lucas. London: Routledge, 84–93.

Hewison, Robert. 1987. *The Heritage Industry: Britain in a Climate of Decline.* London: Methuen.

IPF official website—History. Retrieved 29 June 2007, from http://www.ifp.org .za/History/history.htm.

Kgalema, Lazarus. 1999. *Symbols of Hope: Monuments as Symbols of Remembrance and Peace in the Process of Reconciliation.* Johannesburg: Centre for the Study of Violence and Reconciliation. Retrieved from www. csvr.org.za/papers/papk gal1.htm.

Khumalo, Sipho. 1998. "Let's Value Each Other's Heritage." *Daily News* (17 December).

Kruger, Loren. 2000. "Robben Island Museum." *Public Culture* 12, no. 3: 787–791.

Laband, John. 1995. *Rope of Sand: The Rise and Fall of the Zulu Kingdom in the Nineteenth Century.* Johannesburg: Jonathan Ball.

Lambek, Michael, and Paul Antze. 1996. "Introduction: Forecasting Memory." In *Tense Past: Cultural Essays in Trauma and Memory,* ed. Michael Lambek and Paul Antze. New York: Routledge, xi–xxxviii.

Levinson, Sanford. 1998. *Written in Stone: Public Monuments in Changing Societies.* Durham: Duke University Press.

Maré, Estelle. 2002a. "A Critique of Monuments." Paper presented at the Eighteenth Annual Conference of the South African Association of Art Historians (SAAAH), Pretoria, July.

———. 2002b. "The Aesthetics of Ideology: The Vicissitudes of Monuments." *South African Journal of Cultural History* 16, no. 11: 15–24.

Marschall, Sabine. 2003. "Setting Up a Dialogue: Monuments as a Means of 'Writing Back.'" *Historia: Journal of the Historical Association of South Africa* 48, no. 1: 309–325.

———. 2004. "Gestures of Compensation: Post-apartheid Monuments and Memorials." *Transformation: Critical Perspectives on Southern Africa* 55: 78–95.

———. 2005. "Making Money with Memories: The Fusion of Heritage, Tourism, and Identity Formation in South Africa." *Historia: Journal of the Historical Association of South Africa* 50, no. 1: 103–122.

———. 2008. "Zulu Heritage Between Institutionalized Commemoration and Tourist Attraction." *Journal of Visual Anthropology* 21, no. 3: 245–265.

Mhlanga, Elijah. 2000. "Call for Monument to Indians." *Daily News* (31 January).

Milazi, Abdul. 1998. "Where the River Runs Between . . ." *Sunday Tribune* (20 December).

Naidu, Sanusha. 2000a. "Monumental Mistake Needs to Be Avoided." *Daily News* (14 February).

———. 2000b. "Where Do We Put This 'Indian' Monument?" *Daily News* (24 February).

National Heritage Resources Act (NHRA). 1999. *Government Gazette*, no. 506.

Nettleton, Anitra. 2003. "Can Monuments Speak in African Languages? Interrogating Issues of Style in Post-Colonial African Monuments." *Proceedings of the Nineteenth Annual Conference of the South African Association of Art Historians (SAAAH)*. University of Stellenbosch. 11–13 September.

Nora, Pierre. 1989. "Between Memory and History: Les Lieux de Mémoire." *Representations* 26 (Spring): 7–25.

Pistorius, Penny. 1996. "Legislation *and* the National Monuments Act." In *Monuments and Sites: South Africa,* ed. Janette Deacon. South Africa: ICOMOS (International Council on Monuments and Sites) National Committee, 9–14.

"Racist Remarks Spark Strong Response." 2004. *Courier* (24 December).

Rassool, Ciraj. 2001. "Cultural History in Collections." *South African Museums Association Bulletin* 25, no. 2: 43–49.

Rassool, Ciraj, Leslie Witz, and Gary Minkley. 2000. "Burying and Memorialising the Body of Truth: The TRC and National Heritage." In *After the TRC: Reflections on Truth and Reconciliation in Tourism* (South African ed.), ed. James Wilmot and Linda van de Vijver. Cape Town: David Philip, 115–127.

Ross, Keith. 1998. "Battlefield Reconciliation." *Daily News* (10 November).

Ross, Marc Howard. 2007. *Cultural Contestation in Ethnic Conflict.* Cambridge: Cambridge University Press.

Rowlands, Michael. 1999. "Remembering to Forget: Sublimation as Sacrifice in War Memorials." In *The Art of Forgetting*, ed. Adrian Forty and Susanne Küchler. Oxford: Oxford University Press, 129–145.

South African Government Information. 2000. "Public Announcement About the Disciplinary Enquiry Involving Prof Musa Xulu." Issued by the Department of Arts, Culture, Science, and Technology (22 December).

"This Is Welcome Recognition of Indians' Contribution." 2000. *Sunday Tribune* (6 February).

Wells, Julia. 2004. "Who Owns Heritage? Developing Powers to Traditional

Leadership and Local Government in the Eastern Cape of South Africa." Paper presented at the conference *Heritage in Southern and Eastern Africa: Imagining and Marketing Public Culture and History*, Livingstone, Zambia, July.

Witz, Leslie, Ciraj Rassool, and Gary Minkley. 2001. "Repackaging the Past for South African Tourism." In *Heritage, Museums, and Galleries: An Introductory Reader*, ed. Gerard Corsane. 2005. London: Routledge, 308–309.

Yoganathan, Venilla. 2000. "Monument to Indians Urged." *Mercury* (31 January).

Personal Communication

Desai, Ashwin. Writer and community activist. Personal interview. 22 February 2005.

Gookol, Krish. Chair, 1860 Heritage Foundation. Personal interview. 21 January 2005.

Greeff, Gabriel. Architect. Personal interview. 22 January 2004.

Frescura, Franco. Architect. Personal communications. 2002.

Hall, Andrew (then NMC Regional Manager KZN). Letter to the Director of the Voortrekker Museum (Pietermaritzburg). 15 December 1994. SAHRA Head office file 9/2/447/1, vol. 4.

———. Letter to Hannes Meiring Architect. 16 March 1995. SAHRA Head office file 9/2/447/1, vol. 4.

———. Letter to Barry Marshall, KMC. 21 September 1995. SAHRA Head office file # 9/2/447/1, vol. 4.

Hall, Andrew. Department of Sport, Arts and Culture, Northern Cape Province (ANC). Personal e-mail communication. 20 April 2007.

Maphalala, Jabu. Historian and (IFP) Member of Parliament (KwaZulu-Natal). Personal interview. 4 January 2005.

van Vuuren, James. Amafa. Personal e-mail communication. 13 November 2006.

Chapter 9
Emerging Multiculturalisms in South African Museum Practice
Some Examples from the Western Cape

Crain Soudien

After 1994 a number of new museums opened in South Africa, the most significant of which have been the Nelson Mandela Museum in the small Eastern Cape Province town of Mthatha, the Apartheid Museum and Constitution Hill at the Fort, both in the country's financial capital, Johannesburg, and the Robben Island and District Six Museums in Cape Town. Landmark Exhibitions have included the Democracy X Exhibition at the country's oldest colonial building, the Castle, in Cape Town and the opening of new sites at the Mapungubwe National Park in the Limpopo Province, a province in the northernmost reaches of South Africa. In this chapter, I reflect briefly on this new memory landscape and make the argument that distinctive discourses around "race" have begun to emerge on it. While the broad ambition of these exhibitions has been to cultivate a discourse of inclusion and to establish new critical platforms for representing the past, I argue that much museum practice has struggled to articulate a countermemory to the racialized tropes of self and other in which notions of civilization and savagery, goodness and evil, and beauty and hideousness circulate. While I make occasional observations about exhibitions elsewhere in the country, I focus specifically on how these practices have evolved and developed in the three Cape Town museums, namely, the *Democracy X* exhibition at the Castle of Good Hope, the Robben Island Museum, and the *Digging Deeper* exhibition at the District Six Museum.

Toward making sense of the post-apartheid landscape in museum practice in South Africa, I draw on the work of Barnor Hesse, particularly his interesting assessment of Steven Spielberg's *Amistad*. Hesse

(2002: 152–154) argues that the film "represents one of the most significant Hollywood interventions in remembering the historical contours of Atlantic slavery, if only due to the scarcity of such interventions." "Yet," he goes on to say, "it scarcely remembers slavery at all." In a finely argued essay Hesse draws attention to the fact that in the scheme of things, remembering slavery in the United States, as opposed to *not* remembering it, is a good thing. But that is hardly sufficient. The real question is *how* one remembers. Allied to this is the question too, of who is doing the remembering. Embodied in these questions, I want to argue, is the larger question of who one considers oneself to be in relation to issues of the "self" and the "other."

Drawing on the work of people like Hesse, the argument that I am making in this chapter is that there is a very particular politics of memory in the new South Africa that we need to understand. This politics has, not unexpectedly, a great deal, not everything, to do with the relationship between apartheid and post-apartheid. Central to this politics are the figures of race and power. In the discursive frame of this politics, certain techniques of memory are mobilized that seek to recompose, reorder, and ultimately to re-*authorize* the past and the figures of race (and indeed class and much more) and power within it. These techniques involve a "who" and a "how." To illustrate this with respect to the American past, Hesse argues in his critique of *Amistad*, that what we are seeing in the film is not a narrative of slavery, but a narrative of American justice and the triumph of American justice, brought to its logical conclusion by the heroes of the abolition movement. In the face of this justice stand a group of aberrants, the slaveowners. The practice of slavery in the film is represented as deviance, enacted by, as we now remember them, our vaguely embarrassing ancestors. It is something we have to confess to. Because it is deviant, ultimately justice will prevail, and as Hesse says, it is shown up for the miscarriage of justice that it is, a miscarriage to be ultimately rectified by the courts of justice.

In the South African case, I suggest that we are seeing the emergence and development of certain discourses of memory in our museum work in which many of us are implicated. These discourses carry the heavy imprint of one or other positioning with respect to issues of race and difference. In them are evident the ways of managing the relationship between the past and the present. In this chapter, I argue that discourses shift and evolve but always build on, or take from preexisting discourse. In the South African case the discourses that are evolving in current museum practice are iterations or versions of older discourses that have been on the South African landscape for a long time. In this chapter, I draw attention to what I think these discourses are and offer a suggestion about how we might engage with their politics. Ross's opening remarks in this volume are useful for understanding how these discourses work.

The suggestion I will make is essentially that the focus of our attention must be, as it has been indeed in many spheres of public scholarship and public politics for a long time, on understanding the relationship between the past and the present. Where, currently, our discourses, in their various iterations, render our history as a history of different times, of pre-apartheid time, apartheid time, and post-apartheid time, and embody particular conceptions of culture and the multicultural nature of South African society, I am arguing that we need to renegotiate and reconstitute the terms of the debate and the formal historical distinctions upon which the debate works. With respect to the present, we need to look again at the distinctions that are being made between what we call our new state and the old state, between old approaches to identity and new ones, and the memories that these various understandings of identity and of power authorize. In a word what we need to do is to re-*member* or to bring together the past and the present within a much more vigorous dialogue of critique to understand how much the present remains constituted in a relationship with the past. Within such an approach, we need, specifically, to understand how the figure of race continues to play a role in framing the present and to initiate a discourse that operates beyond the reductive vector of race, recognizing the complex ways in which race is instantiated into, and alongside, other sources of difference.

Beginning there, the question then arises for the purposes of this discussion of whose role it is to remember? I want to argue that we have no alternative to remembering. In these terms it is a role performed by everybody. How we do that, however, is what is at question. Hesse says, "as there is no alternative to remembering, we are always implicated in considering what this something is" that we *ought* to be remembering. It is here that the politics of memory is expressed as a certain kind of economy in which bits and pieces float in relation to each other, where they now assume a high value, then no value at all, but where value is constantly being expressed and enacted. Even forgetting is a move which produces value or disvalue. When we choose to forget, or worse, are placed in positions where memory is repressed, we remember in a very particular way. In the very act of disavowing a memory, whether it is voluntary or not, we reconstitute its value.

Given this, I am suggesting that in confronting the burden of our apartheid past, we have developed a number of remembering discourses. These discourses constitute forms of "re-membering," and consist of ways in which the past and the present are stitched together. As I have argued above, this re-membering is not a process which happens in an abstract way but draws directly from the fabric or raw material of preexisting discourses. In South Africa these discourses sit along a spectrum, and consist on the one hand of discourses of nostalgia, which I am not particularly interested in here, but about which a word is necessary, and, on the other, discourses of reconstruction. These latter are what I think are important. It is among these and from these that a critical memory will emanate.

Briefly, discourses of nostalgia are rooted in both public and private celebrations of colonial conquest and subordination. Manifestations of these discourses exist in places of worship, schools, and even public museums. They present themselves in two forms, namely that of White supremacy and indigenous recidivism. In terms of the first, evident is a Eurocentric address framed around an unproblematized supremacist narrative framed in the language of either a Darwinian racial inevitability or a religious predestination. South Africa has many examples of these. Interesting examples in the Western Cape, the oldest colonial part of the country, include the forensic conceit demonstrated in the permanent exhibition in the museum of Montague, a small town in the arid small Karoo region of the Western Cape. One sees in this exhibition the skeletal remains of a vagabond Khoi highwayman apprehended and executed at the turn of the twentieth century. The remains are presented as an almost biological truth. In them we have the outlines of what a not-quite civilized person might look like—the confluence of anatomy and crime and an attempt to suggest a link between them. A second example is the Taalmonument (Language Monument) on the slopes of the Paarl Mountain, some fifty kilometers outside of Cape Town, which shows the superiority of European civilization over that of the subordinate groups which constitute the country's past. The last example and, in some ways the most controversial is the notorious San diorama at the Iziko: South African Natural History Museum in Cape Town. In this exhibition San people, often referred to as Bushmen, were exhibited alongside stuffed whales and embalmed antelope. Important about the exhibition is the invocation in it to an older biological understanding of race. Evident in it is an evolution thesis constructed around a genealogy of animal and human life and the position of the San within that chain. They are presented as the great link between animals and human beings.

In the second form we see the newly confident indigenous address. This address is framed either by a narrow primordialism or an equally narrow ethnocentrism. Central to this project is the recovery of the identity of the "other" and his or her repositioning as a "subject." Critical about this project is its rehabilitation of a timeless, continuous, and unsullied memory in which the subject emerges as a coherent, unified, and self-determining member of a community with equally stable and wholesome qualities. Often absent in these renderings is a complex awareness of the dialectic of self and other, and self and the tangled social, political, and ecological backdrop of colonialism and apartheid. Where the latter are included they are recruited as stage-sets for the reproduction of timeless nobility and beauty. Key examples in the Cape Town area include the Amlay family museum in the small naval town of Simonstown. In this exhibition we see a genealogy of durable and immutable *Malayness*—Malay being a term used to describe the descendants of the slaves brought to the Cape from modern-day Indonesia and Malaysia during the colonial rule of the Dutch in South Africa—holding fast over three centuries of faithful cultural continuity. It is presented around the artifacts of religious observance, the preservation of the imperatives of probity, and the sublimation of the profanity of daily ritual. Central to the museum, and indeed other exhibitions in this genre at sites such as the Bo-Kaap Museum, a house museum belonging to the Iziko Museums and located in the old slave quarter of the city, is the extrapolation of life from the mundane and the profane and its embeddedness in and loyalty to the order of religious observance. The subject is above all a subject of the imagination of religious observance outside the taint of personal, social, and public desire. Colored somewhat differently but impelled by similar motives are the works of the world-renowned documenter and photographer of the apartheid era, Peter Magubane. Inherent in the work of Magubane is a romance of a noble Africa timelessly reveling in its ethnic virtuosity. That this ethnic aesthetic is a product of colonial displacement and subjugation is not addressed in the representations.

While I am interested in how the nostalgia of indigeneity is mobilized in processes of reconstruction, and will refer to these, this broad discourse is not the focus of this chapter. Much more critical are the discourses of reconstruction and what these discourses do with the challenge of inclusiveness, and multiculturalism. In this chapter, I identify two dominant forms of multiculturalism that are emerging in the museum post-1994 and then draw attention to alternative ways of addressing questions of difference and inclusion that are emerging in museums such as the District Six Museum. The first of the dominant forms is what I would call empirical multiculturalism (or multiculturalism for the record) and the second triumphalist multiculturalism.

The purpose of this chapter, against this introduction, is to ask how the public is constituted in key exhibitions and in key museums in some South African museums. In reflecting on key exhibitions such as *Democracy X* at the Iziko Museum, Cape of Good Hope Castle, *Digging Deeper* at the District Six Museum, *A Decade of Democracy* at Iziko Museums, the

South African National Gallery, the Apartheid Museum, Constitutional Hill in Johannesburg, and the Robben Island Museum in Cape Town, the chapter will look at how the imperative of inclusion—through an examination of issues such as race, class, and gender—has been interpreted to produce a notion of the public and what the implications of these notions are for developing critical practice.

An Empiricist Multiculturalism

In the last ten years, South Africans have been privileged to see a number of key exhibitions. Hilton Judin's *Setting Apart* at the Cape Town Castle in the early 1990s set a standard for prying open the mystique of the colonial imagination and revealing it in its calculated Darwinian obsession with order and hierarchy. Drawing on identity documents and plans for urban development, the exhibition took the viewer into the official colonial mind exposing its eugenicist complexity. A feature of the exhibition was its encyclopedic reach. It sought to show the depth, width, and volume of the colonial desire for control and subordination of what became known as the "nonwhite" peoples. Using both the arcane and the predictable the exhibition showed the extent to which the colonial mind sought to displace the symbolism and currency of precolonial Africa, its awareness of how this currency (to mix one's metaphors) was interstitially distributed within the structure of the everyday and the minutiae that surround and give character to the everyday, and what it would take impose the new symbolic order of colonialism. What Judin had done was to take the empirical and place it within a discursive framework which showed the inner workings of colonial power and the deeper structure of its narrative. Colonial power, in his representation, was made visible not only in the displacement of the iconic world of the other, in the outlawing and disallowing of that symbolic order, but in its totalizing substitution with the discipline, the rules and regulations and the conventions of British colonialism. In the accumulation of detail Judin showed how colonial power understood the necessity of effacing the symbolic currency of the precolonial.

This precedent, in its detail, in its attention to the quotidian and in its understanding of how the sum of the parts is itself significant, had a big impact on the aesthetics of representation. Elements of it came to be reproduced in subsequent exhibitions. A feature of many of the new exhibitions that were to follow, however, was that they were long and even strong on detail, but somewhat short on the conceptual coherence demonstrated by Judin. The empirical as a medium, to show the totalizing reach of the colonial mind, only episodically came to emerge in the major exhibitions that were to follow. Instead, it came to be used as a technique. It is this, in relation to inclusiveness and the multicultural nature of contemporary exhibitions, that I wish to discuss below.

Working from the Hilton Judin *Setting Apart* exhibition, the argument I am making here is that a documentary-style of exhibition emerges after 1994 along the lines of what I would call "empiricist multiculturalism." This discourse is a discourse of collection, or better, of curatorial memory. In this discourse the approach is that of rearranging and recollecting the artifacts of the past and displaying them "experientially" and aesthetically for the curiosity of the onlooker. Exhibitions of this kind are marked by volume, the accumulation of evidence. Their approach pivots on the idea of "filling out" the story. Much of this aesthetic address was, interestingly, apparent and consolidated in the Truth and Reconciliation Commission. In this process evidence—the experience of the apartheid past—was often "enacted" repeatedly for emotionally traumatized commissioners and the general public. A famous example arose where Jeff Benzien, an apartheid-era member of the police's special branch (tasked to obtain information about anti-apartheid activities) demonstrated to the audience how he had wrapped a wet cloth bag around the head of Tony Yengeni, a well-known Cape Town activist. Many exhibitions have followed this style. With respect to those exhibitions that deal with racism, the purpose (see Hesse 2002: 155) has often been to direct attention to the excess of apartheid. Their representational style has often pivoted on the dramatization of the machinery and techniques of oppression: in its most extreme form, the staging-place of the gallows, and in its most immediate, the representation of the passbook. The most important examples of this style are to be found in the interesting new Apartheid Museum, at Gold Reef City in Johannesburg, and the Constitutional Hill Museum, incorporating the Old Fort and the new Constitutional Court in Hillbrow, Johannesburg. Both of these memory sites operate within this broad genre. The Apartheid Museum is a beautifully designed building which takes viewers through the history of colonialism and apartheid and the struggles against these. Its most striking feature is a chamber where a forest of hangman's nooses are suspended from the ceiling, recalling the large number of Black people who would have been executed for fighting against apartheid. The Old Fort is Johannesburg's original jail where famous political, and criminal, prisoners were kept, including Nelson Mandela. The prison was rigidly segregated by race. Much of the exhibition focuses on the differential way in which prisoners were treated.

Significant as this form of address is, I argue that it reduces the complexity of the past to a selective but reified set of routines. Life in this narrative experience tends toward the routinely violent. I suggest that this kind of remembering constitutes a form of emptying out of the fullness of the drama of the everyday, even in the most oppressive of spaces and times. Remembering is dramatized as an act of permanent horror. For many young South Africans, and particularly for white South Africans, out of this horror, I argue, issues disbelief. For many, a set of logics ensues that essentially amounts to denial. It cannot be true that it was so. The moment is too great to engage with, and is so, rather left alone. Omitted in many of these exhibitions, as an approach, are the intensely complex social structures, relations and habits that surround, precede, and follow the horror. Life is presented in its most extreme and egregious forms. The result is an effective disavowal of the reality of their ancestors' lives. And in some way their reactions are understandable, because they are not provided an opportunity of seeing the interior complexity of those lives. Permanent and unabating horror is all they are provided with. Little of the contradiction of everyday life is made available.

One of the most important exhibitions to emerge in modern South Africa has been the *Democracy X: Marking the Present; Representing the Past* at the Cape of Good Hope Castle in Cape Town. The exhibition was listed in the United Kingdom *Royal Academy Journal* recently (Autumn edition) as one of the best fifteen current exhibitions in the world. The exhibition was conceived, as some of its curators argue, "to narrate the cultural history of South Africa in broad sweeps, which departs from traditional representations of the past that rely on documentary evidence or from art exhibitions, in which works are presented in isolation from their historical contexts. It draws on iconic and everyday objects from different historical eras in South Africa" (Oliphant, Delius, and Meltzer 2004: xv). The essential objective of the exhibition was to mark, as part of a series of official year-long events, ten years of democracy in South Africa.

The *Democracy X* exhibition is large, consisting of over 400 objects, including archaeological artifacts, precolonial, colonial, and contemporary art, documents, photographs, sound, and film, and arranged around a timeline beginning at the very dawn of humanity in southern Africa and culminating in the present. The timeline begins chronologically, with the astonishingly beautiful 75,000-year-old perforated shell beads found in the Blombos Cave in the Southwestern Cape, and ends with attractive everyday images of young South Africa, young men and women making statements about the significance of ten years of democracy for them. The timeline flows along a series of chambers in Secunde House, the main building of the Castle, the oldest surviving colonial building in South Africa and also, at various times, the seat of the Dutch and British military governments and also the headquarters of the military serving successive political authorities, including the post-apartheid government. Symbolically, the exhibition is intended to be a narrative of resilience, of overcoming and, finally, of triumph. Rayda Becker (2004), a curator of the exhibition, talks about the exhibition in its thematic around the timeline, as "marking time." The apotheosis of the narrative is the coming of democracy—the culmination of a "great waiting."

The exhibition crucially operates around the critical presumptions evident in the Judin exhibition—of the grand iconography of colonialism and apartheid, the Lydenberg Heads, ancient African full-headed busts, soap-stone bird sculptures from Great Zimbabwe, padraos, intended to be eternal monuments of Portuguese achievement, from the early Portuguese, Dutch, and British voyages of exploration, juxtaposed with the artifacts and materials that signify the everyday. In terms of the everyday, especially in relation to the early period of the Dutch settlement at the Cape, the curators went out of their way to avoid inserting the marks of power of that period, the great tapestries that have come to signify the "civilizing" foresight of the colonist, the imposing statues of the founding fathers gazing across grand vistas and the endless trophies of subjugation. Important in this juxtaposition, as Becker (2004: 273) says, is "What transforms the ordinary into the special? Who makes meaning?"

A major conceptual thread holding the exhibition together was that of challenging conventional South African museum practice. The curators were profoundly aware of the debates around classificatory conventions in museums and the manifestation of these conventions in labeling practices. Talking of these practices, Becker (2004: 273) remarks, "Colonial indifference, reinforced by apartheid thinking, in naming products seems to linger and informs display appearances. Changes are not always visible and this exhibition self-consciously attempted some redress. In the words of Lalou Meltzer (a curator) it was 'really a manifestation of the bringing together of different collections and placing them in a historical context, and in that way, reframing the collections.' Could one say that this was a democratising approach to Iziko's collection?"

Responding to Becker, the exhibition is an important statement in a number of ways. It is a statement of the new South Africa and its desire to be an inclusive state. In these terms the exhibition is a major achievement. It provides guidelines, building on Judin's work, for developing a museum practice that is reflective and aware of the politics of inclusion.

It is a statement too, however, about the aesthetics of the new South African exhibition style. While the exhibition is significantly more self-aware than the exhibitions that have been developed at the Johannesburg Fort on Constitution Hill and the Apartheid Museum at Gold Reef City, and, at points, indicates a wariness of race labels (such as the "bracketing" of "Matabele," an Nguni-language-speaking group formed during the internal diaspora precipitated by conflicts in the early nineteenth century) it remains, simultaneously, caught in (i) the insidious puzzles surrounding description of racial identity and racialization and, (ii) struggles to develop a vocabulary and a representational style, particularly in its labeling, that engages with the questions of colonial and apartheid social hierarchy.

In terms of the first, the difficulties around race and racial description are evident in the tendency in the labels referencing paintings and photographs to avoid commentary on the conditions of production of the imagery. The imagery, much of it susceptible to extensive deconstruction, such as images of African men (see object 102 in catalogue, Oliphant, Delius, and Meltzer 2004: 289), of "Bushmen" driving cattle up a kloof (ravine) called "*Thieves*" (object 104), of Cape Town (image 119), of students and teachers at Lovedale (a college for African men and women in the colonial eastern Cape town of Alice) (images 138 and 139), and many more, is presented empirically. The storyboards preceding the images provide a narrative that is sensitive in so far as they talk of upheavals and so on, but the racial conceits and the racialized production of knowledge evident in many of the images remains unaddressed. Why, for example, portraiture is sometimes conveyed through images of people in skins and sometimes in the deeply layered clothing of "civilized" Europeans is not broached as a question of knowledge production. The discursive decisions that circulate during the production of images such as these are avoided.

Instead, and this leads to the second issue, the aesthetic of the exhibition is, at its most fundamental level, one of "collection." Implicit in the aesthetic is the idea of assembling what amounts to a comprehensive account of life in the timeline of South Africa's history. Comprehensiveness is assumed to be able to capture, contain, and rebut the critique of inclusion and exclusion and hierarchy. There is little in the hierarchy that is not included. What this panoptic avoids, however, is a story of *how* hierarchy is mediated and managed in everyday life. An attempt at explanation is offered in a series of images that deal with strong women (such as images 249 of Olive Schreiner, 253 of Charlotte Maxeke), of ordinary life containing personal memorabilia (images 303 and 304) of boxing gloves, children's shoes (images 306–308), but even these fall down once they are revealed to be about icons of the South African struggle, such as Nelson Mandela and Bram Fischer. The representational style is thus marked by detail, but detail that is often extraordinary and not fully able to show how oppression is instantiated, lived and experienced, and then worked with. Individuals and their possessions and experiences are "collected" and then curated. Absent is a sense of their selves, of an ability to narrate themselves in the context of their histories. The strategy of the exhibition, instead, is to "collect" them inside a larger narrative. What the process of "collection" does is to expand the line of sight for the viewer. The viewer sees more of the story than has hitherto been told, but the thrust of the story remains within a narrative economy of the empirical. The burden of history in this narrative style is to continue assembling and growing. Inclusion proceeds through a process of adding and extending. What is avoided is a history that engages with itself and attempts to understand the politics of its own production and to open up the possibility of contradiction in the lives of the subjects that are assembled within the collection.

Triumphalist Multiculturalism

Triumphalist memory, in some ways now the official state memory, and more about this in a moment, is framed around the ideal of redemption. It is rendered essentially as a memory of the triumph of the human spirit, of the inevitability of goodness. Iconicized by the image and the memory of Mandela, it defines the ideological and cognitive limitations of human identity. Through the act of reconciliation, humanity is rendered, in somewhat Hegelian terms, as having progressed through its contradictions to arriving at a point of perfection. Memory is reorganized in relation to the ultimate inevitability, when good comes to prevail. The timeline, evident in many of our museums, embodies the sense of inevitability dictated by this discourse. All of experience is a preparation for the moment of enunciation. The discourse is like a balm. It is the ultimate feel-good.

What it does is displace the lines of tension within the process of remembering. Its central problem is its erasure of any racialized sense of the country's very specific historical formation. Hollowed out from it are the animating figures of race and racism. Left behind in the discourse is only the trace of race and racism. We see only the victim and then later the victim's redeemed self. The figure has no substance independent of the deviance, the aberration of apartheid that has thrust it into that state. It takes its life entirely from the script of the miraculous emergence from subjugation. The story covers over the substance, the contradictoriness of life within the world of the subordinate, or for that matter, the world of the dominant, it covers over the low-level and perpetual depression, the self-mutilation swirling in and around the consciousness of the oppressed, or, on the other hand, the implicatedness of people with privilege in the production of this misery. In covering over and up these stories it leaves only the question of the mystery of the triumphant spirit. How is it that those who were hurt so much can so readily forgive? This is its redemptive character. It redeems and absolves. It never requires anybody to own up and account for themselves. It is a certain kind of forgetting. Derek Walcott (1995: 373) responds to this kind of remembering: "I say to the ancestor who sold me, and to the ancestor who bought me, I have no father, I want no such father, although I can understand you, black ghost, white ghost, when you both whisper 'history,' for if I attempt to forgive you both I am falling into your idea of history which justifies and explains and expiates, and it is not mine to forgive, my memory cannot summon any filial love, since your features are anonymous and erased and I have no wish and no power to pardon." Within this narrative the entire complexity of race is reduced and then assimilated into the story of the heroic resurgence of the victim. While the victim overcomes his (and rarely is it her) circumstances, the social conditions within which identity is imposed, reacted to and remade are substantially minimized.

Much of this approach is evident in the Robben Island Museum, in some ways, South Africa's premier memory site. Robben Island is a small island ten kilometers off the coast from Cape Town. It was used as a prison, leper colony, and for a variety of other similar purposes by the colonial and apartheid authorities. It has become one of the country's most important heritage sites because it was the prison-home of Nelson Mandela for almost twenty-seven years. It was turned into a museum in the late 1990s. Its broad approach, as a museum, exemplifies the point being made above with respect to redemption. While Nelson Mandela's personal life constantly surprises, to the extent that new facets of a story that is assumed to be well-known continue to emerge, and so throws into disarray the seamless narrative that has come to characterize the iconography of Mandela, interestingly, as a subject of history, the Robben Island Museum and the people who have been incarcerated there and who worked there continue to be rendered in the prescripted language of the hagiographic.

The Robben Island Museum itself, constructed around a guided tour through the prison, is symbolically rendered as a tale of emergence. (Chapter 10 of this volume discusses Robben Island at greater length.) The museum's logo, for example, is of the transformation of prison bars into great resurgent human figures.

The problem with these discourses is that they treat the past—apartheid—as a socially discrete but deviant event. These forms of remembering inadequately engage with memory as a process that comes with consequences. Specifically, they ignore the deep continuities manifest in the figures of race and racism between the past and the present. They ignore the ways in which the apartheid past is inscribed into contemporary racism. Instead, they portray the post-apartheid period as a break, a rupture with racism. Racism in this construction is indissolubly attached to the deviance of apartheid. With the end of apartheid, so went the end of racism.

The question now arises how we should remember the past and who should take responsibility for it. As a point of departure, I argue that our responsibility is to unsettle the new certainties that have taken root in this new order in which we are in where the figures of race and racism continue to permeate and reproduce themselves. Central amid these certainties is the idea that we occupy a different space and time. Instead, what is necessary is a critical examination of the ways in which domination and colonialism continue uninterrupted, perhaps adapted but, unfortunately, sustained. In this process it is necessary to fight against those forms of remembering, whether they are triumphalist or curatorial, that imagine against the evidence, and refuse opportunities for counter-interrogation. Where such discourses present themselves they need to be filled with the substance of the complex past. Necessary is a form of memory that is open to evidence. And central in this process is recovering the memory of the forgotten, the shadowy, and the opaque and to help the emergence of a voice that confronts the conditions of its own production. Necessary is a memory which is aware of itself as production, and which is able to take responsibility for itself as a production. What such a memory does is unsettle the settlements of the current time. It calls for naming and counternaming, an endless commitment to uncovering rather than covering over. To a questioning of the relationship between what is remembered and what is forgotten.

And who will do this? Whose role is it to bring this about? Again, I would argue it is that which belongs to all of us. But how we define ourselves in relation to the project of modern racism, to the question of race is critical. Without a critical understanding of these problems, of our own implicatedness in these projects, of the many, often unspeakable realities of the production and cultivation of our identities as raced identities, we will never even begin to understand what the intellectual and the emotional challenge of developing an ethical memory is all about.

Deconstructionist Approaches

Given the debates about the nature of South Africa, and particularly the racial ways in which hegemonic discourse sought to project it during and before the apartheid era, as *white, African, colored, and Indian,* the oppositional project of the District Six Museum was crafted around an antiracial principle. This shaped the ways in which the museum located itself in relation to the people of District Six, Cape Town, and the larger social canvas of South Africa. (See Chapter 10 in this volume for further description and discussion of the District Six Museum.) In thinking of District Six, the museum deliberately presented itself as an inclusive space. District Six, that space on the foothills of Cape Town's famous Table Mountain from which over 60,000 people of color were removed in the 1970s to the late 1980s, was not the heartland of a dispossessed *colored* community, as some narratives sought to suggest. Instead it was a place which constantly problematized and decentered the totalizing impulses of color, class, religion, gender, and political belief. Its distinctiveness, like that of, but in some ways more thoroughly so, the large, old townships for people of color in major South African cities— Marabastad in Pretoria, South End in Port Elizabeth, Cato Manor in Durban, and Beaconsfield in Kimberley—lay in its ability to take difference and to sublimate it within a community identity.

While the apartheid state's racial project continually overlay, and often overwhelmed discourses of difference in District Six, the district was able, so the popular explanation goes, within the framework of shared and limited public and private resources and spaces, to assert the virtues of civility and public-mindedness. One's life in the district was lived in relation to others, to their needs and interests, and so one found oneself constantly interpellated, positioned but always, also, having to take position and voice. Identity, as a result, was inscribed as elusive and shifting, but always relational. While one would practice a religion, it was seldom that one's religion operated in a self-referential and closed way. Christian, Muslim, or Jewish, as one might be, one was also many other things. One lived one's beliefs in relation to the challenges of good neighborliness.

These readings of District Six strongly influenced how the museum was, therefore, to conduct itself as a space of representation and identification. It tried to present itself as a Museum *of* Cape Town *for* a much more inclusive Cape Town than that offered to history by the variety of readings available in mainstream discourse. The museum has been well documented by a range of South African and international scholars (see, for example, Rassool and Prosalendis 2001; Coombes 2003; McEachern 2001). Its distinctiveness, it has been argued in these texts, lies in its ability to work with the dominant forms of social difference in South Africa, race, class, and religion are critical among these, and to show how these differences were negotiated in District Six. The point to be made in relation to this is that the human dynamic of District Six, and by extension the larger urbanscape of Cape Town, before apartheid solidifies race as a physical reality through the Group Areas Act in the 1960s and 1970s, works to weaken the salience of race, religion, and class. Living in spaces of shared socioeconomic difficulty, people come to deal with each other as human beings. Their racedness is sublimated in the fluid space of the district (see Soudien 2001). In the *Digging Deeper* exhibition much of this approach was evident. The exhibition attempted to show this past. More importantly, it also attempted to reproduce this spirit of inclusion in its curatorial style. It deliberately sought to be inclusivist in what came into the museum, and how what came in was represented. The photographs on the walls, the memorabilia embodied in the furniture and household artifacts, the voices captured in interviews, and much more, were those which the people themselves sought to have within the museum. The photographs and the voices, moreover, were not those of *colored* ex-residents or *Jewish* shopkeepers, but those of individuals with names and histories of their own. Out of this process they emerged as people attempting to tell their own stories. This is the major difference between the curatorial approach of deconstructionism and those of the empirical and triumphal multiculturalisms described above. All three styles are driven and led by curatorial collectives, but the former is not only more democratic, the subjects themselves decide what will be put on display, but, critically, it is marked by what they themselves think is important. What emerges as a result is quite surprising. Identity is reconfigured in this process in relation to a much more complex engagement with the dominant factors of race, class, and religion. These factors do not go away, but they are not, as in the other two approaches, the totalizing schema against which subjectivity is sought and made.

I have argued elsewhere (see Soudien 2001) that this inclusivism was not without its problems. A central problem, I argued, was the sublimation of Africa in the narrative of District Six within a multicultural narrative economy in which the District's European, Asian, and African markers are treated as having, when in fact the reality is otherwise, a covalent status. The sublimation of Africa within this inclusiveness, it could be argued, is a large and unspoken challenge confronting the museum.

This notwithstanding, the museum's approach and its relation to the state of the new South Africa is a considerably more reflective one, premised as it is on the deconstruction of the everyday and the caution it precipitates with respect to processes of identification. Present in this working through of the everyday is a complex overlaying of the personal and the public and an attempt to get at the articulation between them. The museum offers an opportunity for people to take identity and to develop a relationship with the broader South Africa and its diverse publics in a way that relies on reflection. Possibilities for a much more inclusivist public identity arise out of this process.

Conclusion

In assessing how museums have positioned themselves in relation to images of the public in the new South African state, it must be concluded that much work remains. The problem is that institutions which might have been managerially captured remain deeply informed by their colonial origins. They have difficulty in deconstructing memory, and so their only option is to talk against it. The challenge that this represents is that in attempting to constitute a new memory, the new is forced to imagine itself against this old, and in the process, has difficulty in developing repertoires of the self that are more expansive and more fluid. What resources might a new exhibitionary approach call on in attempting to be different from the old? What discursive alternatives, in which identity is represented, could it look to for thinking about a new South African subject?

While the work that has emerged in the major museums in the last ten years has gone a great distance in confronting the specter of race and racism and its role in constituting an understanding of what it means to be a member of the public—a citizen—it has, however, been limited by the generalized difficulty in the public discourse, in some ways authorized by the state itself, of confronting the deep significance of race in public life. The challenge must by no means be underestimated, but there remains the problem of reracialization. More to the point, there remains the difficulty of understanding how profoundly the inherited (and thereby racial) protocols and values of the state need to be opened up for scrutiny to show, and then to provide opportunity for reflection on how these continue to work against a project of critical understanding of its power (and indeed our involvement and complicity as subjects in making and implementing decisions that result in some people being included and some excluded). This difficulty, I suggest, is compounded when the transfer of power to previously excluded people takes place under the aegis of a circumscribed political settlement, where the conditions of transfer effectively prohibit a deep interrogation of the fundamental terms of reference for the exercise of power in society and a deep interrogation of institutions such as the state that carries, represents, and embodies this power. The difficulty we have here, it is suggested, is that the deeply racial ways in which South African history has been presented, as if it had been present at the beginning and the end of the country's history in an undisturbed and pure form, is a major obstacle. This historiography of race continues to operate in the public and official domain and so comes to condition the vocabulary and the terms by which everybody in the new country comes to understand themselves. It is suggested in this chapter that other versions of the articulation of difference in South Africa exist and could be drawn on as resources for imagining the new South Africa in more complex ways. The District Six example is an important illustration of this point.

It is recognized here that cultural institutions such as museums stand in a difficult relationship to institutions of power in South Africa. It is recognized also that they cannot become and offer themselves as alternative sites of power. Whatever else might be suggested, they cannot become new instruments of revolution. By the same token, however, they need not become, either deliberately or unconsciously, the handmaidens of the state. It is their duty, as publicly constituted spaces, to provide opportunity for public education. This education, of necessity, must include opportunity for reflection on civic and public identity.

How they do this is clearly a matter for institutions to work out themselves, but it is suggested that they need to understand the conditions of their own representational and pedagogical practices. They need to develop a practice of rigorously inspecting the internal grammar of the discourses at their disposal—in a way which understands how subjectivity is constituted and presented and how this subjectivity might itself contain possibilities for exclusion. While only knowing this, as opposed to acting upon it, is clearly insufficient for promoting change, it is an infinitely more challenging and indeed defensible position in which public institutions might find themselves.

Bibliography

Becker, R. 2004. "Marking Time: The Making of the Democracy X Exhibition." In *Democracy X: Marking the Present; Representing the Past*, ed. A. Oliphant, P. Delius, and L. Meltzer. Pretoria: UNISA Press, 271–278.

Coombes, A. 2003. *History After Apartheid: Visual Culture and Public Memory in a Democratic South Africa.* Johannesburg: Wits University Press.

Hesse, B. 2002. "Forgotten Like a Bad Dream: Atlantic Slavery and the Ethics of Post-colonial Memory." In *Relocating Postcolonialism*, ed. D. T. Goldberg and A. Quayson. Oxford: Blackwell, 143–173.

McEachern, C. 2001. "Mapping the Memories: Politics, Place and Identity in the District Six Museum, Cape Town." In *Social Identities in the New South Africa. After Apartheid—Volume One*, ed. Abebe Zegeye. Cape Town: Kwela Books and South African History Online, 223–248.

Oliphant, A., P. Delius, and L. Meltzer, eds. 2004. *Democracy X: Marking the Present; Representing the Past*. Pretoria: UNISA Press.

Rassool, C., and S. Prosalendis, eds. 2001. *Recalling Community in Cape Town: Creating and Curating the District Six Museum*. Cape Town: District Six Museum Foundation.

Soudien, C. 2001. "The Uses of District Six in the Non-Racial Discussion." In *Coloured by History, Shaped by Place*, ed. Z. Erasmus. Cape Town: Kwela Books, 114–130.

Walcott, D. 1995. "The Muse of History." In *The Post-Colonial Studies Reader*, ed. B. Ashcroft, G. Griffiths, and H. Tiffin. London: Routledge, 370–374.

Chapter 10
Strategies for Transforming and Enlarging South Africa's Post-Apartheid Symbolic Landscape

Marc Howard Ross

The settings in which people live communicate many messages about the meaning of the past relevant to the present and future. These messages are inscribed across the symbolic landscape, and even when it is literally set in stone, what is told about the past can be fluid in that what people emphasize, worry about, commemorate, and celebrate shifts to meet changing needs in the present. Popular and scholarly accounts of the past change as particular details are selectively remembered and forgotten, and lessons drawn from the past are selectively emphasized. Often changes in the symbolic landscape occur slowly; occasionally they are rapid, as when there is major regime change in a society. In these latter situations, new regimes seek to alter how the past is understood and used, but we do not know a great deal about how this is accomplished.

South Africa is particularly interesting because an important part of the political transition in that country has involved specific strategies to bridge competing narratives and to develop more inclusive cultural expressions that diminish the racial separation that dominated the country in the past where for centuries whites, and especially Afrikaners, dominated the country's symbolic landscape as much as they dominated its politics. Their narrative of racial superiority and civilization gave no space to human rights, equality, and self-determination. By the 1980s pressures for change within South Africa were building and while many were surprised when in 1990 President F. W. de Klerk freed Nelson Mandela and other political prisoners, lifted the ban on the ANC and South African Communist party, and entered into negotiations with them, these public steps were only taken after a decade of planning and secret talks both within and outside the country (Crocker 1992; Sparks 1995).

When regimes quickly change, what happens to previously important sites of memory and commemoration? How is the country's symbolic landscape transformed? Widely cited experiences include beheading church statuary after the French Revolution and the smashing of monuments to Lenin and Stalin after the fall of the Soviet Union. Levinson notes that when there is radical regime change, one of the first tasks of the new rulers is the destruction of the old symbols (Levinson 1998), but he also describes a far less atypical solution found in Hungary, where monuments in Budapest from previous regimes are not destroyed but moved to a park where they are visible as historical, not political, objects. South Africa offers a complex and nuanced example of another option of how a new regime can treat the previous regime's symbols and narratives that dominated the country's symbolic landscape. It suggests how emerging narratives and cultural expressions have helped to address the collective trauma of apartheid and to construct a more inclusive nation in a land that was not long ago organized exclusively on racial lines.

Following the 1990–1994 transition to majority rule, South Africa broke with its past in a number of dramatic and important ways, including the adoption of its new nonracial constitution that removed all the apartheid laws and institutionalized majority rule. At the same time, many of the symbolic changes that some had thought were likely did not occur. For example, there was no destruction of monuments and statues honoring the former white rulers and the apartheid regime, although a few statues and portraits were moved out of prominent locations.[1] There was no construction of a new location for its capitol. There was no closing of monuments and museums associated with the previous regime. There was no wholesale renaming of cities, streets, and public parks.[2]

Post-apartheid South Africa pushes us to consider the extent to which cultural sites presenting not just different, but alternative, narratives can coexist in a society. Can the country allow space for the monuments and narratives that once supported apartheid, while also constructing new sites that recount the trauma of the apartheid years and its ultimate defeat? The tentative answer fifteen years after the 1994 transition is "yes" and to the extent that we can understand the underlying dynamics at work, there may be significant lessons for other postconflict societies.

The absence of decisions to totally recast the symbolic landscape does not mean that South Africa's new rulers failed to think about this question; quite the opposite. They shared the belief that it was necessary to address the past 350 years of race-based inequality, domination, and suffering, but not in a vindictive or exclusive manner that simply produced a politics that was a mirror image of that of the apartheid years. Doing so would be incompatible with the goal of reconciliation and the inclusive political vision that the African National Congress (ANC) and South African Community Party (SACP) had articulated for decades. In discussions about the past, it was widely accepted that whatever was done needed to take place within the ANC's and SACP's long-stated nonracial framework for building an inclusive society and each had long emphasized the role that individuals from all groups played in the anti-apartheid struggle. Finally, Nelson Mandela's statements and actions upon his release from prison strongly reaffirmed the commitment to build a nonracial society based on the equality of all people. It was made clear that whites who wanted to remain in South Africa and participate in a democratic nonracial society would be fully accepted.

Cultural institutions are a major vehicle for articulating and strengthening new narratives that are of particular significance in societies emerging from trauma that accompanies identity conflicts. They present experiences that were previously absent from public consciousness rendering them visible in the country's symbolic landscape, and in so doing help people process their own experiences and feelings of loss, shame, and guilt. To the extent that they serve as sites of grief and mourning as well, museums, monuments, and memorials can contribute to the growth of new community self-images and build new relationships and institutions in the postconflict period. New more inclusive narratives about the past help people make emotional sense of what occurred, serve as vehicles for justice and restitution, and offer visions of a shared future.

In examining museums and memorials, my goal is to consider three strategies for transforming South Africa's symbolic landscape and narratives and making them more inclusive as part of postconflict peacebuilding: *appropriation,* meaning linking the preexisting holidays, symbolic places, and buildings with the new regime's practices and institutions; *modification,* altering existing sites by changing their contents and/or narratives in significant ways to include previously excluded people and events, modifying the story told there, the intended audience, or shifting the objects exhibited; and *addition,* the creation of new symbolic sites where the voices of previously excluded people are heard. While the analytic distinction between these processes is clear, any single site may contain more than one. To examine these strategies I describe three sites—the Voortrekker Monument, Robben Island, and the District Six Museum—to understand the narratives about their past and the voice they give to those who were previously excluded from the symbolic landscape to produce South Africa's more inclusive symbolic landscape in the post-apartheid period.

Competing Narratives in Pre-1994 South Africa

Afrikaner Historical Narrative

For many years, the most publicly visible narrative in South Africa was that of the country's Afrikaners, one that emerged over several centuries illustrating the interaction of identity construction and context (Delmont 1993). It told of the arrival in Cape Town of the first settlers in 1652, their survival, British takeover of the colony, and most important, the decision to leave the coast and undertake the Great Trek into the interior in search of political autonomy when the British abolished slavery in 1833. In this account, the Afrikaners fought hostile natives, had two wars with the British, and succeeded in bringing civilization and Christianity to the interior and finally capturing control of the state in 1948 (Moodie 1975; Thompson 1985).

There are two emotional high points in this narrative. One is the battle of Blood River in Natal, where on 16 December 1838 a group of 450 men led by Andries Pretorius defeated an army of some 12,000 Zulu who attacked them at Ncome. The story is told that the group had earlier vowed that if they survived, they would declare a Sabbath day and build a church to honor God who delivered the victory. Sure enough, the Boer defenders fought off the Zulu, killing some 3,000 attackers, and forcing the remaining warriors to withdraw while suffering only three injuries and no deaths themselves. The battle, named Blood River after the Zulu blood that turned the river red, was memorialized as a testament to the Boers' religious faith and commemorated in Pretorius's church, later built in Pietermaritzburg (Thompson 1985). The second key event was the bloody Second Anglo-Boer War (1899–1902), in which the British defeated the Afrikaners ending the Transvaal's and Orange Free State's independence. During the war, the Afrikaners turned to guerilla tactics and in response the British engaged in a scorched-earth policy putting women and children in concentration camps, where many died. Even though they were defeated militarily and incorporated into the new Union of South Africa, the Afrikaners resisted assimilation and hardliners maintained the vision of a state.

The fortunes of these Afrikaner nationalists rose in the late 1930s when the centenary celebrations of the Great Trek crystallized nationalist fervor. As the anniversary approached, a number of plans were drawn up including the erection of monuments to the Trekkers in both Blood River and Pretoria. However, the most emotionally significant part of the celebration was a symbolic retracing of the steps of the Voortrekkers (Moodie 1975: 176–177). This quasi-religious political pilgrimage began in Cape Town. Following a reading of the sacred vow, two ox-drawn wagons, replicas of those used one hundred years before, wound their way to Pretoria capturing the imagination of many Afrikaners. As the wagons made their way north there were increasing demands for the wagons to visit small towns and villages where religious services were often held (Moodie 1975).

The sacred history was constituted and actualized as a general context of meaning for all Afrikanerdom in spontaneous liturgical re-enactment during the 1938 celebrations. Passionate enthusiasm seized Afrikaans-speaking South Africa. Men grew beards and women donned Voortrekker dress; street after street in hamlet after hamlet was renamed after one or another trek hero; babies were baptized in the shade of the wagons . . . and young couples were married in full trekker regalia on the village green before the wagons. . . . At night folks would gather around the campfires of the trekkers in their hundreds and thousands to sing traditional Afrikaans [folksongs] and the old Dutch psalms, to watch scenes from the Voortrek enacted in pantomime, and to thrill to inspired sermons culled from the depths of civic faith. . . . Wreaths were laid on the graves of all the Afrikaner heroes. . . . Holy ground was thus resanctified by the visit of the wagons. (Moodie 1975: 180–181)

Eventually seven other wagons joined the original two and the celebrations reached their climax in Pretoria, where on 16 December over 100,000 Afrikaners gathered for the celebration and the laying of the cornerstone for the Voortrekker monument. Historians see the intense emotional outpouring linking Afrikaner cultural and political identity as central to the Nationalist Party's electoral victory a decade later in 1948. The following year the massive Voortrekker Monument was dedicated, and the inaugural ceremony celebrated Afrikaner culture while laying out "a vision of society that legitimated the social ordering of South Africa under apartheid" (Crampton 2001: 224). The core themes at the Voortrekker monument's inauguration stressed the Afrikaners as an authentic nation that had brought White Christian civilization to tame the African interior. In many ways, it shares important elements with the American narrative of expansion and settlement in the west in the nineteenth century.

Liberation Struggle Narrative

Over time, a resistance narrative developed in South Africa that at its simplest level shares many elements with many other anticolonial accounts; this chronicle emphasizes that nonwhites lacked even the most basic political and human rights under white rule and that whites turned others into slaves and indentured workers and took their lands.[3] At a deeper level are the details central to accounts of the South African resistance and the liberation struggle and the compelling commitment, dedication, and sacrifice of its leading figures. Resistance in South Africa has a long history and it includes a century of Xhosa wars of resistance against whites moving into the Eastern Cape in the eighteenth and nineteenth centuries, and strong Zulu resistance to Afrikaner encroachment in Natal including major battles, such as Isandlwana in 1879 where Zulu warriors defeated an entire British regiment in one of the most ignominious defeats the British ever suffered.

In 1912, soon after the formation of the Union of South Africa, Africans met to form a single organization that later evolved into the African National Congress to oppose increasing white restrictions such as the Land Act that severely limited African land ownership outside the reserves, and pass laws that severely restricted peoples' movement and forcing Africans to work in the diamond and gold mines or on white farms. Protests took place over the next few decades but did not have much impact. Only when the ANC Youth League, which included Nelson Mandela, Walter Sisulu, and Oliver Tambo, was formed in 1944 did efforts to mobilize a mass struggle really begin. Following the Nationalist Party's victory in 1948 and the imposition of apartheid, opposition to the regime's policies increased as the ANC launched its Defiance campaign stepping up protests against apartheid policies such as the pass laws, population registration act, the Group Areas Act, and the Bantu Education Act.

In 1955 leading anti-apartheid organizations adopted the Freedom Charter at the Congress of the People calling for major changes; the government's response was to label it a communist document and to arrest 156 people (105 blacks, twenty-one Indians, twenty-three whites, and seven coloreds) including almost the entire executive of the African National Congress (ANC), Congress of Democrats, South African Indian Congress, Coloured People's Congress, and the South African Congress of Trade Unions (collectively known as the Congress Alliance). They were charged with high treason and a countrywide conspiracy to use violence to overthrow the present government and replace it with a communist state. In the dramatic trials all the defendants including Mandela were acquitted, but their organizations were weakened from government harassment and having to spend so much time and energy defending themselves.

Still, protests continued and when the Pan African Congress (PAC) gathered at Sharpeville to protest the pass laws, the police fired on the unarmed crowd killing sixty-nine and wounding 196. The government then declared the ANC and PAC illegal under the Suppression of Communism Act, and a year later the ANC took up arms against the government declaring that peaceful protest alone would not work against the regime. They formed the Umkohto wa Sizwe, Spear of the Nation, which carried out some two hundred acts of sabotage in the next year and half. They were no match for the South African security forces, however, and when the police raided the MK's secret headquarters, top leaders were put on trial. Those who could went into exile to continue the struggle, and in June 1964, Mandela and seven others were sentenced to life imprisonment for terrorism. Oliver Tambo managed to escape South Africa to lead the ANC in exile for thirty years.

For the next two decades, internal resistance developed in the townships as students and workers mobilized to oppose apartheid. The black consciousness movement captured the imagination of many and student protests against the imposition of Afrikaans as the language of instruction in schools launched the Soweto uprising in 1976. The next decade saw more protests, school boycotts, and an effort to make the townships ungovernable. In response, the government cracked down hard and in 1985 declared a state of emergency in many parts of the country. Despite the increasingly harsh violence of the regime, resistance continued to spread and South Africa was increasingly isolated internationally. Many realized that neither its small reform steps nor repression were working. By the late 1980s there were serious talks with the ANC and in 1990 it and other resistance organizations were unbanned, Mandela and other leaders were released from prison, and many in exile returned. Negotiations with the government began and in early 1994 the country held its first fully democratic election overwhelmingly selecting Nelson Mandela as president.

Transformation of the Symbolic Landscape

Appropriation

The simplest, and in some ways most visible, forms of appropriation in post-apartheid South Africa were state buildings and institutions. The easiest sites to appropriate were official ones associated with exclusive white rule such as the Parliament in Cape Town and the Union Buildings in Pretoria. The new government and post-apartheid leaders simply took over these sites to conduct government business. For many, the image of Nelson Mandela taking the oath of office as president before hundreds of thousands in front of the Union Buildings evoked intense emotions and signaled the tremendous transformation in the country that had taken place. Likewise, the multiracial character of the new parliament and the new voices heard within it for the first time had a huge symbolic impact on the country.

Following a peaceful, democratic election formerly outlawed and banned groups came to power. The substitution of Nationalist Party apartheid-era officials with those from the ANC and other formerly banned groups including the South African Communist Party was dramatic. Most of the new leaders' faces were black, and they included not only ex-prisoner Nelson Mandela but also the new Defense Minister, Joe Modise, who had headed the ANC's military wing while in exile, and others whom many whites had reviled for years. Just as challenging to many white and black South Africans was the appointment of Whites such as Joe Slovo, the long-exiled, one-time head of the South African Communist Party as Minister of Housing, and Albie Sachs, a high ranking exile leader who the South African Defense Forces had severely wounded in a car bomb attack, as head of the Constitutional Court. There was also a new flag, a new national anthem (which incorporated a verse of the older one), and dozens of small ways that previously excluded people and images became publicly visible.

Some sites were not only appropriated, but then transformed in such dramatic ways so that their former associations are reversed. A particularly notable example is Johannesburg's Old Fort Prison which held political and other prisoners including Gandhi and Mandela; it has been renovated and now houses the country's Constitutional Court. As demonstrated in these examples, appropriation provides simultaneously a kind of continuity through reference to the past, a highlighting of present changes, and suggestions of a very different future. However, appropriation was not the only strategy used in the new government's commitment to an inclusive multicultural nation-building project, and there were no steps taken to appropriate nongovernmental sites associated with specific groups.

Modification

Modification occurs when the group controlling a site alters key elements in the site's meaning and presentation. Modification of a site's symbolic meaning differs from appropriation in that control over the site does not necessarily shift from one group to another although those in control of the site might change as is the case when there is a major governmental shift. In South Africa, modification is visible in the country's local and national museums where there is an effort to present historical events in a more inclusive context. For example, there has been some effort to rename the Second Anglo-Boer War (1899–1902) the South African War, and new exhibits explain that the war was not just between whites, but that blacks were involved in it on both sides and thousands died, often in prison camps.

The challenge to South Africa's apartheid-era sites at the emotional core of Afrikaner identity concerns the possibility of focusing its role in the country's contemporary cultural diversity rather than its political past. For decades, the narrative offered at the Voortrekker monument just outside Pretoria, and at the Blood River battle site was one of conquest that completely merged political and cultural elements and was central to the Nationalist Party's political project and Afrikaner political identity. Given the emotional significance of these sites and their close association with white domination and apartheid, it was not evident what their role would be in the post-apartheid era. There was talk, for example, of tearing down the Voortrekker monument as a way of symbolizing the destruction of apartheid as well as a suggestion to paint it pink and to turn it into a gay nightclub. Another, probably more serious, proposal was made to turn the lower level of the monument that contains the cenotaph and the flame of civilization that some consider the most sacred part of the monument into an exhibition on the struggle against apartheid and the country's political transformation (Kruger 2002: 89).

Modest Modification: The Voortrekker Monument

The Voortrekker monument, a landmark intimately associated with the Afrikaner understanding of history and with the politics of domination under the Nationalist Party from 1948 to 1994, contains many references to the key elements of the Afrikaner historical narrative. In thinking about the problem of transforming the meaning of this well-known structure, Coombes points out the need to ask about the: "possibilities and impossibilities for rehabilitating . . . monument[s] with an explicit history as a foundational icon of the apartheid State . . . how far it is possible to disinvest such an icon of its Afrikaner nationalist associations and reinscribe it with new resonances which enable it to remain a highly public monument despite a new democratic government whose future is premised on the demise of everything it has always stood for" (Coombes 2000: 173–174). She also considers how monuments from the apartheid period are subject to public reinterpretation that can serve as "a staging post for self-fashioning for both black and white constituencies across the political spectrum" (Coombes 2000: 175) through rich and varied examples of how this Afrikaner icon has served as a setting for identity redefinition in recent years.

The monument is a massive stone construction atop a hill just outside Pretoria next to Schanskop Fort, one of four built to defend the city in the Second Anglo-Boer War, and in sight of the Union Buildings (Delmont 1993: 80). At its base, there is a granite laager of sixty-four wagons surrounding the building offering symbolic protection, and on the outside of the monument are statues of three Trekker leaders and an unknown leader. Close to the entrance is a statue of a mother and child that "symbolizes the culture and Christianity that were maintained and developed by the women during the Great Trek" (Heymans 1986: 6). Inside the monument are two significant symbolic spaces. The first is the twenty-seven friezes made from Italian marble that recount the story of the trek to British recognition of the Transvaal Republic in 1852 that fills the walls of the large dome covered room on the entrance level. The second is the monument's lower hall that contains two particularly significant objects that are visible from above: a niche against one wall holding a flame that symbolizes civilization in South Africa, and at the center an empty cenotaph that represents the symbolic resting place of the Trekker leader Piet Retief and his comrades whom the Zulus killed and the Voortrekkers' spirit of sacrifice and suffering (Delmont 1993: 81). It is laid out so that a ray of sunlight shines on the words, "We for thee South Africa" (in Afrikaans) carved on the cenotaph on 16 December, the Day of the Vow.

Given the monument's close association with Afrikaner cultural nationalism and political domination, it was not clear that the building would survive the transition and remain part of the landscape in a new, nonracial South Africa. A psychocultural drama over its future began but escalated far less than many expected.[4] Explaining how this came about is important, and the key is that it required an energetic effort to decouple Afrikaner culture from the politics of apartheid. Not an easy task. Indeed there were calls for the Voortrekker monument's destruction, radical transformation, and appropriation. The new government, however, did not compel any change in the monument and instead encouraged it to operate as an independent cultural institution, although it did not particularly prosper in the early post-apartheid years.

Since 2000, the monument has had a leadership group that has worked to recast the Voortrekker monument as a cultural, rather than a political, site. The challenge is how to operate as an Afrikaner cultural institution while not reviving divisive memories of apartheid among non-Afrikaners and not seeming to abandon the core Afrikaner values which to many people the monument embodies. Working toward this goal is not be easy for while the monument's contents make no explicit references to apartheid, the iconography and many of the objects in it are completely associated with conquest, white rule, and domination. In the twenty-seven marble friezes, for example, most of the images of blacks show them either as fighting with, and often murdering, the Voortrekkers, or being killed by the courageous and inspiring Boers.

The monument's current leadership has taken some initial inclusive steps to present the Voortrekker monument as an Afrikaner cultural institution and distance it from apartheid-era politics. One is an effort to attract black school children to the monument; they report that in some months there are three times more black school children than whites who visit the monument.[5] A second is the development of a new museum-like exhibit in the lower floor of the monument that emphasizes cultural history, rather than political images. It includes a presentation on human migrations throughout world and locates the Great Trek in this more general context. There is also a good deal on Afrikaner heritage through material culture that is presented in displays of nineteenth-century tools, clothing, furniture, and farming that emphasize details about daily life; little evokes the most emotional parts of the political narrative.

Third, the Voortrekker Monument Heritage Site includes more than the monument itself: there is also Fort Schanskop, an amphitheater that can seat 20,000 people, a series of hiking, bike, and horse trails, a picnic area, art gallery, ecology courses, a planned campground, and a Garden of Remembrance that will offer 6,500 niches holding individual last remains following cremation and will address the "growing problems at traditional cemeteries . . . due to the general fall in standards and the high level of crime in the country" (press release, 27 September 2002).[6] These uses emphasize activities separated from any explicit political agenda, and many Afrikaners support the multiple uses of the site. This is not surprising given Cohen's (1969) observations concerning the importance of cultural organizations when explicit political organization around identity is not likely to be productive.

Fourth, there has been an explicit effort to legitimize the monument in part by building bridges to the government agencies and political leaders. This has led to the return of, and then to recent increases in, government funding. In South Africa, there is nothing more valuable for a white cultural group seeking legitimation than a positive word from Nelson Mandela who has spoken out in support of the site. In 2000 he wrote to potential donors asking them to contribute to the monument's renewal projects. Then, in early 2002 Mandela visited the Voortrekker Monument Heritage Site where he delivered a speech and laid a wreath beside the statue of Anglo-Boer war hero Danie Theron. In his remarks Mandela stressed his esteem for the Afrikaner people and their resistance to imperial domination. He said he had learned a good deal from Afrikaner generals and "that shared experience of fighting for one's freedom binds us in a manner that is most profound." Mandela's inclusive comments acknowledged the role of Afrikaners in the country's development noting that Theron's patriotism "would in the present circumstances have translated into a passion that we jointly build and develop this country for the common good of all."[7] Finally, he noted that blacks and Afrikaners shared a common experience in struggling against British colonial rule. Interestingly, while the Voortrekker monument was a gathering place for right-wing Afrikaners during the South African transition, that some right-wing Afrikaner groups loudly protested Mandela's visit in 2002 only serves to further help the new administration separate itself from the apartheid-era policies.

Extensive Modification: Robben Island

Robben Island which housed the prison in which Nelson Mandela and other black political leaders were incarcerated after 1964 recounts the story of "the triumph of the human spirit" through the perseverance and creativity of South Africa's future leaders. Robben Island appropriates a locale of banishment and transforms it into one with an entirely different meaning with lessons about the resistance and community for the new nation. Here, not just the defeat of apartheid, but the detailed account of how the prisoners resisted daily humiliation and degradation and the inner strength with which they emerged from Robben Island, are at the core of the narrative recounted there.

Robben Island, a barren three square miles located in Table Bay, is a half-hour boat ride from Cape Town. It has a long history as a site of banishment for those who opposed the status quo in South Africa. Often compared to Alcatraz, Robben Island long served as a detention center for criminals and political opponents and then as a hospital for the insane, lepers, and the sick poor (Deacon 1998: 162). However, its greatest notoriety came when the apartheid regime turned it into a maximum security prison to hold black political prisoners in the 1960s (white political prisoners, although often subject to the same mistreatment as blacks, were held elsewhere). The island's most famous prisoner, Nelson Mandela, and all of ANC's top leadership not in exile were detained there. Mandela was sent to Robben Island in 1964 and was held there until 1987. In 1996, the government decided to convert Robben Island into a museum. What resulted is one of the most painful, as well as inspiring, places to explore issues of memory and memorialization in South Africa as it recounts the story of resistance and triumph though the actions and sacrifices of men (and an occasional woman) who actively opposed apartheid. In this emerging standard narrative, the details of heroes' lives are a powerful tool for communicating the story of the struggle and for drawing lessons relevant to the country's present and future development.

Nowhere in the country is the story of the apartheid regime's inhumane treatment of opponents, Nelson Mandela's vision and wisdom, the ANC's coordination and control, and the triumph of the human spirit told more powerfully than in Robben Island. The visitor learns how the political prisoners refused to give up the hope that within their lifetime there would be majority rule in South Africa and that the ANC's nonracial vision for the country would prevail. The buildings and setting have not been changed—what differs is the narrative that is told there. Its future-oriented message communicates an inclusive optimism: "While we will not forget the brutality of apartheid, we will not want Robben Island to be a monument to our hardship and suffering. We would want Robben Island to be a monument . . . reflecting the triumph of the human spirit against the forces of evil. A triumph of non-racialism over bigotry and intolerance. A triumph of a new South Africa over the old" (Kathrada 1999). The message of the narrative is clear: no matter how oppressive the system and the guards, the prisoners clung to the belief that they would eventually prevail and become democratic South Africa's rulers. Finally, the narrative emphasizes the fundamentally nonracial spirit of the resistance and stresses that there were whites deeply involved in the struggle against apartheid and that there were Blacks, such as prison guards, police and army officers, and black homeland leaders who profited from, and worked to maintain, apartheid.

Inside the prison an ex-prisoner who serves as the tour guide leads visitors into his former cell and recounts his own treatment and experiences (Figure 10.1). The visit also includes the cell where Mandela was confined for so many years and a visitor gets to reflect on how a person could have so much inner strength and courage living in such as small 8 foot by 8 foot cell. The story one hears about torture, mistreatment, and daily degradation is not pretty. At the same time, the details of what the prisoners endured only make more poignant the inner strength and resistance that sustained their mutual support and shared vision. One also learns about their creative communication methods, self-education, the painstaking translation, copying and distribution of newspapers, and their commitment to focus on governing an integrated country and not pursuing racialized vengeance when they gained power.

Although Robben Island is not readily accessible physically to many South Africans—it is not centrally located in the country and requires a boat ride from Cape Town—it is very available emotionally and is easily South Africa's the most prominent heritage site. The transformation in the island and its meaning from a repressive prison to one of sacrifice and triumph over evil is dramatic, easy to comprehend, and an incredibly optimistic one that even includes accounts of present-day friendships between ex-prisoners and their guards which connect people in all groups. Emphasis on the details of the personal experiences of Mandela and other political prisoners is emotionally engaging and compelling. The ex-prisoners who conduct the visits to their former cells and describe their treatment and the details of prison life have real credibil-

Figure 10.1. Robben Island. A tour guide, who is a former prisoner, recounts his experiences to visitors.

ity and their presence is a compelling reminder that the story of the struggle is not just about a few "great men." Finally, the Robben Island narrative's optimism is inclusive, recognizing the role that people from all groups in South Africa played in opposing apartheid, and inviting people from all groups to participate in nationbuilding.

Addition: District Six

Addition has been the most general strategy for changing the country's symbolic landscape. Some notable examples in and around Johannesburg are the Hector Peterson Museum in Soweto that recounts in detail the 1976 uprising; the Apartheid Museum in Gold Reef City that tells the story of apartheid focusing on the gold rush in the late nineteenth century that brought people to the area and the developments of a segmented labor market and eventually apartheid; and Museum Africa, located in the old fruit and vegetable market in downtown Johannesburg, that contains a permanent exhibit on the 1950s treason trials that emphasizes the multiracial nature of the opposition to apartheid.

Addition is seen particularly clearly in District Six, an old Cape Town neighborhood not far from the city's downtown port where there had been forced removals going back to the arrival of the first Dutch settlers in the mid-seventeenth century. Although there were a number of white residents in District Six in the early part of the twentieth century when many Eastern European Jews lived there, by the mid-1960s, District Six's more than 60,000 residents were primarily colored ("mixed-race" in South African parlance) although there were also blacks and Malays as well. District Six's prime location made it an obvious target for development and in 1966, it was declared a White Group Area under the government's Group Areas Act. Removal of residents to more remote colored and black townships in Cape Flats took until 1982 by which time virtually the only buildings remaining were the District's schools, churches, and mosques.

District Six is only one of many areas in Cape Town and in other cities that were demolished under this legislation. In and around Cape Town, there were some forty areas where nonwhites lived that were declared whites-only under apartheid. In 1988, there was strong support to build a museum that would tell the story of the forced removal. A District Six Museum Foundation was established and held a two-week exhibit that presented photographs from District Six in 1992. In late 1994, a more ambitious exhibit, named *Streets: Retracing District Six* opened. Although it was only scheduled for a few weeks, *Streets* never closed due to the tremendous interest the museum generated in the issues of memory and community (Rassool 2007). Soon the museum expanded its exhibitions, and supported the efforts of former residents and their descendants to pursue land restitution claims.

If Robben Island tells the story of resistance and triumph in South Africa through the lives of national heroes, then the District Six Museum joins memory and politics in a very different way through its grassroots exploration of the community's "archaeology of memory" (Rassool 2007). By emphasizing the daily lives of the area's 60,000 residents before they were shattered through forced removal, their varied forms of resistance to apartheid and exclusive White rule, memories, and a sense of dignity are recovered. Here memory is not just a mechanism for a nostalgic view of the past, but it is mobilized for the restoration of the district's unjustly appropriated land. As a result, since its establishment the museum has pursued two goals: telling the story of District Six and other forced removals and mobilizing "the masses of ex-residents and their descendants into a movement of land restitution, community development and political consciousness" (Rassool 2001a: viii).

Three objects serve as central emotional points for visitors. First there are the old street name signs from District Six that a white foreman who worked on the demolition crew managed to save in his attic rather than throw into Table Bay with everything from District Six as he had been instructed to do (Figure 10.2). The signs that are hung in three vertical columns immediately catch a visitors' eye upon entering the building. To many, their reappearance seemed to almost magically signal the return of the community from the past. The second object that the museum uses that particularly engages visitors and turns them into active participants is a memory cloth on which people are asked to write comments which are later hand embroidered by volunteers. From the outset, people were interested in writing their own memories and comments on the cloth and the tremendous response is perhaps best measured by the fact that it is now far more than a kilometer long.

Third is a large canvas on which a map of the district had been painted. It covers most of the central floor space and former residents and their descendants are invited to write the names of shops and to put their names on the spot of their former homes (Figure 10.3). The map proved to be of particular emotional significance in several ways. McEachern (1998) observed that invariably former residents visiting the museum first locate where they lived on the map and that it is at the center of the personal stories they tell each other or to their children or grandchildren in visits to the museum. She suggests that walking across the map is an active process of recovering what is lost and this helps build popular narratives and "makes *visible* the people in contrast to apartheid making them disappear into Cape Flats. . . . The map works as a mnemonic, allowing the recall of the place . . . [and] in the revalu-

Figure 10.2. District Six Museum, Cape Town. The street signs from the former neighborhood.

Figure 10.3. District Six Museum, Cape Town. The large canvas map showing the former neighborhood where former residents are invited to write their names showing where they once lived.

ing of the District, the walkers achieve distinction and value themselves" (McEachern 1998: 58). Story telling, she argues, is about meaning-making and the stories are both models of District Six and models for South Africa's future (McEachern 1998: 61).[8] McEachern (1998: 55–56) considers the many reactions to, and uses of, the map for eliciting deep memories and notes that for some people their visit to the museum provided their first occasion for talking to their children about District Six. This is not surprising and is consistent with many other reports that people who have experienced trauma often have great trouble talking about and reliving it with close family and friends.

While the museum offers a special place to former residents, its message is far from exclusive and Bohlin suggests that the category of "we" is broadened to encompass all who suffered under apartheid (1998: 181). Outside visitors easily feel like learners and witnesses, not voyeurs. In fact there is a great deal of space for outsiders, including foreign visitors, to identify with the former residents and the goal of recovering memories, community, and their seized land. In the museum's symbolic reappropriation of the land and community that was destroyed, "the memories of the events in District Six are construed as belonging collectively to all South Africans, regardless of race, economic status and political affiliation" (Bohlin 1998: 184). Finally, it is important to note that the suit to recover District Six's undeveloped land was victorious and the process of building homes to allow former residents to return is under way.

Conclusion

The "rainbow" vision of the new government led to a great variety of efforts to recognize the country's past. In South Africa following the end of apartheid perhaps the most immediate need was to recount and publicly acknowledge the trauma that it had inflicted on people. This took many forms, including publication of books and articles, media presentations, the Truth and Reconciliation Commission's public forums, and transformation of the symbolic landscape. This chapter has explored the role of cultural sites and institutions, such as museums and monuments, in this process and analyzed three strategies of transformation: appropriation, modification, and addition. The three cases discussed communicate the complexity of enlarging the country's symbolic landscape and building newer, more inclusive narratives with which a majority of all of South Africa's racial and ethnic groups could identify. In societies that have experienced major transformations, appropriated, modified, and new cultural institutions can serve as both reflectors of these changes and as sources of change that deepen understanding of what the society has experienced.

The analysis here of the strategies of appropriation, modification, and addition offers some hypotheses, but no evidence concerning the extent to which changes in the symbolic landscape have had an impact on how ordinary people understand the past and imagine the future. Although he did not study the country's heritage sites, Gibson's analysis of the Truth and Reconciliation Commission's findings suggests that there is a good deal of support in South Africa for a common national identity and a broad acceptance of the TRC's findings about the abuses of the apartheid era (Gibson 2004). His results are certainly consistent with the hypothesis offered here that narratives found in the country's heritage sites not only reinforce the new national narrative but transmit it in ways that change how many people think about social and political relationships and open possibilities for a continuing inclusive, democratic political life in the country.

In new, or transformed, states great effort and resources are often put into symbolic activities. In South Africa since 1990, there has been great interest in recounting experiences and publicly expressing ideas that previously were explored only in private or protected settings. In particular, there has been a widely felt intense need to have state institutions and the media address the past and to legitimate the experiences of the previously marginalized and powerless. Yet the commitment to give voice to the past says little about exactly whose voice is to be heard and what will be said. The three sites discussed here show great variation in their styles and specific messages. Each, however, offers a narrative that reframes the past in ways that are relevant for the present and future that interact with current politics, and highlight the diverse needs heritage sites can address in a multicultural society.

The Voortrekker monument, once the country's dominant symbol of apartheid, now seeks to position itself as a cultural institution searching for ways to link Afrikaners to South Africans of other backgrounds rather than expressing domination over them. At present, this is probably more successful than most people had expected in part because its meaning has been modified and even appropriated at times so that "Rather than working to disinvest the monolith of its ignoble and oppressive history, the more successfully disruptive 'performances' engage with the past in order to 'domesticate' the apartheid state's symbolic armory as a means of offering the possibility of indifference in the future" (Coombes 2003: 53).

In Robben Island, the narrative of "the triumph of the human spirit over adversity" is at the core of how the ANC and leaders of the country explain both the long struggle against apartheid and the democratic transition. Mandela's creative, long-term responses to his treatment are used as a model for the South African future. The ability of the top leadership in the prison to devise methods of self-education, communication, and mutual support are central themes used in constructing the nation since 1994. Robben Island meets a widespread, basic need to have a coherent explanation about what apartheid did to people, how it ended, a rationale for reconciliation (and nonvengeance), and an optimistic vision for the future, offering the country inspiring heroes and moral principles.

The District Six Museum's narrative begins with many of the same elements found in many other heritage sites—an account of victimization and racism that led to the destruction of a community through forced removal, a common apartheid-era practice. However, in contrast to the Robben Island narrative emphasizing the country's political heroes, this one is deeply embedded in the grassroots narrative of how District Six residents lived their daily lives, both paying the price for apartheid and managing at times to create spaces that insulated themselves from its oppressive presence (Rassool 2001b; Rassool and Prosalendis 2001). The Museum's founders and board have been clear that uncovering memory is intimately linked to political voice and restitution. Recovered truth, in this conception, is needed to redress past injustice, and to do this political consciousness must be built and action strategies developed. What is so compelling in the District Six story told through the street signs, the map with thousands of names, the memory cloth, the sights and sounds of daily life, is how reasonable, even necessary, land restitution appears. To bring people to this conclusion, District Six mobilized the buried memories and objects of everyday life to render the ordinary compelling, and the project depended upon the widespread participation of the dispersed former residents and their descendants. Psychoculturally, District Six addressed the trauma of apartheid on two levels—through testimony about past injustices and through legal action to address its injustices.

At the same time, there are significant challenges remaining in South Africa given the continuing inequalities between groups. Moving too quickly to rectify them threatens to disrupt the country's economic stability, while acting too slowly will produce political disillusionment and protest. The South African transition and its success in the first dozen years of majority rule offer great hope that even the most racially divided societies can find ways to begin to heal past wounds and build a shared future. As Gibson (2004) concludes in his study of public reactions to the TRC process, the answer is a clear "maybe they can." In this day and age of ethnic hatred and clashes of civilization perhaps this is not such a pessimistic conclusion.

Notes

This chapter is drawn from the analysis in Ross (2007: chapters 8–9).

1. For example, the statue of Hendrick Verwoerd, former prime minister who was widely recognized as apartheid's chief architect, was removed from the grounds of the Union Buildings in Pretoria, the seat of the country's executive branch.

2. In recent years there has been conflict over renaming Pretoria and a compromise has emerged to change the name of the region but not the city itself.

3. This section draws heavily from ANC's account of its history found at http://www.anc.org.za/ancdocs/history/.

4. In 1992 "History Workshop" held a conference at which its future was discussed and a poster from the session shows the Voortrekker monument bound in chains and teetering on one side possibly about to be pulled over.

5. It was suggested to me that black teachers are often more willing to bring students to the monument than whites who, because of the monument's association with apartheid, are either uninterested in visiting it or are embarrassed to do so.

6. Obviously this is aimed at Afrikaners for it is not very likely that there will be many non-Afrikaners who seek "a dignified last resting place in a culturally sympathetic environment, in the shade of the Monument" (Press Release, Voortrekker Monument. September 2002. http://www.voortrekkermon.org.za/archive1.php).

7. "Madiba Praises Afrikaner Hero," *Herald*, 7 March 2002, http://www.the herald.co.za/herald/2002/03/07/news/theron.htm.

8. Bar-On (2002) makes a similar point about the value of storytelling as part of healing in his work on the Israeli-Palestinian conflict.

Bibliography

Bar-On, Daniel. 2002. "Conciliation Through Storytelling: Beyond Victimhood." In *Peace Education: The Concept, Principles, and Practices Around the World*, ed. G. Salomon and B. Nevo. Mahwah, N.J.: Lawrence Erlbaum, 109–116.

Bohlin, Anna. 1998. "The Politics of Locality: Memories of District Six in Cape Town." In *Locality and Belonging*, ed. N. Lovell. London: Routledge, 168–188.

Cohen, Abner. 1969. *Custom and Politics in Urban Africa*. Berkeley: University of California Press.

Coombes, Annie E. 2000. "Translating the Past: Apartheid Monuments in Post-Apartheid South Africa." In *Hybridity and Its Discontents: Politics, Science and Culture*, ed. A. Brah and A. E. Coombes. London: Routledge, 173–197.

———. 2003. *History After Apartheid: Visual Culture and Public Memory in a Democratic South Africa*. Durham: Duke University Press.

Crampton, Andrew. 2001. "The Voortrekker Monument, the Birth of Apartheid, and Beyond." *Political Geography* 20: 221–246.

Crocker, Chester. 1992. *High Noon in Southern Africa: Making Peace in a Rough Neighborhood*. New York: W. W. Norton.

Deacon, Harriet. 1998. "Remembering Tragedy, Constructing Modernity: Robben Island as a National Monument." In *Negotiating the Past: The Making of Memory in South Africa*, ed. S. Nuttall and C. Coetzee. Cape Town: Oxford University Press, 161–179.

Delmont, Elizabeth. 1993. "The Voortrekker Monument: Monolith to Myth." *South African Historical Journal* 29: 221–246.

Gibson, James L. 2004. *Overcoming Apartheid: Can Truth Reconcile a Divided Nation?* New York: Russell Sage Foundation.

Heymans, Riana. 1986. *The Voortrekker Monument, Pretoria.* Pretoria: Board of Control of the Voortrekker Monument.

Kathrada, Ahmed. 1999. *Letters from Robben Island: A Selection of Ahmed Kathrada's Prison Correspondence, 1964–1989,* ed. Robert D. Vassen. Cape Town: Mayibuye Books.

Kruger, Cecelia. 2002. "Heritage Resource Management in South Africa: A Case Study of the Voortrekker Monument Heritage Site." *Historical and Heritage Studies.* Pretoria: University of Pretoria.

Levinson, Sanford. 1998. *Written in Stone: Public Monuments in Changing Societies.* Durham: Duke University Press.

McEachern, Christine. 1998. "Working with Memory: The District Six Museum in the New South Africa." *Social Analysis* 42, no. 2: 48–72.

Moodie, T. Dunbar. 1975. *The Rise of Afrikanerdom: Power, Apartheid, and the Afrikaner Civil Religion.* Berkeley: University of California Press.

Rassool, Ciraj. 2001a. "Introduction: Recalling Community in Cape Town." In *Recalling Community in Cape Town: Creating and Curating the District Six Museum,* ed. C. Rassool and S. Prosalendis. Cape Town: District Six Museum Foundation, vii–xii.

———. 2001b. "Memory and the Politics of History in the District Six Museum." Paper presented at the workshop on Mapping Alternatives: New Heritage Practices in South Africa, University of Cape Town, 25–26 September.

———. 2007. "Community Museums, Memory Politics and Social Transformation: Histories, Possibilities and Limits." In *Museum Frictions: Public Cultures/ Global Interactions,* ed. I. Kratz and C. Kratz. Durham: Duke University Press, 286–321.

Rassool, Ciraj, and Sandra Prosalendis, eds. 2001. *Recalling Community in Cape Town: Creating and Curating the District Six Museum.* Cape Town: District Six Museum Foundation.

Ross, Marc Howard. 2007. *Cultural Contestation in Ethnic Conflict.* Cambridge: Cambridge University Press.

Sparks, Allister. 1995. *Tomorrow Is Another Country: The Inside Story of South Africa's Road to Change.* Chicago: University of Chicago Press.

Thompson, Leonard. 1985. *The Political Mythology of Apartheid.* New Haven: Yale University Press.

Chapter 11
Invisible House, Invisible Slavery
Struggles of Public History at Independence
National Historical Park

Charlene Mires

For most of two centuries, the southeast corner of Sixth and Market Streets in Philadelphia stirred little public interest, despite its location one block north of Independence Hall, the landmark birthplace of the Declaration of Independence and the United States Constitution. Along Market Street, a major thoroughfare, eighteenth-century houses gave way to nineteenth-century commercial buildings. When the light industrial zone fell into decay in the twentieth century, entire blocks were leveled to create a vista of landscaped plazas reaching for three blocks north of Independence Hall. The resulting Independence Mall, originally a state park, became the north-south axis of Independence National Historical Park. Situated within the park boundaries, the southeast corner of Sixth and Market Streets served as no more than a convenient site for a women's restroom structure. A simple wayside marker provided only a brief summary of a more notable history: that during the late eighteenth century, this had been the site of a fine mansion owned by the Revolutionary War financier Robert Morris. During the 1790s, when Philadelphia served as the nation's capital, Presidents George Washington and John Adams occupied this house and established the presidency of the new republic within its walls.

In a city as old as Philadelphia, there are no empty lots. Sites may appear to be vacant after features are demolished, buried, paved over, or cast aside, but history remains to be recovered by future generations. Such was the case at the site of the President's House, which became the focus of intense interest and controversy starting in 2002, when new

Figure 11.1. Independence Hall Plaza in Philadelphia showing where President George Washington's residence and its slave quarters were located while Washington lived there from 1790 to 1796.

research raised awareness that the house was not only the home of presidents but also of at least nine enslaved Africans whom George Washington brought from Mount Vernon (Lawler 2002, 2005). Furthermore, this place with a history of slavery as well as freedom overlapped with the site of a new Liberty Bell Center, a nearly block-long exhibit hall for the symbolic bell bearing the inscription, "Proclaim liberty throughout all the land, unto all the inhabitants thereof." As twenty-first-century visitors paid homage to this symbol of liberty, they would be walking directly over a site of slavery—without knowing it, unless steps were taken to change both the exhibits in the Liberty Bell Center and the lack of attention to the history of the adjacent ground.

Such an undeniable convergence of liberty and slavery demanded recognition—but exactly how, and under whose control? These questions forced into conflict, but also into conversation, the federal caretakers of

Figure 11.2. The 2007 excavation of the President's House and its slave quarters abutting the Liberty Bell Pavilion.

the site, historians from outside the National Park Service, and diverse and wide-ranging community groups, most especially African Americans tied by ancestry to the history and legacy of slavery. This was a conflict about one particular plot of ground, but the stakes were much higher. The President's House represented much larger issues of whose histories had been told and whose had been left out (Horton and Horton 2006; Coard 2005; Holt 2005). Grievances directed at the obscured history of slavery at the President's House site were deeply rooted in personal experiences of social and economic injustice. Acknowledging such injustices would call into question the traditional understanding of Independence National Historical Park as a place for celebrating the achievements of American freedom, not its limitations. When the controversy began, the institutional structures and practices of the National Park Service could neither contain, manage, nor resolve the conflict. Only through the disruption of the status quo and the invention of new avenues for public participation could the site of the President's House become a place where the interdependent histories of slavery and freedom could be recognized.

Construction, Curiosity, and a History Revived

Two independent series of events during the late 1990s combined to call new attention to the President's House site. During this decade, Independence National Historical Park underwent a major reorientation which placed new buildings and attractions along its north-south axis. Extending northward from Independence Hall, these included the new Liberty Bell Center which opened in October 2003 in the first block, the Independence Visitor Center in the second block, and the National Constitution Center in the third. The site of the President's House stood directly between the Liberty Bell Center and the Visitor Center across the street, although it did not originally figure into the park's plans. Prior to the Liberty Bell Center's construction, archaeologists did uncover one remnant of the President's House history—a stone-lined pit, nine feet across, which proved to be the remains of an ice house. Once documented, however, the ice house disappeared from public view, "preserved in place" under the Liberty Bell Center, in keeping with standard archaeological practice and NPS regulations (Independence National Historical Park n.d.; Flam 2001).

Meanwhile, a local man with determined curiosity embarked on a personal pursuit of the history of the President's House. Edward Lawler, Jr., a musician and one-time architecture student at the University of Pennsylvania, had shown out-of-town visitors the famous Philadelphia meeting places of the United States Congress and the United States Supreme Court, when one of them asked him where the executive branch of government had been located. Lawler did not know, but he made it his mission to find out. His quest led the Independence Hall Association—a civic group dating to the 1940s creation of the national park around Independence Hall—to formally request in August 2001 that the floor plan of the President's House be marked with stone on the site at Sixth and Market Streets. Then-Superintendent Martha B. Aikens denied the request, stating that such a footprint would not foster public understanding of the nation's first two presidents (Independence Hall Association Board 2001; Aikens 2001).

Lawler's detailed reconstruction of the history of the President's House appeared in January 2002 in the *Pennsylvania Magazine of History and Biography*, the peer-reviewed journal published by the Historical Society of Pennsylvania. To his surprise, the article's greatest impact grew from his documentation of the structural changes that Washington ordered to accommodate his slaves. Historian Gary Nash, visiting Philadelphia during February 2002, amplified and fueled the controversy by charging during a broadcast radio interview that the National Park Service was ignoring the history of slavery as it constructed a new exhibit hall for the Liberty Bell. With Nash's urging, a group of Philadelphia-area historians (called the Ad Hoc Historians) mobilized to intervene, first to persuade the National Park Service to revise the Liberty Bell exhibits to tell a more complex story of liberty and slavery, and then to press for a full interpretation of the history of the President's House (Nash 2006; Nash and Miller 2002). The President's House site also spurred the founding of two organizations of Philadelphia African Americans—the Avenging the Ancestors Coalition (ATAC) and Generations Unlimited—to campaign for a memorial to the enslaved Africans of George Washington's household and recognition of their history (Coard 2005). The controversies over the President's House site and the Liberty Bell exhibits were widely reported in the local and national media (Smith 2002; Teicher and Robinson 2003; Strauss 2003; Kilian 2003; Zucchino 2004).

The path toward presenting the history of freedom and slavery at the President's House was paved with good intentions, but also with anger, frustration, and misunderstandings. Despite the fact that freedom and slavery were entwined in the early history of Philadelphia and the nation, reweaving these narratives with a particular focus on George Washington and his presidency presented difficult challenges. Understanding these challenges requires a look back at how the narratives of freedom and slavery became separated at Philadelphia's leading historic sites. How is it that these two aspects of American history diverged? In part, the answer lies in the history of public memory of the American Revolution. As Michael Kammen and others have shown, constructing and preserving the memory of the nation's founding is closely tied to American national identity (Kammen 1978; Kammen 1986). The memory of the nation's early history also has been contested in ways that reflect John Bodnar's conception of public memory as an interaction between "official" and "vernacular" versions of the past. In the case of historic places within Independence National Historical Park, the National Park Service has offered the official narrative of history, while groups such as those mobilized around the President's House issue have presented alternative interpretations (Bodnar 1992). Finally, the location of the President's House site within an ever-growing and changing urban environment has contributed to the loss and rediscovery of its historic significance. Scholars have viewed cities as sites of "collective memory," but the site of the President's House and the cultural landscape of Independence National Historical Park also point toward a city of selective memory in which the physical remnants of some histories survive while others are allowed to fade from view (Boyer 1994; Hayden 1995; Gross 2000; Mires 2004).

Freedom, Slavery, and the Memory of the Nation's Founding

Public memory of the American Revolution in Philadelphia has been organized to a large degree around the two symbols that anchor Independence National Historical Park: Independence Hall, the setting for the Declaration of Independence and the United States Constitution; and the Liberty Bell, which hung in the bell tower of Independence Hall at the time of the Revolution. Independence Hall, constructed beginning in 1732, began its existence as the Pennsylvania State House. Events within the building during the eighteenth and nineteenth centuries testify to the entwined histories of freedom and slavery. Many of the Pennsylvania Assemblymen who served there were slaveowners (Horle et al. 1997: 55). The Second Continental Congress, also including slaveholders, approved the Declaration of Independence but argued bitterly over the clause in which Thomas Jefferson blamed the King of England for inflicting slavery on the British colonies. The delegates struck out that clause. In 1780, with the building once again serving as Pennsylvania's State House, the Pennsylvania Assembly passed the young nation's first gradual abolition law—but a law so gradual that the child of a slave born on the day the law went into effect could be legally held in bondage until the age of twenty-eight (Nash 1988: 60–63). In 1787, the State House once again became a national stage, this time for the Constitutional Convention, with George Washington presiding. These delegates produced a lasting frame of government for the United States—avoiding the word "slavery" but acknowledging and allowing its continued existence. Through all of these events, it must be remembered, the Pennsylvania State House stood in a city fast becoming the free black capital of the United States, with African Americans living and working nearby and monitoring every action that seemed to promise freedom but more often added constraints to their liberty.

Philadelphia served as the nation's capital from 1790 until 1800. Again, freedom and slavery both remained on the national agenda. Meeting next door to the Pennsylvania State House in the new County Court House (Congress Hall), the United States Congress passed the Fugitive Slave Law of 1793, which provided the enforcement mechanisms for the fugitive slave clause in the Constitution. A block to the north, President George Washington rented the fashionable mansion of Robert Morris at 190 High Street (today's Market Street). Like other slaveholding visitors to Pennsylvania, he took advantage of the state law that allowed slaves brought into the state to continue to be held for a period of six months. The President took care to rotate his household staff back to Mount Vernon at intervals that assured that no enslaved African would reach the six-month limit. While the master tended to the nation's freedom, his slaves were mindful of the limits of their own in the midst of a city with a large and growing free black population. Two of George Washington's slaves asserted their freedom by escaping. One, the President's talented chef Hercules, escaped while en route back to Mount Vernon from Philadelphia. The second, Martha Washington's favorite Ona Judge, escaped from the President's House in 1796 with the help of free black Philadelphians. Quietly, the President of the United States used his executive powers to try to recapture Ona Judge, but she successfully maintained her freedom in Portsmouth, New Hampshire. As he neared the end of his Presidency, George Washington resolved to free the slaves he owned outright after both he and Martha died, but this did not change the fact that slaves worked and lived in the President's House in Philadelphia. For slaves such as Ona Judge, who were owned by Martha Washington or her first husband's estate, Washington's final intentions had no effect (Wiencek 2003: 313–325).

Slavery itself diminished in the northern states through the late eighteenth and early nineteenth centuries, but the issue of slavery did not. In the blocks south of the Pennsylvania State House, African Americans assembled in National Negro Conventions to address the continuing tragedy of slavery in the South. Black Philadelphians had additional battles to fight, against the Pennsylvania Assembly's proposal in 1813 to ban further migration of African Americans into the state; against the American Colonization Society's project to transport free blacks to Africa; and against the 1838 revisions of the Pennsylvania Constitution, which made being "white" a qualification for voting. In these campaigns, African Americans deployed the language of the Declaration of Independence—the rights to life, liberty, and the pursuit of happiness that seemed to have been promised in 1776. Because of the association of the old Pennsylvania State House with the Declaration, the building became both a symbol of liberty and a symbol of liberty denied. Frederick Douglass spoke against slavery in Independence Square in 1844. During the 1850s, when federal courts occupied the second floor of Independence Hall, the building became the setting for hearings to determine the fate of accused fugitive slaves captured under the Fugitive Slave Act of 1850. These hearings resulted in freedom for some, but slavery for others. In at least one case, the freedom of an accused fugitive was purchased in the federal marshal's office inside Independence Hall (Mires 2002: 47–54, 88–99).

How did we lose sight of the powerful convergence of freedom and slavery in the space which later became Independence National Historical Park? For this, we can look to the record of historic preservation and public memory of the American Revolution. Even as the slavery issue continued to inflame public opinion in nineteenth-century Philadelphia, physical reminders of its history in the city itself were lost, remodeled, remembered, or forgotten in ways that separated the narrative of the nation's freedom from the history of slavery. The President's House, which quartered slaves as well as the executive branch of government, became subsumed by the architecture of nineteenth-century commerce. After the nation's capital moved to the District of Columbia, the Philadelphia "White House" was leased to John Francis, who operated it as Francis's Union Hotel. In the early decades of the nineteenth century, the once-elegant home became divided into stores on the first floor with a boarding house above. In 1832, a new owner demolished most of the structure and replaced it with new storefronts facing Market Street (Lawler 2002). In the midst of the growing commercial city, the President's House met a fate similar to Benjamin Franklin's house and the original piazzas of the Pennsylvania State House, also demolished early in the nineteenth century.

Independence Hall, meanwhile, gradually evolved into a shrine honoring the nation's "founding fathers," with George Washington accorded an especially prominent role, in keeping with his stature in public memory in the nineteenth century (Schwartz 1987). In 1855, nativist politicians in control of Philadelphia's city government took the occasion of Washington's Birthday to dedicate their redecoration of the room in which the Declaration of Independence and the Constitution were adopted. A sculpture of Washington by William Rush stood in an honored position surrounded by portraits of other founders. In 1869, a monument to Washington also was erected on Chestnut Street in front of the building. Inside Independence Hall, on the second floor, the federal courts were replaced during the 1850s by chambers for the Philadelphia City Councils, then "restored" to a colonial ambiance during the 1890s by the Daughters of the American Revolution. By the end of the nineteenth century, at the urging of ancestral organizations and Philadelphia elites, Independence Hall became fully dedicated to the memory of the achievement of freedom for the United States through the acts of declaring independence in 1776 and creating the new United States Constitution in 1787 (Mires 2002: 99–106; 139–145). The square and streets around Independence Hall continued to be venues for demonstrations which called attention to the grievances of African Americans, women, immigrants, and organized labor, but such ephemeral activities left no lasting marks on the landscape or on the presentation of Independence Hall as a shrine of liberty.

Cold War Consensus, Persistent Voices

The narrative of freedom served as the rationale for creating Independence National Historical Park in 1948. As defined by Congressional resolution, the park would preserve "for the benefit of the American people . . . certain historical structures and properties of outstanding national significance . . . associated with the American Revolution and the founding and growth of the United States" (Independence National Historical Park 1995: 4). To create a monumental, unobstructed setting for Independence Hall, all "nonhistoric" structures north and east of the landmark building were demolished, creating parks and plazas for three blocks in both directions. The demolition to the north brought down the last vestige of the President's House of the 1790s—surviving walls which had been incorporated into later commercial structures (Lawler 2002). As the blocks north and east of Independence Hall lost the physical remnants of earlier histories that did not fit the script of the enabling legislation, urban redevelopment to the south during the 1950s and 1960s also obscured the long history of Philadelphia's free black community. Redevelopment displaced African Americans and low-income residents of colonial-era structures and the resulting "Society Hill" neighborhood became a quaintly restored, white, upper-income enclave. Mother Bethel African American Methodist Church remained on Sixth Street south of Independence Hall, but the nearby neighborhood lost other connections to its African American history (Pace 1976).

Within Independence National Historical Park, as within other historic sites devoted to early American history, the culture of the Cold War shaped the history that visitors encountered during their vacation visits and school field trips. Independence Hall presented a narrative of freedom achieved through the acts of the Declaration of Independence and the Constitution. George Washington entered into this narrative twice—when appointed as Commander in Chief of the Continental Army and as presiding officer of the Constitutional Convention. Congress Hall offered an additional encounter with Washington, as the President who peacefully gave up the power of his office to the second elected President, John Adams. A monument to George Washington maintained its place on Chestnut Street, joined by plaques in the pavement commemorating later speeches given there by Abraham Lincoln and John F. Kennedy (Mires 2002: 226–239).

The site of the President's House, meanwhile, became obscured in the landscaping of Independence Mall—the designation of the three blocks extending northward from Independence Hall. Although the location of the President's House was not forgotten, the site itself became occupied by a women's restroom structure, built in 1954 and enlarged in 1984 (described jokingly by some tour guides as "the seat of power"). A wayside marker facing Market Street identified the site, but the house and its history were otherwise invisible to passersby. Visitors who stopped to read the wayside could learn about the famous people who lived at the site and about the cabinet meetings, receptions, and celebrations held by the nation's first president. Through its own research program, the National Park Service knew of the site and the presence of enslaved people within Washington's household, but with no physical artifact apparent, the President's House did not figure into interpretive programs (Fanelli 2005).

The narratives of freedom and slavery had been separated by acts of preservation and interpretation (in the case of Independence Hall and Congress Hall) and demolition (in the case of the President's House). But slavery and freedom came together, diverged, and then came together again in the most famous artifact of Independence Hall—the Liberty Bell, with its inscription, "Proclaim liberty throughout all the land, unto all the inhabitants thereof." The bell, ordered for the Pennsylvania State House in 1751, proved sufficiently flexible to represent both aspects of the American story—and, ultimately, to be the wedge for recovering and commemorating the full story of the President's House. The "Liberty Bell" received its name from abolitionists during the 1830s, although its fame grew during the nineteenth century because of the bell's presumed connection with the American Revolution. Taken on tour around the nation seven times between 1885 and 1915, the Liberty Bell achieved increased symbolic power as an icon of American patriotism (Mires 2002: 147–167). Still, its connection to abolitionism did not fade entirely. The abolitionists were mentioned in a history of the bell published in 1926, the sesquicentennial anniversary year of the Declaration of Independence (Rosewater 1926). The connection was further documented by National Park Service historians beginning in the 1950s and called to greater public attention during the 1970s by the noted collector of Afro-Americana, Charles Blockson (Paige n.d.). As a result, when the Liberty Bell was moved out of Independence Hall to its own pavilion in 1976, interpretive talks could address slavery indirectly through the role of abolitionists in naming the bell. With the focus on the campaign to end enslavement, this aspect of the Liberty Bell's history could be knit into the narrative of freedom.

African Americans in Philadelphia, meanwhile, gave the Liberty Bell a central role in a commemoration that called attention to the connected narratives of freedom and slavery. "National Freedom Day," first observed in 1942 and continued each 1 February since then, marks the date when Abraham Lincoln signed the congressional legislation for the Thirteenth Amendment to the Constitution, which ended slavery in the United States. This commemoration, invented by a prominent black Philadelphian who had been born in slavery in Georgia, challenged the traditional narrative of freedom by shifting the date of its achievement from 1776 to 1865. National Freedom Day includes a wreath-laying at the Liberty Bell, but it shifts the accomplishment of freedom from George Washington and the founders of his generation to Abraham Lincoln. Rather than a story with an ending at the American Revolution or even the Civil War, National Freedom Day calls attention to the continuing struggles of African Americans (Wright 1941).

Although National Freedom Day has been an annual occurrence at the Liberty Bell, it has not been widely recognized or well understood beyond its sponsors and participants. In its attention to continuing tensions between freedom and the legacy of slavery, and its identification of these entwined narratives with one of the nation's treasured symbols, this commemoration seems in retrospect to be both prescient and indicative of the challenges that lay ahead for the neglected site of the President's House. For many years, National Freedom Day sustained a part of the story that the official narrative of freedom lacked, especially the continuing economic and political struggles of African Americans.

National Freedom Day also represents another narrative of African American experience that figured prominently in the controversy over the President's House. During the late nineteenth and early twentieth centuries, the African American population of Philadelphia swelled with migrants from the South. For them, the history and legacy of slavery were living memories, not distant histories of the eighteenth century. The founder of National Freedom Day, Richard R. Wright Sr., was among these migrants, moving to Philadelphia during the 1920s to join his children who already had moved north. The migrants fled from the South to northern cities to escape racial violence and to seek opportunity, but their aspirations were often frustrated by discriminatory employment and housing practices. In Philadelphia, their economic opportunities further eroded after the Second World War, as industries abandoned the city and other northern cities and transferred manufacturing to Sunbelt states or locations overseas (Hardy 1989; Gregg 1993; Adams et al. 1991: 30–99).

Forging New Narratives

Forging a new narrative incorporating freedom and slavery has required breaking down barriers of procedure, language, and distrust. These were dramatically illustrated during the first public meeting called to consider a preliminary design plan for marking the site of the President's House and creating a memorial to the enslaved Africans in Washington's household. By the time this meeting was held, in January 2003 at the African American Museum of Philadelphia, the site and its connection with slavery had been a matter of public interest for nearly one year. The Independence Hall Association, the African American citizens' groups, and area historians all had mobilized around the issues of interpretation at the President's House site and in the exhibits of the Liberty Bell Center. By the time of the public meeting about the President's House, the National Park Service had agreed to substantial revisions to the Liberty Bell exhibits so that they would acknowledge the history of slavery as well as abolition, and so that they would include images and text about the President's House and the enslaved Africans of Washington's household (Nash 2006).

Like the revised exhibits for the Liberty Bell Center, the preliminary plans and interpretive themes for the President's House site were created in meetings called by the National Park Service and including invited representatives from groups vitally interested in the site. But the session in January 2003 at the African American Museum was the public's first encounter with the outcome of the planning meetings. Although the designs were intended to be preliminary, their presentation in the form of projected images, narrated by consultants hired by the National Park Service, made the project appear like a finished product. The overflow audience in the museum auditorium was predominantly African American, but the National Park Service officials and all but one of the consultants on the stage were white. Conflict over language, symbols, and perceptions of the history of slavery precluded consideration of the designs themselves. Members of the audience objected to the use of the word "slave" rather than "enslaved Africans," and expressed doubt that anyone who did not know the difference should be involved in creating a memorial. When Professor Clement Price of Rutgers University, the only African American on the stage, described the history of slavery at the President's House site, he characterized George Washington as a relatively benign master—an interpretation that met with vocal disapproval from the audience. A projected title slide of three faces—George Washington, John Adams, and the African American minister Richard Allen—loomed over most of the discussion, prompting a final denunciation at the end of the meeting by a woman angered by the image of George Washington, whom she considered to be a "slave-holding rapist" (Holt 2003; Salisbury 2003).

The frustration in the room also emanated from economic issues and a distrust of the federal government. The audience included individuals who questioned whether African Americans had been given a just share of employment on the various construction projects in Independence National Historical Park, including the soon-to-open National Constitution Center. If the historic sites of Philadelphia were the engines of the city's tourism economy, just where were the profits from this business going? Why were minority contractors not more involved, and why were the designs for the President's House site and slavery memorial entrusted to white consultants? Furthermore, where was the money to pay for the President's House project, which had a price tag of $4.5 million? Members of the audience were unwilling to accept the site design as a good faith effort without funding in place to make it reality.

Nearly two years passed without another public forum on this issue. Among the groups that had mobilized around the President's House site, differences in methods and strategy were clear. Each group proceeded within its own set of cultural or institutional practices for gathering and communicating information; for responding to differences of opinion; and for evaluating the credibility of opponents and allies. Finding ways to bridge these gaps would be necessary if the President's House site was to become anything more than a battleground.

The National Park Service operated from within a long-established set of policies and procedures, some embedded in federal law or regulatory codes. National Park Service professionals compile their research findings in reports for internal use; the reports are public documents, but they are seldom read by the public. Instead, the information filters to the public through historic preservation, public interpretation of historic places, and tourist-oriented brochures and guidebooks. In the case of the President's House, NPS staff members could truthfully assert that the knowledge that George Washington kept slaves in Philadelphia was nothing new. They had known it, and reported it in their customary ways. Furthermore, as part of the NPS Underground Railroad initiative, Independence Park staff members had devoted great effort to incorporating African American history into the park's documentation for the National Register of Historic Places (Toogood 2000, 2001; Fanelli 2005). But from the perspective of the general public, the information about slavery at the President's House site came as a surprise, and its absence from their understanding of Independence National Historical Park seemed to be evidence of a cover-up. When challenged, the park staff responded by inviting controlled numbers of representatives of various viewpoints to the table; but as the meeting in January 2003 demonstrated, this left many others feeling excluded and suspicious of the process.

Discussion about the future of the President's House site also had to overcome the gap between the historiography produced by university-based historians, the ongoing work of the National Park Service, and the public's understanding of the nation's history. While the Cold War-era interpretation of American freedom remained dominant at Independence Park, cemented in place by the park's enabling legislation, historiography underwent a sea change. In 1975, as the park was gearing up for the celebration of the bicentennial of the Declaration of Independence, Edmund S. Morgan dealt with the history of freedom and slavery together in his book *American Slavery, American Freedom: The Ordeal of Colonial Virginia*. For the non-NPS historians who became involved in the controversy over the President's House site, the paradox of freedom and slavery coexisting in the nation's founding seemed to be commonplace knowledge that belonged at the forefront of the public presentation of history. Morgan himself had pointed the way toward a reimagined history at Independence National Historical Park when he wrote:

To a large degree it may be said that Americans bought their independence with slave labor. . . . Virginia furnished the country's most eloquent spokesmen for freedom and equality. . . . A Virginian commanded the Continental Army that won independence. Virginians drafted not only the Declaration of Independence but also the United States Constitution of 1787 and the first ten amendments to it. And Americans elected Virginians to the presidency of the United States under that constitution for thirty-two out of the first thirty-six years of its existence. They were all slave-holders. If it is possible to understand the American paradox, the marriage of slavery and freedom, Virginia is surely the place to begin. (Morgan 1975: 5–6)

Virginia was the place to begin, but the Virginians stepped onto the national stage in Philadelphia. Thirty years after Morgan's book, his observation about the "American paradox" of the interdependency of freedom and slavery suggested the way in which the long-separated narratives at Independence National Historical Park might be brought together. Once the convergence of these themes at the President's House site became a matter of public concern, non-NPS historians insisted that exhibits at the Liberty Bell Center address this paradox; at the invitation of the NPS, panels of scholars reviewed the exhibit plans to rewrite text and add images which would present not only a celebration of freedom but also the struggle to achieve it.

The two African American groups organized in Philadelphia in response to the President's House controversy, the Avenging the Ancestors Coalition (ATAC) and Generations Unlimited, pressed for a monument to the enslaved Africans kept by Washington as well as the broader goal of greater visibility for African American and African history. Both groups engaged in letter-writing campaigns and public demonstrations to ensure that the history of slavery within Independence National Historical Park would not be neglected. They communicated their interests through position papers, signs, and ceremonies recalling African traditions, such as the libation ceremony conducted near the Independence Visitor Center on the day that the new Liberty Bell Center opened to the public for the first time. Both African American groups linked the recognition of the enslaved Africans at the President's House to broader issues of racism and justice. To quote a position paper by ATAC, the commemorative project was a necessary response to a history in which "our ancestors as forced laborers transformed America into the economic world power that it remains today" (ATAC 2004). Generations Unlimited identified its goal as "dismantling racism in Philadelphia by ensuring that the history of Africa, African Americans and their contributions to the world [are] told." Both groups emphasized the human cruelty of slavery; Generations Unlimited placed particular emphasis on violence against enslaved women (Generations Unlimited 2004; Rhodes 2004).

For the Independence Hall Association, the President's House site continued to be a public campaign to mark the footprint of the mansion that accommodated the executive branch of government during the 1790s. But with such public attention focused on the issue of slavery, the association made the marking of the "slave quarters" portion of the President's House a priority in its campaign as well. To generate public interest, the association created an extensive archive of information and news coverage on its web site, ushistory.org, much of it prepared by Edward Lawler, Jr., whose article about the President's House brought the site to public attention. While advocating its positions, the association became the leading source of information about the President's House, with a web presence that far surpassed the information made available on the Internet by Independence National Historical Park itself. The web site also provided a bulletin board for public comment, the great majority of it supporting the marking of the site and decrying the loss of the original structure. In the posted comments, many writers stressed the importance of acknowledging the presence of slavery within the household of the first President of the United States.

During the nearly two years in between the public meetings about the President's House site, steps were taken to bridge some of the gaps among these divergent groups. Significantly, the controversy coincided with a "civic engagement" movement within the National Park Service, initiated by the Northeast Region headquartered in Philadelphia. Between 2001 and 2003, the NPS adopted new policy and sponsored training workshops to encourage "frank and open communication" with the public and "open and inclusive" decision-making. "The word 'no' must not be our first response when we are approached with ideas or requests that may be out of our traditional comfort zone," the new policy directed (National Park Service 2003; Linenthal 2003). In that spirit, the staff of Independence National Historical Park listened to public concern over its plans for another site with significance in African American history. One block north of the President's House site, a bus drop-off point for the National Constitution Center was planned for a site once occupied by the home of James Dexter, a founding member of one of the nation's first African American churches. The National Park

Service initially planned no archaeological investigation of the site prior to the driveway's construction; however, when African American religious leaders called for archaeology to recover the artifacts of their history, park representatives listened rather than rejecting challenges to their decision-making. An excavation in 2003 began with a benediction by African American pastors and allowed public access to the project with a viewing platform overlooking the dig (National Park Service 2004).

Meanwhile, changes in the top management of Independence Park and a reorganization of staff gave responsibility and authority to individuals who were both willing to confront the challenges and open to new approaches to interpretation. Park rangers began offering Underground Railroad tours that included the President's House site and other sites of African American history. After the task of revising the exhibits in the Liberty Bell Center had been completed, Independence Park managers convened a roundtable of park staff, non-NPS historians, and representatives of the interested organizations in November 2003 to review the available evidence about the President's House and its history, including the presence of enslaved Africans. This resulted in a "consensus document" to guide further work on the site (Fanelli n.d.; Lawler 2004). Through the summer of 2004, all of the interested community groups participated in planning a public forum to restart public discussion of how to mark and interpret the site. This forum, held in October 2004, was an event for listening to the public, rather than presenting plans that appeared to be finished.

The 2004 public forum showed once again the diversity of historical narratives and personal experiences that generated such attention to the President's House site. For the occasion, the National Park Service for the first time marked the outline of the President's House on the ground at Sixth and Market Streets. Although temporary, the outline of blue tape on the ground clearly showed the convergence of the site of slavery with the entrance to the Liberty Bell Center. Accomplishing this temporary marking was a milestone for the Independence Hall Association and for Edward Lawler, Jr., who assisted with the project. Another breakthrough occurred when a National Park Service ranger referred to the rear of the structure as the "slave quarters" rather than the "servants' hall," a shift in language that Lawler, the African American groups, and non-NPS historians had long advocated.

The testimony of the participants in the forum once again showed the challenges of making the transition from a Cold War-era, nationalist interpretation of American history to a more pluralistic view recognizing the limitations as well as the achievements of freedom. In the case of the President's House site, it also highlighted the role of personal experiences of Philadelphians, especially those who previously found little reason to pay attention to the history presented at Independence National Historical Park. Some members of the Generations Unlimited group arrived dressed as field hands; their demonstration once again invoked the importance of ancestry and connected with the family histories of the generations of African Americans who had migrated from the South in the late nineteenth and twentieth centuries. Inside the forum, one participant asked why Philadelphia had a statue to the strong-arm Mayor and police commissioner Frank Rizzo, but not a memorial of slavery. This testimony framed the President's House site as a symbol of justice for African Americans who had suffered injustices in their experiences with Philadelphia city authorities. Like the earlier public meeting, the audience was predominantly African American, with many echoing earlier frustrations with the slow pace of progress on the project and an interest in sharing in the economic benefits of tourism. Clearly, many who attended did not feel that their positions had yet been heard by the managers of Independence National Historical Park. But at this session, instead of presenting plans which seemed to be fixed, the park staff attending took notes and responded to questions. They emerged with an understanding of cultural values associated with the President's House site, as expressed by participants in the forum: agency, identity, dignity, truth, ancestry, memory, and the influence of the past on the present (Fanelli 2005; Salisbury 2004).

While the forum in October allowed the airing of public concern, it did not immediately solve the problem of how to commemorate the full history of the President's House, including its connection to slavery. Later that day, several participants in the forum lingered in conversation near the front entrance to the Liberty Bell Center. Tourists entered the center, unaware of the history beneath their feet. The forum participants began to challenge the visitors: "Do you know what was here? Do you know that slavery was here?" Startled and embarrassed, the visitors admitted they did not. They had walked by signs portraying the three faces of Washington, Adams, and Allen (the same images that had prompted protest more than a year before), but even if they had paid attention, the information on the signs was too vague to be helpful. Under the headline, "The Presidents' House in Philadelphia, 1790–1800," the text said simply: "Coming . . . EXHIBITS about the house on this site, the early American Presidency and the free African community in Philadelphia, and a COMMEMORATION of the enslaved Africans who lived here."

After that day, however, steps were taken toward bringing the history of the site, especially the presence of slavery, to greater public attention. Park staff members prepared an informational flyer for distribution to the public, with drafts circulated among the various groups that had taken an interest in the site and its interpretation. The park developed new, more informative wayside markers to replace signs that had featured the staring three faces of Washington, Adams, and Allen. Moving far from the initial resistance to interpreting the site, the park's cultural resources managers regarded the site as a "contact zone" where conflicting views of the past could be acknowledged (Fanelli 2005). Significantly, a new interpretive plan for Independence National Historical Park developed during 2005 and 2006 identified "Liberty: The Promises and the Paradoxes" as a major theme for the park's future programming. This theme recognized the role of slavery in the early republic; if the plan is fully implemented, visitors to Independence will encounter the powerful convergence of freedom and slavery not only at the President's House site but elsewhere in the park where it was previously obscured (Independence National Historical Park 2006).

The greatest remaining hurdle to a full interpretation of the President's House site—funding—was overcome in two phases. On the day the new Liberty Bell Center was dedicated in 2003, Philadelphia Mayor John F. Street pledged $1.5 million for the project—a large sum, but short of the estimated $4.5 million needed for marking the footprint of the house, creating a moment to enslaved Africans, and developing exhibits to tell the story of the entwined histories of the presidency and slavery. The financial barrier was broken in 2005 when Congressman Chaka Fattah announced a $3.6 million federal grant for the project (Slobodzian 2005). With the City of Philadelphia taking the lead by virtue of its financial commitment, the design process was reopened. This time, the public had greater access to the process. Rather than producing a design in a closed meeting with a select few participants, a nationally advertised competition titled "Freedom and Slavery in the Making of a New Nation" produced five finalists whose designs were displayed for public comment at the National Constitution Center and the African American Museum. An Oversight Committee appointed by the Mayor of Philadelphia and representing the various President's House constituencies—including the Independence Hall Association, the Avenging the Ancestors Coalition, and the Ad Hoc Historians—also evaluated the designs, although the final decision rested with the Mayor and the Superintendent of Independence National Historical Park. In 2007, the Philadelphia firm Kelly/Maiello Architects and Planners won the competition with a design that promised to mark the footprint of the President's House and interpret the stories of all of its inhabitants.

The Oversight Committee formed for the design competition became another avenue for bringing issues to the forefront for discussion and possible resolution. Such was the case during the summer of 2007, when archaeologists discovered foundations for the President's House that were thought to have been destroyed by later generations of construction. With the public watching from an observation platform at Sixth and Market Streets, archaeologists uncovered foundations for the bow window where George Washington stood to receive visitors; the kitchen where Hercules toiled; and a previously unknown underground passageway that would have allowed slaves and other servants to move about the house out of view. Such real evidence of slavery and the presidency in such close proximity provoked remarkable conversations about race and American history among visitors to the platform (Salisbury 2007). This dramatic turn of events also posed a new challenge: With the design competition completed, a fixed budget, and the project already far behind its original schedule, what should be done about the archeological findings? The Oversight Committee, along with press reports about public interest in the archaeology, provided a means for expressing opinions about whether the project should be changed. Within a matter of weeks, an initial plan to rebury and "preserve in place" the foundations gave way to considerations of how the new findings could be kept visible. This adaptability stood in marked contrast to events five years before, when strong resistance was necessary to overcome the momentum of budgets and construction schedules so that exhibits inside the Liberty Bell Center could be revised to acknowledge the history of slavery at the President's House.

The President's House site controversy is a case study of divergent histories, contested public memory, and organizational cultures in conflict. In this case, public advocates stood their ground while the official guardian of the site, the National Park Service, changed position in keeping with the "civic engagement" initiative that reshaped its own organizational culture. With the formation of the Oversight Committee in September 2005, National Park Service officials sat at the table with representatives of advocate groups while consultants hired by the City of Philadelphia launched the new design process for the President's House site. If the project is carried forward to completion as planned, the corner of Sixth and Market Streets will no longer appear to be an empty lot. It will represent the powerful convergence of liberty and slavery that lies at the foundation of American history and in the shadow of America's symbols of freedom.

Note

The author writes from the perspective of an advocate for marking the site of the President's House and including the history of slavery as well as the presidency in its interpretation. She is affiliated with the Ad Hoc Historians advocacy group and serves on the City of Philadelphia Oversight Committee for the President's House and Slavery Commemoration.

Bibliography

Adams, Carolyn, David Bartelt, David Elesh, Ira Goldstein, Nancy Kleniewski, and William Yancey. 1991. *Philadelphia: Neighborhoods, Division, and Conflict in a Postindustrial City*. Philadelphia: Temple University Press.

Aikens, Martha B. 2001. Letter to Nancy Gilboy (11 October). Correspondence archived by the Independence Hall Association. Retrieved http://www.ushistory.org/presidentshouse.

Avenging the Ancestors Coalition. 2004. Position statement distributed at public forum (30 October).

Bodnar, John. 1992. *Remaking America: Public Memory, Commemoration, and Patriotism in the Twentieth Century*. Princeton: Princeton University Press.

Boyer, M. Christine. 1994. *The City of Collective Memory: Its Historical Imagery and Architectural Entertainments*. Cambridge, Mass.: MIT Press.

Coard, Michael. 2005. "The 'Black' Eye on George Washington's 'White' House." *Pennsylvania Magazine of History and Biography* 129, no. 4: 461–472.

Fanelli, Doris Devine. n.d. Consensus Document from the President's House Roundtable. Retrieved from http://www.nps.gov/inde/NPS/docs.htm.

———. 2005. "History, Commemoration, and an Interdisciplinary Approach to Interpreting the President's House Site." *Pennsylvania Magazine of History and Biography* 129, no. 4: 445–460.

Flam, Fay. 2001. "Formerly on Ice, Past Unearthed." *Philadelphia Inquirer* (23 February).

Generations Unlimited. 2004. Position statement distributed at public forum (30 October).

Gregg, Robert. 1993. *Sparks from the Anvil of Oppression: Philadelphia's African Methodists and Southern Migrants, 1890–1940*. Philadelphia: Temple University Press.

Gross, David. 2000. *Lost Time: On Remembering and Forgetting in Late Modern Culture*. Amherst: University of Massachusetts Press.

Hardy, Charles Ashley III. 1989. "Race and Opportunity: Black Philadelphia During the Era of the Great Migration, 1916–1930 " Ph.D. diss., Temple University.

Hayden, Dolores. 1995. *The Power of Place: Urban Landscapes as Public History*. Cambridge, Mass.: MIT Press.

Holt, Sharon Ann. 2003. "Object Lessons: Race in the Park." *Common-Place* 3, no. 4. Retrieved from http://www.common-place.org/vol-03/no-04/lessons.

———. 2005. "Questioning the Answers: Modernizing Public History to Serve the Citizens." *Pennsylvania Magazine of History and Biography* 129, no. 4: 473–481.

Horle, Craig W., Jeffrey L. Scheib, Joseph S. Foster, David Haugaard, Carolyn M. Peters, and Laurie M. Wolfe. 1997. *Lawmakers and Legislators in Pennsylvania: A Biographical Dictionary*, vol. 2. Philadelphia: University of Pennsylvania Press.

Horton, James Oliver, and Lois E. Horton, eds. 2006. *Slavery and Public History: The Tough Stuff of American Memory*. New York: The New Press.

Independence Hall Association Board. 2001. Letter to Martha Aikens (15 August). Correspondence archived by the Independence Hall Association. Retrieved from http://www.ushistory.org/presidentshouse.

Independence National Historical Park. n.d. "The Robert Morris Mansion."
Retrieved from http://www.nps.gov/inde/archeology/morris.htm.
———. 1995. *General Management Plan.* Philadelphia: Independence National
Historical Park.
———. 2006. *Long-Range Interpretive Plan for Independence National Historical Park.*
Retrieved from http://www.nps.gov/inde/upload/LRIP.pdf.
Kammen, Michael. 1978. *A Season of Youth: The American Revolution and the Historical Imagination.* New York: Alfred A. Knopf.
———. 1986. *A Machine That Would Go of Itself: The Constitution in American Culture.* New York: Alfred A. Knopf.
Kilian, Michael. 2003. "Plans Made to Mark the 1st 'White House.'" *Chicago Tribune* (8 November).
Lawler, Edward, Jr. 2002. "The President's House in Philadelphia: The Rediscovery of a Lost Landmark." *Pennsylvania Magazine of History and Biography* 126, no. 1: 5–95.
———. 2004. *Roundtable Minority Report.* Retrieved from http://www.ushistory.org/presidentshouse/controversy/minority.htm.
———. 2005. "The President's House Revisited." *Pennsylvania Magazine of History and Biography* 129, no. 4: 371–410.
Linenthal, Edward T. 2003. "Preserving the Memory; Reflections on a Year of Public History Seminars." National Park Service Civic Engagement Bulletin. Retrieved from http://www.nps.gov/civic/newsevents/reflections.pdf.
Mires, Charlene. 2002. *Independence Hall in American Memory.* Philadelphia: University of Pennsylvania Press.
———. 2004. "Race, Place, and the Pennsylvania Emancipation Exposition of 1913." *Pennsylvania Magazine of History and Biography* 128, no. 3: 257–278.
Morgan, Edmund S. 1975. *American Slavery, American Freedom: The Ordeal of Colonial Virginia.* New York: W.W. Norton.
Nash, Gary B. 1988. *Forging Freedom: The Formation of Philadelphia's Black Community, 1720–1840.* Cambridge, Mass.: Harvard University Press.
———. 2006. "For Whom Will the Liberty Bell Toll? From Controversy to Collaboration." In *Slavery and Public History: The Tough Stuff of American Memory,* ed. James Oliver Horton and Lois E. Horton. New York: The New Press, 75–102.
Nash, Gary B., and Randall M. Miller. 2002. "Don't Bury the Past." *Philadelphia Inquirer* (31 March).
National Park Service. 2003. Director's Order 75A, "Civic Engagement and Public Involvement." Retrieved 14 November 2003, from http://www.nps.gov/policy/DOrders/75A.htm.
———. 2004. "We the People: The Decision to Excavate the James Dexter Site." Public Engagement Case Study Bulletin. Retrieved from http://www.nps.gov/civic/casestudies/INDEDexter10–18.pdf.
Pace, Valerie Sue. 1976. "Society Hill, Philadelphia: Historic Preservation and Urban Renewal in Washington Square East." Ph.D. diss., University of Minnesota.
Paige, John C. n.d. *The Liberty Bell: A Special History Study.* Denver: National Park Service, Department of the Interior.
Rhodes, Sacaree. 2004. "Statement at Public Forum" (30 October).
Rosewater, Victor. 1926. *The Liberty Bell; Its History and Significance.* New York: D. Appleton.
Salisbury, Stephan. 2003. "Design of Liberty Bell Site Criticized." *Philadelphia Inquirer* (16 January).

———. 2004. "Forum Furthers Memorial to Slaves." *Philadelphia Inquirer* (7 November).

———. 2007. "Slavery Laid Bare: A Historic Platform for Dialogue About Race." *Philadelphia Inquirer* (20 May).

Schwartz, Barry. 1987. *George Washington: The Making of an American Symbol.* New York: The Free Press.

Slobodzian, Joseph A. 2005. "Independence Mall Slavery Memorial Gets Federal Funding." *Philadelphia Inquirer* (6 September).

Smith, Dinitia. 2002. "Slave Site for a Symbol of Freedom." *New York Times* (20 April).

Strauss, Robert. 2003. "In Pursuit of Liberty." *Washington Post* (10 October).

Teicher, Stacy A., and Walter H. Robinson. 2003. "The Other Side of Liberty." *Christian Science Monitor* (3 July).

Toogood, Anna Coxe. 2000. *National Register Amendment, Independence National Historical Park, Underground Railroad and Anti-Slavery Movement.* Retrieved from http://www.nps.gov/inde/archeology/NRamend.htm.

———. 2001. *Historic Resource Study, Independence Mall, the Eighteenth-Century Development, Block One, Chestnut to Market, Fifth to Sixth Streets.* Philadelphia: Independence National Historical Park.

Wiencek, Henry. 2003. *An Imperfect God: George Washington, His Slaves, and the Creation of America.* New York: Farrar, Straus and Giroux.

Wright, Richard Robert, Sr. 1941. "Banker Works to Make February 1 a National Holiday." *Philadelphia Tribune* (1 November).

Zucchino, David. 2004. "A Historic Clash of Slavery, Liberty." *Los Angeles Times* (30 August).

Chapter 12
Politicizing Chinese New Year Festivals
Cold War Politics, Transnational Conflicts, and Chinese America

Chiou-Ling Yeh

In 1978, the year before the United States normalized its relation with the People's Republic of China (PRC), Nationalist flags—the flags of the Republic of China (ROC, Taiwan)—were prominently displayed on the Chinese New Year parade route in San Francisco while its consul general sat on the reviewing stand.[1] Yet things would quickly change one year later. In the year of the normalization, the representative from Taiwan was no longer present while the Nationalist flag would disappear two years later (Hall 1979: 6). Why did parade organizers shift their political expressions in the wake of the change in American foreign policy? Why did international politics affect a local ethnic cultural celebration? People often perceive the Chinese New Year celebration in the United States as a static cultural practice, directly transplanted from ancient China. On the contrary, Chinese immigrants have invented public celebrations to continue their bonds with the homeland, to create group solidarity, to enlarge their economic and political resources, and, finally, to claim their American membership (Yeh 2008).

Many groups use public celebrations to articulate their identity and, more important, to gain acceptance and membership. Throughout history, immigrant communities were compelled to showcase their political allegiance in public celebrations. April Shultz has shown how Norwegian Americans invoked the image of pioneers to assert their Americanness in the Centennial Celebration, while Bénédicte Deschamps has suggested that Italian immigrants transformed the Columbus Day celebration into a mainstream holiday as part of the way they incorporated themselves into American society. Lon Kurashige has contended that

Japanese Americans used the Nisei Week celebration to negotiate the tensions generated from the United States and Japan conflicts. Public celebrations thus became a means to articulate group loyalty and mitigate tensions within and outside the community (Schultz 1994; Deschamps 2001; Kurashige 2002). Group leaders usually chose certain rituals, which they thought would be acceptable not only by group members but also by the larger society. However, it was usually difficult to reach consensus over what should be included in public expressions of group identity. Even if leaders attempted to claim a unified identity through symbolic rituals, such attempts often resulted in excluding or rejecting certain people. Yet, group members were not powerless. They could resort to various means to articulate their identities: from deconstructing rituals and staging sideshows to simply refusing participation. Meanwhile, the larger society and sometimes international forces had influence over cultural celebrations, which were usually linked to allocation of resources or opportunities. The stakes thus were high for groups to select "correct" forms of public expressions to create group harmony and solidarity, and to gain acceptance or resources from the larger society and other outside forces.

This chapter focuses on how U.S. foreign policy has dictated San Francisco's Chinese New Year Festival and how transnational politics and conflicts are manifested in the ethnic celebrations in the second-half of the twentieth century. The history of the contemporary Chinese New Year Festival in San Francisco is closely entangled with American Cold War politics and the conflicts between the PRC and Taiwan. The legacy of the Chinese Exclusion Act (1882–1943), unfortunately, has persistently perpetuated the image of Chinese Americans as foreigners.[2] As a result, changes in U.S. foreign policy and international political conditions often had a direct impact on Chinese Americans. For example, while World War II elevated Chinese Americans into "good Chinese," as Republican China was then an ally, the tensions in the early Cold War quickly redefined them into "bad Chinese," as Communist China was an enemy who killed Americans in Korea. As I have argued elsewhere, the creation of the contemporary Chinese New Year Festival in San Francisco was the result of U.S. Cold War containment politics and the efforts of Chinese Americans to demonstrate their anticommunist conviction and loyalty to the United States (Yeh 2004).

Ironically, Chinese Americans had to demonstrate their American patriotism through the assertion of a "correct" transnational tie. Whereas Cold War politics compelled Chinese American leaders to denounce Communist China and pledge their allegiance to the Nationalist government of Taiwan, the normalization between the United States and the PRC in 1979 once again created pressures on ethnic lead-crs to bring their political expressions in line with the country's changing foreign policy. This time, however, the ethnic community did not rally behind these new expectations, but instead was divided by it. While Cold War anticommunist hysteria compelled Chinese Americans to reach an anticommunist consensus in its public expressions, the détente between the United States and the PRC, in contrast, created political tensions and conflicts among them. Because the Chinese New Year celebration was the most visible event in the community, it became a medium for Chinese Americans to express their diverse political opinions publicly, but at the same time there were important tensions between the needs of the community and what could be freely expressed without difficulty.

Immigration and Pre–Cold War Ethnic Celebration

San Francisco's Chinatown is the oldest Chinese American community in the United States. Appearing in the 1850s, it quickly expanded from six or eight blocks in 1876 to more than twelve blocks in 1885. The area attracted new Chinese arrivals who opened shops and established their residence there, marking it as a distinct ethnic enclave and increasing its economic vitality (Lee 2001: 9; Chen 2000: 58). Chinatown emerged as a commercial and service center for many Chinese immigrants, and Chinese houseboys and laundry shops served the entire city. Soon, the Chinese successfully entered many light manufacturing industries such as textiles, shoes, and cigars (Chen 2000: 61, 66).

The Chinese immigrants brought old world traditions and rituals—including Chinese New Year celebrations—to the host country. Initially, the celebration was for the most part private and community-oriented. For the Chinese New Year dinner, bachelors gathered at the homes of their fortunate counterparts—those who could afford to have families in the country. For those who worked as houseboys or in the surrounding areas, they came back to Chinatown to participate in the festivities (Baldwin 1880: 73). When district and family associations were soon established to provide social welfare services to members, they sponsored banquets and lion dances to build and strengthen bonds among their members (Scharnhorst 1990: 27; Chen 2000: 119, 137–138; Soo 2002).

Political disenfranchisement had encouraged Chinese immigrants to identify with China during the Chinese exclusion era (1882–1943). Racial discrimination motivated district and family associations to serve as cultural brokers between the ethnic community and the dominant society linking Chinese immigrants and the "home" country. However, old world ritual observances failed to guarantee Chinese Americans a transnational tie, especially when the "home" country experienced a major political change. After the Qing government was overthrown in 1911, the new Republican government abolished the lunar calendar as part of its program to modernize China, and the Chinese New Year celebration was among the traditions it eliminated.

The Chinese Consolidated Benevolent Association (CCBA), the largest family and district association in San Francisco and the United States, considered itself a spokesperson for the Chinese community. When Republican China eliminated the Chinese New Year, the CCBA urged the ethnic community to do so as well, giving it one year to conform. Many ethnic leaders in other parts of the United States also followed the new policy. John Tim Loy, a Chinese American spokesperson in Nevada County, California, claimed that 1912 was the last Chinese New Year celebration. He stated, "The revolutionary movement has brought many things to pass, and now we have president. Next Year we celebrate New Year alle [*sic*] same American on first day of the year" (Tinlogy 1971: 9). As a result, the celebratory spirit was dampened as fewer people honored the ethnic holiday (*Chung Sai Yat Pao* 1911, 1913; "Chinese New Year Passes Quietly" 1919: 9).

Modern China was not the only reason that tempered participation in the ethnic holiday; acculturation within the ethnic community also played an important role. During the 1920s and 1930s Chinese New Year celebrations, observers noted the presence of Chinese American flappers and their male companions dressed in western-style suits. Mainstream newspapers also printed pictures of children clad in store-bought western-style clothing. Meanwhile, community newspapers lamented the decrease of the ethnic celebration in many ethnic communities. They attributed this to the demise of the older generation and the acculturation of the younger one ("Chinese Blend East, West" 1931: 4; "Chinese New Year Is Today" 1926: 8; *Chung Sai Yat Po* 1925: 3).

However, numerous Chinese immigrants continued to honor the Chinese New Year. Days prior to the ethnic holiday, Grant Avenue was filled with booths selling holiday goods such as lilies, fruits, candies, and other delicacies to meet the needs of holiday preparation. Many continued to decorate their houses and hang festoons, flags, and lanterns on the streets, although the scale of festivity was smaller compared to those held earlier. Meanwhile, Chinatown residents insisted on shooting firecrackers when they were allowed. Chinese Americans in other parts of the country also retained the tradition. Los Angeles Chinatown, for example, persistently welcomed the holiday with a dragon dance. Nevertheless, the fight over whether to maintain the ethnic celebrations continued after World War II. Defenders argued that the Chinese New Year celebration enabled Chinese Americans to retain their ethnic ties. Moreover, they contended that the Chinese government should not intervene with this old tradition. Critics, however, insisted that the ethnic community should follow the modern practice, and supporters of the Nationalist government likewise refused to participate in the celebration ("Chinese Celebrate Rainy New Year" 1911: 4; "Chinatown Aglow" 1915: 9; "You Hear Big Noise?" 1920: 8; "New Year Din" 1921: 10; "Chinese Pay Debts" 1923: 7; *San Francisco Chronicle* 1924: 7). Ironically, it was the Cold War that ended the debate because Chinese American leaders considered the ethnic celebration as a valuable tool to publicly express support for the United States' Cold War policy. Meanwhile, the pressure to maintain the ethnic celebration among Chinese Americans compelled the CCBA and other ethnic organizations to resume festivities and host Chinese New Year banquets or celebratory events which they had once abandoned (*Chung Sai Yat Po* 1912: 1; 1919: 1; 1931: 1–2; "Chinese New Year Is Today" 1926: 8).

Cold War Years—"You're One of the Enemies"

The "loss" of mainland China to communism in 1949 and the outbreak of the Korean War the next year (1950–1953) created a difficult political and economic situation for San Francisco's Chinese Americans. In 1949, when communists took over the mainland and established the PRC, Chiang Kai-shek took his Nationalist government to Taiwan. The United States government encouraged Chinese Americans to support his regime, as it considered the latter to represent "Free China." The Nationalist government seized this moment of anticommunist hysteria to become the dominant political power in San Francisco's Chinatown. For twenty years it cooperated with the Federal Bureau of Investigation (FBI) and the Immigration and Naturalization Service (INS) to suppress leftists and pro-PRC supporters, and the old establishment was rewarded with business opportunities and government positions in Taiwan (Lai 1992: 42–52).

Economic sanctions against China and their impact on Chinatowns across the United States further exacerbated the effects of political repression. The U.S. embargo on Chinese goods forced the closure of Chinese dry good, grocery, and apothecary shops. Many curio shops and gift stores were forbidden to replenish goods from China, thereby reducing Chinatown's attraction to tourists. Moreover, many restaurants lost business because the resentment felt toward the Chinese was transferred to Chinese Americans. As a Chinese American woman, Betty Lee Sung, recalled, "People would look at you in the street and think, well, you're one of the enemies" (Yung 1986: 83).

Chinatown residents also suffered from political persecution. The

McCarran-Walter Act of 1952 armed federal agents with new powers to deport anyone who had connections to communist regimes even if they had been naturalized (Zhao 2002: 160). The INS saw this as a perfect opportunity to crack down on illegal immigration, as they could use the search for communists to hunt for illegal immigrants. After 1953, the federal government began to suspect a strong connection between immigrants and the "Red" Chinese, and they often randomly stopped Chinese Americans in various Chinatowns to see if they had proper documents (Lee 1960: 368). As Maurice Chuck of San Francisco recalled, "They would stop you on the street. Harassed you and asked you all sorts of questions, push you around. It became a daily part of our lives in Chinatown during that time" (Chen 2001). The FBI even questioned children in playgrounds and schools, thereby compelling some parents to instruct their children how to answer questions. As one resident recalled, "One day, my mother told me to use a different name in school" (Lowe interview 1998). This harassment was a constant source of anxiety for many, especially those who entered the country as "paper sons" (people claiming to be the sons of merchants or US citizens, two of the exempt classes permitted to enter the United States during the exclusion era). While real sons were among these "paper sons" to assume their derivative citizenship, many Chinese used this practice to circumvent the Chinese Exclusion Acts. If the real identity of a "paper son" was uncovered, he would be deported to China. This anxiety was not specific to the Bay Area. Helen Zia recalled that her father, who lived in suburban New Jersey, was suspected to be a communist for often expressing his political opinions in Chinese newspapers. FBI agents likewise questioned Tung Pok Chin, a laundry operator in New Jersey, for the same reason, even though Chin had served in the U.S. Navy during World War II (Chen 2001; Zia 2000: 11; Chin 2000: 68–71, 83–88, 126–129).[3]

The Making of the Contemporary Chinese New Year Festival

To rescue Chinatown businesses and to showcase Chinese American anticommunist conviction, San Francisco's Chinatown leaders staged a Chinese New Year Festival in 1953. Although various organizations previously had staged public celebrations for the ethnic holiday, this was the first festival that organizers linked the celebration to Cold War political conditions. They articulated the Chinese American anticommunist pledge in festival announcements and events, which included Chinese art shows, street dancing, martial arts, music, sports, a fashion show, and an evening grand parade. The following year, it added a Miss Chinatown beauty pageant contest, which became a nationwide Miss Chinatown USA competition in 1958.

Using the false accusation that Communist China had eliminated the Chinese New Year, Chinese American leaders championed celebrating it as a way of denouncing communism and of displaying one kind of American democratic practice that trumpeted ethnic diversity. To defuse foreign criticism of its race relations, the United States began to champion its multicultural image, in part by encouraging ethnic cultural expressions. Accordingly, the State Department often sent speakers abroad to affirm the freedom and equality enjoyed by nonwhite people, and they clearly believed that the Chinese New Year celebration was a good way to mute the criticism from the PRC, one of the strongest critics on U.S. racial policy (Dudziak 1994: 567; Dudziak 2000: 39). As a result, a broadcast team was sent to Chinatown to record the event so that the ethnic celebration could be publicized to the PRC (*Chinese Pacific Weekly* 1953: 24).

To further disassociate itself from Red China, the Chinese New Year parade included a car from the Anti-Communist League. Ethnic leaders in San Francisco formed the Anti-Communist League on 14 November 1950, to "let the American people know that the Chinese are not communists and to rally all overseas Chinese people against communism and to support the Republic of China" (Nee and Nee 1972: 211). The anticommunist loyalty pledge was not specific to San Francisco. The All-American Overseas Chinese Anti-Communist League was established in New York in 1954 to assure that Chinese Americans were not communists (Takaki 1989: 415).

Veterans were showcased in the parade to demonstrate Chinese American loyalty. This was not surprising since many ethnic and racial minorities often militarized their celebrations in the Cold War period, and veterans usually replaced pioneers, a main feature of public celebration in the 1920s (Schultz 1994; Bodnar 1992: 138–166). In 1953 Chinese veterans of three wars (World War I, World War II, and the Korean War) marched in the parade, led by Grand Marshal Corporal Joe Wong and two enlisted Air Force women, Jessie Lee and Anna Tome (*San Francisco Chronicle* 1953: 1). In 1954 Marine Lieutenant Thomas Lee, a Chinese American officer recovering from wounds suffered on the Korean front, was selected to lead the parade (*San Francisco Chronicle* 1954: 9). The presence of these veterans showcased Chinese American participation in the country's major battles, a demonstration of their patriotism. The female veterans also embodied a representation different from the hyperfemininity and exoticism of beauty queens, one of the main attractions in the parade.

The Miss Chinatown beauty pageant was designed to change the per-

Figure 12.1. The national flags of China, Taiwan, and the United States displayed together in Chinatown during the Chinese New Year festival in San Francisco in 2005. Photo by Kuo-Tung Li.

ception of Chinese Americans from an inscrutable, scheming, communistic people, to a docile, exotic, feminized minority. Chinatown had hosted beauty contests as early as 1915 to raise money for the community, and ethnic organizations had previously used the beauty pageant to showcase Chinese American acculturation (Yung 1995: 148; *Asian Week* 1981; *East/West* 1970; see Wu 1997: 5–31; Lim 2003: 188–204). However, in contrast to the preceding years, the *cheong-sam* (a Chinese long gown) was presented as official dress at the height of the Cold War (Finnane 1996: 99–131). The *cheong-sam* was introduced to Chinatown in the 1930s, when the Chinese image began to shift from "yellow peril" to heroic defenders against the Japanese invasion (Hu [Woo] 1991: 530). The gown conjured up the picture of Madame Chiang Kai-shek attired in a *cheong-sam*, a popular image in American society and in Chinese American communities during World War II (Wong 2000: 181). The adoption of such gowns also signified that certain leaders wanted to claim nationalist China as their "ancestral country" since the *cheong-sam* was "the national female dress of Guomindang [Kuomintang] China" (Finnane 1996: 119). At the same time, the adoption of the *cheong-sam* was a refutation of the Mao suit and thus a manifestation of a Chinese American anticommunist position. In this way, the *cheong-sam* not only denounced the elimination of gender difference in Communist China, but also upheld an American gender ideology that considered women as sexual objects. Finally, the *cheong-sam* catered to the mainstream perception of the "China doll" fantasy, which was affirmed by community newspaper reports that described many male "westerners" happily spending one dollar to purchase raffle tickets for their favorite beauty pageant candidates (*Chinese Pacific Weekly* 1954: 25).[4]

Meanwhile, the rhetoric that pledged loyalty to the United States, ironically, became a loyalty pledge to the Nationalist government of Taiwan because the United States saw it as a democratic and capitalist ally to contain communism. Chinese American leaders therefore deliberately showcased their support for Taiwan during the festival. Each year, the Nationalist flag was prominently displayed on the parade route, either carried by a parade float or by one of the Chinese school teams. Beginning in 1954, the Taiwanese Consul General was invited to be a parade float judge or honored guest while his wife was a beauty pageant judge (Wu 1997: 11).[5] The winners of the national Miss Chinatown USA beauty pageant were sent on a trip to Taiwan after their coronation. They sometimes even participated in the Double Ten festivities (the celebration of the collapse of imperial China) in Taipei and were photographed with top government officials there.[6] In this way, the community's political loyalties were expressed in festival publications. For example, the 1968 Chinese New Year festival booklet equated Double Ten with other important ethnic holidays such as the Chinese New Year ("Souvenir Program" 1968). In addition, parade organizers went to Taiwan to procure "authentic" Chinese goods, supporting the idea of the Nationalist government as the guardian of traditional Chinese culture. Parade organizer David Lei, for instance, acquired a Qing Dynasty wedding procession from Taiwan for the 1977 Chinese New Year parade ("Spring Festival" 1977: 1; Chang 1977: 6).

Many liberals and China supporters, however, were opposed to this politicization of the festival. Although political persecution at the height of the Cold War virtually wiped out Chinatown leftist organizations, several community liberals such as Gilbert Woo denounced the political oppression by the Nationalist government and were branded as "communists" by the old establishment. However, Chinese American radicals began to emerge in the late 1960s with the influence of civil rights movements and the Black Power movement. The Red Guard Party, formed in 1969, was one example. Their members went to nearby Oakland to study Marxism and Mao Tse-Teng's ideology with the Black Panthers (Ho and Yip 2000: 286–287). In addition, not only did the Red Guard Party hang Mao's picture in its headquarters in Chinatown, but it also brought its pro-Communist China ideology into the public arena, when on 7 May 1969, the flag of the PRC was displayed in Portsmouth Square, the most visible place in Chinatown. The Red Guard Party also urged the United States to normalize its relationship with the PRC, again enraging the old establishment who denounced communism (Lyman 1973: 20; "Red Guard" 2000: 402).

Despite challenges such as these, political differences were seldom visible in ethnic celebrations in the 1950s and 1960s. While an affinity with the Nationalist government was clearly showcased in ethnic festivals, any association with Communist China was deliberately minimized to comply with U.S. containment policy. The Red Guard Party's distribution of Mao's Red Book in the 1969 Chinese New Year Festival was a rare exception (Yeh 2002: 341). Nevertheless, the relaxing tensions between China and the United States would soon end the prominence of the Nationalist government in San Francisco's Chinese New Year Festival.

After Nixon's Trip—"Now It Was Okay to Be Chinese"

President Richard Nixon's trip to the PRC in 1972 opened a new era for many Chinese Americans. They were proud of this new relationship because they no longer feared being associated with "enemy agents." As one Chinese American woman explained the impact, "Nixon's visit elevated the status of Chinatown. In a way, now it was okay to be Chinese. We could be proud to be Chinese. And China, instead of being an enemy, became a friend" (Laguerre 2000: 39). Other Chinese Americans also felt empowered by the change. Philip Choy, an architect and a historian, stated: "I felt a feeling of pride watching Nixon and Chou meet (on television). For the first time, a representative of China meets a representative of the Western world as equals. Before, foreign visitors came to China arrogantly and dictated terms before cutting her up" (Wong 1972: 7). Once China was seen as an equal entity to the United States, these Chinese Americans could proudly refer to China as their "homeland" and reaffirm their ethnic ties.

The lessening hostility indeed permitted Chinese Americans to renew both personal and economic transpacific ties. Visits to the PRC had been cut off after the outbreak of the Korean War. The new Sino-American relation allowed Chinese Americans to visit their families or relatives. It also generated trade interests in the Chinese American community and in mainstream society, and lifting the embargo in 1971 allowed Chinatown business people to import "authentic" Chinese goods to attract tourists and to cater to the needs of the local Chinese American population. Chinese medicinal herbs were the first goods to be shipped to the United States (Power 1971: 9). Most businesspeople, however, were hesitant to trade with China because the United States had imposed a stiff tariff ranging from 70 to 80 percent of import duty tax. It was only in 1979, when the two countries signed a mutual agreement granting a most-favored-nation tariff, that trade took off.

New organizations began to emerge to create trading opportunities with the PRC. In 1977 professionals formed the National Association of Chinese Americans to "promote U.S.-China friendship" (Lai 1999: 14). In San Francisco, a group of Chinese American business people formed the Chinese American Association of Commerce (CAAC) in 1980 to meet new demands as the Chinese Chamber of Commerce, the major sponsor of the Chinese New Year Festival, mainly dealt with Taiwan and refused to trade with the PRC. The founding members of CAAC numbered 110, but after one year, membership increased to more than 200. San Francisco's city hall made similar efforts to increase business opportunities with China. The city not only hosted a merchandise exhibition from China in 1980, but Mayor Dianne Feinstein also proclaimed September of that year as "China Month" ("Mayor Feinstein" 1980: 1).

Nixon's visit and the subsequent normalization with China, coupled with the rise of the New Left, fueled great interest in Chinese cultures and Chinese food within and beyond the ethnic community. Before Nixon's trip, Chinese American radicals such as the Red Guard Party had attempted to introduce communist ideology, but they often suffered from police harassment. The situation changed soon after Nixon's visit. Chinatown institutions began to bring in mainland Chinese artists and sport teams. In 1972 the Chinese Cultural Foundation in San Francisco sponsored a lecture on contemporary Chinese revolutionary art. The tours from a Peking opera troupe and a ping-pong team from China met with great enthusiasm among Chinese Americans (Wang 1972: 2). To go along with the trend, Miss Chinatown USA beauty pageants included Chinese music and dance. In 1977, pageant organizer Louella Leon organized the ethnic beauty pageant in the form of a Chinese opera (Springer 1980: 6; Wu 1997: 21). Chinese food also became fashionable. The Chinese dishes from Nixon's trip became the hottest foods. Instead of being satisfied with chop suey, Americans now requested more of the "authentic" flavor of Chinese food. Chinese liberation uniforms, Mao's red book, Chinese canned food, ping-pong, and Chinese artifacts likewise enjoyed popularity in mainstream society (*San Francisco Journal* 1972: 1).

Nixon's trip encouraged people in the community to openly endorse the PRC and challenge the old establishment's support for Taiwan. Shirley Sun, director of San Francisco's Chinese Culture Foundation (CCF), was among the first to visit the PRC in 1971 after the United States had lifted the ban on travel to China. Sun was known for supporting PRC art and artists. She also blasted the Chinese New Year celebration for being "politically tied to Taiwan." As a result, the old establishment boycotted the activities sponsored by the CCF (Lai n.d.: 26–37, 47; "The 'Costs' of Chinese Celebration" 1977).

Pro-Taiwan groups and anticommunist supporters clearly were unhappy with the easing of animosity between China and the United States. Although the *San Francisco Journal,* a bilingual weekly newspaper welcomed the normalization, the *World Journal* and the *Young China,* both Chinese-language daily newspapers, considered it as a betrayal of an ally (Draper 1979: 10). Meanwhile, some refugees from mainland China were still bitterly against the communist regime. For example, Peter Eng's immigrant father, who fled to Hong Kong to escape the communists, vowed that he would never return there under communist rule (Eng 1982, punch 3–1). At the same time, most of the Chinatown establishment, including the CCBA and the Chinese Chamber of Commerce, still remained committed to the Nationalist government (Lai 1999: 14).[7] Not all organizations, however, maintained this position. Four of the seven largest family associations, which were part of the CCBA, no longer raised the Nationalist flag on the first day of the normalization while in the past all of them did (Hall 1979: 6).

Although the rise of professionals and the increasing number of Chinatown residents who were not part of the old establishment began to destabilize the pro-Nationalists' influence, they still controlled significant material and personal resources in the community. The eighty-four

Figure 12.2. A protester voices his discontent with the 2004 Taiwanese presidential election at the 2005 Chinese New Year parade in San Francisco. Photo by Kuo-Tung Li.

family and district associations in fact owned 50 to 75 percent of Chinatown property (Iwata 1990; Nee and Nee 1972: 232).[8] Because the majority of the old establishment had close political and economic relationships with Taiwan, it perceived the growing support of the PRC as a threat to its leadership.

This conflict within the Chinese American community was not limited to the power center. One community leader commented that the antagonism was "most evident with recent immigrants—you can always hear them fighting about politics" ("The 'Costs' of Chinese Celebration" 1977). Competition for political support resulted in public confrontations. On 20 May 1978, more than one hundred persons rallied at Portsmouth Square, the most visible place in Chinatown, to denounce the inauguration of President Chiang Ching-kuo, eldest son of Chiang Kei-shek. They then marched to the Kuomintang (Nationalist Party) headquarters and encountered the pro-Chiang group who gathered inside to celebrate the inauguration. Violence soon broke out between the two groups and resulted in several injuries (Editorial 1978: 2).

In order to ease the tensions between these two groups, several Chinatown community leaders urged Chinese Americans to disassociate themselves from transnational conflicts. One argued, "We're Chinese-Americans. We can't fight these foreign wars . . . we've got our own life to live" ("The 'Costs' of Chinese Celebration" 1977). An editorial in the *East/West*, a bilingual community newspaper, likewise held the same opinion: "Political influence from the other side of the Pacific has been a most unhealthy element in our communities. It alienates our leaders. It confuses priorities. It misuses our community organizations. Its presence has frightened many from participation in genuine community services" ("Get Rid of Foreign Influence" 1973: 2). Critics therefore called for a form of political assimilation which discouraged Chinese Americans from getting involved in transnational politics.

On New Year's Day of 1979, the year that the United States recognized the PRC, people in Chinatown could sense the hostility between pro-China and pro-Taiwan groups. That morning, the pro-Taiwan group rallied first at St. Mary's Square in Chinatown, then about one thousand marched through Chinatown, chanting "Free China, go, go, go; Communist, no, no, no." The march ended at one P.M. but about three hundred pro-Taiwan supporters proceeded to Portsmouth Square, where eight hundred people gathered to celebrate the normalization. The pro-Taiwan supporters stopped on Clay Street across from Portsmouth Square chanting "Long Live Free China!" Despite more than 140 police positioned between two groups to prevent a collision, violence still broke out and four persons were injured ("Thousands Turn Out" 1979: 1; "Normalization Celebration" 1979: 1; "S.F. Police Prevent" 1979: 2).[9] The big rallies from both sides were clearly indicative of the severe political division within the ethnic community. This political division not only produced tensions in the public space, but also created disagreements over political expressions in the ethnic celebration, as Chinese Americans had no consensus over transnational political affiliations. The San Francisco city government also intervened in political expressions of the ethnic celebration to ensure that Chinese Americans complied with U.S. foreign policy. The Chinese New Year parade became a contested site for various groups or entities.

Ethnic Celebrations After Normalization

Since its staging in 1953, San Francisco's Chinese New Year Festival had been the community's most publicized event, attracting not only ethnic, but also mainstream and international spectators. Chinatown residents anticipated that pro-China and pro-Taiwan supporters would use this occasion for their respective political agendas, and because the 1979 Chinese New Year parade would be broadcast live on television, any political expressions or confrontations would gain even greater exposure ("Thousands Turn Out" 1979: 1; "Normalization Celebration" 1979: 1). However, both sides showed restraint and the recognition of the PRC produced no disturbance, despite widespread expectations that it would (*Chinese Pacific Weekly* 1979: 4).

However, the absence of violent confrontation by no means meant that politics was absent at the 1979 Chinese New Year Festival. When the relationship between China and the United States was normalized, Taiwan lost its privileged status. As a result, the San Francisco Mayor pressured the Chinese Chamber of Commerce not to show the Nationalist flag or any slogans that supported Taiwan. The Chinese Chamber of Commerce was supposed to comply with the policy. However, Chinese Central High School, Kin Kuo Chinese School, and Taiwan's China Airlines were seen either marching with the Nationalist flag or displaying it on their float in the parade ("KMT Flags" 1979: 8; *Chinese Times* 1979: 1, 1980: 6).[10]

Politics remained an issue in the 1980 Chinese New Year Festival. As mentioned earlier, San Francisco's Chinese Chamber of Commerce had invited Taiwanese representatives to the parade since the second year of the festival. Even though the United States now recognized China rather than Taiwan, the Chinese Chamber of Commerce had no intention of inviting the Chinese Consul General, Hu Dingyi, to the 1980 parade. Knowing this, Mayor Dianne Feinstein pressured the Chinese Chamber of Commerce and it finally invited the Chinese Consul General along with Taiwan representative H. P. Chung. In the end, rather than cave in to political pressure from the city and have both representatives in the parade, the Chinese Chamber of Commerce withdrew both invitations at the last minute. Dennis Wong, publicity chairman of the Chinese Chamber of Commerce, candidly admitted that "It [has] been our tradition not to deal with the mainland" (Hsu 1980: 5). Moreover, the parade committee continued to allow Chinese schools to carry Taiwan flags in the parade, which also infuriated Mayor Feinstein and prompted her to announce, "This is the last time city funds will be used for this event" ("China Rep Problem" 1980: 1).[11]

Not only did this incident anger the mayor, but it also enraged some Chinese Americans. Victor Seeto, vice president of the Chinese American Democratic Club (CADC), insisted that the public was "outraged that the Taiwan flag was prominently displayed within the parade by some of the marching units." The CADC promptly asked its chief administrative officer, Roger Boas, to undertake a "thorough investigation" of the "possible misuse of public funds for improper and illegal political purposes by the sponsor of the Chinese New Year parade" ("Demo Club" 1980: 1). Seeto even asked that the parade be put under "new sponsorship" if "improper and illegal political purposes" were found (Chan 1980: 1). An editorial in the *East/West* also concurred: "A parade of this nature, supported by public funds, should not be used for partisan politics, not to mention foreign politics ("The New Year Parade" 1980: 2). Not only did China sympathizers object to any political associations with Taiwan, but other Chinese Americans also believed that the Chinese New Year parade, the most significant and publicized event in the ethnic community, should have no association with foreign governments.

Others, however, questioned the politics of the city government. One reader of the *East/West* pointed out that people should not overreact, and argued that even though the U.S. government ended normal relations with Taiwan, state and city governments had not made a clear break with it. San Francisco remained a sister city with Taipei, and just a month earlier, city hall had accepted a pavilion from Taipei to be installed in Golden Gate Park (Lu 1984: 12).[12] In addition, San Francisco's mayor arranged trips to Taipei as well as to Shanghai and Peking. These policies made some Chinese Americans think that the mayor cared little about the changes in foreign policy and wondered why she made a big fuss over the issue of representation in the Chinese New Year parade (*East/West* 1980: 15).[13]

City politics, nevertheless, had a lasting impact on the ethnic celebration. Again in 1981 Mayor Feinstein requested that the Chinese Chamber of Commerce only allow American flags to be displayed. As a result, several Chinese schools withdrew their parade participation ("New Year Parade" 1981: 2). Since then, no foreign flags have appeared in the festival. In 1982 though fourteen British Parliament members were in the Chinese New Year parade reviewing stand, no official representatives came from China or Taiwan, and the Chinese Chamber of Commerce began to adopt a neutral position on issues of transpacific politics. As Rose Pak, the main power behind the Chinese Chamber of Commerce, claimed, "This is a community event. We want to keep international politics out of it" (Lattin 1982: 2). This incident illustrates the pressures Chinese Americans experience to not express their political differences in public spaces, especially during the Chinese New Year Festival. While early Cold War politics pressured them to express support for Taiwan by displaying the Nationalist flag in the parade, once U.S. policy changed, it became intolerable to city hall. Nevertheless, some parade spectators still carried the Nationalist flag along the parade route (*Young China* 1982: 8). In addition, not every city in the United States responded to the policy shift in the same way. For example, in Washington, D.C., a small-scale Chinese New Year parade hosted by the local Chinese Consolidated Benevolent Association continued to hang Taiwan flags along the parade route and distributed them to spectators in the 1980s (Hsu 1987).

As this chapter has demonstrated, the tenuous political status of Chinese Americans propelled them to use public cultural expressions to gain acceptance from the larger American society. Ethnic leaders were encouraged to demonstrate their affiliation with the Nationalist government in the Chinese New Year parade to comply with U.S. Cold War politics. Anticommunist hysteria compelled the ethnic community to reach a consensus over political expressions. However, once the anticommunist consensus disappeared, the division within the ethnic community over the conflict between China and Taiwan resurfaced in the ethnic celebration. Changes in American foreign policy again dictated the political expression of the Chinese New Year parade. Because the dominant society continues to perpetuate Chinese Americans as foreigners, and the relationship between the United States and the PRC remains tenuous, Chinese Americans are unlikely to cease showcasing their patriotism during their ethnic celebrations. The replenishment of new immigrants from the conflicted areas themselves will continue to involve the ethnic community in transnational politics and encourage members to voice their political opinions in the ethnic celebrations.

Notes

1. I use the PRC to refer to the People's Republic of China and Taiwan to refer to the Republic of China.

2. The first Chinese Exclusion Act was enacted in 1882 to exclude Chinese laborers from immigrating to the United States for ten years. This is the first race-based immigration exclusion law. The law was renewed several times until its repeal in 1943.

3. Often, a merchant or U.S. citizen reported the birth of a son or daughter after a visit to China, which then created a "slot" to bring in a child. In the 1950s, the United States could not deport all illegal immigrants because the nation did not have diplomatic relations with China, nor were Taiwan and Hong Kong willing to accept the deportees. Though some were spared from deportation, they were still stigmatized by the status of suspended deportation, which meant they had no rights in the United States and could not reenter the country once they left.

4. At this time, Chinese-language newspapers often used "westerners" to refer to the general non-Chinese public.

5. The festival included a best float competition.

6. The trip later included China when the Chinese Chamber of Commerce and other old establishments recognized the potential commercial interests in China. In addition, Taiwan eased travel restrictions to China.

7. After normalization, the PRC started a similar campaign to gain support

from Chinatown organizations, as did its Taiwan counterpart. The competition resulted in factions within organizations.

8. According to Victor Nee and Brett De Bary Nee, 65 percent of the land and property in the core area of Chinatown belonged to family and district associations (Nee and Nee 1972: 232).

9. *Chinese Times* reported that pro-Taiwan supporters were about 2,000 (*Chinese Times* 1979: 1).

10. China Airlines, a Taiwanese airline, has been actively involved in the Chinese New Year Festival. It usually sponsored a float in the parade and in some years its flight attendants offered entertainment at the Miss Chinatown USA beauty pageant.

11. The City of San Francisco contributed the following amounts to the festival: $27,500 in 1976–1977, $29,700 in 1977–1978, and $19,899 in 1979 ("Parade Safety" 1979: 1; *East/West* 1980: 6).

12. San Francisco signed its sister city agreement with Taipei in 1969.

13. San Francisco later became a sister city to both Taipei and Shanghai. Mayor Feinstein made a remark that "We tried not to get into politics. We're a friendship and trade group" (Lu 1984: 1, 15).

Bibliography

Asian Week. 1981. (12 February).

Baldwin, Catherine. 1880. "Chinese in San Francisco—The Sixth Year of Qwong See." *Harper's New Monthly Magazine* 62, no. 367 (December): 70–78.

Bodnar, John. 1992. *Remaking America: Public Memory, Commemoration, and Patriotism in the Twentieth Century.* Princeton: Princeton University Press.

Chan, Doug. 1980. "City Investigates Charges of Parade Funds Misuse." *San Francisco Journal* (9 April): 1.

Chang, Lester W. 1977. "400,000 Jam Parade Route to See Dragon Usher in the New Year." *East/West* (9 March): 6.

Chen, Amy. 2001. *The Chinatown Files* [motion picture]. New York: Filmmakers Library. VHS.

Chen, Yong. 2000. *Chinese San Francisco, 1850–1943: A Trans-Pacific Community.* Stanford: Stanford University Press.

Chin, Tung Pok. 2000. *Paper Son: One Man's Story.* Philadelphia: Temple University Press.

"China Rep Problem Mars New Year Parade." 1980. *East/West* (5 March): 1.

"Chinatown Aglow on Eve of Year 2466." 1915. *San Francisco Examiner* (12 February): 9.

"Chinese Blend East, West in New Year Fete." 1931. *San Francisco Chronicle* (1 January): 4.

"Chinese Celebrate Rainy New Year." 1911. *San Francisco Chronicle* (30 January): 4.

"Chinese New Year is Today." 1926. *San Francisco Chronicle* (13 February): 8.

"Chinese New Year Passes Quietly by Police Ban." 1919. *San Francisco Chronicle* (1 February): 9.

Chinese Pacific Weekly. 1953. (14 February): 24.

———. 1954. (12 January): 25.

———. 1979. (4 January): 4.

———. 1981. (12 March).

"Chinese Pay Debts." 1923. *San Francisco Chronicle* (16 February): 7.

Chinese Times. 1979. (2 January): 1.
———. 1979. (12 February): 1.
———. 1980. (6 March): 6.
Chung Sai Yat Po. 1911. (14 February): 3.
———. 1912. (14 February): 1.
———. 1913. (5 February): 2.
———. 1915. (9 February): 9.
———. 1919. (31 January): 1.
———. 1925. (19 January): 3.
———. 1926. (13 February): 1, 2.
———. 1931. (17 February): 1, 2.
"Demo Club Asks City Hall to Investigate New Year Parade." 1980. *East/West* (March 26): 1.
Deschamps, Bénédicte. 2001. "Italian Americans and Columbus Day: A Quest for Consensus Between National and Group Identities, 1840–1910." In *Celebrating Ethnicity and Nation: American Festive Culture from the Revolution to the Early Twentieth Century,* ed. Geneviève Fabre, Jürgen Heideking, and Kai Dreisbach. New York: Berghahn Books, 124–139.
Draper, George. 1979. "Chinese Dailies in S.F. Are Angry." *San Francisco Chronicle* (5 January 5): 10.
Dudziak, Mary L. 1994. "Josephine Baker, Racial Protest, and the Cold War." *Journal of American History* 81, no. 2 (September): 543–570.
———. 2000. *Cold War Civil Rights: Race and the Image of American Democracy.* Princeton: Princeton University Press.
East/West. 1970. February 18 (Chinese Section).
———. 1980. (March 6), 6.
———. 1980. (March 26), 15 (Chinese Section).
"Editorial." 1978. *East/West* (31 May): 2.
Eng, Peter. 1982. "The Worlds Between My Father and Me." *San Francisco Chronicle* (6 June): punch 3–1.
"Falungong Row Overshadows Australia's Chinese New Year Preparations." 2005. *Agence France Presse* (8 February).
Finnane, Antonia. 1996. "What Should Chinese Women Wear? A National Problem." *Modern China* 22, no. 2 (April): 99–131.
"Get Rid of Foreign Influence." 1973. *East/West* (25 July): 2.
Hall, Stephen. 1979. "Bring Problems to Chinatown." *San Francisco Chronicle* (31 March): 6.
Ho, Fred, and Steve Yip. 2000. "Alex Hing: Former Minister of Information for the Red Guard Party and Founding Member of I Wor Kuen." In *Legacy to Liberation: Politics and Culture of Revolutionary Asian Pacific America,* ed. Fred Ho et al. San Francisco: AK Press, 279–296.
Hsu, Evelyn. 1980. "Wrangle over Envoys at Chinese Parade." *San Francisco Chronicle* (29 February): 5.
———. 1987. "A Bang-up Celebration in Chinatown: 3,000 Gather for Parade and Fireworks to Welcome 4685, Year of the Hare." *Washington Post* (2 February): 4e.01.
Hu, Jingnan (Gilbert Woo). 1991. *Hu Jingnan wenji* [Gilbert Woo Anthology]. Hong Kong: Xiangjiang chuban youxian gongsi.
Iwata, Edward. 1990. "Beneath Serene and Thriving Surface, Old Battles Live On." *Los Angeles Times* (15 January).
Joe, Glenda Kay. 1981. "We Should Put Aside the PRC/Taiwan Debate and Look to Community Problems." *East/West* (18 February): 2.

"KMT Flags in City-Funded Chinese New Year's Parade." 1979. *San Francisco Journal* (14 February): 8.

Kurashige, Lon. 2002. *Japanese American Celebration and Conflict: A History of Ethnic Identity and Festival, 1934–1990.* Berkeley: University of California Press.

Laguerre, Michel S. 2000. *The Global Ethnopolis: Chinatown, Japantown and Manilatown in American Society.* New York: St. Martin's Press.

Lai, Him Mark. n.d. "Thirty Years of the Chinese Culture Foundation and Twenty-Two Years of the Chinese Culture Center of San Francisco." Unpublished manuscript.

———. 1992. "To Bring Forth a New China, To Build a Better America: The Chinese Marxist Left in America to the 1960s." *Chinese America: History and Perspectives* 6: 42–52.

———. 1999. "China and the Chinese American Community: The Political Dimension." In *Chinese America: History and Perspectives,* 1–32.

Lattin, Don. 1982. "165,000 at Chinatown Parade." *San Francisco Sunday Examiner and Chronicle* (31 January): 2.

Lee, Anthony W. 2001. *Picturing Chinatown: Art and Orientalism in San Francisco.* Berkeley: University of California Press.

Lee, Rose Hum. 1960. *The Chinese in the United States of America.* London: Oxford University Press.

Lim, Shirley Jennifer. 2003. "Contested Beauty: Asian American Women's Cultural Citizenship During the Early Cold War Era." In *Asian/Pacific Islander American Women: A Historical Anthology,* ed. Shirley Hune and Gail M. Nomura. New York: New York University Press, 188–204.

Lowe, Joan (pseudonym). 1998. Personal interview. 14 July.

Lu, Elizabeth. 1984. "SF Mayor's Trip to Far East Brought Business, Social Ties with Shanghai." *East/West* (5 December): 12.

Lyman, Stanford. 1973. "Red Guard on Grant Avenue: The Rise of Youthful Rebellion in Chinatown." In *Asian-Americans: Psychological Perspectives,* ed. Stanley Sue and Nathaniel N. Wagner. Ben Lomond, Calif.: Science and Behavior Books.

"Mayor Feinstein Proclaims September 'China Month.'" 1980. *East/West* (2 March): 1.

Nee, Victor, and Brett De Bary Nee. 1972. *Longtime Californ': A Documentary Study of an American Chinatown.* New York: Pantheon Books.

"New Year Din Rings Through Sun Francisco Chinatown." 1921. *San Francisco Chronicle* (7 February): 10.

"New Year Parade." 1980. *East/West* (26 March): 2.

"New Year Parade." 1981. *East/West* (18 February): 2.

"Normalization Celebration." 1979. *San Francisco Journal* (3 January): 1.

"Parade Safety, A Major Concern." 1979. *East/West* (7 February): 1.

Power, Keith. 1971. "China Trade Policy, Herbs May Be First Through Bamboo Curtain." *San Francisco Chronicle* (12 June): 9.

Ramirez, Raul and Ken Wong. 1978. "Chinatown Cool to New Agreement." *San Francisco Chronicle* (17 December): 20.

Red Guard, Appendix I: Red Guard Program and Rules. 1969 [2000]. In *Legacy to Liberation: Politics and Culture of Revolutionary Asian Pacific America,* ed. Fred Ho. San Francisco: AK Press.

San Francisco Chronicle. 1919. (1 February): 9.

———. 1924. (4 February): 7.

———. 1929. (11 February): 10.

————. 1953. (16 February): 1.
————. 1954. (6 February): 9.
San Francisco Journal. 1972. (March 22), 1 (Chinese Section).
Scharnhorst, Gary, ed. 1990. *Bret Harte's California: Letters to the Springfield Republican and Christian Register, 1866–67.* Albuquerque: University of New Mexico Press.
Schultz, April. 1994. *Ethnicity on Parade: Inventing the Norwegian American Through Celebration.* Amherst: University of Massachusetts Press.
"SF Police Prevent a Clash in Chinatown." 1979. *San Francisco Chronicle* (2 January): 2.
Soo, Annie (Shew). 2002. Personal interview. 9 January and 15 February.
"Souvenir Program, San Francisco Chinese New Year Festival." 1968. San Francisco: Chinese Chamber of Commerce, Public Library, Chinatown Branch.
"Spring Festival." 1977. *East/West* (2 March): 1.
Springer, Richard. 1980. "The New Look at This Year's Beauty Pageant." *East/West* (27 February): 6.
Takaki, Ronald. 1989. *Strangers from a Different Shore: A History of Asian Americans.* New York: Penguin Books.
"The 'Costs' of Chinese Celebration." 1977. *San Francisco Examiner* (February 15).
"Thousands Turn Out to See Parade." 1979. *East/West* (14 February): 1.
Tinlogy, Patrick. 1971. "Nevada County's Chinese." *Nevada County Historical Society* 25, no. 1 (January): 1–10.
Wang, Ling-Chi. 1972. *San Francisco Journal* (22 March): 2.
Wong, K. Scott. 2000. "War Comes to Chinatown: Social Transformation and the Chinese of California." In *The Way We Really Were: The Golden State in the Second Great War,* ed. Roger W. Lotchin. Urbana: University of Illinois Press.
Wong, Ken. 1972. "Chinatown Is Proud and Booming." *San Francisco Sunday Examiner and Chronicle* (27 February): 7.
Wu, Judy Tzu-Chun. 1997. "Loveliest Daughter of Our Ancient Cathay! Representations of Ethnic and Gender Identity in the Miss Chinatown USA Beauty Pageant." *Journal of Social History* 31, no. 1 (September): 5–31.
Yeh, Chiou-Ling. 2002. "Contesting Identities: Youth Rebellion in San Francisco's Chinese New Year Festivals, 1953–1969." In *The Chinese in America: A History from Gold Mountain to the New Millennium,* ed. Susie Lan Cassel. Walnut Creek, Calif.: Alta Mira Press, 329–350.
————. 2004. "In the Traditions of China and in the Freedom of America: The Making of San Francisco's Chinese New Year Festivals." *American Quarterly* 56, no. 2 (June): 395–420.
————. 2008. *Making an American Festival: Chinese New Year in San Francisco's Chinatown.* Berkeley: University of California Press.
"You Hear Big Noise? New Year in Chinatown." 1920. *San Francisco Chronicle* (15 February): 8.
Young China. 1982. (2 February): 8.
Yung, Judy. 1986. *Chinese Women of America: A Pictorial History.* Seattle: University of Washington Press.
————. 1995. *Unbound Feet: A Social History of Chinese Women in San Francisco.* Berkeley: University of California Press.
Zhao, Xiaojian. 2002. *Remaking Chinese America: Immigration, Family, and Community, 1940–1965.* New Brunswick, N.J.: Rutgers University Press.
Zia, Helen. 2000. *Asian American Dreams: The Emergence of an American People.* New York: Farrar, Straus and Giroux.

Chapter 13
Paddy, Shylock, and Sambo
Irish, Jewish, and African American Efforts to
Ban Racial Ridicule on Stage and Screen

M. Alison Kibler

In 1910 an editorial in *B'nai B'rith News* observed: "Now we have a protest against the 'stage Jew.' Some time ago a crusade was made against the 'stage Irishman.' The colored people have from time to time protested against the 'stage Negro.' And *Uncle Tom's Cabin* can not to this day 'show' in many sections of the South because of the caricature of southern characters."[1] This description is an apt introduction to the overlapping campaigns against racial ridicule in the early twentieth century. Irish nationalists threw rotten eggs and vegetables at several types of characters on stage—drunken, lascivious Irish women, and lazy, ape-like Irish men. Irish and Jewish activists urged performers and managers—often members of their own race—to stop perpetuating these stereotypes for profit. Jewish businessmen pulled advertising from publications that ran offensive stories and cartoons about the miserly, cheating Jew. Jewish, Irish, and African Americans also tried to harness the power of race-based censorship, by lobbying for the passage of bans on racial ridicule and turning bans on racially inflammatory productions to their own goals. In addition, Southern censors suppressed plays and films that challenged white superiority. With supporters from different racial and ethnic groups and opposing political sides, race-based censorship often had surprising outcomes. For example, civil rights leaders who fought to ban the racist film, *The Birth of a Nation*, relied in some cases on the statutes designed to ban *Uncle Tom's Cabin* because both inflamed racial feeling.

This essay examines the nationalists and civil rights leaders who supported race-based censorship in the early twentieth century. It shows how different ethnic and racial groups often supported one another (sometimes inadvertently) and used similar justifications for race-based censorship. In particular, Irish, Jewish, and African American groups advocated a pluralist mass culture and denounced racist images as indecent. But they also undercut each other; Irish and African American protesters often blamed Jews for the misrepresentation of other groups. These intertwined cases demonstrate that censorship in the early twentieth century was broader than the focus on sex and violence (Vasey 1996).[2] Furthermore, as historian Francis Couvares has already argued, the history of progressive or "good censors" shows that the history of censorship is more complicated than an "old-fashioned 'heroic' tale of expressive freedom versus moralism" (Couvares 1994: 234).

To understand the drive to censor racial ridicule, it is important to compare the demographic characteristics and political aspirations of the African American, Irish, and Jewish communities in the United States around the turn of the twentieth century. Irish, Jewish, and African Americans were improving, in different degrees, through migration, economic advances, and political organizing in the early twentieth century, but they shared a sense of being outsiders from mainstream American society. Around 1900, the American-born children of Irish immigrants from the Irish famine of the late 1840s became the dominant force in Irish American life (Meagher 2005: 103). The status of the Irish in America improved from one wave of immigration to the next, and from one generation to the next. Only 10 percent of Irish immigrants in Boston had white-collar jobs in 1890, but 40 percent of second-generation Irish had moved up to white-collar occupations (Miller 1985: 496). Around the turn of the twentieth century, the Jewish families from western and central Europe—the "German" Jews—who had migrated in the 1830s and 1840s, encountered large numbers of eastern European immigrants. The German leaders of the Jewish community were concerned about how the new masses of Yiddish-speaking Orthodox Jews would fare in the United States. Although their success did not match the German Jews' accumulation of wealth, eastern European Jews and their children still achieved "remarkable . . . occupational and economic mobility" (Sorin 1992: 152; Diner 1995: 15).

The status of African Americans did not improve as much as immigrant groups, but the dramatic migration of African Americans from the rural south to the urban north offered some relief from violence, poverty, and political disenfranchisement. Chicago's black population, for example, more than doubled between 1910 and 1920. Life in the North was not free of racism (segregation and rioting marked northern urban history), but African Americans still gained political influence and developed a robust artistic scene—the Harlem Renaissance—in the North.

African Americans, despite improved security in the North, had fewer opportunities than Irish and Jewish citizens. African Americans still received the lowest wages and the lowest skilled jobs; upward mobility was "virtually impossible" (Greenberg 2006: 18).

Despite social and political improvements, all three groups faced slights, coercion, and discrimination because they were outside of the Anglo-Saxon ideal. A movement for strict Americanization, centered on. Anglo-Saxon supremacy, emerged at the end of the nineteenth century and peaked during World War I. The emphasis on Americanization had a humanitarian, progressive trajectory, including assistance for immigrants, but it increasingly emphasized loyalty, naturalization, and an uncompromising "100 per cent Americanism" (Higham 1963: 247). During World War I, in the name of national unity, social workers, businessmen, and civic leaders encouraged immigrants to give up old-world customs. Henry Ford, for example, established a compulsory English school for his immigrant workers (Higham 1963: 247–248). The second Ku Klux Klan, established in 1915, advocated white supremacy and 100 percent Americanism as it popularity increased in the 1920s (Dumenil 1995: 236). Lynching accelerated to become a terrifying weapon against African Americans in the South between 1890 and World War I. Jewish newspapers in the United States—in English and in Yiddish— condemned mob violence against African Americans. Jews were shocked by the lynching of one of their own in 1915. In 1913 Jewish businessman Leo Frank was accused of sexually assaulting and killing his employee at his Atlanta pencil factory. The main evidence in Frank's trial was the testimony of the only other suspect, an African American janitor, Jim Conley. Frank was convicted and sentenced to death, but, in response to the explicit anti-Semitism of Frank's trial, the governor of Georgia commuted Frank's death sentence to life in prison. A vigilante mob took Frank out of prison and lynched him in 1915. Frank's murder was a powerful reminder of the Jews' marginal and maligned status in the United States. After Frank's murder and after encountering more African Americans in northern cities, Jewish concern with the status of African Americans "intensified" (Diner 1995: 20).

In response to this emphasis on conformity, many Irish, African American, and Jewish leaders called for a pluralistic model of American national identity and championed their uniqueness. The Gaelic League challenged the supremacy of Anglo-Saxons in the United States by delineating the Celtic contributions to the United States and by pointing to the diversity at the heart of American life (Jacobson 1995: 189–191). The National Association for the Advancement of Colored People, founded in 1910, also emphasized racial pride and equal rights. In 1913, the same year as Frank's trial, the International Order of B'nai B'rith—a Jewish fraternal order established in 1843—created the Anti-Defamation League to battle anti-Semitism, including stereotypes in the press, theater, and film. Louis Brandeis, the first Jewish Supreme Court justice, championed a new American nationality that "proclaims that each race or people, like each individual, has the right and duty to develop, and only through such differentiated development will high civilization be attained" (Greenberg 2006: 39). The attempts to censor racial stereotypes grew out of this debate over conformity and pluralism.

Irish American "Practical Censorship"

Jewish and African American activists often acknowledged their debt to Irish nationalists' attack on the Stage Irish.[3] Indeed, Irish American nationalism had become "the standard by which all other subversive nationalisms in the United States were to be judged" (Guterl 2001: 94). In the 1890s, radical Irish nationalists turned against the "stage Irish" as a way to rejuvenate Celtic race pride, including the revival of the Gaelic language and the elimination of Anglo influence in American culture. These radical nationalists supported the use of force to achieve Irish independence, as opposed to parliamentary negotiations for Home Rule. It is not surprising then that these Irish activists were often willing to disrupt theatrical space and risk arrest. Riots broke out over *McFadden's Row of Flats* in Philadelphia in 1903 because of the image of the Irish man as a green-whiskered ape, the flirtatious Irish woman on stage, and a pig living in the Irish family's house. Riots followed in New York City over the Russell Brothers' vaudeville act in 1907 (Kibler 2005).

These Irish nationalists championed this kind of direct action in theaters as "practical censorship," but they also occasionally turned to state censorship. Their approach to John Millington Synge's controversial play *The Playboy of the Western World* demonstrates their use of both "practical" and "state" censorship. On 15 January 1912 at the debut of *The Playboy* in Philadelphia at the Adelphi Theatre, Irish spectators hissed and shouted when Pegeen Mike's father departs, leaving her with "the playboy" overnight. Various nationalists stood up to speak against the play; they interrupted actors and tried to shame spectators into leaving. Joseph McLaughlin, vice president of the Ancient Order of Hibernians (an organization with a radical nationalist stance at this time), took the floor to denounce the play. Some spectators who recognized him shouted, "Put the saloonkeeper out." The police did just that. Twenty-nine Irishmen were ejected; two were arrested.[4] At the second production, fourteen men were arrested after they disrupted the play with hisses, coughs, and cries of "shame." Press reports acknowledged that the Philadelphia protesters, unlike their New York brethren, did not throw "substantial missiles" at the opening night in this city, although they did resort to tossing eggs and cakes following production.[5] Forewarned by the conflicts in New York City, police were well prepared for the disruption in Philadelphia.

Irish American activists tried to get the play banned because it insulted the Irish race, but they found little sympathy among city officials for this argument. Rather, they pressed their objections to the play in terms of decency and public order, with marginal references to the play's racial harm. A committee of Irish nationalists, including representatives from the Ancient Order of Hibernians and the Clan na Gael (an organization supporting violent revolt against the British), visited Mayor Blankenburg, a recently elected reformer, who answered, "If an Irish Mayor of Boston does not object to the play, there seems to be no justification for action by myself."[6] The mayor of New York had concluded, "A play may offend against good taste, truth, racial pride, national tradition and religious conviction, and yet not be of such an immoral character as to call for suppression."[7] The Irish nationalists noted Philadelphia's refusal to recognize the racial prejudice in the play, particularly in comparison with the apparent sympathy of the Pittsburgh press to this argument. "Anything that aggravates racial or religious prejudices is to be deplored."[8]

The protesters tried a new tactic on 17 January 1912. Based on affidavits drawn up McGarrity, the Irish players were arrested for violation of the state's McNichol Act of 1911, which prohibited "lascivious, obscene, indecent sacrilegious or immoral" plays. McGarrity claimed that the play was immoral, blasphemous, and a misrepresentation of the Irish.[9] It was a bold move for the liquor dealer, Joseph McGarrity, to claim the upper hand in morality. This failed also, however, as the players were released on bail and continued to perform the play. A judge quickly dismissed the charges without explanation. McGarrity, perhaps, was interested in pressing his claims of decency against those who cast him as unrefined. In addition, the Clan na Gael focused on the misrepresentation of Irish peasant women's sexuality in the play, making charges of indecency compatible with their claims of racial insult. Arguing that the "barelegged" peasant girls on stage and their sexual advances to the playboy were not typical of Ireland, Irish nationalists also asked, "What meaning has the word morality in Lady Gregory's mind?"[10]

The drive to censor *The Playboy of the Western World* ultimately relied on the dominant rationale for censorship: the bad tendency test. According to historian David Rabban, the protection of public welfare from the "alleged bad tendency of speech" was the most common approach to First Amendment questions between the end of the Civil War and World War I. Speech that caused unrest or harmed community "morals" was not protected by the First Amendment (Rabban 1997). Officials at this time recognized obscenity or indecency as speech with a bad tendency more consistently than they acknowledged racist images and rhetoric as speech with a bad tendency.

Irish nationalists in America had a difficult relationship with state censorship. They were not as confident in it as many Jewish and African American organizations and did not lobby city and state censorship boards as extensively as Jewish and African American groups, perhaps because they had experienced the suppression of their own publications during World War I. Several Irish American papers, including the radical nationalist paper, the *Gaelic American*, were suppressed by the United States Post Office because of their anti-British stance during the war. The *Gaelic American* denounced the "petty tyranny" of postal censorship, while the more conciliatory newspaper, the *Irish World*, accepted the censorship of its galley proofs prior to publication (Mulcrone 1993: 316–317). Despite these intrusions on the Irish American press, some Irish nationalists seemed to take a pragmatic approach to censorship, favoring the suppression of anti-Irish images, yet opposing the censorship of Irish political speech. Irish nationalist Jeremiah O'Leary supported the censorship of *The Playboy of the Western World* and advocated a revised licensing ordinance in New York City that would ban productions that included racial ridicule, even though he had been imprisoned during World War I for speaking out against conscription, a violation of the Espionage Act (Mulcrone 1993: 265). In 1927 Irish nationalists called for an expansion of New York City film censorship, from a refusal to license "immoral" or "indecent" motion pictures to a ban on licenses for films that "disparage any race, creed or nationality."[11] But even this push for censorship seemed uncertain. Some activists claimed that their efforts were not in fact "censorship." One Irish leader asserted his belief in liberty and explained that the Irish had been forced to "resort to legal measures." He then explained how censorship could enhance freedom: "Let us make it [this free country] free from prejudice."[12]

Jewish Censorship

Organized Jewish efforts to eliminate the Stage Jew acknowledged a debt to the Irish campaign. At an early meeting of Jewish activists, Irishman James Shaughnessey, gave advice about how to battle offensive representations. Accounts of this meeting noted that the "the agitation of the Irish Americans which brought the elimination of stage lampoons on the Celtic race was commended."[13] The founding of the Anti-Defamation League (ADL) of B'nai B'rith in 1913 has been considered the "key year" in the organized campaign against the "stage Jew" (Erdman 1997:

150). As John Roche explains, Jewish organizations were "vigorous supporters of 'censorship' in their campaign to eliminate anti-Semitism
from popular culture" (Roche 1963: 95). The ADL, for example, joined
with the American Jewish Committee (AJC) and responded to the discrimination against Jewish vacationers at summer resorts by lobbying for
the passage of civil rights laws that prohibited advertisements stating that
hotels would refuse accommodations on the basis of a "patron's race,
color or creed." They succeeded in getting New York's civil rights law
amended to include a ban on defamatory advertising in 1913 (Schultz
2000). In the ADL's first annual report, published in 1915, the organization's president, Sigmund Livingston, elaborated, "The chief evil is not
the discrimination but in the method by which that discrimination is
made known."[14]

When the ADL first looked systematically at anti-Semitism in motion
pictures, it believed that the large number of Jews involved in making
motion pictures would work in their favor. But the ADL was disap-
pointed when these Jewish manufacturers merely told the ADL that it
was "supersensitive" when these manufacturers ignored the ADL altogether.[15] The ADL then turned more strongly to censorship, surveying
existing censorship boards about their policies toward movies "which
grossly and maliciously caricature any people" and then drafting its own
model ordinance to stop movies that were obscene, portray unlawful
activity, disturb the peace, or defame a religious sect.[16] In just a few years,
the ADL reported that movie producers began to take them more seriously, largely as a result of the ADL's success pressuring state and city
censors and its warnings to its representatives in cities around the country about films that had been previously censored.

The ADL reported that it had "caused a motion picture censorship
ordinance to be introduced in a number of larger cities."[17] The Maryland board of censors, in 1922, clarified that its standards included the
"elimination of scenes and titles calculated to stir up racial hatred." The
attempt to stop films that created racial hatred was used, in some cases,
to support conservative efforts to ban productions like *Uncle Tom's Cabin*,
but the ADL apparently tried to use the rule for its own purposes. The
Mexican government and the "Anti-Jewish Defamation League" [*sic*]
urged many cuts from films based on that rule, according to the board.[18]

The ADL maintained a close relationship with city and state censorship boards in the early twentieth century. In 1914 the ADL's *Motion Picture Bulletin* described the organization's close relationship with the
Chicago Board of Censors. For example, the ADL lobbied the board to
make cuts in *Fagin*, a film based on the Dickens story, which features an
immoral Jewish peddler who corrupts Rose O'Brien, a "beautiful young
girl."[19] In one case, the Chicago Board notified the ADL about an objec-

tionable film, *The Fatal Wedding*.[20] In 1914 some Jewish leaders pressured the National Board of Censorship of Motion Pictures (a voluntary association of New York reformers, established in 1909 and later renamed National Board of Review) to suppress or modify *The Fatal Wedding* and *Rose of the Alley*. Sarah Kendall, of the Seattle Board of Censors, wrote to the National Board of Censorship to tell it about Jewish complaints: "The Hebrew people," she noted, "seem to feel especially singled out for such impersonation."[21] The National Board explained to Kendall that it had already issued a bulletin asking filmmakers to "avoid the showing of the Jew in a malicious, slanderous way." It reported that many had "complied with our request."[22] But the National Board of Censorship concluded that it could only move ahead in an "advisory way." The ADL was dissatisfied with the lax and inconsistent approach of this organization.

The ADL's and AJC's enthusiasm for state censorship and group libel laws contrasts with Reform rabbis' conflicted involvement with the anti-obscenity crusade in the early twentieth century. Historian Andrea Friedman shows that Reform rabbis became active in this movement "as much in response to anti-obscenity campaigns as to the existence of obscenity. They hoped their participation could undermine Christian beliefs about the lax morals among Jews and they tried to counter the argument of many anti-obscenity activists that cultural decay was caused by Jewish producers. Reform rabbis also found that their work against obscenity conflicted with "Reform Judaism's self-definition as a modern religious movement, in an era when individual autonomy and relaxed sexual mores were two of the primary denoters of modernity" (Friedman 2000: 140, 145). The enthusiasm of Jewish leaders for censorship thus seems to vary, depending on the images and topics that were under attack.

Civil Rights and Conservative Southern Censors

Along with Irish and Jewish organizations, African Americans were heavily invested in struggles over group representation in mass culture in the early twentieth century. Their campaign against *The Birth of a Nation* is the premier example of race-based censorship in this period. Three key texts were at heart of efforts to regulate the representation of African Americans in the early twentieth century—*Uncle Tom's Cabin*, *The Clansman* (and its movie version, *The Birth of a Nation*), and films of Jack Johnson's heavyweight fights. These examples show that race-based censorship served white supremacy and civil rights campaigns; in fact, legislation intended to protect white southerners from *Uncle Tom's Cabin* was later used to ban racist images. Activists in the early twentieth century understood that *The Clansman, The Birth of a Nation,* and Jack Johnson's fight films responded to the preceding texts and that censorship of any one affected the others. *The Clansman* was advertised as "the other side of the picture" from *Uncle Tom's Cabin* and films of African American heavyweight Jack Johnson's victories, banned in many cities, were shown in Chicago as a response to *The Birth of a Nation.*[23]

Theatrical versions of Harriet Beecher Stowe's antislavery novel *Uncle Tom's Cabin* were popular throughout the late nineteenth and early twentieth centuries. Though some versions of the "Tom show" included minstrel show characterizations and happy endings that idealized the Plantation South, one production, by George Aiken and George How-ard, stayed true to the "abolitionist pathos" of Stowe's book (Williams 1996: 119). The play ended with the death of Uncle Tom and did not romanticize plantation life. Southern lawmakers targeted this version, according to film historian Linda Williams, by passing laws against plays that incited racial prejudice, intended to mean black prejudice against whites. In the South the play was controversial because, as some critics argued, it "slurred the fair name of Southerners" and was likely to "inflame race prejudice among the large class of Negro citizens" (Waller 1995: 44). An early "Uncle Tom's Cabin bill" in Lexington, Kentucky, passed in 1905 at the urging of the Daughters of the Confederacy, outlawed theatrical performances that "tend to create racial feelings and prejudice" (Waller 1995: 45). In 1906 the Kentucky state legislature passed a law banning "any play that is based upon antagonism between master and slave, or that excites racial prejudice" (Grieveson 1998: 63; also see Williams 1996: 123).

Around the same time as southern politicians were legislating against *Uncle Tom's Cabin,* African American leaders and other reformers were beginning to campaign against a new play, *The Clansman,* based on Thomas Dixon's second book (Waller 1995: 44). The Woman's Christian Temperance Union of South Carolina unanimously denounced "in unmeasured terms the unspeakable play *The Clansman,* the presentation of which is calculated to arouse race hatred."[24] Several newspaper editors criticized the play for encouraging lynching and audiences hissed the play in Columbia, South Carolina.[25] In Brooklyn, New York a committee of African Americans objected to the play because it "tended to excite race hatred."[26]

Dixon's racist views were well-known. At one meeting he asserted, "God ordained the Southern white man to teach the lessons of Aryan Supremacy."[27] In 1906 Dixon offered particularly inflammatory commentary on the recent Atlanta race riot, predicting that "there would be outbreaks of whites against negroes until the latter are outside of this country." And he blamed the riots on African American assertiveness:

"The insolence of the negro in Atlanta has grown greatly," said Dixon.[28] He also predicted that bloody riots, far worse than that of Atlanta, would occur in New York and Chicago in the near future, because of the "liberties the negro is allowed in the North."

The Atlanta race riot precipitated the most pronounced African American reaction to Dixon's play, perhaps partly due to Dixon's incendiary rhetoric. *The Clansman* became much more controversial in Philadelphia after the Atlanta riot of 1906.[29] *The Clansman* controversy in Philadelphia is important for two reasons: the confrontation at the Walnut Theater became the basis for later NAACP claims that the movie based on the play would cause a riot; and the censorship of the play was based not on laws against racial ridicule, but on bans on immoral plays or plays likely to cause a breach of peace. This pattern was followed in many other cases.

The play had appeared during the previous season in Philadelphia and African American preachers objected then too. But by October 1906 black leaders were more adamant about suppressing the play because of the recent Atlanta riots. During the summer of 1906 tensions increased over lynchings in Atlanta and Chattanooga. White leaders complained of a "rape menace" and elected officials and press reports lent sympathy to white men's efforts to "protect our women" (Crowe 1969: 152). On 22 September, in the midst of a "general sexual hysteria," armed white men gathered in on the outskirts of the African American neighborhood and attacked black-owned saloons, pool halls, and restaurants (Crowe 1969: 153). Calm did not return to the city until 27 September. Twenty-five African American men died and several hundred were wounded.

African American preachers in Philadelphia, complaining that "lynchings of negroes have been encouraged by the play,"[30] sent out "a call to action" on 20 October 1906: "We, the citizens, have determined that it shall not play at the Walnut Street Theatre during the coming week."[31] Three days later a crowd of African Americans gathered outside the Walnut Street Theatre when *The Clansman* was scheduled. One report estimated that 2,000 African Americans came to protest and another 1,000 whites came to observe the event.[32] At the start of the play, one African American man threw an egg at the stage from the gallery. Someone shouted, "We want no Atlanta here" (referring to the recent Atlanta race riots) and then African Americans ran from the gallery to join the crowd on the street.[33] Police arrested the egg-thrower, Henry Jenkins, and, according to one report, clubbed him on the head and led him, with a bleeding scalp, outside. *The Philadelphia North American* noted that "hundreds of Negroes swarmed" around Jenkins and threatened the police.[34] When the Director of Public Safety tried to break up the crowd, the crowd surged around him, but ministers calmed the crowd and it eventually dispersed quietly: "That there was largely no bloodshed is largely due to the action of a number of negro ministers and leaders, who moved among the crowd of angry men and urged them to be quiet."[35]

Republican Mayor Weaver banned *The Clansman* because he believed it was "calculated to produce disorder and endanger lives."[36] Although he remained concerned about the behavior of the African American crowd, he upheld the protesters' claims about the play's harm. "The play holds up a whole race to ignominy and ridicule," he concluded, "instead of bringing all races together."[37] The mayor's decision was controversial because he seemed to be censoring the play for being racially insulting, even though that was not an established category for censorship in the city. As one letter explained in 1906:

> *The Clansman* has been stopped. Very good—if *The Clansman* is immoral, or if *The Clansman* in any way disturbs the peace and tranquility of the city, let it be stopped. But a way to stop it! . . . Was it *The Clansman*, which incited violence or was it a party of negroes—the sort aping social equality, a thing which can never exist—that incited the mob of low negroes to such disgraceful conduct as was exhibited the other night?[38]

It is important to note the conflicting accounts of the Philadelphia protest. While a protester threw an egg on stage, leaders outside reportedly restrained the crowd from pursuing police officers who were violent. Indeed, African American preachers denied that the protest was a riot: "The play incites to riot. . . . It is not the colored people who are rioters."[39] Nine years later, however, the NAACP referred to this event as proof that the film version of *The Clansman*, *The Birth of a Nation*, was likely to cause violence.[40]

When Dixon tested the Mayor's order in court, he encountered an even more spirited defender of the African American protesters—Judge Mayer Sulzberger. Dixon said to the judge, "It is a grave commentary on civilization that a mob of colored rioters can constitute themselves as censors of the drama and . . . close a historic theatre." But Sulzberger replied by asking Dixon about the conclusion of the play, in which the Ku Klux Klan arrests the villain of the play: "Oh!, Then the government of the State is displaced and usurped by a body of citizens who run things to suit themselves."[41] When Dixon complained about the egg-throwing in the theater, Sulzberger again disagreed, "So you make yourselves the judge and police the audience, I see. . . . The audiences may applaud, but may not show their disapproval."[42]

Sulzberger may have been sympathetic to the leading African American advocates of Philadelphia because he was involved with organizations that were turning their attention to the harm of the Stage Jew. Several months before he heard the *Clansman* case, Sulzberger started his six-year term as president of the new American Jewish Committee. Although the AJC was primarily concerned with battling anti-Semitism overseas, it also became involved in drafting civil rights legislation to stop discrimination against Jews at American resorts. In 1907, for example, Louis Marshall, another leader of the AJC, began the process of amending an 1895 New York civil rights law to prohibit hotels from printing advertisements that announced Jews were not welcome there (Schultz 2000).

Whereas officials and protesters often claimed that the play should be banned as immoral or as encouraging violence, the city of Des Moines censored the play because of its racial defamation. S. Joe Brown, an African American attorney in Des Moines, had introduced the bill banning exhibitions and performances that inflamed racial feeling.[43] Brown's Des Moines ordinance states: "No person shall . . . exhibit, sell, or offer for sale any . . . book, picture magazine or other thing for exhibit or perform or assist in the performance of an indecent, immoral, lewd or inflammatory play . . . calculated to encourage or incite rioting, breaches of the peace or lawlessness of any kind of to create a feeling of hatred or antipathy against any particular race, nationality or class of individuals."[44] In 1907, when the play returned to Des Moines, Brown announced that the play was "destructive of good morals and good order, productive of race hatred and mob violence and has been prohibited in a number of the leading cities of the country."[45]

Critics and activists in the early twentieth century noted how *The Clansman* reversed many aspects of *Uncle Tom's Cabin*. "The protest entered by the colored people against *The Clansman* is very different from the protest of southern people against *Uncle Tom's Cabin*. If *Uncle Tom's Cabin* is overdrawn it is not for the purpose of belittling people struggling against great odds to improve their condition. . . . *Uncle Tom's Cabin* presented at a critical time a tremendous argument for human liberty, and its exaggerations may be forgiven or at least overlooked."[46] At a hearing in Philadelphia, protesters laughed when they noted that *The Clansman* had been forbidden in Kentucky because "it accidentally came under the provisions of the law forbidding the production of *Uncle Tom's Cabin*."[47] James Weldon Johnson, in his March 1915 editorial in the *New York Age*, also explained a legal link between the two cases. Censorship of *The Clansman* was justified, he said, partly because *Uncle Tom's Cabin* had been revised many times under the pressure of angry whites.[48]

Scholars have shown that *The Clansman* reversed several of the features of *Uncle Tom's Cabin*, while both share basic melodramatic elements.[49] *The Clansman* switched the innocent hero from a suffering female slave threatened by a brutal white master to a suffering white virgin, pursued by a violent black man. With this transformation, *The Clansman* reversed the moral positions and popular feelings of *Uncle Tom's Cabin*. But Linda Williams argues that the two texts are not in opposition, because both are melodramas with innocent, feminine (or emasculated) heroes.

Four years after *The Clansman* first toured, many state and municipal officials banned the showing of films of the African American boxer Jack Johnson beating white fighters. Films of his 1908 world title fight were suppressed when they arrived in the United States in 1909. Attacks on his fight films accelerated when he defeated Jim Jeffries, a retired fighter who returned to the ring to rescue the white race (Grieveson 2004: 124). The Woman's Christian Temperance Union declared that these fight films aroused an "ungovernable spirit" in young men in the theaters (Grieveson 2004: 122). And the federal government banned the interstate trade in fight films in 1912, after Johnson defeated Jim Flynn, another white fighter. The controversy over boxing was not new; prizefighting was generally regarded as an affront to respectability. But the reaction to films of Johnson's victories over whites was also based on how these films threatened the racist hierarchy in American society. Censors reacted to Johnson's behavior inside and outside of the ring. His victories challenged the scientific view of the day—that a black man could not be heavyweight champion of the world (Grieveson 2004: 123). His lifestyle outside the ring also flouted American racial conventions. He dated and married white women, wore fancy clothes, and generally did as he pleased. The chairman of the Atlanta police board stated the racial politics clearly: "We don't want Jack Johnson down in this part of the country" (Grieveson 2004: 129).

Critics feared that the *Jeffries-Johnson Fight* (1910) would lead to the same kind of race riots that followed the fight itself in Reno (Streible 1989, Grieveson 2004). Part of the concern about a violent response to the film was based on the assumed childlike nature of the African American audience, their desire to imitate the action on screen, and the undesirable outcomes of the spread of black pride, like the integration of movie theaters. According to film historian Lee Grieveson, "In much of the rhetoric surrounding these films there was a clear sense that images of black power onscreen would lead directly to expressions of the same power outside of the space of exhibition" (2004: 123).

The Birth of a Nation was the next focal point in this chain of controversies over the appropriate representation of African Americans on stage and screen. The film, based on Reverend Thomas Dixon's book and play, *The Clansman*, melded Griffith's artistry and sentimental approach to American race relations, with Dixon's violent white supremacy. The movie pictured the disasters of the Civil War and Reconstruction, including free black men menacing white women, black legislators wreaking havoc in the South Carolina state house, and unruly black soldiers. In January of 1915, the NAACP, launched a campaign against the film, with the help of other organizations, such as the Urban League and the National Equal Rights League, and the Negro Welfare League. Throughout the movie's national run (and then in subsequent releases in the twentieth century) the NAACP tried to stop the film through government censorship, pressure on advertisers, printed editorials, sermons, boycotts, and confrontations at movie theaters. Race-based censorship regulations were central to the NAACP campaign. The NAACP succeeded in suppressing the film in some cities by pressuring existing movie censorship boards and other public officials and by working to get new race-based legislation passed.

Activists noted the connection between *The Birth of a Nation* and previous controversies were prominent, sometimes using previous censorship controversies to support their demands for a ban, and at other times, referring to previous cases as a cause for caution about legal censorship. Some protesters demanded a ban on *The Birth of a Nation* under the laws regulating boxing movies (Cripps 1977: 59). But NAACP leader Joseph Spingarn was reluctant to embrace censorship of *The Birth of a Nation* because any suppression of *The Birth of a Nation*, he reasoned, could also be used to censor *Uncle Tom's Cabin* (Lennig 2004: 123).

In 1915 the National Board of Censorship approved the release of *The Birth of a Nation*. The NAACP pressured the National Board to reconsider its decision. The Board's General Committee then voted fifteen to eight to cut some scenes from the film, including an African American man's sexual pursuit of a white woman. Frederic Howe, the head of the National Board of Censorship at the time, favored banning the film entirely. Howe felt that the film would cause violence and "race troubles" (Couvares 1994: 324–325). Upset by the Board's decision, Howe resigned his position soon after *The Birth of a Nation* began its national run.

The NAACP's initial and overriding complaint was that the movie portrayed African Americans in a negative light, based on a distortion of historical facts. As the run of the film continued, the NAACP often shifted to more expedient arguments; it began to emphasize the movie's incendiary quality—riots would result from the film. And the NAACP also charged that the film subverted public decency (Lennig 2004: 126). Sometimes the criticisms were separate; in other cases, the attack on public decency was the instigation of racial prejudice.

The uproar surrounding this movie significantly expanded race-based censorship in the early twentieth century. While the NAACP relied on some preexisting race-based censorship, such as Des Moines's law against *The Clansman*, it also worked to pass new legislation. The NAACP advised its chapters around the country to work for the passage of an ordinance like the Des Moines law (Lennig 2004: 126). Five cities passed new laws or amended old ones, to stop racially inflammatory plays. Wilmington, Delaware, and Tacoma, Washington both passed new laws to stop *The Birth of a Nation*. Dr. John Hopkins, the only African American city council member in Wilmington, introduced the ordinance in June 1915: "No person, firm or corporation shall exhibit within the limits of the city of Wilmington, any moving picture that is likely to provoke ill-feeling between the white and black races" (Fleener-Marzec 1977: 330). A few months later Tacoma amended its statute to cover not just obscene or immoral performances, but also those that tend "to incite race riot or race hatred" (Fleener-Marzec 1977: 330). Denver, St. Paul, and Wichita also passed laws to censor *The Birth of a Nation*. The laws did not always have the intended result. Despites its new law, Tacoma did not suppress *The Birth of a Nation*. The Denver city council voted to censor the film, but a court injunction allowed the film to be shown (Fleener-Marzec 1977: 331).

Some state legislatures also responded to criticism of *The Birth of a Nation* by amending censorship laws to include bans on racial prejudice. After the Boston Mayor Curley refused to stop the movie because it did not violate obscenity rules, the Massachusetts legislature gave local officials the authority to ban films they believed would "excite racial or religious prejudice or tend to a breach of the public peace."[50] Boston authorities, however, did not suppress *The Birth of a Nation*. In 1917 Illinois passed a law against any public exhibition that "portrays depravity, criminality, unchastity or lack of virtue of a class of citizens, or any race, color or religion" (Fleener-Marzec 1977: 338).

Three court cases in 1915 rejected the argument that *The Birth of a Nation* would "incite racial prejudice because of the uncomplimentary stereotyping of blacks" (Fleener-Marzec 1977: 109). When the Pittsburgh mayor banned *The Birth of a Nation* in 1915, even though the State Board of Censors had approved the film, the Allegheny County Court of Common Pleas enjoined the mayor because his action was not based on the two justifications for censorship—"apt to cause a breach of peace" or "subversive of public morality."[51] The judge acknowledged that the film had "scenes that might excite race prejudice" in people who were not educated about American history; but this was not a justification for stopping the film, in his view (Fleener-Marzec 1977: 113). Illinois Superior Court Judge William Fenimore Cooper agreed. He stopped the Chicago mayor, William Thompson, from banning the film because he did not believe that the portrayal of one race in an unfavorable light was grounds for censorship. "No one race or nationality has greater right under the law than any other has. Any race or nationality so offended can best give the lie to the bad characters so presented by continuing to conduct themselves as law abiding citizens, who do not expect greater rights from the law than it allows all other men or nationalities."[52]

In the campaign against *The Birth of a Nation*, opponents of the film used laws banning films that were racially inflammatory, but when these laws did not exist in particular locations, they also tried to ban the film using more common terms of censorship laws—immorality and incitement to violence. Some cities and states censored the film because it was immoral, thus fitting the film into existing movie censorship, without race-based rules. Throughout the campaign against the film, the NAACP referred to the film's racial defamation and its threat to public decency. At a hearing in Boston, African American critics lambasted both the film's racial hatred and its sexual excesses (Cripps 1977: 59). And in New York City, the NAACP referred to the film as an offense against public decency . . . and an unjust appeal to race prejudice" (Fleener-Marzec 1977: 222).

In several cases, city officials refused to ban the movie because the defamation of African Americans fell outside of the city's censorship laws, which covered immorality and obscenity. Baltimore police declined to take action because they could only suppress the film if it was "vulgar or indecent" (Fleener-Marzec 1977: 240). In St. Paul, police would not intervene because the law called for suppression of movies that were "immoral or obscene," not racially insulting. Protesters then charged that the entire film was immoral, and won several cuts from the film.[53] In Boston, Mayor Curley said he found the movie to be an "outrage upon colored citizens" but he could not stop the play.[54] He cut two scenes probably because he believed they were immoral or obscene, in keeping with the censorship statute (Fleener-Marzec 1977: 234). But a Boston judge overruled him and cut only one scene from the play—Gus's pursuit of Flora—because of immorality; he did not consider race in his censorship of the film, in accordance with the law against "obscene or immoral work" (Fleener-Marzec 1977: 255). Spokesmen for the NAACP responded by arguing that immorality should be "construed in a broad sense as anything hostile to the welfare of the general public" (Fleener-Marzec 1977: 108).

Different grounds of censorship did not just coexist and overlap; they were also in conflict with each other. For example, critics of censorship accused civil rights activists of using charges of indecency as a cover for the real reason for censorship—racial animosity. In 1939 police censors shut down the film after African American leaders argued that the film violated local laws against obscene or immoral movies. The ACLU responded angrily: "I see great danger in a precedent that would allow the obscenity and indecency of *The Birth of a Nation* to be used as the cloak under which it its showing is denied and the real reason is its incitement to race hatred" (Fleener-Marzec 1977: 251).

Conclusion

These three campaigns reinforced each other in two ways. First, Irish nationalist activism in the late nineteenth and early twentieth centuries set the stage for other racial groups to complain about (and protest vigorously against) misrepresentation in the early twentieth century. The Jewish activists regularly claimed to be indebted to the Irish model and referred to Irish successes as a way to motivate their own constituency. "The Jews are not the only ones who are protesting against insulting caricatures," wrote one Jewish leader, "nor have they gone as far in the matter as have the Irish."[55]

Second, Irish, Jewish, and African American leaders added a different voice to these early-twentieth-century culture wars: They demanded a pluralist popular culture, in which no race was maligned, and sought to defend their particular group by reforming representation. For example, the *Gaelic American* explained in 1907: "In a country where the theory is to give every one a chance it is an unwise thing to attempt ridicule of race elements. . . . In cosmopolitan America no man has a right to poke fun at this neighbor because of some peculiarity of race or mode of thought."[56] B'nai B'rith leaders objected to racial ridicule because it "tends to narrowness and prejudices that are, to say the least, un-American."[57] Similarly, the *American Israelite* complained about racial caricature, asserting that the "stage is a cosmopolitan institution. It ought to be above this sort of cheap exploitation."[58]

These three campaigns, however, also threatened each other in two ways. First, each group turned on the others. Their proclamations of tolerance and pluralism had their limits. Irish activists, in particular, turned to anti-Semitic theories of cultural control in their campaign against the Stage Irish. "The gross caricatures of the Irish," explained a nationalist editorial in the *Gaelic American*, "are part of a propaganda, conducted mainly by Jews, to hold the Irish up to contempt. Having possession of practically all the theatres, as they have of nearly all the New York papers, the Jews are able to take care of themselves."[59] Irish and Jewish nationalists also advocated more for their own group's status, than for pluralism overall. As one Jewish critic wrote, "The Irish resent them [libels on their race] keenly. The Americans know this, and they are less keen on making enemies of the Irish than they are careless about offending any other nationality."[60]

Second, critics sometimes viewed the multiple challenges to defamation as a sign of the impracticality of reforming culture. One article in the *New York Globe* in 1915 concluded: "Our citizenry is composed obviously of extraordinary elements. If Africans are to have their say and oppose the production of a play . . . to which they object, why should not the Jews, Hungarians, Czechs, Teutons, French, Italians, Slavs, Scandinavians, Irish and Anglo-Saxons also have the same privilege? The prospect is appalling."[61] Similarly, Illinois Superior Court Judge William Fenimore Cooper defended *The Birth of a Nation* against censorship because "every night in every theater there is produced the debased type of the white race of different nationalities and if representative groups of the various nationalities so presented became acutely sensitive, that such individual portrayal would cause them to suffer race hatred of their race, and all the plays in which a villain had played were stopped on that account, the theater as an educator and entertainer of the people would become a memory of the past."[62]

Campaigns for race-based censorship extended beyond a black and white racial divide to a conversation among African American, Irish, and Jewish activists. These groups approached state prior-restraint with varying degrees of enthusiasm and success. They were often selective censors, supporting state suppression of racist material, but opposing censorship on other grounds. This history of race-based censorship has many surprises—as activists and politicians used laws in unintended ways or ignored laws altogether. The attempts to censor "Shylock," "Paddy," and "Sambo" reveal that attempts to ban racial ridicule were widespread, yet tenuous. Race-based censorship, with support from leading Irish, Jewish, and African American organizations, expanded during the early twentieth century through chains of theater and film controversies. Yet it often hid behind or blended together with more secure justifications for censorship—public order and decency. For these protesters, racial ridicule was indecent and incendiary.

Notes

1. "The Stage Jew," *B'nai B'rith News*, October 1910: 17.
2. Ruth Vasey (1996) has shown that Hollywood had to soften or eliminate images of foreign villains to satisfy censors in France, Spain, and Mexico.
3. The phrase "practical censorship" is taken from "Reform It Altogether," *Irish World*, 11 April 1903: 12. A few months later, in a debate over another cartoon theatrical, *Happy Hooligan*, the *Irish World* again explained that "a matter of shaving off green whiskers has little or nothing to do with the case. The Stage Irishman must go, with or without whiskers" ("Gaelic Notes," *Irish World*, 9 May 1903: 8). Edited by Patrick Ford, *The Irish World* had a circulation of 125,000 by the 1890s, while the *Gaelic American*, published by rival nationalist and Clan na

Gael leader John Devoy, reached only 30,000 by 1913. Before 1886 Ford supported a variety of radical causes, including civil rights for African Americans, before becoming more conservative in the late 1880s and increasingly concerned with "respectability" (Rodechko 1976: 50).

4. "Cops Throw Out 29," *North American*, 16 January 1912: 1.

5. "Cops Throw Out 29," *North American*, 16 January 1912: 1. The *North American* reported that a currant cake hit an actor, but no "solid vegetables" were thrown ("Play Is Again Halted by Riots, Police Arrest 14," *North American*, 17 January 1912: 6).

6. "Philadelphia Spanks the Playboy," *Gaelic American*, 20 January 1912: 1. The mayor of Boston refused to suppress the play because it was not immoral or obscene. His "censor" William N. Leahy reported that "Now the language in this play, wisely softened from the original by the players themselves, is still rather coarse in parts. . . . But . . . If obscenity is to be found on the stage in Boston, it must be sought elsewhere, and not at the Plymouth Theater" ("Yeats Cables Tale of Glorious Victory," *Gaelic American*, 4 November 1911: 1).

7. "Robinson Cables Lie to Dublin," *Gaelic American*, 16 December 1911: 1.

8. "Pennsylvania Air Bad for Playboy," *Gaelic American*, 27 January 1912: 1.

9. "Pennsylvania Air Bad for Playboy," *Gaelic American*, 27 January 1912: 1.

10. "Lady Gregory's Inane Talk," *Gaelic American*, 27 January 1912: 4.

11. "Film Men Absent at Censor Hearing," *New York Times*, 15 October 1927: 21.

12. "Film Men Absent at Censor Hearing," *New York Times*, 15 October 1927: 21.

13. "To Boycott the Stage Jew," *New York Times*, 25 April 1913: 3.

14. *Report of the Anti-Defamation League Together with Principles of League and Correspondence* (International Order of B'nai B'rith 1915) box 59, B'nai B'rith Klutznick National Jewish Museum, Washington, D.C.

15. *Report of the Anti-Defamation League* 1915: 6, box 59, BBKNJM.

16. *Report of the Anti-Defamation League* 1915: 54, 62, box 59, BBKNJM.

17. *ADL Bulletin*, Number 3 (1915, 1916?) box 2, folder 10, David Philipson Collection, Jacob Marcus Rader Center, American Jewish Archives, Hebrew Union College, Cincinnati, OH (hereafter cited as AJA). See also Jacob Sable, "Some American Jewish Organizational Efforts to Combat Anti-Semitism, 1906–1930" (Ph.D. diss., Yeshiva University, 1964), 247.

18. Letter to Governor Albert C. Ritchie 1922, Papers of the Maryland Board of Censors, State Archives of Maryland, Annapolis. The ADL reported that "in energetically endorsing and helping the enactment of these ordinances, the League feels that it is doing a work that will rebound not only to its credit, but will benefit all classes of people" ("ADL Bulletin" Number 3, [1915–16?] box 2, folder 10, David Philipson Collection, AJA.

19. ADL, "Motion Picture Bulletin," Number 8, 28 October 1914, box 2, folder 10, David Philipson Collection, AJA. The 3 September 1914 bulletin describes the Chicago Board of Censors rejection of *The Master Cracksman* in August 1914.

20. ADL, "Motion Picture Bulletin," Number 10, 6 November 1914, box 2, folder 10, David Philipson Collection, AJA.

21. Sarah Kendall, Seattle Board of Theatre Censors, to National Board of Censorship of Motion Pictures, 21 November 1914, box 104, folder "Controversial Films Correspondence. Evangeline-Fatal Wedding," National Board of Review of Motion Pictures Collection, Manuscript and Archives Section, New York Public Library (hereafter cited as NBR).

22. Executive Secretary, National Board of Censorship, to Sarah Kendall, 27 November 1914, box 104, folder, "Evangeline-Fatal Wedding," NBR.

23. "Amusements This Week," *Public Ledger*, 21 October 1906: 7 and *Chicago Defender*, 4 September 1915: 1. Also see Grieveson (2004: 129).

24. "The Clansman Denounced," *New York Times*, 2 January 1906: 8.

25. "South Carolina Editor Denlee Charges Made by Thomas Dixon Jr.," *New York Times*; "The Clansman Hissed," *New York Times*, 16 October 1905: 9.

26. "Seek to Suppress a Play," *New York Times*, 25 November 1906: 9.

27. "The Clansman Hissed," *New York Times*, 16 October 1905: 9.

28. "Will be Riots Here—Dixon," *New York Times*, 24 September 1906: 2.

29. "The play is not new to Philadelphia, having been here last season . . . its bid for popular favor seems to be entirely based upon an appeal to race prejudice" ("The Clansman—Walnut," *Philadelphia Record*, 23 October 1906, clipping, scrapbook 126, William Henry Dorsey Collection, Cheyney University of Pennsylvania).

30. "Negroes Excited over Giving of 'Clansman,'" *Public Ledger*, 22 October 1906: 16.

31. "3000 Negroes Start Riot Trying to Stop the Play They Dislike," *North American*, 23 October 1906, clipping, scrapbook 126, Dorsey Collection.

32. "Riot of Negroes over Class Play Halted by Police," *Record*, 23 October 1906, clipping, scrapbook 126, Dorsey Collection.

33. "Riot over Class Play Halted by Police," *Record*, 23 October 1906, clipping, scrapbook 126, Dorsey Collection.

34. "3000 Negroes Start Riot Trying to Stop the Play They Dislike," *North American*, 23 October 1906, clipping, scrapbook, Dorsey Collection. The crowd outside was described as a "swaying mass of negroes [that] blocked both Walnut and Ninth Streets." Protesters in the crowd shouted out their claim that the play portrayed the negro as a "beast of the jungle" ("Negro Mob Causes Trouble at Theatre," *Public Ledger*, 23 October 1906: 1).

35. "3000 Negroes Start Riot Trying to Stop the Play They Dislike," *North American*, 23 October 1906, clipping, scrapbook 126, Dorsey Collection.

36. *New York Times*, 24 September 1906: 9.

37. "Mayor Stops Play," *North American*, 24 October 1906, clipping, scrapbook 126, Dorsey Collection.

38. "The Stopping of the Clansman," *Bulletin*, 1 November 1906, clipping, scrapbook 126, Dorsey Collection.

39. "Clansman Closed by Mayor Weaver," *Philadelphia Public Ledger*, 24 October 1906: 1.

40. Arthur Lennig argues that the confrontations over *The Birth of a Nation* were not as "sensational as later commentators would lead us to believe" (2004: 136). He argues that riots did not occur in Los Angeles, New York City, or Boston, though he does not consider Philadelphia.

41. "To Enjoin Mayor in Theatre Case," 25 October 1906, clipping, scrapbook 126, Dorsey Collection.

42. "To Enjoin Mayor in Theatre Case," 25 October 1906, clipping, scrapbook 126, Dorsey Collection.

43. In 1918, Brown corresponded with a Des Moines newspaper editor about capitalizing "Negro," "which has been adopted as the name of a Race of people." Lowercase type suggested disrespect, according to Brown. The editor agreed to change the practice (S. Joe Brown to W. E. Battenfield, 20 November 1918, folder "Des Moines, Iowa, 1916–1934," box G–68, Branch Files, NAACP Papers, Library of Congress).

44. "Negroes Against the Clansman," *Des Moines Register and Leader,* 1 March 1907: 6.

45. "Negroes Against the Clansman," *Des Moines Register and Leader,* 1 March 1907: 6.

46. "Protest Against the Clansman," *Des Moines Register and Leader,* 2 March 1907: 4.

47. "Extra! Mayor Prohibits Clansman Being Played," *Evening Bulletin,* 23 October 1906, clipping, scrapbook 126, Dorsey Collection.

48. Johnson, "Uncle Tom's Cabin and The Clansman," *New York Age,* 4 March 1915; as quoted in Lawrence J. Oliver and Terri L. Walker, "James Weldon Johnson's New York Age Essays on 'The Birth of a Nation' and the 'Southern Oligarchy,'" *South Central Review,* 10, no. 4 (Winter 1993): 4–5.

49. One review described *The Clansman* as similar to *Uncle Tom's Cabin:* "It was the sort of applause, however, that is invariably showered upon melodrama of this type, and if the story unfolded upon the stage had been that of *Uncle Tom's Cabin* there would probably have been the same noisy approbation" ("The Clansman at the Walnut," *Inquirer,* 24 October 1906, clipping, scrapbook 126, Dorsey Collection).

50. Oliver and Walker, "James Weldon Johnson's *New York Age* Essays," 9; The *Boston Guardian* noted Curley's decision about the film falling outside of obscenity ordinances (17 April 1915). See Fleener-Marzec (1977: 311).

51. *Nixon Theatre Company v. Joseph Armstrong,* box 10, folder 1, Records of the Department of Education—State Board of Censors (Motion Pictures), R–22, The Pennsylvania State Archives, Harrisburg.

52. *Joseph J. McCarthy v. City of Chicago* (1915), NBR.

53. 3 November 1915, folder, "Films and Plays: Birth of a Nation," October 1915, C–300, NAACP Papers, Part I, Library of Congress.

54. Joseph Prince Loud to Miss Nerney, 15 April 1915, folder, "Films and Plays, Birth of a Nation," April 1915, C–300, NAACP Papers, Part I, Library of Congress.

55. "Jottings," *American Israelite,* 2 March 1911: 7.

56. "Exit the Stage Irishman," *Gaelic American,* 2 March 1907: 8.

57. "Race Insults," *B'nai B'rith News,* October 1910: 17.

58. "Libeling Nations on Stage," *American Israelite,* 8 February 1917: 7.

59. "Hooted Off the Stage," *Gaelic American,* 2 February 1907: 5.

60. "Libeling Nations on Stage," *American Israelite,* 8 February 1917: 7.

61. New York *Globe,* 4 March 1915, as cited in Lennig (2004: 124).

62. *Joseph J. McCarthy v. City of Chicago* (1915), NBR.

Bibliography

Couvares, Francis. 1994. "The Good Censors: Race, Sex and Censorship in the Early Cinema." *Yale Journal of Criticism* 7, no. 2: 233–251.

Cripps, Thomas. 1977. *Slow Fade to Black.* New York: Oxford University Press.

Crowe, Charles. 1969. "Racial Massacre in Atlanta, September 22, 1906." *Journal of Negro History* 54, no. 2 (April).

Diner, Hasia R. 1995. *In the Almost Promised Land: American Jews and Blacks, 1915–1935.* Baltimore: Johns Hopkins University Press.

Dumenil, Lynn. 1995. *The Modern Temper: American Culture and Society in the 1920s.* New York: Hill and Wang.

Erdman, Harley. 1997. *Staging the Jew: The Performance of an American Ethnicity, 1860–1920.* New Brunswick, N.J.: Rutgers University Press.
Fleener-Marzec, Nickieann. 1977. "D. W. Griffith's The Birth of a Nation: Controversy, Suppression and the First Amendment as It Applies to Filmic Expression, 1915–1973." Ph.D. diss, University of Wisconsin—Madison.
Friedman, Andrea. 2000. *Prurient Interests: Gender, Democracy, and Obscenity in New York City, 1909–1945.* New York: Columbia University Press.
Greenberg, Cheryl Lynn. 2006. *Troubling the Waters: Black-Jewish Relations in the American Century.* Princeton: Princeton University Press.
Grieveson, Lee. 1998. "Fighting Films: Race, Morality, and the Governing of Cinema, 1912–1915." *Cinema Journal* 38, no. 1 (Autumn): 40–72.
———. 2004. *Policing Cinema: Movies and Censorship in Early Twentieth-Century America.* Berkeley: University of California Press.
Guterl, Matthew Pratt. 2001. *The Color of Race in America, 1900–1940.* Cambridge, Mass.: Harvard University Press.
Higham, John. 1963. *Strangers in the Land: Patterns of American Nativism, 1860–1925.* New York: Atheneum.
Jacobson, Matthew Frye. 1995. *Special Sorrows: The Diasporic Imagination of Irish, Polish and Jewish Immigrants in the United States.* Cambridge, Mass.: Harvard University Press.
Kibler, M. Alison. 2005. "The Stage Irishwoman." *Journal of American Ethnic History* 24, no. 3 (Spring): 5–30.
Lennig, Arthur. 2004. "Myth and Fact: The Reception of *The Birth of a Nation.*" *Film History* 16: 117–141.
Meagher, Timothy J. 2005. *The Columbia Guide to Irish American History.* New York: Columbia University Press.
Miller, Kerby. 1985. *Emigrants and Exiles: Ireland and the Irish Exodus to North America.* New York: Oxford University Press.
Mulcrone, Michael Patrick. 1993. "The World War I Censorship of the Irish-American Press." Ph.D. diss., University of Washington.
Rabban, David. 1997. *Free Speech in Its Forgotten Years.* Cambridge: Cambridge University Press.
Roche, John. 1963. *The Quest for the Dream: The Development of Civil Rights and Human Relations in Modern America.* New York: Macmillan.
Rodechko, James. 1976. *Patrick Ford and His Search for America: A Case Study of Irish-American Journalism, 1870–1913.* New York: Arno Press.
Schultz, Evan P. 2000. "Group Rights, American Jews and the Failure of Group Libel Laws, 1913–1952." *Brooklyn Law Review* 66 (Spring): 77.
Sorin, Gerald. 1992. *A Time for Building: The Third Migration.* Baltimore: Johns Hopkins University Press.
Streible, Dan. 1989. "A History of the Boxing Film." *Film History* 3, 235–257.
Vasey, Ruth. 1996. "Foreign Parts: Hollywood's Global Distribution and the Representation of Ethnicity." In *Movie Censorship and American Culture*, ed. Francis Couvares. Washington, D.C.: Smithsonian Institution Press, 212–236.
Waller, Gregory. 1995. *Main Street Amusements: Movies and Commercial Entertainment in a Southern City, 1896–1930.* Washington, D.C.: Smithsonian Institution Press.
Walsh, Francis. 1990. " 'The Callahans and the Murphys' (MGM 1920): A Case Study of Irish-American and Catholic Church Censorship." *Historical Journal of Film, Radio and Television* 10, no. 1: 33–45.
Williams, Linda. 1996. "Versions of Uncle Tom: Race and Gender in American Melodrama." In *New Scholarship from BFI Research*, ed. Colin MacCabe and Duncan Petrie. London: British Film Institute, 111–140.

Epilogue

Edward T. Linenthal

These rich, evocative essays introduce readers to a dizzying array of case studies in which symbolic and physical ownership of site, story, and identity are up for grabs. We encounter a Hindu temple, the restless bodies of the dead, parades and flags, scarves, language, monuments and museums, historic sites, the stage, and the changing dress of Miss Chinatown USA. A head scarf is as much a site of bitter conflict as an Afrikaner memorial in a transformed South Africa. The use of regional languages can indicate an opening—or closing—of national stories as much as a capacious or limited museum exhibition. These case studies also reveal a host of strategies through which personal and social identity is proclaimed, subverted, stereotyped, and redefined.

In this brief epilogue, I wish to comment on the three core elements of these essays: site, story, and identity. I am particularly fascinated with Roger Friedland and Richard Hecht's (2005) assertion that a sacred site "has power because it has absorbed memory and that memory has not been erased either by the passage of time or the use of [this site] for other purposes." I am reminded of a National Park Service historian who worked for many years at the Little Bighorn Battlefield National Monument. My colleague was a member of the Crow tribe, and like some other tribal members, would not stay at the battlefield after sunset because, I was told, the site contained a powerful "presence."

My friend's words took on greater significance during my first research visit to the Little Bighorn in December 1980. I was staying in a ranger's cabin on site for a week, and one unseasonably warm and very dark December night I started to drive to the Reno-Benteen site, a five-mile winding drive through the heart of the battlefield. (In 1876 this was the location of the remnants of Major Marcus Reno's troops after they had been bloodied and scattered during their ill-fated attack on the

Indian village in the valley. They were soon joined by the late-arriving troops of Captain Frederick Benteen. This beleaguered force remained at the site until the Native Americans moved on, and did not witness the demise of Custer's troops.) I went only several miles, turned around and went back to the cabin. I too felt an overpowering presence, and I "knew" that I was not supposed to be driving through the battlefield at night.[1]

I already hear the predictable responses: "Please, don't be so dramatic. You are merely projecting your own fascination, fear, vivid imagination. Places *aren't capable of this kind of agency. They can't 'speak.'*" Fair enough. But once activated—by witnesses, by visual clues (entering a clearly defined National Park Service site, for example)—such sites do seem to speak, at least for some. *Event transforms place.* For those who are tone-deaf, or better, site-deaf, these places will remain flat, ordinary space. Nothing that has been absorbed will ooze out to enrich or impoverish identity, to simplify, or complicate stories, to demand that attention be paid.

The labor of memory becomes even more challenging when there are few physical remains. At the District Six Museum in Cape Town, South Africa, the symbolic excavation of the neighborhood is itself a moving commemorative act, allowing former residents to bear witness to what is both physically gone but alive in memory. I am reminded of the archival reconstruction of Greenwood, the African American area of Tulsa that was destroyed in the 1921 race riot. The Tulsa Race Riot Memorial Commission's indefatigable archival and oral history efforts offered an opportunity for an imaginative mapping of an area now so different in appearance that the physical landscape offers few clues about its turbulent past. The community was "rebuilt" through, for example, "records and papers long presumed lost, if their existence had been known at all. Some were official documents. . . . Some were musty legal records. . . . Briefs filed, dockets set, law suits decided. . . . Overlooked records from the National Guard . . . lost after-action reports, obscure field manuals, and self-typed accounts from men who were on duty at the riot. Maybe there was a family's treasured collection of yellowed newspaper clippings; an envelope of carefully folded letters, all handwritten, each dated 1921." Through maps, property records, death certificates, photographs, and other materials, the Greenwood area was re-created, and elderly survivors could bear witness immersed in the official context of archival memory. Both they and members of the commission believed that this reconstruction of site was a crucial component of the reconstruction of memory of an intentionally forgotten horror that needed to be visible in local, state, and national narratives (Oklahoma Commission 2001: 4).

When I visited the Little Bighorn, the meaning of the site is filtered through the symbolic sediment of many years of interpretive expression. Once upon a time, the Little Bighorn sparked my childhood fascination with the pathos and drama of the "Last Stand." More recently, I have managed a more mature analysis of this place as a graduate student and then as an author deeply immersed in the biography of the site. Where one stands certainly determines what one sees. Standing on the site of the huge Indian village jolted me into a different way of seeing that complicated the stories through which I inhabited the Little Bighorn. I was no longer a little boy imagining myself standing with Custer and the remnants of his command as the pathos and drama of the Last Stand unfolded on that hilltop. I tried, rather, to envision the battle from the perspective of a Sioux mother or child, watching in fear as Reno's command charged the village.

The controversial name change—from the Custer Battlefield National Monument to the Little Bighorn Battlefield National Monument—the emplacement of the Indian Memorial, the evolution of the small museum in the National Park Service Visitor Center from an almost singular focus on Custer and the Seventh Cavalry to a more inclusive story of the "clash of civilizations," added more layers to what is continually being absorbed and expressed. Narrative revision, spatial displacement, and memorial construction are indeed, in Friedland and Hecht's (2005) words, "extensions of identity into space." In this case, a national identity that includes Native Americans as agents of history, not mere props in a narrative about the "civilizing" of the west.

"Contestation" is certainly the dynamic that drives these essays. What for some people is an enrichment of narrative, a welcome physical memorial alteration, a parade sacralizing foreign space, the insistence of a particular language as an intimate element of identity, or a celebration of the physical destruction of what is perceived as an alien symbolic structure, registers for others as acts of desecration, be they violations of the purity of place or attempts to claim ownership of story and site. Desecration registers as a threat to cherished identities.[2]

In ritual, what individual, group, narrative, is at the center, the periphery, consigned to oblivion, treated with uncritical reverence, with disdain? Who owns the means of representation? One of the significant interpretive transformations at the Little Bighorn has been not just the alteration of museum exhibits in order to include Native Americans in an expanded narrative, but an evolving sensitivity on the part of the National Park Service that Native Americans should share in ownership of interpretation and ritual expression.

Not so many years ago, the Little Bighorn was one of the most volatile sites in the National Park Service. Since the dedication of the Indian memorial, however, there do not seem to be significant struggles for ownership of site and story. In fact, there is no longer a full-time NPS superintendent at the site! Why is the Little Bighorn no longer one of the "razor's edge" historical sites? Is the often violent history of Native American-white relations on the northern Plains no longer threatening to cherished national narratives of innocence, progress, the price of westward expansion? Are these expanded narratives "shared" history, or are they stories told side-by-side, segregated rather than shared? My unease about the concept of "collective memory" arises from these questions. I much prefer James Young's concept of "collected" memory—the "many discrete memories that are gathered into common memorial spaces and assigned common meaning." Individuals, Young argues, "cannot share another's memory any more than they can share another's cortex" (1993: xi).

Do the new and revised memorials in South Africa symbolize shared history, "collective" memory, or are these common spaces where collected memories are stitched together into multiple narratives that may sit uneasily side by side? It may well be that South Africans must by the curse of geography inhabit the same space of history—although the contents of what is "shared" make it almost impossible for me to understand how perpetrators and victims can inhabit the same story, site, identity. With no disrespect intended to the moving, compelling construction of particular cultural processes of engagement with the aftermath of apartheid, might it be premature to declare that civic rituals of reconciliation have drained toxicity from these sites, stories, identities? Or might the allure of violent identity, convinced of the need for purification through bloodletting lurk beneath the surface in South Africa and elsewhere? It is dangerous, I believe, to think that memory work is by definition "healing" for individuals and communities. Such processes can tear apart as well as bring together. It may be as instructive for scholars to write about sites, stories, identities that are *not* amenable to negotiated settlements, failed labors of memory, sites haunted by stories resistant to the illusory rhetoric of "never again," or "the lessons of history."

Notes

1. For an examination of processes of veneration, defilement, and redefinition of five sites: Lexington and Concord, the Alamo, Gettysburg, the Little Bighorn, and Pearl Harbor, see Linenthal (1993).

2. On various types of desecration, see Chidester and Linenthal (1995).

Bibliography

Chidester, David, and Edward T. Linenthal. 1995. *American Sacred Space.* Bloomington: Indiana University Press.

Friedland, Roger, and Richard Hecht. 2005. "Place, Memory and Identity: Some Theoretical Reflections on the Power of Place." Paper presented at *Contesting Culture: Narratives, Dramas and Representing Identity,* conference at Bryn Mawr College, Pa., 24–26 February.

Linenthal, Edward T. 1993. *Sacred Ground: Americans and Their Battlefields.* 2nd ed. Champaign: University of Illinois Press.

Oklahoma Commission. 2001. *Tulsa Race Riot: A Report by the Oklahoma Commission to Study the Tulsa Race Riot of 1921.*

Young, James E. 1993. *The Texture of Memory: Holocaust Memorials and Meaning.* New Haven: Yale University Press.

Contributors

DOMINIC BRYAN is Director of the Institute of Irish Studies at Queens University, Belfast, Chair of Democratic Dialogue, Ireland's first think tank, and has worked with the Northern Ireland Human Rights Commission and the Community Relations Council. He is an anthropologist researching political rituals, public space, and identity in Northern Ireland. His book *Orange Parades: The Politics of Ritual Tradition and Control* (Pluto Press, 2000) used theories of rituals to examine parades organized by the Orange Order in Ireland. He also works on issues around public order policing, human rights, ethnic politics, and sectarianism and has done comparative work in South Africa and the United States. His present research is on the use of symbols in Northern Ireland since the signing of the multiparty agreement in 1998.

BRITT CARTRITE is Assistant Professor of Political Science at Alma College and a former postdoctoral research fellow at the Solomon Asch Center for Study of Ethnopolitical Conflict at the University of Pennsylvania. His research focuses on ethnopolitical mobilization in Western Europe, emphasizing the preconditions from which politically active movements emerge. Currently he is engaged in research in Shetland and Orkney, exploring the potential for ethnopolitical mobilization in reaction to the very successful Scottish nationalist movement. In addition, Cartrite conducts research using agent-based computer simulation.

RICHARD H. DAVIS is Professor of Religion and Asian Studies at Bard College. He is the author of *Ritual in an Oscillating Universe* (Princeton University Press, 1991) and *Lives of Indian Images* (Princeton University Press, 1997). His primary interests include the history of Hindu traditions and the politics of religions images. He is currently working on a cultural history of early India.

GREG JOHNSON is Assistant Professor of Religious Studies at the University of Colorado. He is the author of *Sacred Claims: Repatriation and Living*

Tradition (University Press of Virginia, 2007). His research focuses on contemporary Native American and Native Hawaiian religious life, particularly in legal and political contexts. Repatriation issues (NAGPRA, especially) are at the center of his current research. His recent publications include "Narrative Remains: Articulating Indian Identities in the Repatriation Context" and "Naturally There: Discourses of Permanence in the Repatriation Context."

M. Alison Kibler is Associate Professor of American Studies and Women's Studies at Franklin and Marshall College. She is the author of *Rank Ladies: Gender and Cultural Hierarchy in American Vaudeville* (University of North Carolina Press, 1999) and is currently working on a book project entitled *Paddy, Shylock, and Sambo: Irish, Jewish, and African American Protests Against Mass Culture, 1890–1930.*

Edward T. Linenthal is Professor of Religion at the University of Indiana and serves as the editor of the *Journal of American History*. He is also a consultant for the National Park Service. His books include *Sacred Ground: Americans and Their Battlefields* (1994); *Preserving Memory: The Struggle to Create America's Holocaust Museum* (1995); *The Unfinished Bombing: Oklahoma City in American Memory* (2001); and, coedited with Tom Engelhardt, *History Wars: The Enola Gay and Other Battles for the American Past* (1996). He is a member of the Flight 93 Memorial Task Force and Federal Commission in Shanksville, Pennsylvania.

Sabine Marschall is Associate Professor and academic coordinator of the Cultural and Heritage Tourism Programme at the University of KwaZulu-Natal in Durban and the author of *Community Mural Art in South Africa*. In addition, she has written a number of articles about memorials and regime change in South Africa.

Charlene Mires is Associate Professor of History at Villanova University and author of *Independence Hall in American Memory* (University of Pennsylvania Press, 2002). She is affiliated with the Ad Hoc Historians, a group concerned with the quality of interpretation at historic places, especially the President's House Site in Philadelphia. Currently she is completing a book entitled *Capitals of the World: Big Cities, Small Towns, and Bold Dreams at the End of the Second World War.*

Marc Howard Ross is William R. Kenan, Jr. Professor of Political Science at Bryn Mawr College. He recently published *Cultural Contestation in Ethnic Conflict* (Cambridge University Press, 2007) and is the author of a number of books and articles on culture and conflict. He has done research in East Africa, France, Northern Ireland, the Middle East, Spain, and South Africa. His current work has two major themes: (1) the role that cultural performance and memory play in the escalation and deescalation of ethnic conflict and (2) social science theories of conflict and their implications for conflict management.

LEE A. SMITHEY is Assistant Professor in the Department of Sociology and Anthropology at Swarthmore College where he also serves as the chair of the Peace and Conflict Studies Program. He studies social conflict and social movements, especially identity conflict and the use of nonviolent methods. He has worked extensively in Northern Ireland, and some of his publications have addressed parading disputes and anti-Catholicism, as well as the role of nonviolent social movements in the fall of the Soviet Bloc. He is currently completing a book on postsettlement reconciliation and the Northern Irish Protestant community.

CRAIN SOUDIEN is Professor and Head of the School of Education at the University of Cape Town where he teaches sociology and history of education. His research interests include race, culture, and identity, school and socialization, youth, teacher identity, school effectiveness, and urban history. He has published eighty articles, reviews, and book chapters in the areas of race, culture, educational policy, educational change, public history, and popular culture. He was the Chairperson of the Ministerial Review Committee into the Status of School Governance in South Africa. He is also the coeditor of two books on District Six, Cape Town, and is actively involved in a number of social and educational projects, including the Iziko Museums of Cape Town, the District Six Museum, which he and colleagues established in 1989, the Cape Town Festival, the Independent Examinations Board, and a number of other educational and cultural initiatives in the city and in the country.

CLIFFORD STEVENSON is Lecturer in Psychology at the University of Limerick. His previous research included the investigation of group identities and intergroup relations in conversation and political rhetoric in Northern Ireland. His current research applies both qualitative and quantitative methods to investigate how national and ethnic identities are manifest through crowd behavior and other public displays of identity.

ELAINE R. THOMAS is Assistant Professor of Political Science at Bard College. Her research focuses primarily on contested claims to political membership in the context of French and British racial and immigration politics. She has also written on recent developments in European nationality law and the effects of issue framing on the quality of interethnic political communication. Her publications include recent and forthcoming articles in the *Journal of European Social Theory*, *Ethnic and Racial Politics*, and the *Journal of European Area Studies*. She is currently completing *Who Belongs? Immigration and Contested Definitions of Political Membership in France and Britain*.

CHIOU-LING YEH is Assistant Professor in the Department of History at San Diego State University. She has recently written *Pageants and Performance: Chinese New Year Festivals in San Francisco Chinatown* (forthcoming). She was a Kevin Starr Fellow in California Studies at the University of California Humanities Research Institute in 2001–2002. Her article "In the Traditions of China and in the Freedom of America" appeared in *American Quarterly* (June 2004), and her essay "Contesting Identities: Youth Rebellion in San Francisco's Chinese New Year Festivals, 1953–1969," is included in the anthology *The Chinese in America: A History from Gold Mountain to the New Millennium* (Alta Mira Press, 2002).

Index